GLENCOE

LITERATURE

The Reader's Choice

INTERACTIVE Reading Sourcebook

American Literature

New York, New York   Columbus, Ohio   Chicago, Illinois   Peoria, Illinois   Woodland Hills, California

Glencoe/McGraw-Hill

A Division of The ***McGraw-Hill*** *Companies*

Send all inquiries to:
Glencoe/McGraw-Hill
8787 Orion Place
Columbus, OH 43240-4027

ISBN 0-07-825195-8

Printed in the United States of America

1 2 3 4 5 6 7 8 9 10 066 08 07 06 05 04 03 02

Table of Contents

Unit 2 A New Nation

Theme 2 Breaking Free

Theme 3 Gaining Insight

Unit 3 The Civil War and Its Aftermath

Theme 4 The Union Is Tested

Theme 5 Two New American Voices

Unit 4 Regionalism and Realism

Theme 6 The Energy of the Everyday

Unit 5 Beginnings of the Modern Age

Theme 7 New Directions

Theme 8 The Harlem Renaissance

UNIT 6 MIDCENTURY VOICES

THEME 9 Personal Discoveries

THEME 10 Acting on an Idea

UNIT 7 INTO THE TWENTY-FIRST CENTURY

THEME 11 Generations

Theme 12 Variety Is Richness

PART 3

To the Teacher

The **Interactive Reading Sourcebook** presents unified scaffolded lessons for students who are reading below grade level. The research-based strategies in the Sourcebook are designed to support comprehension as they help students become more fluent and competent readers. Each selection in *Glencoe Literature* has an associated lesson in the **Interactive Reading Sourcebook.**

The companion to the **Interactive Reading Sourcebook** is the **Interactive Reading Workbook.** This workbook gives students opportunities to practice word study, vocabulary, comprehension, and critical thinking skills and strategies as they read the selections. Reading Guides in the workbook provide support for longer, more complex literature selections. Interacting with Text workbook pages each contain a segment of text reprinted from a literature selection. Accompanying exercises give students practice in using reading skills and strategies while improving their abilities to pinpoint specific information in text.

The Interactive Reading Lessons are organized into **Before Reading**, **During Reading**, and **After Reading** segments. In each segment the **Interactive Reading Sourcebook** features clearly defined, practical reading strategies and literature skills that focus on the complex process of reading. An emphasis on building vocabulary encourages students to explore concepts that surround words critical to understanding the selections. The scaffolded lessons develop efficient readers who internalize the critical reading strategies and skills that allow them to understand, interpret, analyze, evaluate, and, most importantly, enjoy literature.

The **Interactive Reading Sourcebook** consists of three parts:

Part 1 The Teaching of Reading
Methods, models, explanations, definitions, and examples to guide the teaching of reading

Part 2 Interactive Reading Lessons
Scaffolded research-based instructional strategies for each selection in *Glencoe Literature*

Part 3 Interactive Reading Workbook—Teacher Annotated Edition
Fully annotated **Interactive Reading Workbook,** including reading guides and Interacting with Text pages

PART 1

The Teaching of Reading

The Teaching of Reading

Effective Teaching Methods

The following approaches are among many that can help you teach reading to your students. Beginning as a whole-class activity and continuing in small-group reading sessions, **Reciprocal Teaching** is a system of working through a text in a way that maximizes student involvement and comprehension. **Modeling** is a method of presenting reading and thinking processes with the goal of having students apply these processes on their own. **Exploring Expository Texts** provides keys that help students access informational texts.

Reciprocal Teaching

Reciprocal teaching (Palinscar and Brown, 1984) is a method of checking understanding during reading. The teacher guides a group of students to apply four reading strategies in a prescribed way, with the goal of achieving comprehension of a segment of text. As students become familiar with the process, the teacher's role gradually changes from leader to facilitator, and the students take over the process themselves, alternating in the role of group leader. **The order of the strategies may vary depending on teacher preference.** However, students should learn and use the strategies in a consistent order. Here is a brief description of the reciprocal teaching process.

Reciprocal Teaching Process			
Questioning After students have read a portion of text, the leader asks the group questions about what they have just read. For student leaders, formulating such questions causes them to determine the important ideas in the text. Answering such questions causes all students in the group to review what they have learned and to look back in the text to find answers.	➡ **Clarifying** The leader points out places in the text that he or she found difficult and also invites group members to bring up anything that they found confusing. Students discuss these troublesome places and use information in the text and their own knowledge to clear up confusing points or difficult terms or concepts.	➡ **Summarizing** The leader then summarizes the segment of text. Orally summarizing requires student leaders to actively evaluate ideas in the text and to determine the key ideas that should be included in a summary. Members of the group also must evaluate the significance of ideas. They respond by suggesting additions or alterations to the summary that the leader has proposed.	➡ **Predicting** The leader makes predictions about what will happen next on the basis of what the group has already read. Group members participate by suggesting changes to the predictions or by proposing new predictions. Students use their predictions to prepare themselves to read the next segment of text.

Modeling

Modeling is a means of demonstrating a thinking process. To model, the teacher usually first reads aloud a segment of text as students follow along in their books. Then, using everyday language, the teacher reasons aloud. The purpose of modeling is for students to understand the steps that readers follow to solve a reading problem or to analyze a text. The goal is to have students apply similar reasoning procedures during their own reading processes. The following example of modeling shows how using context clues helps the reader to understand an unfamiliar word.

> **Modeling** I wonder what the word *vacant* means. From the first sentence in the passage, it seems that *vacant* is a kind of seat on a bus. The narrator goes on to say that she "took" the vacant seat. *To take a seat* means "to sit down." The narrator would most likely sit only in an empty seat. So *vacant* probably means "empty."

To complete the modeling cycle, individual students are asked to think aloud, demonstrating their own thinking processes as they employ the reading strategy or skill. Reasoning aloud makes students more aware of what they actually do as they read. Listening to a student think aloud shows the teacher how the student's abilities are developing and where the student needs support and guidance in applying the strategy (Duffy, Roehler, Herrmann, 1988).

Recognizing Text Structures

Noticing the way ideas are organized in a piece of writing helps students anticipate the ideas they will encounter and prepares them to comprehend the text, whether the text is narrative or expository.

Narrative Writing **Narrative writing** is writing that tells a story. The writing may be fiction or nonfiction (as in a personal narrative or an autobiography).

From the time students first hear and read narratives, they begin to internalize the structure of stories. They develop certain expectations of how stories will be presented and what the stories will include.

For a lesson on **Plot Elements,** see page T156.

This predictable story structure is called **story grammar.** Narrative stories are typically structured to include the following elements:

- a beginning, a middle, and an end
- characters, setting, plot, and theme
- a conflict, a progression of events, and a resolution
- chronological order

For a lesson on **Expository Texts,** see page T63.

Expository Writing **Expository writing** is nonfiction writing that explains, informs, or persuades—for example, essays, articles, and reports. Expository writing whose primary purpose is to provide specific or technical information about a topic or event is sometimes called **informational text.** The most crucial informational text that students will encounter is found in content-area textbooks, such as science, social studies, and math textbooks. Other kinds of informational texts include Web site resources, proposals, brochures, manuals, policy statements, and sets of instructions.

Exploring Expository Texts

Unlike narratives, which usually have a story-grammar structure, the organization of ideas in expository writing may have one of several **text structures.** Teaching students to recognize the text structure will help prepare them for reading and comprehending the text (Armbruster, Anderson, and Ostertag, 1989).

For a lesson on **Cause-and-Effect Relationships** in expository text, see page T160.

The most common text structures are time order, compare-contrast, description, cause-and-effect, and problem-solution. While an expository selection may make use of a variety of text structures, one text structure almost always predominates in a piece of writing. For example, an author may compare and contrast two ideas in an essay with an overall cause-and-effect text structure.

Examples of **signal words** listed in the following chart can help the reader determine the text structure.

Text Structure	Signal Words
time order Arranges events or steps in sequential order	on, before, during, after, first, last, now, when, then, next, finally
compare-contrast Shows likenesses and differences	in contrast, in comparison, on the other hand, similarly, like
description Gives the characteristics or qualities of a subject so that a reader can form mental pictures from textual details	*Details in spatial order:* near, beside, in front of *Details in order of importance:* first, most important
cause-and-effect Explains outcomes caused by various situations	because, as a result, consequently, since, due to, therefore, thus
problem-solution Presents a problem and offers one or more solutions	because, if/then, as a result, therefore

Various **graphic organizers**—concept webs and organizers for compare/contrast, cause-and-effect, problem-solution, and sequence—can help students deconstruct and analyze a text's structure. A graphic organizer can also provide a kind of map or an outline for reviewing the selection.

Considerate Text Considerate text is "text that facilitates understanding, learning, and remembering" (Armbruster and Anderson, 1985). Such text is well organized and ideas are developed logically. Connective words and phrases (such as *however*, *and*, *thus*, and *as a result*) help the reader understand the relationship between ideas. Examples of characteristics that might be found in considerate text are clearly stated main ideas, specialized vocabulary defined at the point of use, and unified paragraphs that do not contain extraneous ideas. Introductions and summaries that pull together main ideas also help to make a text "considerate."

Text Features Text features can also contribute to considerate text.

Text Features

- Headings and subheadings reveal the hierarchy of ideas in a segment of text.
- Boldfaced type points out key vocabulary and concepts.
- Footnotes and captioned illustrations and graphics clarify concepts.
- A logical layout highlights the author's progression of ideas.

Text that does not contain these features can be difficult to navigate and comprehend. Such text is called "inconsiderate text."

Skills and Strategies for Reading Expository Texts

While all the active reading strategies listed on pages T13–T16 are important for reading both narrative and expository texts, strategies such as those listed below are especially helpful for exploring expository writing.

Suggested Strategies for Before Reading

- **Previewing**

  1. Have students preview the **text's structure.** Noticing the organization of ideas will prepare them for the types of information they will receive.
  2. Have students preview the **concepts** in the text by looking over the text features such as headings and subheadings, charted information, illustrations, captions, and graphics.
  3. Have students preview footnotes and boldfaced terms to become familiar with the **specialized vocabulary.**

- **Activating Prior Knowledge and Building Background**

  Prepare students to take in new knowledge by helping them bring to mind what they already know. Use the key concepts and boldfaced terms in the text to frame general questions that encourage students to think about the topic and to share ideas. Then provide specific information that will enhance their understanding of the subject.

- **Setting a Purpose for Reading**

  Guide students to set a purpose for reading. For example, if a heading in the text is "Endangered Animal Species," ask them what they would like to know related to this topic, such as why some animals have become extinct.

Suggested Strategies for During Reading

- **Varying Reading Rate**

  Teach students to adjust their reading rate. They need to slow down when they encounter difficult concepts, connections to previous ideas, new vocabulary, or text that contains a great deal of information.

- **Monitoring Comprehension**

  Students should be aware of their own reading process and notice when they have missed something. They can monitor comprehension by questioning themselves as they read. If they do not understand an important idea, they need to reread, review, or read on to clarify what is unclear.

- **Identifying Main Ideas**

  Students should identify main ideas as they read. Text features—such as headings, subheadings, boldfaced terms, and graphics—are good indicators of main or key ideas.

For a lesson on identifying **Main Ideas and Supporting Details** in expository text, see page T60.

- **Tracking Information**

  Direct students to list key ideas as they read. They may make a list of ideas, create an outline of main points, or write a series of notes. Graphic organizers such as Venn diagrams, problem-solution charts, concept webs, and cause-and-effect charts can also be effective organizational tools to aid comprehension and retention.

Suggested Strategies for After Reading

- **Reviewing**

  Students can use their lists, outlines, notes, graphic organizers, or the text features in the text itself to review critical ideas. Through discussion, students can summarize, analyze, and evaluate ideas to help them process and retain what they have read.

Effective Classroom Procedures

Reading Arrangements

Use flexible classroom organization to provide varying degrees of support and guidance to struggling readers. Students might

- read aloud to partners who can help with difficult words
- read silently with partners, having partners "on-call" to help with difficult places in the text
- read silently
- take turns reading aloud in small groups
- follow along in their books as they listen to a taped reading or as the teacher, a volunteer, or a designated group of students reads aloud
- take turns reading in a whole-class activity
- participate in the choral reading of a text

Independent Reading

Following are some suggestions to encourage independent reading.

- Set up a classroom library of books that have special interest to your students.
- Assign time in the library for groups or individuals to explore subject areas related to the reading selection or additional books by an author.
- Establish in-class discussion groups (literature groups) where students work together to focus on topics connected to the literature they are reading.
- Assign independent reading of at least thirty minutes a day, to be done outside of class.
- Have students create products such as reports, posters, or multigenre writing to express and share what they have learned.
- Via newsletters, suggest that parents or guardians read aloud from the literature selections. Encourage parents or guardians to call attention to items in newspapers and magazines that relate to the literature or that are of special interest to the family.

Teaching Word Study

For a lesson to review **Homophones,** see page T136.

Homophones (Sound-Alikes) *Homophones* are words that sound the same but have different meanings and usually different spellings.

bare (empty)	**base** (foundation)	**sighs** (exhalations)
bear (animal)	**bass** (deep tone)	**size** (amount)

For a lesson to review **Homographs,** see page T102.

Homographs (Look-Alikes) *Homographs* are words that are spelled the same but have different meanings and different origins. Some homographs have different pronunciations.

bill (statement of money owed)	**wound** (injury)	**fan** (admirer)
bill (beak)	**wound** (turned tightly)	**fan** (cooling device)

Synonyms *Synonyms* are words that have similar meanings.

bite, nibble, munch	mistake, error, blunder	run, dash, dart

For a lesson to review **Antonyms,** see page T200.

Antonyms *Antonyms* are words that have opposite meanings.

correct—wrong	busy—idle	dim—bright

For a lesson to review **Compound Words,** see page T212.

Compound Words A *compound word* is a word made up of two or more distinct words.

classroom	worldwide	merry-go-round
underground	sunrise	sparrow hawk

For a lesson to review **Denotation and Connotation,** see page T233.

Denotation/Connotation *Denotation* is a word's dictionary definition. *Connotation* is the emotional value associated with a word.

House and *home* are synonyms, but *home* has a warm, personal meaning that is not stated in its dictionary definition.

My *house* is by the shore.	My *home* is by the shore.

Syllabication A *syllable* is a spoken part of a word. A syllable always contains a vowel sound. Breaking a word in syllables and sounding out each syllable help students decode longer words.

Rule 1: When two consonants fall between two vowels, divide the syllables between the two consonants. However, never separate a blend, cluster, or digraph.

VC/CV	bat/ter	in/dex	

Rule 2: In words with two vowels separated by a consonant, the syllables may be divided before or after the consonant. If the first vowel has a long sound, divide the syllables before the consonant. If the first vowel has a short sound, divide the syllables after the consonant.

V/CV	spo/ken	ba/con	
VC/V	com/ic	sev/en	

Rule 3: When a word ends with a consonant and an *le,* the consonant goes with *le* to form the final syllable.

V/C *le*	ca/ble	sta/ple	trou/ble

Rule 4: A prefix or a suffix (except for common word endings such as *-ed*) usually forms a separate syllable.

Affixes	**prefix/base**	dis/charge	
	base/suffix	joy/ous	

Rule 5: Divide compound words between the distinct words.

Compound Words	ship/wreck	blue/bird	

Effective Vocabulary Instruction

Research tells us that general vocabulary knowledge is a critical component to understanding text (Anderson and Freebody, 1981). As students build both oral and print vocabulary knowledge, they increase their comprehension skills and their ability to read strategically.

The **Interactive Reading Sourcebook** and the **Interactive Reading Workbook** provide vocabulary lessons and activities that develop students' knowledge of larger concepts as well as their understanding of individual words. The vocabulary instruction provides both direct and indirect ways for students to interact with words before, during, and after reading and encourages an ongoing curiosity about language.

The key vocabulary terms provided are words and phrases critical for understanding a selection. They may also be unfamiliar words that promise to be difficult. For struggling readers, it is especially useful to teach key vocabulary before students read. Activating prior knowledge and building background for unfamiliar vocabulary give students a hook on which to hang what they learn. Reinforcement of key vocabulary during and after reading offers students additional exposure to unfamiliar words and concepts as well as to known words used in new ways.

Strategies for Teaching Vocabulary

Because there is a clear connection between readers' vocabulary knowledge and their ability to understand what they read, vocabulary instruction is essential to developing interactive, strategic readers. Vocabulary learning is not an isolated activity. Rather, students build vocabulary through repeated encounters with words in rich oral and written contexts (Nagy, 1988). Teachers reinforce listening, speaking, writing, and reading vocabulary by encouraging students to read across the content areas, to use dictionaries and other word references, to participate in classroom discussions, and to read aloud or listen to oral readings. Each encounter with a word provides new clues to its meaning. Students' understandings of those meanings build and deepen over time. The following strategies provide ways for teachers to offer a variety of interactive opportunities that will involve students in the process of building vocabulary.

For a lesson on using **Context Clues,** see page T217.

Using Context Clues Students can often determine the meaning of a word they do not know by using **context**—the words and sentences that surround an unfamiliar word. The following chart shows specific context clues for students to use as they read.

Type of Context Clue	Examples
Synonym Look for a synonym to the unfamiliar word. Synonyms often appear in context when two things are compared.	The service at this restaurant is *quick*. Is the service at that restaurant just as **expeditious?**
Antonym Look for an antonym to the unfamiliar word. Antonyms appear in context most often when two things are contrasted.	Yesterday Sam was **despondent,** but today he's *cheerful*.
Definition Look for a phrase that defines or describes the unfamiliar word. Commas, dashes, or parentheses often surround a phrase that gives this type of clue.	In **hieroglyphics,** *the writing of ancient Egypt*, picture symbols are used to represent ideas.
Example Look for examples that reveal the meaning of the unfamiliar word.	He can't decide which one of the **martial arts** to study—*karate, judo,* or *tae kwon do*.

Using General Context Sometimes the context does not provide a specific clue to the meaning of an unfamiliar word; however, the general context contains clues. Direct students to study the main idea of a passage to see if it unlocks the meaning of an unknown word.

Example

Since this was the boy's first **infraction** of the rules, the principal let him go with just a warning.
(*infraction*: breaking or violating something)

Techniques for Using Context to Determine Meaning

- Ask students to look before, at, and after the unfamiliar word for a context clue.
- Have students connect what they already know with what the author has written.
- Have students predict a possible meaning.
- Have them apply the meaning in the sentence.
- Ask students if their meaning makes sense. If not, have them try again.

Using Words Parts (Structural Analysis)

Many words can be divided into parts: *prefix*, *base word* or *root*, and *suffix*. Knowing the meanings of common word parts can help readers unlock the meanings of unknown words.

Prefixes

A **prefix** is a word part that comes before a base word or a root and changes the meaning of the word.

For a lesson to review **Prefixes**, see page T53.

Prefix	Meaning	Examples
dis-	opposite of	disobey, displease, disown, dislike
re-	back, again	return, rewrite, redo, relive
pre-	before	prejudge, prepay, preview, preheat
in-	not	inactive, incorrect, inability, incomplete
non-	without	nonfat, nonstop, nonresident, nonvoter

Suffixes

A **suffix** is a word part that comes after a base word or a root. It may change the meaning of the word or the way the word is used in a sentence.

For a lesson to review **Suffixes**, see page T44.

Suffix	Meaning	Examples
-less	without	careless, powerless, fearless, hopeless
-ish	like	greenish, childish, smallish, foolish
-ful	full of	playful, thoughtful, joyful, helpful
-ist	a person who	biologist, artist, violinist, dentist
-ous	full of	joyous, nervous, spacious, curious

Roots

A **root** is the part of a word that contains its basic meaning. Unlike a base word, a root is not a word by itself. Many roots come from Greek or Latin.

For lessons to review **Greek and Latin Roots,** see pages T80 and T86.

Root	Meaning	Examples
bio	life	biology, biography, biosphere
tele	distant	television, telescope, telegraph
dent	tooth	dentist, trident, indent
port	carry	porter, portable, transport
spec	look	spectacles, introspective, circumspect

Using Language Structure Clues

Look for passages that contain **parallel** structures—words arranged in similar ways. Words that have parallel functions often contain clues to unknown words.

> At the zoo, we saw a *herd* of zebras, a ***pride*** of lions, and a *pack* of wolves in free-roaming environments.
> (*Herd*, *pride*, and *pack* are all words for groups of animals.)

Using Classifying and Categorizing Current research indicates that the brain is a pattern detector (Caine and Caine, 1994). Students enjoy grouping items by similarities or separating items by differences. Word sorts—open sorts (where students choose how to label categories) and closed sorts (where teachers provide the categories)—offer opportunities for students to organize ideas. Whenever students can see how words fit into a larger category, they expand their vocabulary knowledge.

Using Word Maps Many teachers routinely use maps to explore and teach vocabulary in the classroom. A map can be any kind of graphic that is designed to show relationships between words or concepts. A commonly used word map or concept web shows a central bubble containing a key word or idea. Bubbles that surround the center bubble may be used to show semantic relationships or to explain structure relationships. **For a reproducible web graphic organizer, see page T27.**

Using a Concept-Definition Map A concept-definition map (Schwartz and Raphael, 1985) is a way to define a word visually. The top section of the graphic asks *What is it?* The next section asks *What is it like?* The last section asks *What are some examples?* Students use their prior knowledge about words and concepts to complete the map. **For a reproducible concept-definition map graphic organizer, see page T25.**

Using a Semantic-Features Chart Use a semantic-features chart (Anders, Bos, and Filip, 1982; Johnson, Toms-Bronowski, and Pittleman, 1982) to help students focus on the discriminating features of items in a group. Ask students to complete a grid with marks to indicate a positive (+), negative (–), or possible (?) correlation. **For a reproducible semantic-feature analysis chart graphic organizer, see page T26.**

Animals	Fur	Feathers	Four legs	Two legs
cat	+	–	+	–
canary	–	+	–	+
seal	?	–	?	?

Using Possible Sentences Possible Sentences (Beck and McKeown, 1983; Moore and Moore, 1986) is a strategy that allows students to speculate about word meanings. It is especially useful for teaching selections dense with new concepts or unfamiliar words. Teachers choose approximately ten key vocabulary terms and write them on the board. Teachers may construct sentences using the words either correctly or incorrectly. They then ask students to comment on whether the sentences are "possible." As an alternative to providing sentences, teachers may ask that, before reading a selection, students construct approximately five sentences from the key terms, taking educated guesses about unfamiliar words or phrases. As students encounter the key vocabulary during reading, they note each term's usage in the selection's context. After reading, students return to their possible sentences to discuss meanings and to rewrite their own sentences as necessary.

Using Story Elements to Teach Vocabulary Fictional and nonfictional narratives share many of the same elements. Both contain characters, settings, a problem or conflict, actions or events, a resolution to a story's problem, and a theme or message. These elements make up the story's structure. Students can use their anticipation of such structures and their knowledge of other stories to categorize key vocabulary words under story-element headings before they read (Blachowicz, 1986). Those categorizations then become students' predictions for what might happen in a selection. Conventional story maps also help students organize and remember fictional works by asking them to use story structure to keep track of key elements during reading.

Teaching Active Reading Strategies

In the past, reading has been described as more of a skill than an active mental process. We now know that reading is a highly interactive process in which students construct meaning from text (Anderson and Pearson, 1984). Readers do not passively receive an author's ideas.

No two students understand a selection exactly the same way, because each brings a unique background and set of experiences to the task (Rosenblatt, 1978, 1994). Comprehension depends on those individual reader experiences. It also depends on the characteristics of the written text, the learning context that defines the reader's task, and the strategies that are consciously applied by the reader to construct meaning from the printed words on a page.

We know that students learn what they are directly taught and what they have an opportunity to practice. The **Interactive Reading Sourcebook** provides carefully scaffolded unified lessons that develop students' strategic reading behaviors. Through explicit instruction, teachers model the most effective reading strategies and provide opportunities for students to practice and eventually internalize the behaviors of effective readers.

Strategies are carefully-thought-out plans that readers use adaptively to make sense of what they read. The strategies that follow help students develop interactive reading behaviors that build comprehension of all types of text.

Previewing

For a lesson on **Previewing,** see page T194.

When students preview, or look over, a selection before they read, they begin to activate what they already know and begin to see what they will need to know to make sense of the text. As students look at the title, illustrations, headings, picture captions, and graphics, teachers can guide students to offer what they already know about a specific topic or about the author, genre, or ideas in the text. As students formulate questions about the text that they are previewing, they can predict the selection's content and thereby set a purpose for reading.

Activating Prior Knowledge

For a lesson on **Activating Prior Knowledge,** see page T48.

By discussing what students already know about a topic, teachers can capitalize on opportunities to build background where student knowledge is weak. They can also offer students a chance to learn from the prior knowledge of others. Most important, they actively cultivate the cognitive soil where future knowledge can be planted. What students learn from the selection is most effectively attached to what they already know. Using a KWL graphic organizer (Ogle, 1986) helps students activate what they know, encourages them to generate questions about what they will read, and helps them record and review what they learn. Elaborated KWL organizers (Carr and Ogle, 1987) invite students to consider questions for further research and to specify where information will be found and how it will be organized. **For a reproducible three-column chart graphic organizer, see page T34.**

Predicting

For a lesson on **Predicting,** see page T46.

One excellent way for readers to interact with text is to make an informed guess about what they will read. When students make predictions, they use their prior knowledge and the information they gather from previewing to create an expectation for what they will read. This expectation then provides a purpose for their reading and generates interest in the selection. As students read, they adjust or change their predictions on the basis of new information they encounter in the text, or they confirm that their prediction was accurate.

Questioning

For a lesson on **Questioning,** see page T54.

Several types of questioning are important in reading strategically. Students need to ask general questions about the text before, during, and after they read. They also need to question their own understanding of the content as they read—that is, they need to conduct a running dialogue with themselves as part of the metacognitive process of thinking about their own thinking. This metacognitive process will naturally lead students to ask specific questions to clarify text. Finally, students need to ask themselves questions about what information is most important in a selection and about what concepts or information teachers will require them to know.

For a lesson on **Monitoring Comprehension,** see page T90.

Monitoring Comprehension

Research suggests that the most efficient readers have mental conversations with themselves as they read (Dickson et al., 1998). They notice when something does not make sense, and they apply fix-up strategies appropriate to the selection organization and to their own learning styles. Often good readers accept a certain amount of ambiguity in the text and forge ahead, looking for ways to clarify ideas as they read further. But at times they may decide to reread sections or to adjust their reading rates. Students need to internalize a variety of fix-up strategies and to use the strategies flexibly, depending on their own learning preferences, the structure of the text, or the demands of the reading task.

For a lesson on **Visualizing,** see page T43.

Visualizing

One of the most powerful aids to comprehension, especially for younger readers, is visualizing (Pressley, 1977). Effective readers form mental pictures based on a writer's descriptions and on their own prior experiences. These mental pictures help students understand what they read and increase their ability to recall the information for later use. Visualizing is helpful for both expository texts and descriptive fiction. Picturing the steps in a process is as powerful an aid to comprehension as picturing the descriptive details about characters or setting in a short story.

For a lesson on **Interpreting,** see page T111.

Interpreting

Students need to use higher-level thinking skills to attach meaning to events or to information. When students interpret, they construct meaning from their own understandings about the world and about the text.

For a lesson on **Analyzing,** see page T157.

Analyzing

When students look critically at the separate parts of a selection in order to understand the entire selection, they are analyzing. For example, students may break apart a story to look at character, setting, plot, and theme so they will understand the story as a whole. They may bring in outside information about the author to help with their analyses. In a nonfiction selection, students analyze the causes and effects of volcanoes to understand a selection on the eruption of Mount Saint Helens. Whenever students use the organizational pattern of a piece of writing to help determine the main ideas and the author's message, they are analyzing text structure.

For a lesson on **Connecting**, see page T52.

Connecting

Students who actively connect what they read to events in their own lives as well as to other selections they have read establish a conduit for constructing meaning in text. By connecting ideas, emotions, and events to themselves, students also increase their enjoyment of a selection and increase their ability to comprehend and recall information and ideas.

For a lesson on **Responding**, see page T187.

Responding

When students offer personal responses as they read, they are interacting with a text in an important way. Teachers can help students become engaged in a selection by asking questions about what students like, what they do not like, what surprises them, and how they feel about characters in a story or ideas in a nonfiction selection.

Reviewing

As students read, teachers should pause at various points to review. Periodic review is especially important when students read informational text dense with new concepts. Reading guides help students negotiate their way through difficult text and keep struggling readers on task. These guides are also helpful models to use when reviewing a selection. Outlines, charts, graphic organizers, and other visual aids help students organize information as they read. They are also valuable aids for reviewing information after reading.

For a lesson on **Evaluating**, see page T201.

Evaluating

As students have access to increasingly larger amounts of print materials, including a variety of electronic resources, they need to be able to evaluate what they read. Evaluating requires making a judgment or forming an opinion. For example, students evaluate when they form an opinion about characters in a story or when they judge a writer's ability to present compelling description. They also evaluate expository texts—newspapers, editorials, advertisements, and essays—when they distinguish between fact and opinion. To evaluate the reliability of information, students should pose questions such as the following: *Is the author qualified to write on this subject? Is the point of view biased? Is there another point of view not expressed here? Are opinions backed up with facts, statistics, and examples?*

Teaching Reading and Thinking Skills

Effective readers use active reading strategies to maneuver meaningfully through text. They apply these strategies flexibly and internalize good reading behaviors so that those behaviors become automatic. To become independent readers, however, students also need to acquire the reading and thinking skills supported by those strategies.

For a lesson on identifying **Main Idea and Supporting Details,** see page T212.

Identifying Main Idea and Supporting Details

Trying to find the **main idea** of a passage is a difficult task—it requires the critical thinking skill of distinguishing between what is most important and what is secondary. Determining **supporting details** means locating the ideas or examples that extend the main idea or that give additional information about it. Students should be reminded that the main idea of a paragraph is often found in the topic sentence; however, they will sometimes need to infer the main idea of a paragraph by using prior knowledge and the information presented in the paragraph.

Teaching students to find main ideas and supporting details during and after reading helps students prepare to summarize. By activating prior knowledge and previewing text before reading, students learn to anticipate what main ideas they will find.

Techniques for Determining Main Ideas and Supporting Details

- Ask students to share prior knowledge about an author or a topic.
- Lead students to anticipate what might be important in a selection.
- Look at the text structure of a selection to see how the author organizes ideas in a selection, for example, cause and effect, compare and contrast, problem and solution, or time order.
- Invite students to read one paragraph of text and to ask questions such as the following: *What one idea are all the sentences in this paragraph about? How does that idea fit in with what I know about this topic? About this author? How is this selection organized? What sentences add information to the most important idea?*
- Remind students to look for headings, captions, illustrations, and other text features to help them determine main ideas in a selection.

For a lesson on **Summarizing,** see page T84.

Summarizing

To **summarize,** students need to be able to determine the most important ideas in a selection and then to restate those ideas in a logical sequence in their own words.

Summarizing teaches students to reduce information and to rethink what they have read. They learn material more deeply and are better able to retrieve what they have learned for subsequent academic tasks.

Summarizing is a skill that can be used as both an oral and a written activity. Students can summarize as often as necessary to monitor their understanding of a selection. Teachers should encourage students to summarize more frequently when text material is difficult.

Techniques for Summarizing

- Ask students: *What is this passage about?*
- Invite students to begin their summaries by answering *who, what, where, when, why,* and *how?*
- Remind students that only main ideas should be included in a summary but that all the main ideas should be included.
- To determine whether students have included all main ideas, ask: *Can your summary be easily understood by someone who has not read the selection?*
- To help students determine whether they have included unnecessary information, ask: *If this information were excluded, would your summary still sound complete?*

For a lesson on **Making Inferences,** see page T161.

Making Inferences

Making inferences requires that students use their reason and their experience to take educated guesses about what an author implies or suggests. Because writers often do not directly state what they want readers to know, making inferences is essential to constructing meaning in a selection.

Selections that encourage character analysis or that suggest a theme for discussion provide good opportunities for students to learn how to make inferences.

Techniques for Making Inferences

- Guide students to look for text clues. Encourage them to notice descriptions, dialogue, events, or relationships that might signal information a writer is suggesting.
- Ask students to think about what they already know—either from prior text clues or from their own experiences.
- As students read, ask questions that require them to think beyond the literal events of a selection.
- Model your own process of inferring when you read aloud.

For a lesson on **Drawing Conclusions,** see page T222.

Drawing Conclusions

A **conclusion** is a general statement that can be made and explained with reasoning or with supporting details. Drawing conclusions is part of the process of inferring. For example, if students read three separate selections about tornadoes—a fictional story about a boy who loses his family in a tornado, an informational selection about how weather forecasters chart wind speeds and directional paths of tornadoes, and an autobiographical piece by someone who survived a tornado—they may conclude that tornadoes are monumental forces of nature that can inflict unimaginable damage. Students may draw conclusions about character traits of people in stories on the basis of the events and dialogue within a selection.

Drawing conclusions helps students see connections between ideas and events as they read. It is useful both in constructing meaning in fiction and nonfiction and in analyzing and interpreting ideas.

Techniques for Drawing Conclusions

- Ask students to notice specific details about characters, ideas, and information as they read.
- Invite students to use the information they have and their own prior knowledge to think about a larger or more general statement that might be made.
- Caution students not to overgeneralize and not to draw unsound conclusions based on insufficient or inaccurate information.

For a lesson on **Understanding Sequence,** see page T179.

Understanding Sequence

The order in which thoughts are arranged is called **sequence.** When writers present the steps in a scientific process or provide technical directions for operating machinery, they follow a logical sequence. Cookbooks rely on a specific sequence to help readers follow a recipe. Some writers arrange their ideas by order of importance, placing the most important idea either first or last. In narrative writing, chronological order is used most often.

If a written sequence is either illogical or incomplete, readers may fail to complete an important task, follow a complicated thought process, or understand events as they occur.

One of the best ways for teachers to help students recognize sequence in a selection is to teach them to look for signal words, transitional words and phrases that indicate chronological order, steps in a process, or order of importance. **For a reproducible chain graphic organizer, see page T32.**

Techniques for Identifying Sequence

- Have students preview the selection. Does the author intend to tell a story? To explain how something works? To present information?
- Ask students to consider what sequence might be most logical given the writer's purpose.
- Direct students to look for signal words to help them determine sequence.
- Have students restate the sequence in their own words.

For a lesson on **Determining Fact and Opinion,** see page T229.

Determining Fact and Opinion

A **fact** is a statement that can be proved or tested. An **opinion** is a statement of belief that cannot be proved. Writers often lend validity to their opinions by gathering support from experts and by supporting opinions with facts.

The ability to distinguish fact from opinion has never been more important than it is today. Internet resources provide a vast amount of information that is not always accurate. Whenever students read expository texts, they need to distinguish fact from opinion. **For a reproducible two-column chart graphic organizer, see page T33.**

Techniques for Determining Fact and Opinion

- Ask students what information is presented.
- Have students determine the source or sources of the information. How is the information supported? Can it be proved? How reliable are sources used to prove statements?
- Is the author or source of information qualified to speak with authority? What are his or her credentials?
- Invite students to evaluate the motivation of the writer. Sometimes writers slant information to convince readers to agree with them.

For a lesson on **Analyzing Cause-and-Effect Relationships,** see page T187.

Analyzing Cause-and-Effect Relationships

A **cause** is an action or event that makes something happen; an **effect** is the result of that action or event. A single cause (for example, a tornado) can produce multiple effects. Similarly, a single effect (for example, a war) may have several causes. Writers may use clue words to indicate cause-and-effect relationships.

Students who can determine why something occurred and what happened as a result can more clearly see relationships that will allow them to interpret, analyze, and evaluate ideas in a selection. **For a reproducible cause-and-effect chart graphic organizer, see page T29.**

Techniques for Analyzing Cause-and-Effect Relationships

- To help students find the cause in a passage, ask the question *Why?*
- To help students find the effect, ask the question *What is the result?*
- Ask students to look for clue words that signal cause-and-effect relationships, such as *because*, *since*, *as a result*, *so*, *the reason that*, and *consequently*.
- Caution students that causality is not necessarily established just because one event precedes another.

For a lesson on **Comparing and Contrasting,** see page T214.

Comparing and Contrasting

Comparing means looking at the way items, people, or ideas are similar. **Contrasting** means looking at the way items, people, or ideas are different.

When writers compare items, they frequently use signal words such as *both*, *same*, *alike*, *like*, *also*, and *similarly* to provide clues.

Signal words such as *unlike*, *but*, *although*, *yet*, *however*, *on the other hand*, *instead*, and *even though* provide clues to contrasting items.

Writers may juxtapose two dissimilar characters or ideas to make each more distinct. They may also compare an unfamiliar person or idea with someone or something familiar to help students understand and interpret what they read. **For a reproducible Venn-diagram graphic organizer, see page T31.**

Techniques for Comparing and Contrasting

- Ask students to look carefully at the descriptions and other details an author includes in a selection.
- Have students look for clue words that signal that the author is comparing or contrasting items.
- Invite students to think about why a writer might compare or contrast things or people. Is there a larger purpose or idea that an author may wish to convey?
- Tell students that sometimes there are no signal words to indicate comparison or contrast. Students must use descriptive details in those instances to infer similarities or differences between items.

For a lesson on **Analyzing Problem and Solution,** see page T87.

Analyzing Problem and Solution

In both fiction and nonfiction, readers often need to identify a particular problem and its solution. Certainly story grammar is organized around a **problem,** or conflict, and a series of events that leads to a **solution,** or resolution. Informational texts and other expository materials may also ask readers to reflect on a problem or challenge. Sometimes writers provide solutions they think are logical and appropriate, and sometimes they ask readers to consider what steps or actions might work to solve a particular problem.

Helping students identify and analyze a problem in a selection enables them to see the complexity of an issue or an idea that a writer presents. Asking them to define, evaluate, or even determine a solution to a given problem gives students practice in thinking logically and systematically. **For a reproducible problem-solution chart graphic organizer, see page T30.**

Techniques for Analyzing Problem and Solution

- Ask students to identify the main problem in a passage or selection.
- How or where does a character in the story encounter the problem?
- Is the problem part of an academic task (such as a math problem) or the explanation of a process (such as a science experiment)?
- What logical steps or actions may be taken to solve the problem? Are possible or partial solutions presented? If so, what are they?
- What happens as a result of the steps or actions taken?
- What other actions may be taken to provide a more permanent solution?
- Ask students to evaluate why a solution did or did not work. How might they have solved the problem differently?

Reproducible Graphic Organizers

To enhance your teaching of reading skills and strategies, see the reproducible graphic organizers that follow the bibliography. These graphic organizers may be duplicated for in-class use. They may also be made into transparencies for use on the overhead projector.

Bibliography

For more information about the topics, skills, and strategies discussed here, please see the following resources.

Reciprocal Teaching

Brown, A. L., A. S. Palincsar, and B. B. Armbruster. 1984. Instructing comprehension-fostering activities in interactive learning situations. In R. B. Ruddell, M. R. Ruddell, and H. Singer (eds.), *Theoretical models and processes of reading* (4th ed.). Newark, DE: International Reading Association.

Marks, M., M. Pressley, J. D. Coley, S. Craig, R. Gardner, T. DePinto, and W. Rose. 1993. Three teachers' adaptations of reciprocal teaching in comparison to traditional reciprocal teaching. *Elementary School Journal* 94(2), pp. 267–283.

Palincsar, A. S., and A. L. Brown. 1984. Reciprocal teaching of comprehension-fostering and comprehension-monitoring activities. *Cognition and Instruction* 1, pp. 117–175.

Modeling

Duffy, G. G., L. Roehler, and B. A. Herrmann. 1988. Modeling mental processes helps poor readers become strategic readers. In R. L. Allington (ed.), *Teaching struggling readers: Articles from* The Reading Teacher. Newark, DE: International Reading Association.

Heller, M. F. 1986. Modeling critical thinking in the English classroom. *Highway One* (1986, Spring), pp. 87–90.

Kann, R. 1984. Increasing motivation and reading comprehension of exceptional learners: Three modeling techniques. *The Pointer* 29(1), pp. 20–21.

Nist, S. L., and K. Kirby. 1986. Teaching comprehension and study strategies through modeling and thinking aloud. *Reading Research and Instruction* 25(4), pp. 254–264.

Text Structures

Armbruster, B. B., T.H. Anderson, and J. Ostertag. 1989. Teaching text structure to improve reading and writing. *The Reading Teacher* (1989, November), pp. 130–158.

Coté, N., S. R. Goldman, and E. U. Saul. 1998. Students making sense of informational text: Relations between processing and representation. *Discourse Processes* 25(1), pp. 1–53.

Englert, C. S., and C. C. Thomas. 1987. Sensitivity to text structure in reading and writing: A comparison between learning disabled and non-learning disabled students. *Learning Disability Quarterly* 10(2), pp. 93–105.

Lenski, S. D., M. A. Wham, and J. L. Johns. 1999. *Reading & learning strategies for middle & high school students*. Dubuque, IA: Kendall/Hunt.

Meyer, B. J. F., and R. O. Freedle. 1984. Effects of discourse type on recall. *American Educational Research Journal* 21(1), pp. 121–143.

Richards, J. C., and J. P. Gipe. 1995. What's the structure? A game to help middle school students recognize common writing patterns. *Journal of Reading* 38(8), pp. 667–669.

Simonsen, S. 1996. Identifying and teaching text structures in content area classrooms. In Lapp D., J. Flood, and N. Farnan (eds.) *Content area reading and learning: Instructional strategies* (2nd ed.). Needham Heights, MA: Allyn & Bacon.

Tierney, R. J., J. E. Readence, and E. K. Dishner. 1995. *Reading strategies and practices: A compendium* (4th ed.). Needham Heights, MA: Allyn & Bacon.

Considerate/ Inconsiderate Text

Armbruster, B. B. 1996. Considerate texts. In Lapp, D., J. Flood, and N. Farnan (eds.), *Content area reading and learning: Instructional strategies* (2nd ed.). Needham Heights, MA: Allyn & Bacon.

Armbruster, B., and T. H. Anderson. 1985. Producing "considerate" expository text: Or easy reading is damned hard writing. *Journal of Curriculum Studies* 17(3), pp. 247–252.

Gordon, J., J. S. Schumm, C. Coffland, and M. Doucette. 1992. Effects of inconsiderate versus considerate text on elementary students' vocabulary learning. *Reading Psychology* 13(2), pp. 157–169.

Konopak, B. C. 1988. Eighth graders' vocabulary learning from inconsiderate and considerate text. *Reading Research and Instruction* 27(4), pp. 1–14.

Schumm, J. S., D. S. Haager, and A. G. Leavell. 1991. Considerate and inconsiderate text instruction in postsecondary developmental reading textbooks: A content analysis. *Reading Research and Instruction* 30(4), pp. 42–51.

Word Study

Bear, D., M. Invernizzi, S. Templeton, and F. Johnston. 2000. *Words their way: Word study for phonics, vocabulary, and spelling instruction*. Upper Saddle River, NJ: Prentice Hall.

Fry, E., J. Kress, and D. Fountoukidis. 1993. *The reading teacher's book of lists*. Paramus, NJ: Prentice Hall.

Honig, B., L. Diamond, L. Gutlohn, and J. Mahler. 2000. CORE: *Teaching reading sourcebook*. Novato, CA: Arena Press.

Pinnell, G., and I. Fountas. 1998. *Word matters: Teaching phonics and spelling in the reading/writing classroom*. Portsmouth, NH: Heinemann.

Vocabulary Instruction

Anders, P., C. Bos, and D. Filip. 1984. The effect of semantic feature analysis on the reading comprehension of learning-disabled students. In J. A. Niles and L. A. Harris (eds.), *Changing perspectives on research in reading/language processing and instruction*. Rochester, NY: National Reading Conference.

Anderson, R. C., and P. Freebody. 1981. Vocabulary knowledge. In J. T. Guthrie (ed.), *Comprehension and teaching: Research reviews.* Newark, DE: International Reading Association.

Beck, I. L., and M. G. McKeown. 1983. Learning words well—A program to enhance vocabulary and comprehension. *The Reading Teacher* 36, pp. 622–625.

Blachowicz, C. L. Z. 1986. Making connections: Alternatives to the vocabulary notebook. *Journal of Reading* 29, pp. 643–649.

Blachowicz, C., and P. Fisher. 1996. *Teaching vocabulary in all classrooms.* Englewood Cliffs, NJ: Prentice-Hall.

Davis, F. B. 1968. Research in comprehension in reading. *Reading Research Quarterly* 3, pp. 499–544.

Freebody P., and R. C. Anderson. 1983. Effects of vocabulary difficulty, text cohesion, and schema availability on reading comprehension. *Reading Research Quarterly* 18, pp. 277–294.

Johnson, D. D., S. Toms-Brownowski, and S. D. Pittelman. 1982. *An investigation of the effectiveness of semantic mapping and semantic feature analysis with intermediate grade level students* (Program Report No. 83-3). Madison, WI: Wisconsin Center for Education Research, University of Wisconsin.

Nagy, W. E. 1988. *Teaching vocabulary to improve reading comprehension.* Newark, DE: International Reading Association.

Schwartz, R. M., and T. E. Raphael. 1985. Concept of definition: A key to improving students' vocabulary. *The Reading Teacher* 39, pp. 198–205.

Comprehension Skills and Strategies

Anderson, R. C., and P. D. Pearson. 1984. A schema-theoretic view of basic processes in teaching comprehension. In P. D. Pearson (ed.) *Handbook of reading research.* New York: Longman.

Caine, R. and G. Caine. 1994. *Making connections: Teaching and the human brain.* Menlo Park, CA: Addison-Wesley.

Caine, R. N., and G. Caine. 1995. Reinventing schools through brain-based learning. *Educational Leadership.* (1995, April), pp. 43–47.

Carr, E. and D. Ogle. 1987. K-W-L plus: A strategy for comprehension and summarization. *Journal of Reading* 30, pp. 626–631.

Lapp, D., J. Flood, and N. Farnan (eds.). 1996. *Content area reading and learning: Instructional strategies* (2nd ed.). Needham Heights, MA: Allyn & Bacon.

McNeil, J. D. 1992. *Reading comprehension: New directions for classroom practice* (3rd ed.). Los Angeles: Harper Collins.

Ogle, D. 1986. K-W-L: A teaching model that develops active reading of expository text. *The Reading Teacher* 39, pp. 564–570.

Rosenblatt, L. M. 1978. *The reader, the text, the poem: Transactional theory of the written word.* Carbondale, IL: Southern Illinois University Press.

Rosenblatt, L. 1994. The transactional theory of reading and writing. In R. Ruddell, M. R. Ruddell, and H. Singer (eds.), *Theoretical models and processes of reading,* (4th ed.). Newark, DE: International Reading Association.

Tierney, R. J., J. E. Readence, and E. K. Dishner. 1995. *Reading strategies and practices: A compendium* (4th ed.). Needham Heights, MA: Allyn & Bacon.

Concept-Definition Map

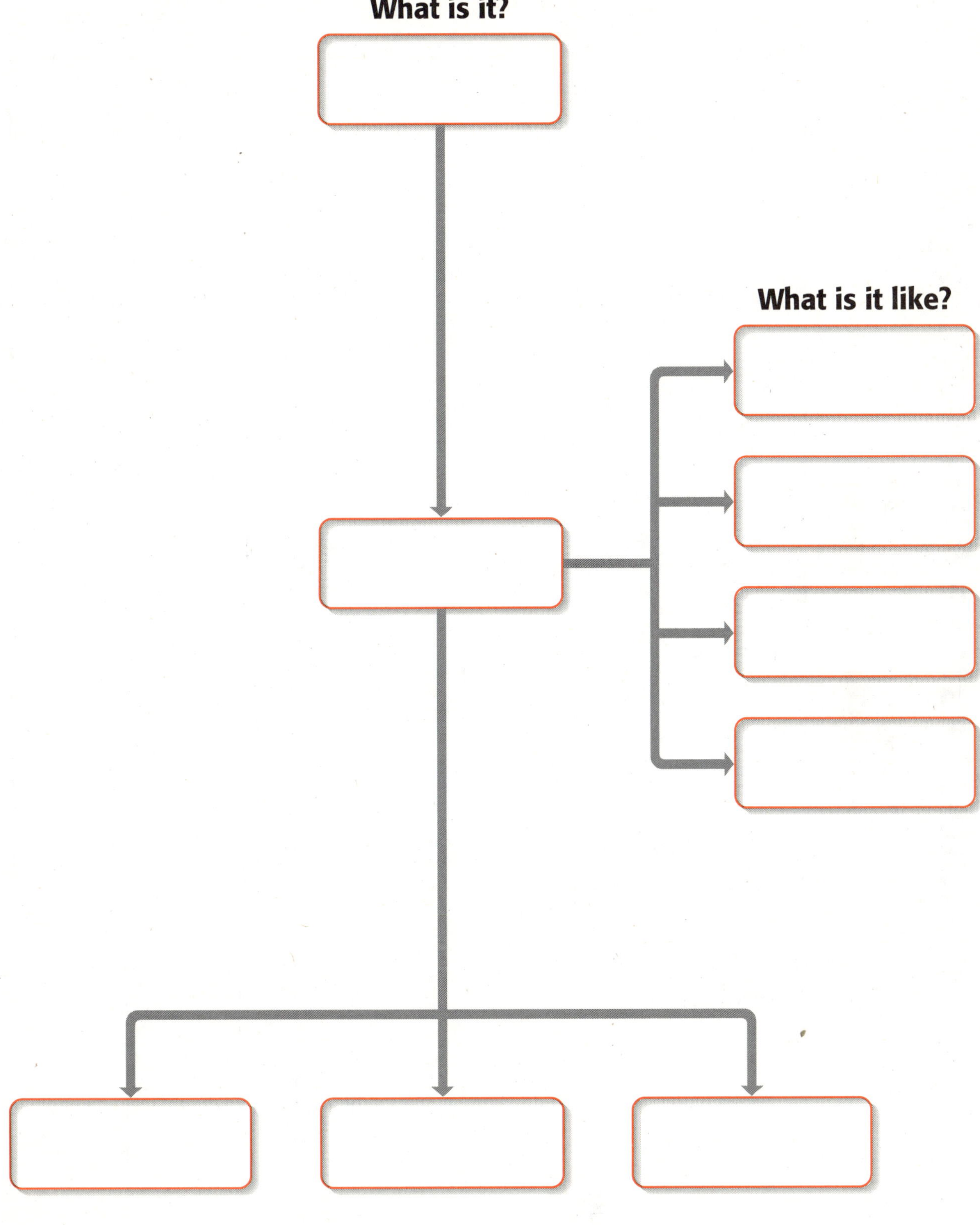

What are some examples?

Semantic-Feature Analysis Chart

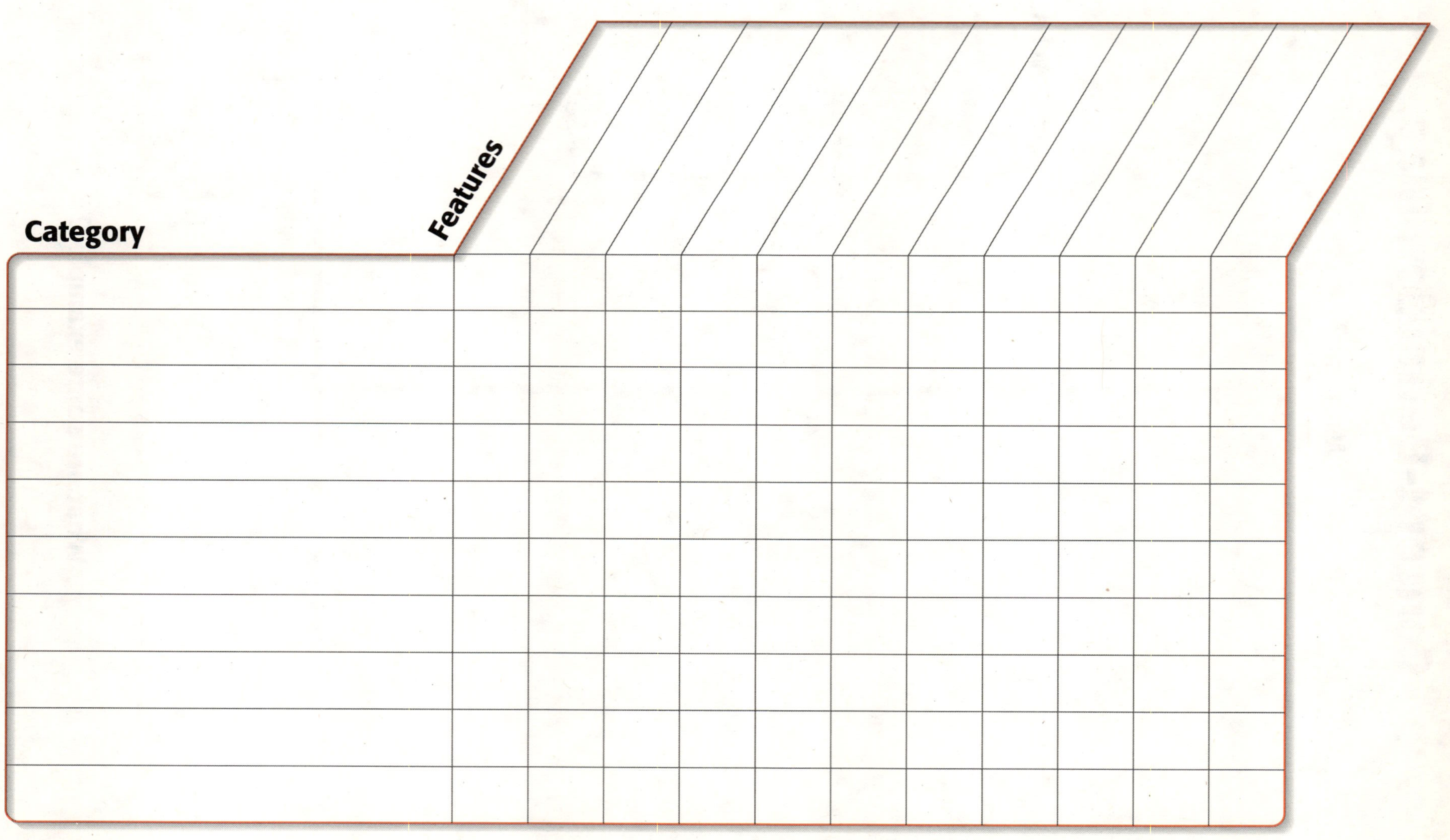

Web

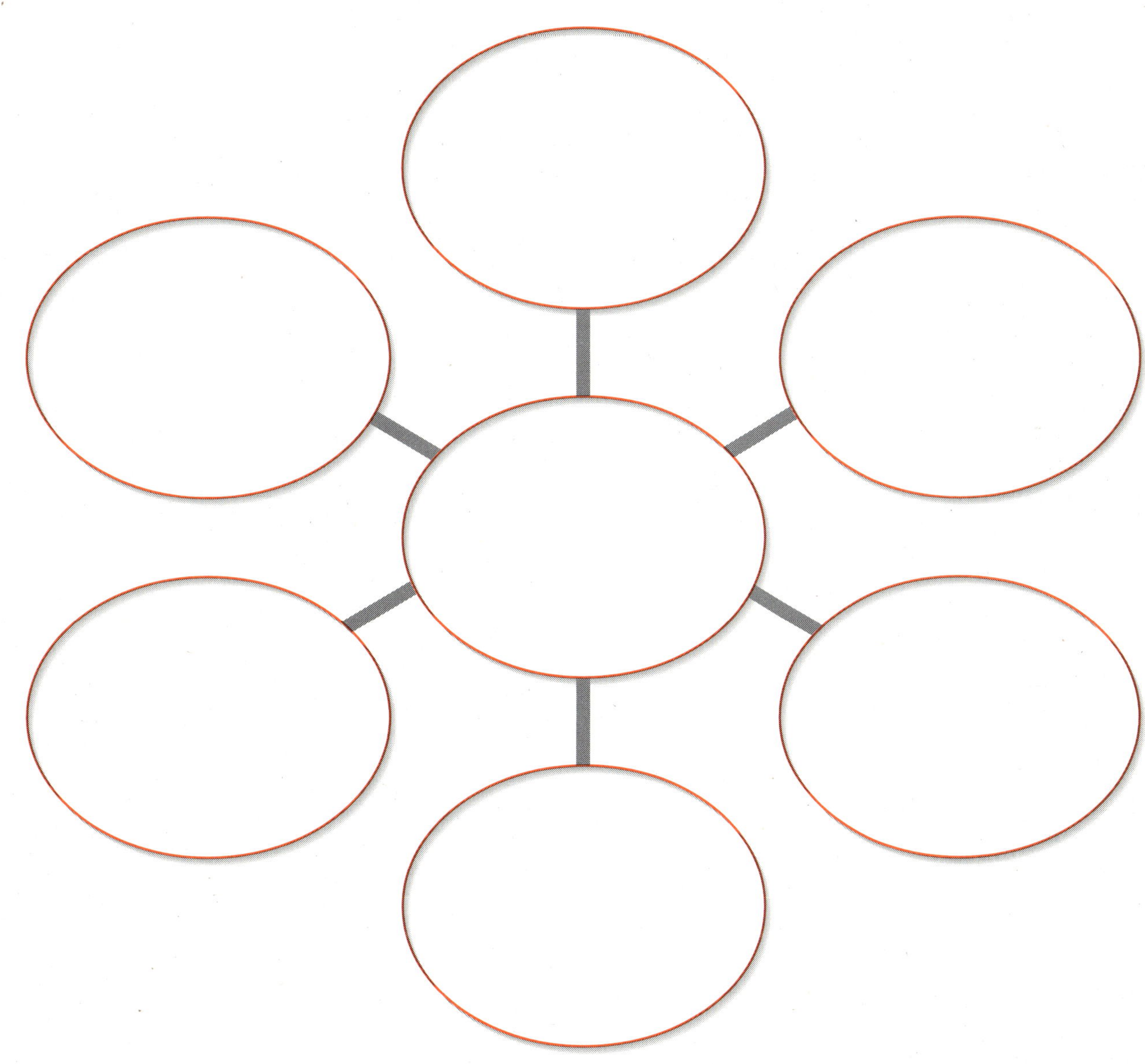

Story Map

Title ________________________________

Setting

Characters ______________ ______________

______________ ______________

______________ ______________

Plot/
Conflict

Event 1 ________________________________

Event 2 ________________________________

Event 3 ________________________________

Event 4 ________________________________

Event 5 ________________________________

Outcome/
Resolution

Theme

Cause-and-Effect Chart

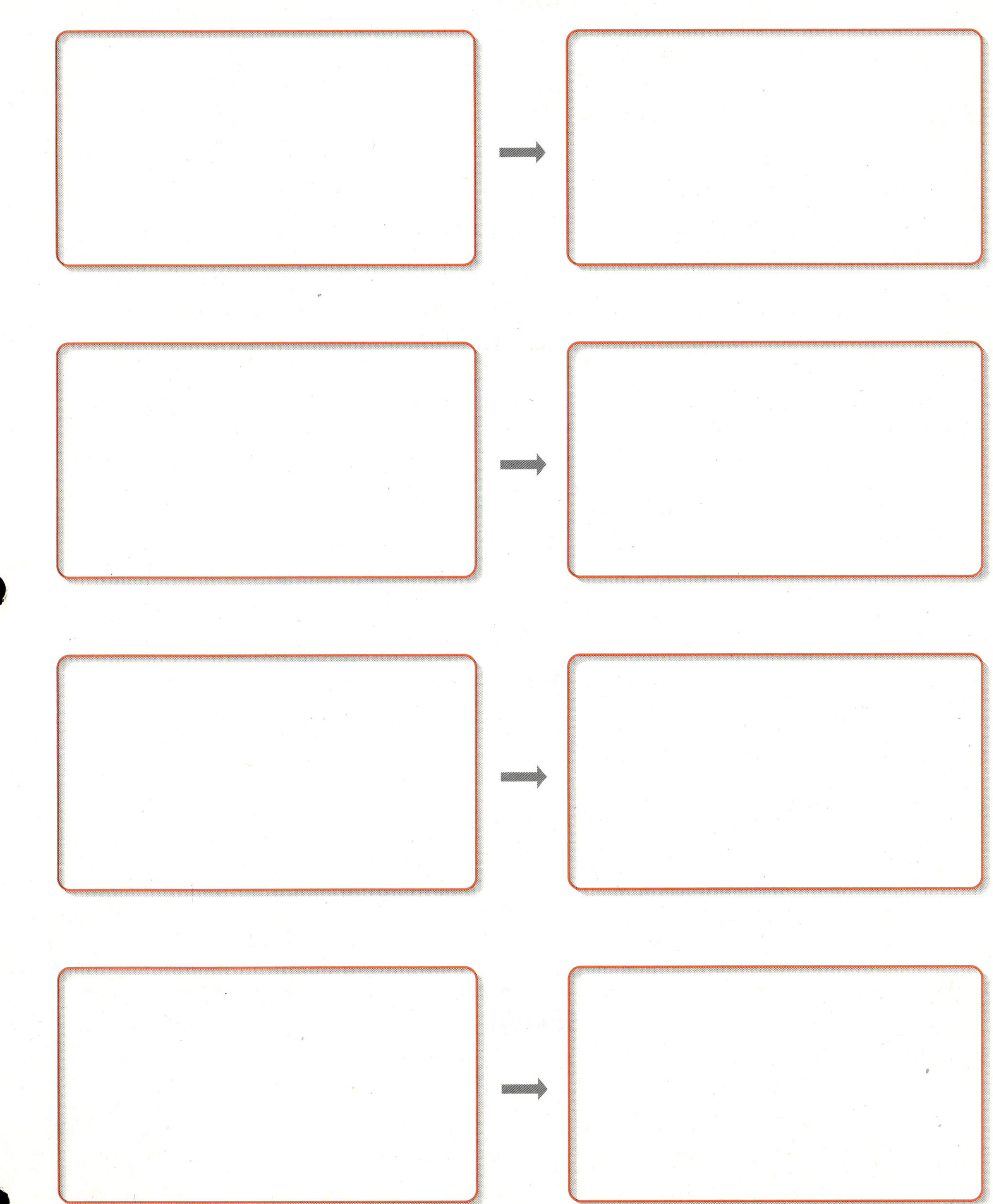

Problem-Solution Chart

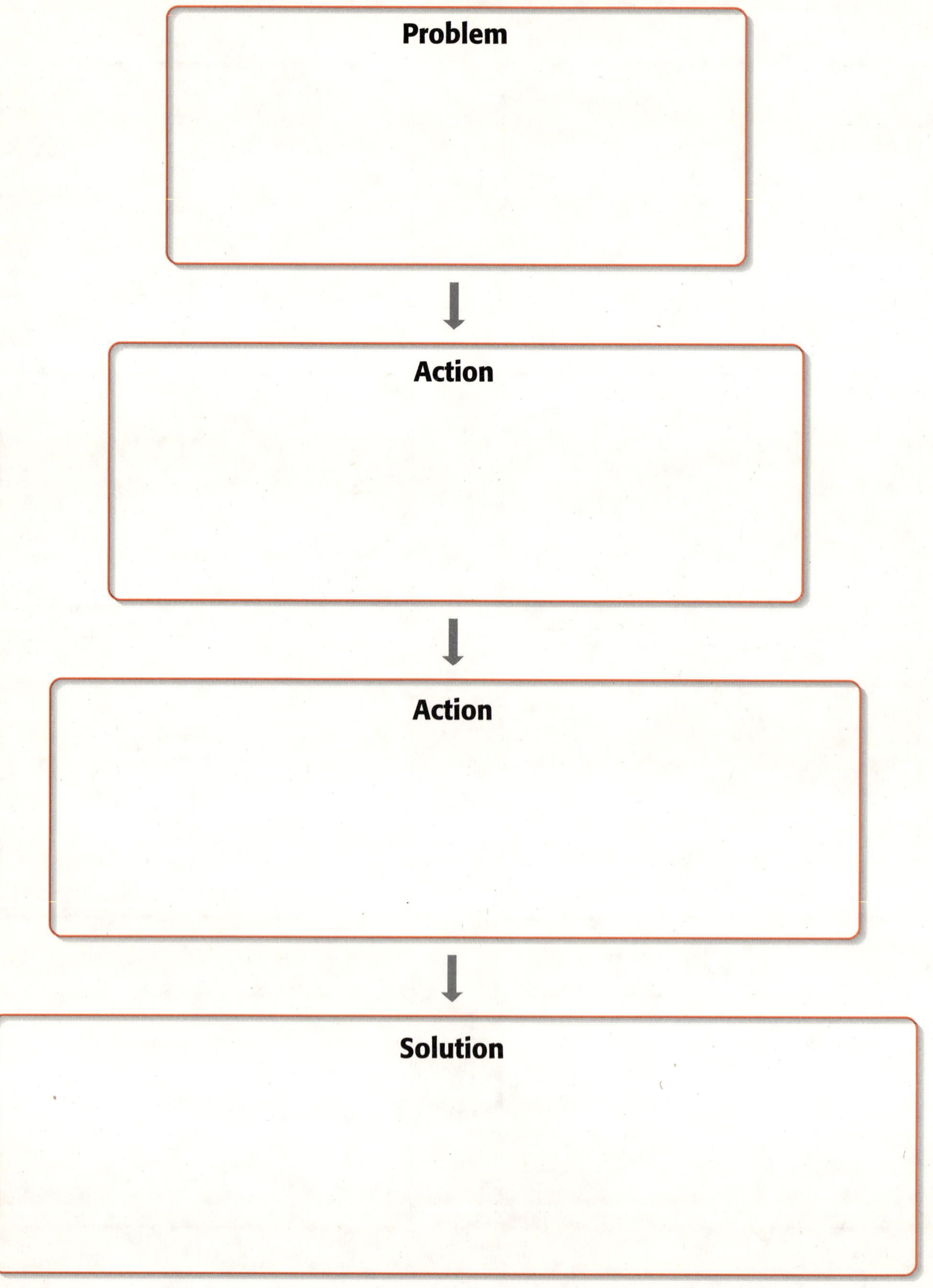

Venn Diagram

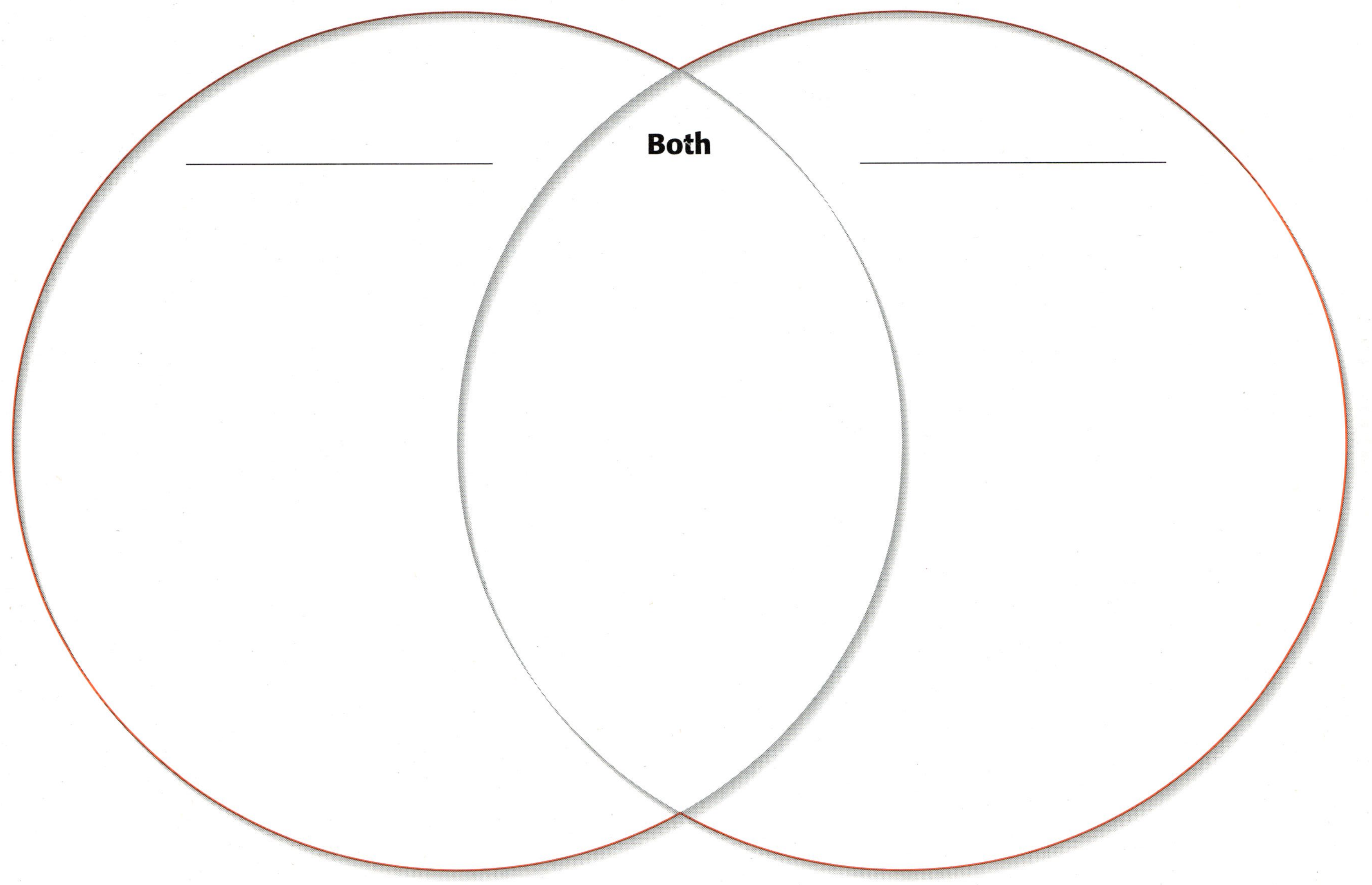

Chain

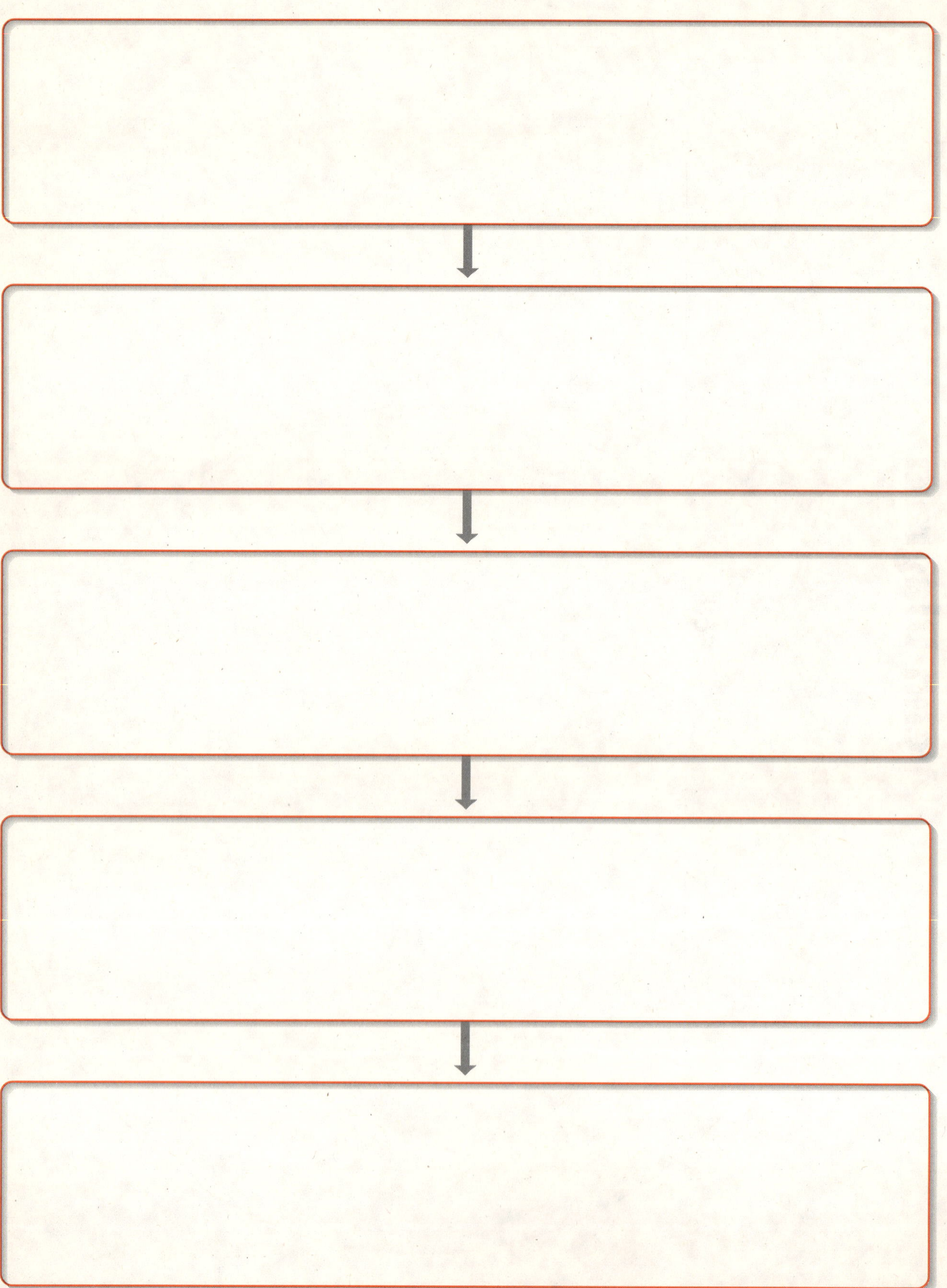

Two-Column Chart

Three-Column Chart

PART 2

Interactive Reading Lessons

OBJECTIVES

- To recognize dialect; to identify themes

The Life You Save May Be Your Own

Flannery O'Connor

Before Reading

Building Background Explain to students that "The Life You Save May Be Your Own" is set in the rural South. To spark discussion, ask students to suppose they were writing a story set in the area where they live. What unique characteristics of the place and the people might they describe? Then have students read "Meet Flannery O'Connor" and the Building Background note in *Glencoe Literature*. Point out that O'Connor is known as a regional writer. She set most of her fiction in the rural South. Her themes and unique portrayals of Southern characters have earned her a reputation as a major literary voice of the American South.

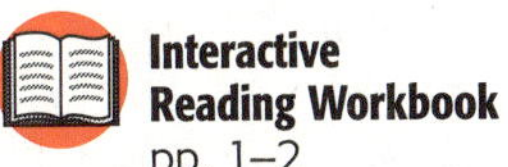
Interactive Reading Workbook pp. 1–2

Building Vocabulary Refer students to Interactive Reading **Reading Guide,** student workbook page 1. Read through Key Vocabulary and Terms with students and discuss the words. Have students make up sentences, using each vocabulary word, that convey the word's meaning. Then call students' attention to the footnotes and glossary notes at the bottom of story pages in the textbook. Encourage students to refer to these notes as they read.

Word Study: Connotation Remind students that the term **connotation** relates to an emotion or an underlying value that accompanies a word's **denotation,** or dictionary meaning. Explain that O'Connor uses vivid adjectives to describe her characters. On the board, write the followings words, without definitions: *gaunt* (thin and hollow-eyed), *sullen* (withdrawn, gloomy), *morose* (bad-tempered), *bitter* (resentful, unforgiving), *depressed* (dejected, sad), and *oppressed* (burdened). Have students tell whether each word has a positive, negative, or neutral connotation. (*All are negative.*) Discuss the meanings of the words with students. Ask students what kinds of characters they would expect to encounter in a story with characters fitting these descriptions. As students read, encourage them to find at least three adjectives that have negative connotations.

Setting a Purpose for Reading Have students read the story to find out whether they agree with the critic who said that author O'Connor is "highly unladylike . . . with a style of writing as balefully direct as a death sentence."

During Reading

Using the Reading Guide Have students turn to their reading guides, student workbook pages 1–2. Tell students that the reading guide will help them keep track of details, characters, and key events in the story. Together with students, read the Key Characters list. Have students complete their reading guides as they read the story.

Recognizing Dialect **Have small groups of students read the story silently.** Remind students that **dialect** is a variation of a language spoken by a particular group, often within a particular region and time. **Write the following sentence on the board and have a volunteer read it aloud.** *"I was raised thataway and there ain't a thing I can do about it."* Point out the words "thataway" and "ain't" and explain that the words are examples of dialect. Ask volunteers to read aloud dialogue and to point out words and phrases that are considered dialect.

Identifying Theme Remind students that the **theme** is the central message of a work of literature that readers can apply to life. To identify the theme of a story, encourage students to pay attention to the story title, the names of characters, any symbols or other objects that appear often, significant speeches by characters, and the plot. Model the process of identifying theme.

> ***Modeling*** The story is about some strange people. I've never met anyone like them. How can I learn something about people in general from them? One way is to look at some of the interesting things Tom Shiftlet says. For example, when he first meets Mrs. Crater, he tells a long story about a doctor's taking out a human heart. He says, "if he was to take that knife and cut into every corner of it, he still wouldn't know no more than you or me." I realize that he is talking about the human heart in a figurative way. Shiftlet's words and his behavior, and even his unusual name, make me think the theme may be that we can never be sure of the intentions and motivations of others.

Point out that a story may have more than one theme. Ask students whether the title may reflect a theme of the story and, if so, how. (*Possible response: The title does not reflect a theme; it reflects the motto of the characters, which can be restated thus: Protect your own interests. Mrs. Carter wanted a husband for Lucynell as well as a handyman; Shiftlet wanted money and creature comforts. Mrs. Carter and Shiftlet try to serve their interests by manipulating each other. Ironically, by leaving Lucynell, Shiftlet saves himself from a life with a woman he does not love, and Mrs. Carter and Lucynell are spared from living with the irresponsible Shiftlet.*) Have students discuss possible themes of the story.

After Reading

You may also use the selection questions and activities in *Glencoe Literature*.

Purpose for Reading Follow-Up Ask students: *Why is O'Connor's writing described as "highly unladylike"?* (The term *ladylike* is often applied to a delicate, polite manner of living and interacting with others. O'Connor's story is shocking in its honesty; it shows people's cynicism, crudeness, selfishness, and exploitation of others.)

OBJECTIVE

▸ To identify figurative language

The Fish

Elizabeth Bishop

Before Reading

Activating Prior Knowledge Tell students that "The Fish" is about the speaker's reaction to a fish she has caught. Invite volunteers who have fished to share fishing experiences. Ask: *What is it like to catch a big fish? How do you feel? Do you ever think about or regret the fish's dying?*

Building Vocabulary On the board, write the following words, without definitions: *barnacles* (marine crustaceans permanently fixed to rocks, boats, or fish), *rosettes* (ornaments resembling a rose), *infested* (having parasites living in or on), *peony* (a bush that produces multiflora blooms), *tarnished* (dulled or discolored), *sullen* (gloomily or resentfully silent or repressed). Have students define the words. Ask students what most of the words have in common. (*The words pertain to nature.*) Have them add the words and definitions to their vocabulary logs or journals.

During Reading

Interactive Reading Workbook p. 3

Identifying Figurative Language Remind students that **imagery** is created through the use of descriptive language that appeals to one or more of the five senses—sight, hearing, taste, smell, and touch. Help students recall that **figurative language** is the expression of truths or ideas that go beyond the literal level. **Call on volunteers to read the poem aloud.** Point out that the poem includes **similes**—nonliteral comparisons of basically unlike things in which the word *like* or *as* is used. (Example: "the pink swim-bladder like a big peony.") Point out that the poem also has several **metaphors**—nonliteral comparisons of basically unlike things in which one thing is spoken of as being another. Ask: *In lines 37–40, are the fish's irises literally backed by tinfoil? Are the lenses literally made of isinglass?* (No, the poet suggests that the fish's eyes have tinfoil behind them and are made of isinglass to help listeners picture the fish's iridescent eyes.) Have students complete Interacting with Text **Identifying Figurative Language,** student workbook page 3.

After Reading

You may also use the selection questions and activities in *Glencoe Literature*.

Interpreting Tell students that **interpreting** is using personal knowledge and experience to attach meaning to what is read. Ask the following questions to help students interpret the poem.

1. How would you characterize the speaker of the poem and her attitude toward nature? (*She is observant; she respects nature.*)
2. How do you respond to the speaker's letting the fish go? Why? (*Possible response: Because the fish is so vividly described, I share the speaker's respect for it. I felt relief when the speaker released the fish.*)

OBJECTIVES

- To use the reading strategy of questioning; to review main ideas

Thoughts on the African-American Novel

Toni Morrison

Before Reading

Activating Prior Knowledge Explain to students that the selection "Thoughts on the African-American Novel" is an essay by Toni Morrison. Ask students: *Why do you read novels? What purpose do you think novels fulfill in society?* Then have students read "Meet Toni Morrison" and the Building Background note in *Glencoe Literature*.

Building Vocabulary On the board, write the following words, without definitions: *peasants* (uneducated persons of low social status), *profoundly* (in a way that shows intellectual depth and insight), *accede* (to express approval or give consent), *clinical* (analytical or coolly dispassionate). Have students write each word and a synonym for each word in their vocabulary logs or journals. Students may consult a thesaurus or a dictionary to verify synonyms.

Word Study: Context Clues Tell students that **context clues** are words or phrases in text surrounding an unfamiliar word that help readers determine the meaning of the unfamiliar word. Context clues can be categorized as antonyms, synonyms, definitions, examples, or explanations. **Read aloud the following sentence** from the essay and ask students to notice the use of the word *peasants*: " . . . there emerged a new class of people who were neither peasants nor aristocrats." Ask students to point out a context clue that helps them understand the meaning of *peasants*. Guide students to understand that the word *aristocrats* (people of noble birth or high social status) is an antonym for *peasants* (people of common birth or low social status). These antonyms define two extremes of society. Urge students to use context clues as they read to help them determine the meanings of unfamiliar words.

Setting a Purpose for Reading Have students read the essay to find out how Toni Morrison thinks that the African American novel should differ from other novels.

During Reading

Questioning **Have students read the essay silently.** After they have read, point out that one good way for students to make sure that they understand a nonfiction selection such as an essay is to use the reading strategy of

questioning, or asking themselves questions as they read. Explain to students that the questions may concern the general meaning of the passage or a specific point that they do not understand. **Read aloud the third paragraph of the selection.** Model using the reading strategy of questioning.

> ***Modeling*** Near the end of the third paragraph, Morrison writes, "Now in a book, which closes, after all—it's of some importance to me to try to make that connection—to try to make that happen also." I ask myself: What connection is she speaking of? What does she want to "happen also"? And what does closing the book have to do with anything? I will reread the paragraph. (*Reread paragraph three.*) Morrison gives examples of connections. A "Black preacher" makes connections to the congregation by involving members in oral response; this increases the power of the sermon. Musicians make connections to the audience that bring about a response and thus enhance the music. Similarly, an author creates a "connection"—a response in readers that causes them to "feel something profoundly"—as the congregation does when listening to a "Black preacher," as the audience does when listening to music. Morrison's saying that a book closes means that the process of reading a book ends. However, the connection the author makes can carry the author's ideas and the meaning of the piece of literature into readers' lives.

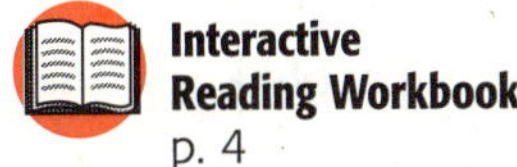

Ask students each to write one or two questions about the content of the essay and to share their questions and answers with the class. Have students complete Interacting with Text **Questioning,** student workbook page 4.

Reviewing Main Ideas Remind students that the main ideas are the most important ideas in a literary work. Point out that Morrison's essay discusses theoretical issues about literature and presents suggestions for how novels should be written. Have pairs of students review the essay and record the practical advice that Morrison gives or implies about writing an African American novel.

You may also use the selection questions and activities in *Glencoe Literature*.

Reviewing Help students review by asking them the following questions.

1. Summarize the definition of the novel that Morrison gives in the first part of her essay. (*A novel is prose that is longer than a short story and that communicates information about life and how to live.*)
2. According to Morrison, why was the novel created? Whom did it serve? (*The novel was created to teach people manners and the rules of society, such as how to get married. It was created for the new middle class, which emerged after the Industrial Revolution.*)
3. What quality seems most important to Morrison in the African American novel? (*The novel must have the characteristics of oral language with a chorus or responsive element.*)

OBJECTIVES

- To analyze cause-and-effect relationships; to visualize the setting and events in a literary work

How the World Was Made

(Cherokee–Great Smoky Mountains)

Retold by James Mooney

The Sky Tree

(Huron–Eastern Woodland)

Retold by Joseph Bruchac

Before Reading

Building Background Ask volunteers to read aloud the definitions of the words *myth*, *creation myths*, and *origin myths* from the Literature Focus preceding the selections in *Glencoe Literature*. Then have students brainstorm for a list of questions they may have asked as children about natural events; for example, Why does it get dark at night? What causes thunder? Why does it rain? Tell students that people throughout the ages have asked questions about the causes and effects of natural occurrences. Explain that, before people knew the principles of modern science, they made up stories to explain natural events. For example, in Norse mythology, Thor was the god of thunder and lightning. Whenever the powerful Thor threw his hammer, lightning was created. Thunder was the noise of his chariot riding through the sky.

Building Vocabulary On the board, write the following words, without their definitions: *suspended* (hanging down), *anxious* (eager), *buzzard* (large slow-moving bird of prey), *endured* (lasted), *multiply* (increase in number), and *toppled* (tumbled down). Have volunteers read the words aloud. Then ask students to write these words in their vocabulary logs or journals and to use what they already know to write a synonym for each word. Ask students to describe a buzzard. (*a large bird of prey*) Then ask them to describe the action of toppling. (*falling as if top-heavy*) Continue the process with the other words.

Word Study: Multiple-Meaning Words Point out to students that the words *suspended, anxious, endured,* and *multiply* have more than one meaning. For example, explain that the word *suspended* can mean "barred temporarily from a privilege or office." Another meaning for *suspended* is "hung so as to be free on all sides except at the point of support." *Anxious* means "worried," though it is often used informally to mean "eager"; *endured* means "suffered" as well as "lasted"; *multiply* means "to perform multiplication" as well as "to become greater in number" or "to breed." Discuss these meanings with students. Encourage them to note each word and its meaning in context as they read the selection. Remind them to consult a dictionary when they are unsure of the meaning of a word.

Setting a Purpose for Reading Encourage students to read to find out about Native American myths that explain the origins of Earth and to note the roles that plants, animals, and people play in the myths.

During Reading

Visualizing **Have students read "How the World Was Made" silently with partners.** Point out that the setting of the selection differs from the world as we know it. In addition, the myth describes a series of events instead of related events that make up a typical plot. Remind students that **visualizing** is using the words of a story to picture a character or a scene. **Read aloud the second paragraph of the selection** and model the process of visualizing for students.

> ***Modeling*** As I read, I try to picture the action of the Water-beetle and its location in relation to the other animals. To understand exactly what is being described, I reread each detail so that I can picture in my mind the Water-beetle going in different directions on the water. I understand the story better when I picture all the animals above the water in some kind of structure in the sky. Then I picture the beetle skimming across the top of the water and diving to the bottom.

Have students read "The Sky Tree" silently with partners. Encourage them to share their visualizations of the setting and the events with their partners as they read.

Analyzing Cause-and-Effect Relationships Ask students what *cause* and *effect* mean. (*A **cause** is an action or occurrence that makes something happen; an **effect** is the result of that action or occurrence.*) Point out to students that the selection "How the World Was Made" describes a cause-and-effect relationship, because it answers the question *why—Why is the world the way it is?* Explain that within the myth other specific causes and effects are described. Suggest that pairs of students fill in a cause-and-effect chart as they read. Distribute copies of the Cause-and-Effect Chart to each pair of students. Use an overhead transparency of a cause-and-effect chart to guide students. Have them follow along as you mark the transparency.

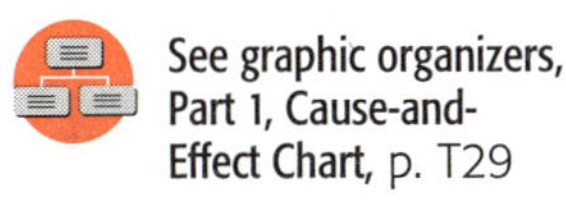
See graphic organizers, Part 1, Cause-and-Effect Chart, p. T29

For practice recognizing causes and effects in "The Sky Tree," have students complete 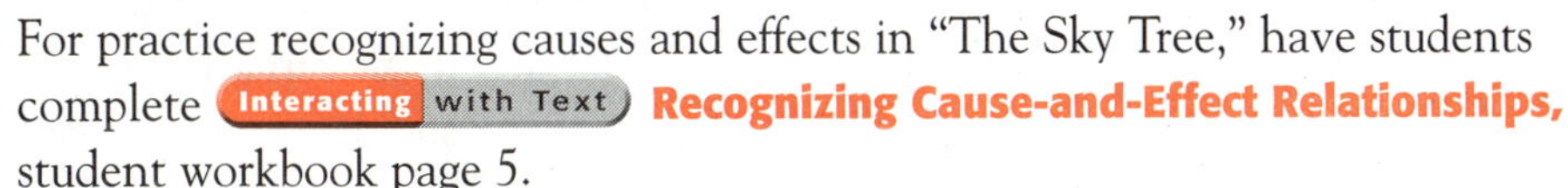

Recognizing Cause-and-Effect Relationships, student workbook page 5.

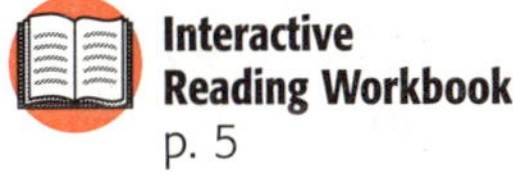
Interactive Reading Workbook p. 5

After Reading

You may also use the selection questions and activities in *Glencoe Literature*.

Analyzing Help students use the following questions to help them think critically about what they have read.

1. What human traits do the animals in "How the World Was Made" have that cause the world to turn out as it does? (*curiosity: "They wonder what was below the water"; ambition: "It was very much crowded, and they were wanting more room."*)
2. What sentence in "How the World Was Made" might explain why the sun's path is an arch rather than a straight line as it moves across the sky? (*"They raised it another time, and another, until it was seven handbreadths high and just under the sky arch."*)

OBJECTIVES

- To summarize; to understand figurative language

FROM

The Iroquois Constitution

Dekanawida

Before Reading

Activating Prior Knowledge Have students read Building Background in *Glencoe Literature*. Then have them, as a group, read the title of the selection. Ask students to name another constitution they have heard of and to describe its purpose. Lead students to understand that the U.S. Constitution was written to set forth the country's laws and system of government and to define the rights of the people of the United States. Explain that the U.S. Constitution was written in 1787, shortly after the United States had won independence from Great Britain in the Revolutionary War. The Iroquois Constitution was written by an Iroquois named Dekanawida about 1570. It was written more than two hundred years before the U.S. Constitution. Ask students what they would expect to find in the Iroquois Constitution, on the basis of their knowledge of the U.S. Constitution.

Building Vocabulary On the board, write the following words, without their definitions: *confederate* (joined with others for a special purpose), *transacted* (carried on), *ascend* (to rise), *allies* (nations united for a special purpose), *respective* (individual), *birthright* (a right or privilege that a person is entitled to by birth), *lineal descent* (in the direct line of descent), and *rites* (solemn ceremonies). Ask students to write the column headings *Nouns*, *Verbs*, and *Adjectives* on a sheet of paper. Then help students find each vocabulary word in the selection. Have them put each word under the correct heading. (nouns: *allies*, *birthright*, *lineal descent*, *rites*; verbs: *transacted*, *ascend*; adjectives: *confederate*, *respective*) As students find the words and categorize them, discuss their meanings in context. Encourage students to record each vocabulary word and its definition in their vocabulary logs or journals.

Word Study: Suffixes Write the words *confederate* and *confederacy* on the board. Ask students to identify the endings that differentiate the two words. (*-ate*, *-acy*) Explain that the suffix *-ate* in the word *confederate* indicates that the word is an adjective. (The suffix *-ate* can also indicate that a word is a verb, as in the words *populate* and *validate*.) Point out that the suffix *-acy* indicates that *confederacy* is a noun. Have students change the word *accurate* into a noun by adding a suffix. (*accuracy*)

Setting a Purpose for Reading Encourage students to read the selection to find out what issues were essential in bringing Native American tribes together.

During Reading

Summarizing Ask students what summarizing means. (***Summarizing*** *is creating a brief statement of the main ideas and the most important details of a passage or selection.*) Then have students read the section titled "The Clans." Ask volunteers to summarize the selection. (*The original clans of the Five Nations are the only owners of their land, and members of those clans must recognize other members of their clan as relatives. Family trees of the Five Nations people are based on their female ancestors, who own the land.*)

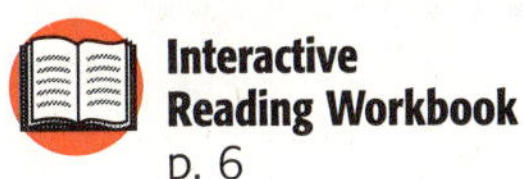
Interactive Reading Workbook p. 6

Have small groups of students read the selection silently, one section at a time. Tell students to pause after the first section and to jot down notes for a summary of the section. Have groups compose oral summaries immediately after reading each section. Then have students complete **Interacting with Text Summarizing,** student workbook page 6.

Figurative Language Explain that **figurative language** is descriptive language used to convey ideas or emotions. A **symbol,** one type of figurative language, is a tangible, physical item that stands for an idea. **Read aloud the section entitled "The Leaders"** and model the process of understanding figurative language.

> ***Modeling*** **Dekanawida describes the thick skin of the leaders of the Confederacy of the Five Nations. He says it "shall be seven spans." I know that skin cannot literally be seven spans thick, because one span is about nine inches. I think Dekanawida is using a symbol. Skin is a physical item. The role of skin is to protect the body. Dekanawida is using the symbol of leaders' thick skin to represent the idea of the leaders' not allowing themselves to be easily angered, hurt, or offended.**

Point out the last paragraph under the heading "The Laws of the Council." **Have a student read the paragraph and its footnote aloud.** Ask students: *What is the league of nations compared to?* (a house) Explain that the beam Dekanawida mentions is not a literal piece of wood. Ask students: *What does a "new beam" represent in the passage?* (a new rule to help support the league) Explain that the author is using a **metaphor**—a comparison between two unlike things—a law and a ceiling beam. A law and a ceiling beam are alike, however, in that they both support something larger than themselves. Explain that both metaphors and symbols are forms of figurative language. They help readers understand abstract ideas. Suggest that students reread, when details do not make sense, to see whether figurative language is being used.

After Reading

You may also use the selection questions and activities in *Glencoe Literature.*

Reviewing and Analyzing Ask the following questions to help students review and analyze the selection.

1. How are the names of the clans and the names of the festivals that Dekanawida mentions similar? What do they tell you about the Five Nations' way of life? (*They are based on names of plants and animals and other aspects of nature. Natural elements and the growing season were central to the people's daily lives.*)
2. Explain the meaning of the symbol of the "Eagle who is able to see afar." How do symbols such as the Eagle and the Tree of the Great Peace make the constitution more powerful? (*The Eagle is a symbol of strength that will keep the league safe from danger. This and other symbols characterize the constitution as powerful, well-developed, and spiritually strong.*)

OBJECTIVES

- To predict narrative events; to analyze character and mood in a nonfiction narrative

FROM

La Relación

Álvar Núñez Cabeza de Vaca

Translated by Martin A. Favata and José B. Fernández

Before Reading

Building Background Have students read "Meet Álvar Núñez Cabeza de Vaca" and Building Background in *Glencoe Literature*. Have students brainstorm to compile a list of facts they already know about the early explorers. Ask: *What European explorers came to the New World before Cabeza de Vaca in 1528?* (Columbus came to the West Indies, 1492; Amerigo Vespucci came to the West Indies, 1499; Ponce de León came to Florida, 1513; Cortés came to Mexico, 1519.) *What hardships did these explorers face in voyages across the ocean?* (lack of food, storms, no modern navigational instruments, unknown destinations) *What did they find once they arrived in America?* (unfamiliar wilderness sparsely populated with groups of Native Americans who had unfamiliar customs and spoke unfamiliar languages) Encourage students to visualize an expedition under these circumstances. Have them discuss what they visualize.

Building Vocabulary On the board, write these words, without their definitions: *sounding* (a measurement of depth), *provisioned* (provided with food and drink), *capsize* (to overturn), *attire* (dress), and *untutored* (not educated). Have students volunteer sentences that use the vocabulary words. On the board, write a sentence for each word and discuss the definition of the vocabulary word. Encourage students to use synonyms, antonyms, and appositives to make the meanings of the words clear in their sentences. An example is "My brother likes casual clothes, but I prefer more formal *attire*." Have students write the sample sentences in their vocabulary logs or journals.

Word Study: Specialized Vocabularies Remind students that many subjects, such as science, sports, and music, have specialized vocabularies. Ask students to suggest words that pertain to a particular sport, such as tennis or football. Explain that sailing also has a specialized vocabulary. As students read, have them list in their vocabulary logs or journals the terms used in the selection that are related to sailing or the sea. Point out that some definitions appear in the selection. Encourage students to check the dictionary for clarification of the meanings of unfamiliar words. Words related to the sea or sailing include *sailing master, tiller, breakers, sounding, fathoms, oar, stern, overboard, launch, shore, capsize,* and *surf.*

Setting a Purpose for Reading Have students read to find out what kinds of disasters awaited the European explorers of America in the sixteenth century.

During Reading

Predicting Remind students that **predicting** what will happen next in a narrative is a good way to improve comprehension. **Have students read the first**

two pages of the selection independently. When they have finished reading, ask: *How do you think the voyage will turn out?* Have students write their predictions on a sheet of paper. Then model the process of predicting for students.

> ***Modeling*** **When I read that the men are going to set out on the ocean again, I predict that the outcome will not be good. The men are still weak and unprepared. I know that it is November and the weather has been bad. Cabeza de Vaca does not say the weather has improved.**

Have students finish reading the selection independently to find out whether their predictions are validated.

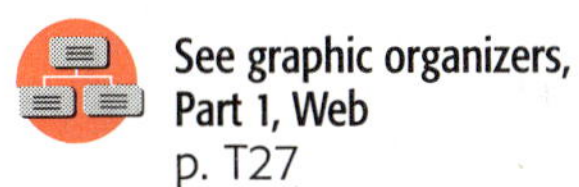

See graphic organizers, Part 1, Web
p. T27

Analyzing Characterization Create two webs on the board to describe the character of Cabeza de Vaca. Point out that, because the narrative is written by Cabeza de Vaca about his own life, he is able to present a positive picture of himself. However, less-positive aspects of his character are also revealed. On the first web, write *Cabeza de Vaca: Positive View* in the center circle. Have students name positive traits. (Example: He is *strong* when he steers the boat despite his exhaustion.) On the second web, write *Cabeza de Vaca: Negative View* in the center circle. (Example: He seems to be *biased*, *suspicious*, and *self-righteous*.) Discuss how the sets of traits together characterize Cabeza de Vaca.

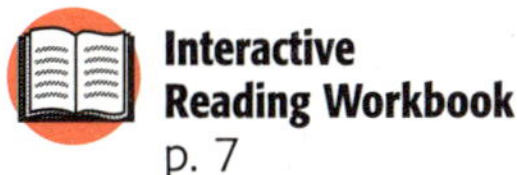

Interactive Reading Workbook
p. 7

Analyzing Mood Ask a volunteer to explain what is meant by the mood of a literary work. (*The* ***mood*** *is the feeling or atmosphere that a writer creates for the reader.*) Then discuss with students how a writer's choice of language, subject matter, setting, and tone contribute to the mood of a selection. Point out that Cabeza de Vaca, to impress readers with the hardships of his expedition, creates a particular mood. Ask students: *How would you describe the mood of the selection?* (dark, sad, and tense) Have students find and read aloud passages that demonstrate the mood. Have students complete **Interacting with Text** **Analyzing Mood,** student workbook page 7.

Predicting Follow-Up Have students write a paragraph analyzing the reasons their predictions were accurate or were off the mark. Encourage students to include quotations from the selection that support their predictions.

After Reading

You may also use the selection questions and activities in *Glencoe Literature*.

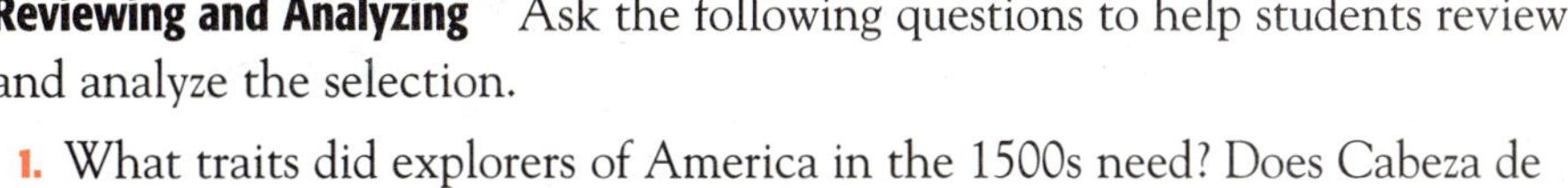

Reviewing and Analyzing Ask the following questions to help students review and analyze the selection.

1. What traits did explorers of America in the 1500s need? Does Cabeza de Vaca exhibit these traits? (*Explorers needed to be curious, courageous, physically strong, and open-minded. Cabeza de Vaca seems to have some of these traits, but he does not seem open-minded about meeting new people.*)
2. What does the Indians' response to the explorers' tragedy show about the Indians' character and their society? (*Their social order seems to be based on maintaining friendships and on helping others through troubled times.*)

OBJECTIVES

- To paraphrase; to analyze an author's style

FROM

Of Plymouth Plantation

William Bradford

Before Reading

Activating Prior Knowledge Have students silently read "Meet William Bradford" and Building Background in *Glencoe Literature*. Ask students to think about what they know about the Pilgrims, who came to America in 1620. Start a KWL chart on the board about the Pilgrims. Ask students to contribute facts they already know. Write them in the first column. Then have students suggest what they would like to learn. Record that information in the second column. Distribute individual KWL charts (see graphic organizers, Part 1) and have students individually complete the first two columns.

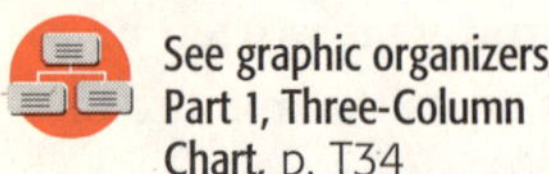

See graphic organizers, Part 1, Three-Column Chart, p. T34

Pilgrims

What I Know	What I Want to Learn	What I Learned
Came to America on the *Mayflower*	How many Pilgrims came on the *Mayflower*?	
Celebrated the first Thanksgiving	How did the Pilgrims interact with Native Americans?	

Building Vocabulary On the board, write the following words, without their definitions: *commonwealth* (a nation, state, or other political unit), *deliberation* (discussion and consideration by a group of persons), *habitation* (a dwelling place), *lamentable* (to be regretted or mourned), *inaccommodate* (not helpful or obliging), *beholden* (indebted for a favor or gift), *skulking* (moving in a stealthy or secretive manner), *aloof* (distant, either physically or emotionally), *discourse* (a verbal interchange of ideas). Read the words aloud with students. Then model how to figure out the meaning of an unfamiliar word.

> ***Modeling*** I've never seen the word *inaccommodate* before, but I recognize parts of the word. I know that if people *accommodate* my needs, they help me. I know that the prefix *in-* can mean "not," as in *incapable*, which means "not capable." So I can figure out that *inaccommodate* as an adjective means "not helpful."

Ask students to discuss the meaning of each vocabulary word and to tell what clues helped them figure out the definition. Encourage students to record the words and their meanings in their vocabulary logs or journals.

Word Study: Connotation Remind students that most words have one or more denotative dictionary definitions. Explain that words also have positive, negative, or neutral **connotations**, additional suggested or implied meanings. For example, the word *habitation* has a neutral connotation. However, the synonym *home* has a positive connotation, whereas *shack* has a negative connotation. Point out that the word *skulking* has a negative connotation, suggesting cowardliness or fear. Ask: *What kind of connotation does the word* aloof *have?* (negative) *Why?* (The dictionary definition is "at a distance," but *aloof* implies being stuck up or snobbish.) Encourage students to note connotations of words as they read to help them recognize bias on the part of the writer.

Setting a Purpose for Reading Encourage students to read the selection to find out what the Pilgrims were like.

During Reading

Paraphrasing Explain to students that they will find William Bradford's writing different from contemporary writing in terms of diction (word choice) and sentence construction. Suggest to students that they stop to paraphrase passages that they find difficult to understand. Remind them that in **paraphrasing** they put the passage into their own words. **Ask students to read the first two sentences of the selection silently** and then have a volunteer paraphrase it. (*The sea was treacherous, and for several days the ships' passengers were forced to stay in the hull below. When John Howland ascended to the deck, he was swept overboard. Luckily he grabbed onto a rope trailing in the water to save himself.*) **Ask students to read the selection silently with partners.** Have them pause after reading each titled section to paraphrase the passage.

Analyzing Style Explain to students that an author's style is shown in elements such as diction, sentence length, and sentence construction. Analyzing an author's style can help readers better understand the content as well as appreciate the literature. **Ask a volunteer to read aloud the first sentence of the second paragraph.** Then ask students what they notice about the way the sentence is written. Lead them to notice the use of parentheses and semicolons, unusual phrases such as "they fell with that land" (meaning "they landed"), and the unusual use of the negative phrase "not a little joyful" (meaning "very joyful"). Point out to students that noticing unusual stylistic elements may help them paraphrase the passage. Ask students how they would characterize William Bradford's style. (*complex, calm, formal, and old-fashioned*) Have students complete Interacting with Text **Analyzing Style,** student workbook page 8.

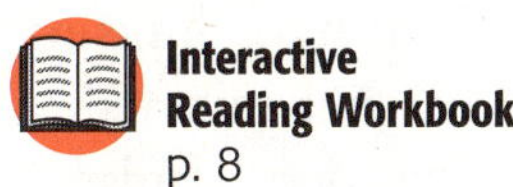
Interactive Reading Workbook
p. 8

After Reading

You may also use the selection questions and activities in *Glencoe Literature*.

KWL Chart Follow-Up Have students complete their KWL charts. Encourage them to include details in the third column that add to what they already know and that answer their "What I Want to Learn" questions. Have students suggest items for the third column of their charts. Discuss the items they have included.

Drawing Conclusions Ask students what conclusions they can draw about the character traits of the Pilgrims. Encourage students to point out specific details about the character traits of the Pilgrims in the selection. (*Possible response: According to the information in the text, the Pilgrims seem courageous, hardworking, religious, wise, cooperative, and grateful for their blessings.*)

OBJECTIVE

- To paraphrase a poem

Upon the Burning of Our House July 10th, 1666 and *To My Dear and Loving Husband*

Anne Bradstreet

Before Reading

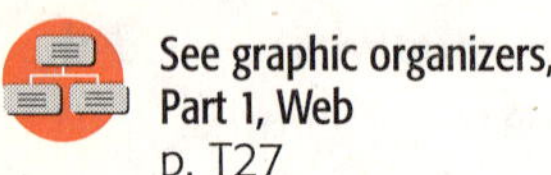
See graphic organizers, Part 1, Web p. T27

Activating Prior Knowledge Draw a concept web on the board. Write the word *Puritans* in the center circle. Explain to students that the Puritans have gained a certain reputation; for example, prudish attitudes are sometimes called puritanical. Ask students to brainstorm to list what they know about the character traits of the Puritans. (*Possible responses: hard working, religious, rigid, unemotional, and strict.*) Have students complete their own webs. After they have read the poems, students should compare their responses to the poems to what they have written on their webs.

Building Vocabulary On the board, write the following words: *piteous, mold'ring, persevere, thy, thee,* and *thou.* Read the words aloud with students. Have students give definitions for *piteous* (similar to *pitiful*) and *persevere* (to persist despite discouragement). Explain that *mold'ring* is a contraction of *moldering* and have them look up its definition ("crumbling into particles"). Explain that *thy* (your), *thee* (you), and *thou* (you) are pronouns that were commonly used in England and the colonies in the 1600s, and later than that in literature and religious speech. Encourage students to record the vocabulary words and their meanings in their vocabulary logs or journals.

During Reading

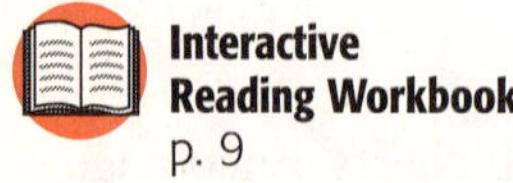
Interactive Reading Workbook p. 9

Paraphrasing **Ask several students to take turns reading aloud "Upon the Burning of Our House."** Have readers pause after lines 12, 20, 28, 36, 42, and 54. Ask volunteers to paraphrase four-line segments. If students have difficulty interpreting the meaning, have them paraphrase lines by changing inverted word order to regular word order (subject/verb), substituting modern words for words such as *thy* and *'twas*, and substituting simple words for unfamiliar words. Have students complete Interacting with Text **Paraphrasing,** student workbook page 9.

After Reading

You may also use the selection questions and activities in *Glencoe Literature.*

Responding Ask students what they liked or did not like about each poem. Then direct their attention to the concept web that they created in Activating Prior Knowledge. Ask: *Which of the character traits that you wrote for the Puritans are demonstrated by Anne Bradstreet, and which are not?* For example, Bradstreet exhibits a very religious attitude. However, she is distressed and emotional about her house's burning. She is not rigid but is able to change her attitude toward her tragedy by reflecting on what is most important in her life. If students thought that Puritans lacked passion, this idea is contradicted by the feelings expressed by Bradstreet in "To My Dear and Loving Husband."

OBJECTIVES

- To visualize setting and events in a narrative; to recognize theme

FROM

A Narrative of the Captivity and Restoration of Mrs. Mary Rowlandson

Mary Rowlandson

Before Reading

Building Background Have students read "Meet Mary Rowlandson" and Building Background in *Glencoe Literature*. Then have students read the selection title. Ask them what *restoration* refers to. (*Mary Rowlandson's release and return to her home*) Ask students to brainstorm to list situations they have heard about in which people were captured or kidnapped. Help students consider two kinds of kidnappings: kidnapping for ransom (for example, kidnapping a member of a wealthy family strictly for money) and political kidnapping (taking hostages or prisoners of war for ideological reasons). Ask students how they would feel in either of these situations. (*frightened, depressed, worried, homesick*)

Building Vocabulary On the board, write the following words, without their synonyms: *prosperity* (wealth), *bespeaking* (requesting), *abode* (temporary stay), *miscarriage* (corruption), and *withal* (besides). Have students write the words in their vocabulary logs or journals. As they read, ask them to write a synonym for each word as it is used in the selection. If they are unsure of the meaning, encourage them to check a dictionary.

Word Study: Changing Verb Forms and Spellings On the board, write the words *shewed*, *spake*, *bad*, *bade*, and *travelling*. Have students find these words in the selection and define them. Explain that the author uses *spake* as the past tense for *speak*. Ask: *What is the past tense of* speak *that we use?* (spoke) The author uses the verb *bid* (to issue an order to or give expression to), a verb that is not often used today. The past tense appears as both *bad* and *bade*. The author spells *showed* "shewed" and *traveling* "travelling." Explain that although *travelling* is an accepted British spelling, in the United States we most often use one *l* when adding *-ed* or *-ing* to *travel*. Ask students what generalization they can make about the English language from these verb forms and spellings. Guide students to understand that the English language is constantly changing. Explain that new words are added while others fall out of use. As students read, have them list words that are not common today. (Examples include *removes*, meaning "moves," and *fain*, meaning "obliged.")

During Reading

Visualizing Remind students that **visualizing,** using the words of a selection to help them picture characters, scenes, and events in their minds, can help them better understand the story and connect to it. **Read aloud the paragraph that**

begins **"My son being now about a mile . . . "** and model visualizing for students.

> ***Modeling*** The author describes "travelling over hills and through swamps," looking for her son. As I read, I picture the rough wilderness that covered North America in the 1600s. I visualize this woman, sad because of her tragedies and weak from hunger, getting lost in this wild landscape.

Have students read the selection independently. Encourage students to visualize each event as they read. Have them share scenes that they find particularly vivid. Ask them to point out sensory details that help them visualize.

Changing Pace **Have a volunteer read aloud the paragraph that begins "*The second remove.*"** Ask students whether they have problems understanding passages like this. Help students recognize that the author uses long sentences. The rhythm differs from the rhythm of modern speech. Readers may find some sentences monotonous and may lose track of a sentence's meaning. When this happens, suggest that students slow down the pace of their reading and that they paraphrase one or two sentences to make sure they understand them.

Recognizing Theme Remind students that the **theme** of a work of literature is the central message that readers can apply to life. Explain that poems and stories of lasting value often teach one or more valuable lessons that can be stated in a sentence. **Ask a volunteer to read aloud the last paragraph of the selection.** Have students write down a generalization about life that they think is the message of the selection. Have students share their statements of theme. (*Possible themes: People should not get upset about minor issues. Undergoing a great tragedy teaches a person to put into perspective the important and unimportant events in life.*) Have students complete **Interacting with Text** **Recognizing Theme,** student workbook page 10.

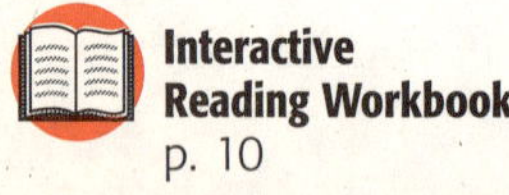

Interactive Reading Workbook
p. 10

After Reading

You may also use the selection questions and activities in *Glencoe Literature*.

Analyzing Character Traits Distribute copies of the Venn diagram. Have students list the character traits of Mary Rowlandson and of the Indians who held her captive. Use an overhead transparency of a Venn Diagram to guide students in listing the traits. Write *Mary Rowlandson's Traits* in one circle of the diagram and *Indians' Traits* in the other circle. Write *Shared Traits* in the center section where the circles overlap. Have students discuss their findings. (*Possible answers: Mary Rowlandson—religious, brave, loving, persevering; Indians—warriors, fair, resourceful; Shared Traits—helpful, generous, kind, compassionate*)

See graphic organizers, Part 1, Venn Diagram
p. T31

Connecting Remind students that, when they **connect,** they think about how events in their lives are similar to or different from the events they have read about. Explain that Mary Rowlandson was surprised because the Indians did not act as she had expected them to act. Ask students to discuss whether they have ever had an expectation about the way an individual would act. Were they surprised by the way the individual did act? Why? Have students write their answers in their journals.

OBJECTIVES

- To analyze conflict; to analyze dialogue

FROM

Stay Alive, My Son

Pin Yathay with John Man

Before Reading

Building Background Have students read "Meet Pin Yathay" and Building Background in *Glencoe Literature*. Show students a map of Southeast Asia and have a volunteer point out Cambodia and Vietnam. Explain that Southeast Asia has been the site of much political strife. Ask students to tell anything they know about Cambodia or Vietnam during the 1960s and 1970s. Lead students in a brief discussion about the Vietnam War. Explain that the Communists, the Viet Cong, revolted against the South Vietnamese government. The United States helped South Vietnam, fighting the Viet Cong from 1965 until 1973. About 58 thousand Americans, 1 million South Vietnamese, and more than 500 thousand North Vietnamese died in the war.

Building Vocabulary On the board, write the following words: *partition*, *contemplate*, *evading*, and *morgue*. Have students write the words in their vocabulary logs or journals. Ask students to locate each word in the selection as they read it. Have them write a definition of each word and a sentence or two explaining why the word is particularly meaningful in the selection. After reading the selection, students will discuss their definitions for each word and tell why each word is meaningful in the selection.

Word Study: Prefix *in-* On the board, write the following words: *inevitable*, *irrevocable*, *impossible*, and *irredeemable*. Have students read each word and its definition as it appears in the footnotes of the selection. Ask what the words have in common. (*All have prefixes that mean "not."*) Explain that the prefix *in-* is spelled *ir-* when it is used before a word beginning with *r*. It is spelled *im-* when it is used before a word beginning with the letters *p* or *m*. Have students write at least one more word that contains each prefix: *in-*, *ir-*, and *im-*. (*Examples:* inactive, irresponsible, *and* immature.) As students read, have them note words that have the prefix *im-* or *ir-*. Tell them to make sure the prefixes mean "not" in the words they identify. (*Examples:* irredeemable, impossible, irrevocable.)

Setting a Purpose for Reading Encourage students to read the selection to find out how a man responds to the problem of how to save the lives of himself and his family.

During Reading

Analyzing Conflict Explain that the selection is a **nonfiction narrative**. It tells a true story from the first-person point of view. However, as in fictional stories, the events are arranged artistically in order to emphasize elements such as character and conflict and to create suspense. **Have students read the selection independently.** Then discuss the **conflict**—that is, the problem around which the events are centered. Ask volunteers to identify the conflict. Write student responses on the board. (*Possible response: Pin Yathay wants to save the lives of himself, his wife, and his son, but he knows that if he stays with them, they will all die. If he runs away, they may all live.*) Ask students: *How does this conflict affect characterization in the narrative?* (Readers judge Pin Yathay on his proposing to leave and considering whether to do so; they see Any in light of her response to the proposal and Nawath as a potential victim of the proposal.) *How does the conflict affect the tone of the narrative?* (Because the conflict is a matter of life and death, it gives a somber, sad, grave tone to the narrative.)

Analyzing Dialogue Remind students that **dialogue** shows the exact words of characters in a narrative. Point out that a nonfiction narrative may include dialogue, just as a fictional narrative does. In both cases, dialogue makes a narrative realistic; it helps characterize the people, and it helps move the plot along. Assign two students the characters of Yathay and Any. Have them read aloud the dialogue on the last two pages of text. Then ask the following questions: *What emotions do Yathay and Any show in the dialogue?* (The dialogue shows Yathay's pain in making his decision and his love for his wife and son. It shows Any's love for her husband and dependence on him, and yet it shows her ability to fight him when she thinks he is wrong.) Have students complete Interacting with Text **Analyzing Dialogue,** student workbook page 11.

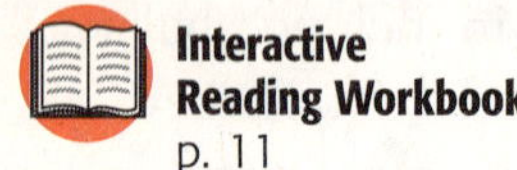
Interactive Reading Workbook
p. 11

Questioning Explain that one way to understand and appreciate a literary work is continually to ask oneself questions while reading the text. Questioning makes reading active instead of passive. **Read aloud the first page of the selection** and model the process of questioning for students.

> ***Modeling*** I read about Yathay's change of attitude after almost surrendering to his fate. First I ask, *What steps will he take to save himself?* Then I ask myself, *How will Yathay justify his decision? and How will Any react to his decision?* These questions increase my suspense and help me focus on the narrative's most important issue.

Have students write two questions they might ask as they read the last page of the selection.

After Reading

You may also use the selection questions and activities in *Glencoe Literature.*

Vocabulary Follow-up Have students discuss the vocabulary words from the selection that they wrote in their vocabulary logs or journals. For each word, ask several students to read aloud their definitions and to tell why the word is particularly meaningful in the selection. For example, Nawath is described as sleeping behind a cloth *partition* (an interior dividing wall). This device suggests the simplicity of the family's lifestyle. The word *contemplate* (to meditate on) implies the thoughtful spiritual process Yathay experiences to make his decision. The word *evading* (avoiding facing up to) describes Yathay's fear of not accepting responsibility. The word *morgue* (a place where bodies are kept) is used figuratively to describe the hospital.

OBJECTIVES

- To analyze problem and solution; to understand figurative language

FROM

Sinners in the Hands of an Angry God

Jonathan Edwards

Before Reading

Building Background Have students read "Meet Jonathan Edwards" and Building Background in *Glencoe Literature*. Remind students that the Puritans originally came to America to practice their religious beliefs as they chose. Therefore, religion was an important part of the colonists' lives. Explain that the colonists were expected to observe the Sabbath by praying all day and by refraining from doing work. Much time was spent in church, listening to preachers such as Edwards.

Building Vocabulary On the board, write the following words, without their synonyms: *executions* (performances), *refuge* (shelter), *arbitrary* (random), *uncovenanted* (unpromised), *forbearance* (patience), *wrath* (anger), *singe* (burn), and *induce* (cause). Have students write a synonym for each word. Encourage students to refer to a dictionary if they cannot think of a synonym. Point out to students that the word *executions* has multiple meanings; in the selection, it means "the act of carrying out." Have students share the synonyms they have written. Encourage students to record each word and its synonym in their vocabulary logs or journals.

Word Study: Emotionally Charged Words On the board, write the following words: *hell*, *wrath*, *devil*, *brimstone*, *wickedness*, *serpent*, *damnation*, and *salvation*. Ask students what the words have in common. Lead students to notice that all the words provoke strong emotional reactions. Ask students: *How does using emotionally charged words help speakers or authors accomplish their purpose?* (The words inspire strong emotions such as fear or guilt and might cause some readers and listeners to change their lives.) *How might using emotionally charged words backfire for a speaker or an author?* (The words might cause some people to react negatively and rebel against doing what the speaker or author suggests.) As students read the selection, they should note the emotionally charged words and list the number of times each word is used.

Setting a Purpose for Reading Have students read the selection to find out the techniques one early American preacher uses to encourage his congregation to find God.

During Reading

Analyzing Problem and Solution Have students read the selection in small groups. Suggest that they take turns reading the first few paragraphs aloud. Then have them read silently, sharing particularly vivid or difficult passages.

As students read, they should look for the problem and the solution that the author presents.

Monitoring Comprehension When students are finished reading, ask the following questions: *Jonathan Edwards spends much of the sermon discussing the major problem that people face. What is this problem?* (He says that God is angry and that people are one step from hell.) *In the last two paragraphs of the sermon, Jonathan Edwards presents a solution to the problem. What is the solution?* (People can accept Christ as their savior, ask for forgiveness, and change their lives by putting God first.)

Understanding Figurative Language Explain to students that the author relies on vivid imagery and figurative language to make an impression on his listeners. Remind students that a **simile** is a comparison between two unlike things, in which the word *like* or *as* is used. **Read the following sentence aloud:** "Your wickedness makes you as it were heavy as lead, and to tend downwards with great weight and pressure towards hell." Ask students: *What is the simile in the sentence?* ("Your wickedness makes you as . . . heavy as lead.") *What two unlike things are being compared?* (wickedness and lead) Explain that the comparison of wickedness with something familiar (lead) provides the reader with a vivid image of an idea.

Now ask students: *What is a metaphor?* (A **metaphor** is a comparison made between two seemingly unlike things without the use of the word *like* or *as*.) Model the process of analyzing metaphors for students. **Read aloud from the paragraph that begins with "O sinner!" Read to "damned in hell."**

> ***Modeling*** In this passage, the author is comparing hell to a "great furnace of wrath, a wide and bottomless pit, full of the fire of wrath." This metaphor creates a vivid, horrifying picture of hell in my mind. I cannot help but picture hell from the author's point of view. Obviously, this is what he wants his listeners to do.

Interactive Reading Workbook p. 12

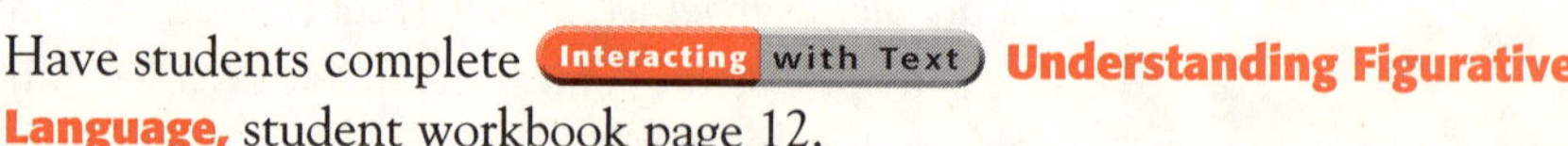
Have students complete Interacting with Text **Understanding Figurative Language,** student workbook page 12.

After Reading

You may also use the selection questions and activities in *Glencoe Literature*.

Reviewing and Analyzing Ask the following questions to help students review and analyze the selection.

1. What is the author's purpose? (*to frighten people into accepting God*)
2. What methods does the author use to accomplish his purpose? (*He uses emotionally charged language, vivid images, and figures of speech to evoke an emotional response.*)
3. Explain why you think Jonathan Edwards is or is not successful in accomplishing his purpose. (*Possible responses: Persuading through emotions is effective; appealing through reason is fairer and more effective.*)

OBJECTIVES

▶ To identify main idea and supporting details

Offer of Help

Canassatego

Before Reading

Activating Prior Knowledge Engage students in a discussion about cultural traditions. Ask volunteers to describe cultural celebrations or other traditions of their ethnic heritage. Ask students to discuss why they think learning about and respecting various cultural traditions is important.

Building Vocabulary On the board, write the following words and definitions: *maintenance* (support), *provinces* (areas of a country), *counsellors* (people who give advice or provide counseling), and *obliged* (put in debt as a result of a favor or service). Ask students to write sentences using each word. Encourage students to use synonyms, antonyms, appositives, or other context clues to make each word's meaning clear. Have volunteers read their sentences. Have students record their sentences in their vocabulary logs or journals.

During Reading

Recognizing Tone Remind students that **tone** reflects the author's attitude toward his or her subject matter. "Offer of Help" was written in response to the colonists' offer to educate several young Native American men. **Have a volunteer read aloud the first two sentences of the selection.** Ask students to make predictions about Canassatego's answer. **Then have a volunteer read aloud the remainder of the message.** Ask students to describe their response to the conclusion of the message. Guide them to recognize the contrast between Canassatego's polite, grateful tone and the pointed meaning of his ideas.

Main Idea and Supporting Details Ask students to tell what the **main idea** is in a piece of writing. (*the key idea; the idea that all the details are about*) Then explain that the author of "Offer of Help" provides details about the skills considered important for young Onondaga men and the skills considered important for the young men of Virginia. Have students complete Interacting with Text **Main Idea and Supporting Details,** student workbook page 13.

Interactive Reading Workbook
p. 13

After Reading

Analyzing Ask students: *On the basis of Canassatego's words, what three roles should young men of the tribe assume?* (Well-trained young men should be able to act as hunters, warriors, and counselors.) *Why does Canassatego offer to train twelve sons of Virginia gentlemen?* (On the surface, Canassatego wants to teach the young men to live as Native American men; his real goal is to make the point that each culture values different skills and knowledge.)

You may also use the selection questions and activities in *Glencoe Literature*.

OBJECTIVES

- To analyze setting; to make generalizations

FROM

The Autobiography of Benjamin Franklin and

FROM

Poor Richard's Almanack

Benjamin Franklin

Before Reading

Activating Prior Knowledge Ask students to discuss what they know about Benjamin Franklin. Record the information in brief form on the board. For example, students may recall that he signed the Declaration of Independence, wrote *Poor Richard's Almanack*, and made important discoveries about electricity. Ask students whether they can quote any famous proverbs written by Franklin, such as "A penny saved is a penny earned."

Characteristics of Genre: Autobiography Explain to students that the prefix *auto-* means "self." Then ask: *What does **autobiography** mean?* (the story of a person's life told by himself or herself) Ask: *What are the advantages of reading the story of a person's life written by that person as opposed to reading a biography written by someone else?* (As a first-person account, an autobiography can describe emotions, thoughts, and perspectives that others cannot know.) *What are the disadvantages of reading an autobiography as opposed to a biography?* (A person may create a biased view of his or her own actions and the actions of others.)

Building Vocabulary Write on the board the following words, without their definitions: *obliging* (helpful), *passage* (a specific act of traveling by sea), *hospitable* (given to generous and cordial reception of guests), *squander* (to spend extravagantly or foolishly). Have students write the words in their vocabulary logs or journals. Ask them to look for the words as they read the selection. Then, for each word, have them write in their own words a definition that is based on the word's context in the selection.

Word Study: Antonyms Write on the board the following words, without their antonyms: *obliging* (unaccommodating), *hospitable* (unfriendly), *ignorant* (educated), *squander* (save). Explain to students that knowing antonyms can help them understand new words. Have students write an antonym, in their vocabulary logs or journals, for each word on the board. Then ask students to write a sentence for each pair of antonyms. An example, "*Jane was afraid her new supervisor would be unaccommodating, but he was actually quite obliging.*"

Setting a Purpose for Reading Encourage students to read the selection from *The Autobiography of Benjamin Franklin* to find out what Philadelphia was like for a young man visiting it for the first time in the 1720s.

During Reading

Analyzing Setting **Have students read the selection from *The Autobiography of Benjamin Franklin* independently.** Ask students: *What does the term* **setting** *mean as it applies to a literary work?* (The term applies to the time period and the place presented in the literary work.) Ask: *What is the setting in the selection?* (the route from Boston to Philadelphia and Philadelphia itself during the 1720s) Encourage students to jot down details as they read that describe the setting. Have students describe the mood created by each detail. (*Sample details/mood: The rain on the way to Burlington and the poor inn create a lonely, depressing mood. Franklin's description of coming back to the Market Street wharf with a roll creates a cheerful, optimistic mood.*) Have students complete 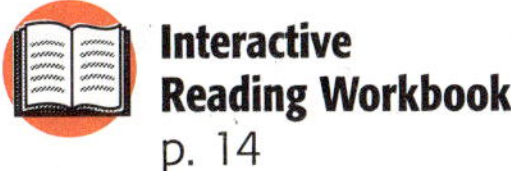 **Analyzing Setting,** student workbook page 14.

Interactive Reading Workbook
p. 14

Making Generalizations Remind students that **making a generalization** is forming a general rule or conclusion on the basis of several particular facts or examples. Then ask students: *What was travel like in America during the 1700s?* From information in the selection, guide students to make a generalization. **Read aloud the first two paragraphs** in the selection from *The Autobiography of Benjamin Franklin* and model the process of making a generalization.

> ***Modeling*** As I read, I see that Benjamin Franklin crosses on the ferry, walks fifty miles to Burlington, and then catches another boat. I can make the generalization that travel may have been difficult in early America. When making a generalization, I try to find several facts or examples to back up my statement. I would want to check other sources to learn more about travel in early America to be sure that my generalization is valid.

Ask students the following question, using the same procedure: *How did people behave toward strangers in Benjamin Franklin's time?* (1. "Dr. Brown . . . became very obliging and friendly." 2. An old woman "was very hospitable." 3. "I fell fast asleep and . . . some one was kind enough to rouse me." Possible generalization, which would require checking other sources for validation: In Franklin's time, most people were kind and willing to help one another.)

Have students read the selection from *Poor Richard's Almanack* independently. As a class, discuss the sayings from *Poor Richard's Almanack*.

After Reading

You may also use the selection questions and activities in *Glencoe Literature*.

Analyzing Characters Have students list, in order, the characters Franklin encounters in the selection from *The Autobiography of Benjamin Franklin*. Ask students to write a brief description of each encounter. Have them meet with a partner and share their lists. (*Franklin encounters Dr. Brown, an old woman who offers lodging in Burlington, the people on the boat to Philadelphia, a boy with bread, the person at the bakery, his future wife, a woman and a child from the boat, and people at the Quaker meeting-house.*)

OBJECTIVES

- To identify main idea and supporting details; to understand figurative language

Dichos

Américo Paredes

Before Reading

Activating Prior Knowledge On the board, write the proverb *Every cloud has a silver lining.* Ask students to explain what the proverb means. (*There is something good in difficult or challenging experiences.*) Have students discuss the possible circumstances in which someone might use this saying. Ask: *Do you, your friends, or your family members ever use sayings like this? What are some sayings you recall hearing recently?* Encourage students to discuss specific proverbs and their meanings. Ask students why people use these sayings. Encourage them to recognize that the sayings are colorful ways to state beliefs that are based on experiences that people often have in life. Explain that most cultures use sayings of this type. Then have a student read aloud the boldface quotation from "Meet Américo Paredes" in *Glencoe Literature.* Have the class read "Meet Américo Paredes" and Building Background silently.

Building Vocabulary On the board, write the following words, without their definitions: *ox, ewe* (female sheep), *ram* (male sheep), *wolves, donkeys, lamb* (young sheep), and *burro* (a small donkey used as a pack animal). Ask students what all the words have in common. (*They are names of animals.*) Have students describe each animal, looking up in a dictionary any words they are unsure of. Point out that there are special words for the gender and the young of many kinds of animals. For example, a female horse is a *mare,* a male a *stallion,* and a baby a *colt.* Have students suggest other examples, such as *kid* (a young goat), *cub* (a young bear), and *joey* (a young kangaroo). Ask students to note the use of animal names in the selection and to consider why the proverbs might contain so many animal names. Encourage students to record each word and its meaning in their vocabulary logs or journals.

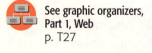

See graphic organizers, Part 1, Web p. T27

Word Study: *Folk* Write the word *folk* on the board. Explain to students that *folk* means "people" when it is used as a noun. When it is used as an adjective (*folk medicine*) or as part of a compound word (*folklore*), it means "originating or traditional with the common people of a country or region and reflecting their lifestyle." Create a web graphic organizer and display it on an overhead projector. Write the word *folk* in the center circle. Have students contribute words for the web that contain the word *folk,* such as *folklore, folk song, folktale,* and *folk medicine.* Explain that Américo Paredes calls proverbs a form of "folk poetry."

Setting a Purpose for Reading Ask students to read the selection to learn about "the wisdom of many," Mexican American sayings that state common beliefs.

During Reading

Identifying Main Idea and Supporting Details Remind students that the overall **main idea** of a paragraph is the most important idea in the paragraph that most or all of the details in the paragraph are about. Explain to students that the author uses a structure of main ideas and supporting details to inform the audience about Mexican American proverbs. **Have students read silently the explanatory material at the beginning of the selection up to "True Proverbs."** Then have them brainstorm in small groups to compile a list of the main ideas discussed in this section. Have students discuss the main ideas. (*The main ideas include the following: Proverbs express the attitudes of many people in the witty words of one person.* Dichos *are used in ordinary conversation by many Mexican Americans. Individual* dichos *may express contradictory advice. There are two main kinds of* dichos. *One is the true proverb, which is a complete sentence and uses poetic effects such as alliteration. The other is a comparison, which is not a complete sentence and is usually based on a story.*)

Connecting Explain that the proverbs are examples that help demonstrate the ideas in the first part of the selection. **Have groups of students take turns reading the proverbs aloud in English.** (You may wish to encourage Spanish-speaking students first to share their readings of the proverbs in Spanish.) Then have each student choose one proverb and explain how it applies to a situation he or she has encountered. Also, encourage students to mention proverbs they have heard in English that have similar meanings to the ones in the selection. For example, "Walk a mile in someone else's shoes" expresses an idea comparable to "He who shoulders the bag knows what he carries in it."

Understanding Figurative Language Explain to students that some of the *dichos* are **literal**; that is, the meanings are exactly the dictionary meanings of the words. For example, "No food is bad when you're good and hungry" has a mostly literal meaning. Other *dichos* use figurative language (such as similes, metaphors, or symbols) to make their points. Ask students to define the following types of figurative language: **simile** (*comparison between two unlike things in which* like *or* as *is used*); **metaphor** (*implied comparison between two unlike things*); **symbol** (*a person, place, or thing with a concrete meaning that represents something abstract*). Then model understanding figurative language.

> ***Modeling*** When I read "Like a sick man's gruel," I know this is a simile because it includes the word *like*. Because gruel is a thin porridge, this *dicho* is a comparison to something that is boring, distasteful, or sickening. In the *dicho* "Pray to God, but keep hammering away (at your problem)," *hammering away* is a metaphor for "working hard."

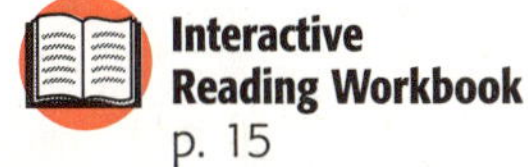
Interactive Reading Workbook
p. 15

Have students complete Interacting with Text **Understanding Figurative Language,** student workbook page 15.

After Reading

You may also use the selection questions and activities in *Glencoe Literature.*

Drawing Conclusions Ask students what they can conclude about the references to animals in many of the proverbs. Elicit recognition that *dichos* are a form of "folk poetry"; they describe the everyday lives of common people. People have always depended on animals, using them as pets, as workers, and as food. They recognize "human" traits in animals. Ask students to read their favorite *dichos* that mention animals and to discuss their meanings.

OBJECTIVES

- To identify persuasive techniques; to use word-attack skills

Speech to the Second Virginia Convention

Patrick Henry

Before Reading

Building Background In his "Speech to the Second Virginia Convention," Patrick Henry says, "But different men often see the same subject in different lights." Ask students to discuss what they think the statement means. (*People view the same thing differently.*) Explain that in 1775 Great Britain governed America. Have students discuss how it might affect citizens of the United States if, instead of having our own form of government, our country were governed by Great Britain. Then ask students to read "Meet Patrick Henry" and Building Background in *Glencoe Literature*. Explain to students that Patrick Henry strongly believed that Americans should govern themselves. However, in 1775 Americans had never ruled themselves, and some Americans felt loyalty to the British.

Building Vocabulary On the board, write the following words, without including definitions or parts of speech: *anguish* (extreme pain or distress—noun), *solace* (to soothe—verb), *reconciliation* (the state of being restored to friendship—noun), *implements* (tools—noun), *submission* (the act of submitting to the authority or control of another—noun), *contempt* (lack of respect or reverence for something—noun), *inestimable* (incapable of being estimated or computed—adjective), *formidable* (causing fear or dread—adjective), *treason* (disloyalty towards one's own country—noun), *invincible* (incapable of being conquered or subdued—adjective). For each word, ask a volunteer to give its meaning. Encourage students to look up in a dictionary each word whose meaning is unclear. In their vocabulary logs or journals, have students write each word and its definition. Students might create charts having the headings *Noun*, *Verb*, and *Adjective* and record their vocabulary words and definitions on the charts.

Word Study: Concrete/Abstract Write the terms *concrete* and *abstract* on the board. Explain that **concrete nouns** are things that we can see or touch; **abstract nouns** are ideas, qualities, or characteristics that cannot be seen or touched. Point out that Patrick Henry uses many abstract words, such as *patriotism* and *subjugation*. Explain that concrete objects sometimes are used to symbolize abstract ideas. For example, an American flag might symbolize patriotism; chains might symbolize subjugation. Symbols help people understand abstract terms. As students read, have them identify at least three abstract nouns in the selection. (Examples: *freedom*, *anguish*, *reconciliation*, *peace*.) Encourage students to discuss concrete symbols that might be used to symbolize the abstract nouns they identify.

Setting a Purpose for Reading Suggest that students read the selection to find out why Patrick Henry's speech is one of the most famous American speeches.

During Reading

Identifying Persuasive Techniques Point out that, in his speech, Patrick Henry uses several persuasive techniques. **Have students read the selection silently with partners.** Encourage them to read aloud to their partners any parts they find difficult and then to summarize these parts.

On the board, write the following terms, without their definitions: **Loaded Language** (words that evoke strong positive or negative feelings); **Rhetorical Questions** (questions asked for effect and not in expectation of answers); **Figures of Speech** (nonliteral comparisons used for effect); **Specific Facts** (information that can be proven to be true); and **Literary Allusions** (references to literary works such as the Bible or Shakespeare's plays). Discuss each term and its definition with students. Ask students to make a two-column chart in their vocabulary logs or journals, listing the terms in the left column. Together with students, identify examples for each term. For example, a literary allusion to the sirens of the *Odyssey* is found in the sentence "We are apt to shut our eyes against a painful truth, and listen to the song of that siren till, she transforms us into beasts." As students read, have them fill in the right column of their charts with specific examples from the speech. Have students complete Interacting with Text **Identifying Persuasive Techniques,** student workbook page 16.

p. 16

Using Word-Attack Skills Encourage students to figure out the meaning of a challenging word by using word parts they already know. **Read aloud the second paragraph on the last page of the selection,** "They tell us, sir, that we are weak . . . ," and model the process of using word-attack skills.

> **Modeling** I'm not sure what the word *irresolution* means, but I think it must be based on the base word *resolve*. If I resolve to do something, I make a firm decision. I know that the prefix *ir-* means "not." I also know that the suffix *-tion* means "action" or "process." So I think *irresolution* means "the act of not being decisive." If I try this meaning in context, it fits.

Encourage students to use word parts—prefixes, suffixes, and base words or word roots—and the context to help them figure out word meanings.

After Reading

You may also use the selection questions and activities in *Glencoe Literature*.

Persuasive Techniques Follow-Up After students read the selection, discuss the charts that they created. Have students share, with the class, items from each category. (*Examples—loaded language: "Noble struggle"; rhetorical question: "Shall we resort to entreaty and humble supplication?"; figure of speech: "I have but one lamp by which my feet are guided . . . "*)

OBJECTIVES

- To recognize author's purpose; to analyze problem and solution

FROM

The Crisis, No. 1

Thomas Paine

Before Reading

Building Background Ask students whether they have ever been given a pep talk by their friends, parents, or coaches. Ask a volunteer to describe the circumstances of one of these talks. Have the student describe the talk's purpose and tell whether it was accomplished. Then have students read "Meet Thomas Paine" and Building Background in *Glencoe Literature*. Help students understand that Thomas Paine's pamphlets were like pep talks to support the war effort. Ask: *How do you think Americans probably felt during the Revolutionary War when the American army was facing defeat? What effect do you think the morale of the public might have had on the outcome of a war?*

Building Vocabulary On the board, write the following words with their definitions: *crisis* (an unstable time in which a decisive change is impending), *consolation* (comfort), *dearness* (expensiveness), *celestial* (suggesting heaven or divinity), *repulsed* (drove or beat back), *earnestly* (gravely, seriously), *pretense* (a claim made but not supported by fact), *duration* (the time during which something exists or lasts), *peculiar* (particular), *reflection* (consideration of some idea or purpose). Call on students to make up a sentence based on the definition provided for each word. Have students record the words and their definitions in their vocabulary logs or journals.

Word Study: Multiple-Meaning Words On the board, write the words *dearness*, *repulsed*, *pretense*, *peculiar*, and *reflection*. Point out that each word has a meaning other than the meaning used in Paine's essay. Have students give meanings in their own words for each word on the board. Ask students to explain how they know which definition to use when they read a word. Model the process of recognizing the appropriate meaning of a word with multiple meanings.

> ***Modeling*** In the first paragraph of the essay, I read the sentence "What we obtain too cheap, we esteem too lightly: it is dearness only that gives everything its value." The main definition of *dearness* I know is "a high value to oneself." This definition might fit in this context, but it doesn't exactly make sense with the first part of the sentence. I know that the British sometimes use *dear* to mean "costly" or "expensive." If I substitute *costliness* for *dearness*, it makes more sense. The word contrasts with the idea of cheapness in the first part of the sentence.

Have each student write two sentences for each word. In one sentence ask them to use the word as it is used in the selection and in the other sentence ask them to use another definition of the word. (*repulsed*: aroused disgust; *pretense*: false show; *peculiar*: odd; *reflection*: the production of a mirror image)

Setting a Purpose for Reading Encourage students to read the selection to find out the techniques one man used to rally support for a cause.

During Reading

Recognizing Author's Purpose **Have students read the selection independently.** Ask: *What are three ways in which Paine tries to make the war personal and specific to the American people? Why do you think he does this?* (Paine mentions "the spirit of the Jerseys" and "some Jersey maid to spirit up her countrymen," and he compares the British acts to a thief's breaking into his house and burning and killing him. All these details are meant to make Americans take the war personally so that they will have a vested interest in winning it.) *Which Americans does Paine criticize? Which does he commend?* (He criticizes "sunshine patriots," people who are patriotic until their loyalty is put to the test in difficult times, and "secret traitors," Tories who pretend to be loyal Americans. He commends patriotic Americans who work hard and remain loyal.) Read the descriptions of people that Paine gives on the last page. *What effect is Paine trying to achieve?* (He uses emotionally charged language—"The heart that feels not now is dead" and "it is the business of little minds to shrink"—to make the national issue personal and to shame and exhort people to display loyalty.) Have students complete Interacting with Text **Recognizing Author's Purpose,** student workbook page 17.

Interactive Reading Workbook
p. 17

See graphic organizers, Part 1, Problem-Solution Chart p. T30

Analyzing Problem and Solution Distribute copies of the Problem-Solution Chart. Create a transparency of the Problem-Solution Chart and display it on the overhead projector. Ask for volunteers to state the main problem according to Paine. (*The problem is a lack of support for the American cause.*) In the same box, under the problem statement, ask students to list three details that support the problem statement. (*1. There are "sunshine patriots," those who are patriotic only when things are going well. 2. People quickly give up when a struggle, like that for freedom from the British, is too difficult. 3. There are traitors in the colonies, secret Tories who do not support the war.*) Then ask for volunteers to state the solution that Paine advocates. (*The proposed solution is to be strong, join the cause, and support the fight for freedom and independence from Britain.*) Ask students to fill in the action boxes with two details to support the solution statement. (*1."Lay your shoulders to the wheel." 2. "Come together in a great cause."*)

After Reading

You may also use the selection questions and activities in *Glencoe Literature*.

Responding Ask students to brainstorm about a national crisis they recall, such as a contested election, a power shortage, or a disastrous economy. Ask students to describe the mood of the public during the crisis. Encourage them to recognize that there is a sense of anxiety and a need to see decisive action. Ask students to imagine that they are American colonists reading Thomas Paine's essay. How will they respond? Have them discuss whether they think the essay is effective in inspiring the colonists to come together to support the American cause in the Revolutionary War. Why or why not?

OBJECTIVES

- To identify sequence of events; to analyze dialogue in a narrative

FROM

The Histories

Herodotus

Translated by Aubrey de Sélincourt

Before Reading

Activating Prior Knowledge On the board, draw a concept web with the words *ancient Greece* in the center. Encourage students to contribute any ideas that relate to ancient Greece, such as *city-states, Sparta, Athens, the Acropolis, mythology, the Olympics, Homer, architecture,* and *Socrates.* Write the terms in the web. Encourage students to give facts they know about each term. Emphasize that the Greeks had many important achievements in government and the arts that have had a lasting impact on the world. Explain that the Golden Age of Greece (477–431 B.C.) occurred soon after the events described by Herodotus. During this time, Socrates taught philosophy, the Athenian government advanced democracy, and drama was created at festivals.

Building Vocabulary On the board, write the following words, without definitions: *advisability* (prudence), *reinforcements* (fresh additions, such as soldiers, that strengthen or increase), *absurd* (ridiculously unreasonable), *unaccountable* (unable to be explained), *foretold* (predicted), *folly* (lack of good sense or normal prudence), *innumerable* (too many to be counted), *slackened* (slowed up), *seer* (one that predicts events or developments), *circuitous* (having a circular or winding course). Discuss the meanings of the words. Ask students to write three sentences in their vocabulary logs or journals, using one of these words in each sentence. Have students read their sentences. Discuss with students the meanings of the vocabulary words in their sentences.

Word Study: Suffix *-able* On the board, write the words *advisability, unaccountable, innumerable,* and *inevitable.* Ask the class what the words have in common. (*All include a form of the suffix* -able.) Ask students what the suffix means. (*capable of being, fit for,* or *worthy of*) Lead students to analyze the parts of each word and their meanings. For example, in *unaccountable, account* means "to explain." The suffix *-able* adds the meaning "capable of being." The prefix *un-* adds the meaning "not." So *unaccountable* means "not able to be explained." Repeat the process of analyzing word parts for each word on the board. Have a volunteer point out the suffix in *advisability.* (*-ability*) Explain that *-ability* is the noun form of the suffix *-able.* Explain that the word *inevitable* is somewhat different in that *evit* is a word root. *Evit* means "to avoid." Point out that the word *inevitable* means "incapable of being avoided" and ask students to identify the word parts that create this meaning. (*in-*, "not"; *evit*, "to avoid"; *-able*, "capable of being")

Setting a Purpose for Reading Suggest that students read the selection to find out what behavior the ancient Greeks considered courageous during war.

During Reading

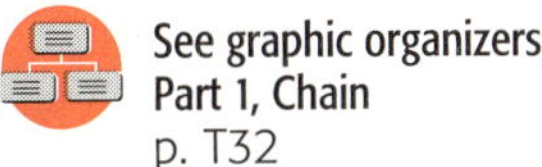

See graphic organizers, Part 1, Chain p. T32

Identifying Sequence of Events Explain to the students that the selection from the *Histories* presents a series of events concerning a battle. **Have students read the selection independently.** Then have partners work together to list the important events in the selection. Distribute copies of the Chain graphic organizer and have partners use their listing of key events to summarize briefly these events in the boxes of the graphic organizer. Call on volunteers to share their summaries. (*1. Xerxes, leader of the Persian army, sends a spy to view the Greek force. The spy notices only the Spartan army, one army in the Greek force, and reports back. Xerxes cannot believe that the small army will fight the Persian army. 2. Xerxes' forces attack the Spartans but do not prevail; fighting continues. 3. A messenger tells Xerxes about an unguarded pass. 4. The Greek leaders realize that the Persians will attack from the rear; some men desert. 5. The Greek forces fight valiantly but are defeated by the Persians. Leonidas, commander of the Greek forces, is killed.*)

Analyzing Dialogue Ask: *What is dialogue?* (**Dialogue** is conversation between characters in a literary work.) Explain to students that Herodotus, in the selection, does not include a great deal of dialogue. However, students can gain understanding of the events and insight into how the events are presented by analyzing the conversation between Xerxes and Demaratus. **Read aloud Demaratus's speech starting with** "Once before . . . " and ending with " . . . and with the bravest men." Model the process of analyzing dialogue.

> ***Modeling*** **In reading the speech that Demaratus gives to Xerxes about the Spartans' intentions, I notice that Demaratus says, "You have now to deal with the finest kingdom in Greece, and with the bravest men." I think Herodotus, as a Greek historian, is expressing his own bias. As I read on, I see that Xerxes has difficulty believing that the small Spartan force could effectively battle against the large Persian army.**

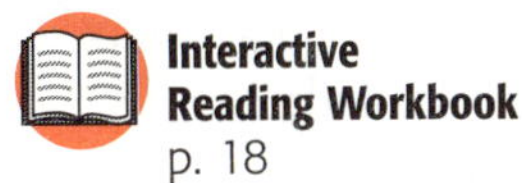

Interactive Reading Workbook p. 18

Lead students to understand that readers can gain insight into Herodotus's account by noticing that he portrays the Greeks in a positive light. Ask students what Demaratus's speech may indicate about Herodotus's account of events. (*Herodotus's bias in favor of the Greeks may make his account of events questionable.*) Have students complete Interacting with Text **Analyzing Dialogue,** student workbook page 18.

After Reading

You may also use the selection questions and activities in *Glencoe Literature.*

Reviewing and Analyzing Ask the following questions to help students review and analyze the selection.

1. What was Herodotus's purpose in writing the narrative? (*Herodotus's purpose was to record the events of the battles and to make sure the brave deeds of the Greek warriors were recognized and remembered.*)
2. What acts does he define as courageous? (*Herodotus calls the following acts courageous: fighting bravely for one's country despite great odds, resisting to the bitter end, and not being intimidated by tales of the opposing army's strength.*)
3. According to Herodotus, what rewards will brave warriors have? (*They will gain glory and be remembered.*)

OBJECTIVES

- To summarize and paraphrase; to analyze problem and solution

Declaration of Independence

Thomas Jefferson

Before Reading

Activating Prior Knowledge Have students read "Meet Thomas Jefferson" and Building Background in *Glencoe Literature.* Draw two columns on the board with the headings *pro* and *con.* Have students contribute, as items to the pro column, reasons to support independence from Great Britain and, as items to the con column, reasons to remain under British rule. (*Pros might include throwing off the tyrannical rule of the British king, getting rid of unfair taxes, and enabling Americans to make their own laws. Cons might include facing war with Britain over the issue, having to become financially independent, and having to create a new government.*)

Building Vocabulary On the board, write the following words and definitions: *dissolve* (bring to an end, terminate), *abolish* (destroy), *transient* (passing quickly into and out of existence), *relinquish* (give up), *annihilation* (destruction), *harass* (annoy persistently), *abdicated* (discarded), *plundered* (took by force or theft), *desolation* (devastation, ruin), *constrained* (forced), *unwarrantable* (not able to be justified). Ask students to record the words and their meanings in their vocabulary logs or journals. Then have them complete the following exercise.

1. Write two verbs that describe acts of breaking up or doing away with. (*dissolve, abolish*)
2. Write two verbs that describe acts of casting off or discarding something. (*relinquish, abdicated*)
3. Write two verbs that describe acts of annoyance or theft. (*harass, plundered*)
4. Write two nouns that describe destruction or ruin. (*annihilation, desolation*)
5. Write a verb that means "forced." (*constrained*)
6. Write two adjectives and give their definitions. (*transient*: passing quickly into and out of existence; *unwarrantable*: not able to be justified)

Word Study: Suffix *-tion, -ation* On the board, write the selection words *usurpations, annihilation, dissolutions, appropriations,* and *desolation.* Ask students how the suffix *-tion* (or *-ation*) affects the meaning of a word. (*It means "action" or "process of"; it changes a verb or adjective into a noun.*) Have students work in pairs, using a dictionary as needed, to write the verb or adjective to which *-tion* has been added. (*usurp + -ations, annihilate + -tion, dissolute + -tion, appropriate + -tion, desolate + -tion*). As students read the selection and notice words with the *-tion* suffix, encourage them to figure out the meaning of each word.

Setting a Purpose for Reading Have students read the selection to find out why the American colonists thought that they had to cut ties with Great Britain.

During Reading

Summarizing and Paraphrasing Remind students that a **summary** briefly states the main ideas of a passage. **Have students read the selection independently.** Then have students scan the document with you, to determine its structure. Explain that the first three paragraphs give background information about why the colonists want to be independent from Great Britain. Ask a volunteer to summarize the first three paragraphs. (*Sample summary: When one people declares independence from another, it is only fair to explain the reasons. The colonists believe that they have the God-given rights of "life, liberty, and the pursuit of happiness." If a government does not ensure these, it should be rejected. A government should not be rejected lightly, but when its offenses are serious, the people are obliged to reject it.*) Point out that the next several paragraphs begin with the pronoun *He*. Ask students to skim the previous text to find out whom this refers to. (*the king*) Encourage students to **paraphrase,** or put into their own words, the formal language of the selection. **Read aloud the paragraph** that begins "He has endeavored to prevent . . ." and then model the process of paraphrasing.

> ***Modeling*** **I know the language is formal. I can change many parts into more common language. I can also simplify the sentence structure to help me understand the main idea. A paraphrase of the paragraph might sound like the following: *He has kept the population of the colonies down by not allowing foreigners to come to live here and by making it hard to add new lands to our states.***

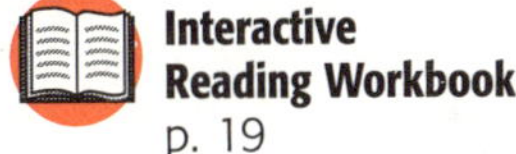
Interactive Reading Workbook
p. 19

Have students complete **Interacting with Text** **Summarizing,** student workbook page 19.

Analyzing Problem and Solution Point out that the Declaration of Independence describes a problem and a solution to the problem. Ask: *Does Jefferson pay more attention to the problem or to the solution?* (the problem) *Why do you think he chose this structure?* (Jefferson knew that the colonists were taking a risk and apparently considered it important to let the British government, the British people, and the colonists know exactly why the colonists were doing so.) Say: *State the problem in one sentence.* (The American colonists are being treated unfairly by the government of Great Britain.) *Summarize the solution that Jefferson proposes to the problem.* (The United Colonies declare themselves independent states with no further political connection to Great Britain.)

After Reading

You may also use the selection questions and activities in *Glencoe Literature*.

Interpreting Ask: *From reading the Declaration of Independence, what qualities or attributes would you ascribe to Thomas Jefferson and the other colonial leaders?* (Possible response: The colonial leaders were intelligent, wise, reasonable, and patriotic, and they were independent thinkers.) *Do you think Jefferson was a rebel, or do you think he respected tradition? Explain.* (Possible response: Jefferson respected tradition and made it clear that breaking free of Great Britain was a last resort.)

OBJECTIVES

- To paraphrase and summarize a poem; to analyze personification

To His Excellency, General Washington

Phillis Wheatley

Before Reading

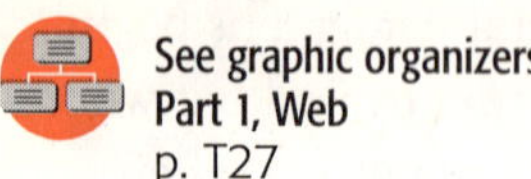

See graphic organizers, Part 1, Web p. T27

Building Background Have students read and discuss "Meet Phillis Wheatley" and Building Background in *Glencoe Literature*. Ask students to share what they know about George Washington. Record the students' responses on a concept web. Use an overhead transparency of the Web graphic organizer in Part 1 to get students started. After students have discussed ideas, provide the following additional information about Washington: *Washington had been unanimously elected commander-in-chief of the Continental (American) army at the beginning of the Revolution. He became known for his great skill, strength, and courage in leading the Americans to victory in the war. After the war, the Electoral College unanimously voted him president for two terms.*

Building Vocabulary On the board, write the following words, without definitions: *realms* (spheres), *toils* (struggles), *tempest* (uproar), *martial* (relating to army or military life), *implore* (beg), *prevails* (triumphs), *pensive* (sadly thoughtful), *lament* (express regret). Discuss the definitions with students and have them write the definitions in their vocabulary logs or journals.

Word Study: Formal Language **Read aloud the first two lines of the poem.** Ask students to point out words in the lines that they would identify as **formal**: words appropriate for important speeches or occasions—as opposed to words used frequently in everyday life. (*Formal words include* celestial, enthron'd, realms, glorious, *and* toils.) Then ask students what the advantages and disadvantages are of the poet's use of formal language. (*Advantages: formal language is appropriate to communicate Washington's greatness and express Wheatley's admiration for him; disadvantages: formal language makes the meaning of the poem somewhat difficult to understand; it also makes the tone seem today to be exaggerated or overblown.*) As students read the selection, have them note the use of formal words and phrases.

Setting a Purpose for Reading Have students read to find out how a contemporary viewed General Washington.

During Reading

Paraphrasing and Summarizing **Have students read independently the "letter" that precedes the poem.** Remind students that **summarizing** is stating the main ideas of a passage. Ask a volunteer to summarize the "letter." (*Wheatley tells Washington that she has written a poem about him because he is a great man and an inspirational leader.*) **Then have pairs of students take turns reading sections of the poem aloud.** Have them write a summary for each of the following lines: 1–8, 9–12, 13–20, 21–28, 29–38, and 39–42. Explain to students that they may need to paraphrase parts of the poem first to clarify the meaning of the groups of lines. Model the process of paraphrasing.

> ***Modeling*** **I have a hard time understanding line 28, "Hear every tongue thy guardian aid implore!" Maybe it's because the poet uses unusual words instead of common ones and an inverted word order instead of the usual subject–verb–direct-object order. So first I change the formal words into common ones: "Hear every voice your guarding help ask for." Then I change it into logical word order: "Hear every voice ask for your guarding help." Now I understand the meaning of the line.**

Ask a student to talk through a paraphrase of line 22, "Where high unfurl'd the ensign waves in air." (*The unfolded flag waves high in the air.*) Then have students read line 36 and ask them to put the words in logical order. (*While the rising hills of dead increase around.*) Encourage students to paraphrase when they are unsure of the meaning of a passage.

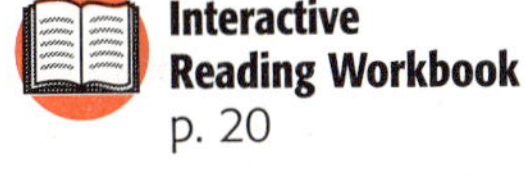
Interactive Reading Workbook
p. 20

Analyzing Figurative Language: Personification Explain that one kind of figurative language is personification. In **personification,** an animal, an object, a force of nature, or an idea is assigned human qualities or characteristics. For example, in the poem "To Autumn," Keats calls autumn "Season of mists and mellow fruitfulness, / Close bosom friend of the maturing sun." A season cannot literally be a friend, but Keats makes the point that, as friend would work with friend, the season works with the sun to create the harvest. In "To His Excellency General Washington," Phillis Wheatley compares America to the goddess Columbia. Ask students what human traits of this goddess the poet describes. (*She is beautiful; her passion for freedom and righteous anger when freedom is threatened have brought her many supporters. These traits are applicable to America.*) Have students complete Interacting with Text **Analyzing Personification,** student workbook page 20.

After Reading

You may also use the selection questions and activities in *Glencoe Literature.*

Summarizing Follow-Up Have pairs of students take turns reading their summaries of portions of the poem. Make sure they recognize the main ideas—similar to the following: (Lines 1–8) *The poet is writing about America's struggle for freedom, which is watched anxiously by Mother Nature, other nations, and heaven.* (Lines 9–12) *America has beauty and grace.* (Lines 13–20) *America's army, on the move like a storm, calls attention to its strength and noble cause.* (Lines 21–28) *As the army goes to war, the speaker wonders whether it is necessary to tell Washington how the soldiers praise him. She concludes that it is enough that the army does its job with glory. Meanwhile, everyone, aware of Washington's courage and goodness, will pray for his safety.* (Lines 29–38) *In the mid-1700s, America fought France in the French and Indian War. Now the world watches and hopes for America's victory over Great Britain, which strives for power, ignoring America's objections.* (Lines 39–42) *The speaker wishes Washington well as he proceeds with the war. Goodness is on his side. He deserves earthly rewards and eternal glory.*

OBJECTIVES

- To recognize author's purpose; to make generalizations

Letter to Her Daughter from the New and Unfinished White House

Abigail Adams

Before Reading

Building Background Have students discuss what they know about the United States government during the late 1700s and early 1800s. Ask: *Who was president of the United States from 1789 to 1797?* (George Washington) *Who became president in 1797?* (John Adams) Explain that President Washington lived in New York City and in Philadelphia, where the nation's capital was located at the time. Washington, D.C., was a brand-new city that did not exist before 1791. In 1800 the city's population was about 8,000. Have students read Building Background in *Glencoe Literature*.

Building Vocabulary On the board, write the following words, without definitions: *interspersed* (placed at intervals among other things), *vessels* (ships), *agues* (chills), *expended* (used up), *procure* (obtain by particular care and effort), *habitable* (capable of being lived in), *venison* (flesh of a game animal, especially a deer). Have students write the words in their vocabulary logs or journals. Challenge them to write a synonym for each word. Then have students work in pairs to compare their synonyms. Encourage students to look up in a dictionary each word whose meaning is unclear.

Word Study: Outdated Words and Phrases Write the following words on the board: *cot*, *levee-room*, *billet*, *agues*, and *procure*. Have students read the words aloud; then review with them the meanings of some of the words, as provided in the selection footnotes. Explain that most of these words, although commonly used during the 1800s, are not often used today or are used with different meanings. As students read the selection, have them list words, terms, or phrases that they identify as outdated or old-fashioned or that represent an earlier way of life. (*Examples: parlor, drying-room, drawing-room, to secure, render, chambers.*) Encourage students to discuss the definitions of such words, checking the words' context in the selection when needed.

Setting a Purpose for Reading Have students read the selection to find out how life in the White House in 1800 was different from life in the White House today.

During Reading

Recognizing Author's Purpose **Have students read the selection independently.** Ask: *What is an author's purpose in writing a piece of literature?* (An **author's purpose** is to accomplish one or more of the following goals: to persuade, to inform, to explain, to entertain, or to describe.) *What is the author's purpose for writing "Letter to Her Daughter from the New and Unfinished White House"?* (Adams's purpose is to entertain and inform her daughter by making the circumstances and events of her daily life vivid.) *How is Abigail Adams's purpose reflected in the details she uses?* (Abigail Adams wants her daughter to know the basic details of her daily life, so she talks about lighting lamps and hanging clothes instead of more public matters.) *How does Adams's intended audience affect the details she uses?* (Because she is writing to a close family member, Adams is frank and gives the practical details of daily life that one usually tells only close friends and family members.) *Do the author's audience and purpose make the letter more interesting and useful to modern readers or less so?* Explain. (The letter is more interesting and useful to modern readers because it contains details that are difficult to find in more formal histories.)

Making Generalizations Remind students that **making generalizations** is thinking of a statement that can apply to several instances or to a group. Ask students to make a generalization about what travel was like in the United States in the year 1800, according to the selection. (*In the area of Washington, D.C., which was a new city, travel and transportation were extremely unsophisticated.*) Lead students to understand that a generalization is based on details that support the generalization. **Read aloud the first paragraph in the selection** and model the process of making a generalization.

> ***Modeling*** I can use specific details from Adams's letter to make a generalization about life in America in 1800. She talks about going eight or nine miles through the woods on her way from Baltimore to Washington. She must have been on foot or on horseback. From this detail, I can generalize that travel was very difficult: There were few roads in this era; wandering through woods and getting lost were not unknown. To be sure that this generalization is valid, I would check other sources.

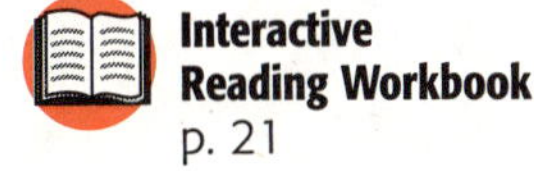
Interactive Reading Workbook
p. 21

Have students complete Interacting with Text **Making Generalizations,** student workbook page 21.

After Reading

You may also use the selection questions and activities in *Glencoe Literature*.

Analyzing Character Traits Help students analyze the character traits of Abigail Adams by asking the following questions.

1. Give three examples of what Abigail Adams says about herself. How does what she says reveal her character? (*Examples: She is funny—"I arrived here on Sunday last, and without meeting with any accident worth noticing." She is busy—"Yesterday, I returned fifteen visits." She is adaptable—"I could content myself almost anywhere three months."*)
2. Give an example of what Adams says about other people. How does what she says reveal her character? (*"with a billet from Major Custis, and a haunch of venison, and a kind, congratulatory letter from Mrs. Lewis, . . . with Mrs. Washington's love, inviting me to Mount Vernon"—Adams seems to be well-liked. She is friendly and appreciative.*)
3. Give an example of the type of mother Adams is to her children. (*She is an affectionate mother—"Give my love to your brother, and tell him he is ever present upon my mind. Affectionately your mother"*)

OBJECTIVES

- To analyze cause-and-effect relationships; to analyze characterization

FROM

The Life of Olaudah Equiano

Olaudah Equiano

Before Reading

Activating Prior Knowledge Explain to students that they will be reading an autobiographical account of a formerly enslaved person's life. Ask students what they know about Africans who were kidnapped from Africa by slave traders, sold into slavery, and brought to the New World. Students may point out that the captured people were put on slave ships. Ask what happened to the enslaved people aboard the ships. (*Possible responses: They were packed closely together, starved, and maltreated.*) On the board, begin a KWL chart. Fill in the first column with facts students know about slavery and the second column with facts they want to find out. Following is an example of the beginning of a KWL chart.

What I Know	What I Want to Learn	What I Learned	Where I Found Information
Enslaved people were kidnapped in Africa.	What was life like on slave ships going from Africa to America?		
Enslaved people were separated from their family members and sold.	Why did slave sellers separate families? How did the enslaved people react when they were taken from their families?		

Have students read "Meet Olaudah Equiano" and Building Background in *Glencoe Literature.*

Building Vocabulary On the board, write the following words, without definitions: *dejection* (lowness of spirits), *indulge* (to give free rein to), *salutation* (greeting), *stench* (stink), *flogged* (whipped), *quartered* (lodged or sheltered), *inconceivable* (impossible to comprehend), *wretches* (miserable persons, those in great misfortune), *accursed* (being under an evil curse or misfortune), *mariners* (sailors), *pacify* (soothe), *avarice* (excessive desire for wealth). Ask students to give synonyms or definitions for each word and to make up sentences using each word. Have students record the words and definitions in their vocabulary logs or journals.

Word Study: Latin Roots Write the selection words *perspirations* and *respiration* on the board. Explain that both words come from the Latin root *spirare*, "to breathe." Have students define *respiration*. (breathing) Explain that the prefix *per-* means "through." Therefore, *perspire* means "to breathe through (the skin)." Have students use their knowledge of prefixes to figure out the meanings of *expire* and *inspire*. (ex- *means "not,"* so expire *means "not breathing"*; in- *means "in, within, or into,"* so inspire *means "breathe [thoughts or influence] into."*) As students read the selection, have them use word parts to help them determine the meaning of an unfamiliar word.

Setting a Purpose for Reading Ask students to read the selection to find out about the feelings and experiences of a person taken from Africa to North America on a slave ship.

During Reading

Identifying Cause-and-Effect Relationships **Have students read the selection independently.** Remind students that, in a **cause-and-effect relationship**, one event or action causes one or more other actions or events. Encourage students to consider some of the cause-and-effect relationships described in the narrative. Ask: *Why were those on the ship transporting Africans?* (The slave traders would be paid large amounts of money for their captives.) *Why did the slave traders crowd so many Africans into the ship?* (The slave traders were greedy and apparently did not consider that large losses of life would make their journey less profitable.) Model the process of identifying cause-and-effect relationships for students. **Read aloud the part of the text that begins "The closeness of the place, and the heat . . . "** and ends " . . . thus falling victims to the improvident avarice, as I may call it, of their purchasers."

> ***Modeling*** As I read, I notice that there is a direct cause-and-effect relationship—the number of enslaved people crowded onto the ship in horrible conditions **caused** many of them to die. The suffocatingly close quarters brought on sickness and the final **effect**—death.

Have students work in pairs to identify at least three cause-and-effect relationships in the selection.

Analyzing Characterization Ask students what **characterization** refers to in a literary work. (*It refers to the ways a writer reveals the personality of a character.*) Explain to students that Equiano characterizes the slave traders by describing their characteristics, appearance, and actions. Have students find one example of each method of characterization. (*Examples: "the improvident avarice"; "those white men with horrible looks, red faces, and long hair"; flogging a white man to death.*) To provide students with further practice, have them complete Interacting with Text **Analyzing Characterization,** student workbook page 22.

After Reading

You may also use the selection questions and activities in *Glencoe Literature*.

KWL Chart Follow-Up Encourage students to be aware of general cause-and-effect relationships, in addition to specific cause-and-effect relationships described in the narrative. Ask: *What effects might narratives like that of Olaudah Equiano have had on society?* Bring out the idea that such narratives let people know the extent of slavery's cruelty. Encourage students to suggest information for the last two columns of the KWL charts.

OBJECTIVES

- To analyze characterization; to identify conflict in a short story

The Devil and Tom Walker

Washington Irving

Before Reading

Activating Prior Knowledge Ask students to read the Building Background notes in *Glencoe Literature*. Point out to students that Washington Irving set "The Devil and Tom Walker" in the 1720s, a time approximately one hundred years prior to the time in which Irving wrote the story. Explain that social values in the United States were changing dramatically in the 1700s. Traditional Puritan values were shifting and beginning to allow for and encourage the accumulation of wealth. Use an overhead transparency of a web or draw a web on the board. Write *Puritan Values* in the center circle of the web and have students suggest traits associated with Puritan values. Attach their ideas to the web. (*Possible responses: simple lifestyle, faith in God, hard work, family loyalty, and strict moral standards.*)

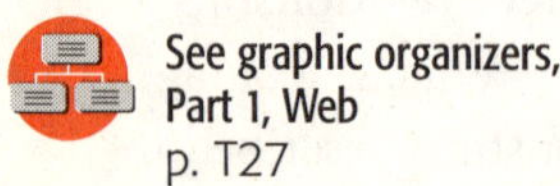

See graphic organizers, Part 1, Web p. T27

Characteristics of Genre: Tall Tale Ask students what they know about folktales. Remind them that a **folktale** is a traditional story, often with variations provided by various contributors to the tale, that is passed down orally for a long time before being written down. Explain that a **tall tale** is a kind of humorous folktale, often associated with the American frontier, that contains wild exaggerations and invention. As students read the story, encourage them to notice the elements of a tall tale.

Interactive Reading Workbook pp. 23–24

Building Vocabulary Have students turn to Interactive Reading **Reading Guide,** student workbook pages 23–24. Review with students the Key Vocabulary and Terms for the first section of the story. Before students read the next section of the story, have them review that section's vocabulary.

Word Study: Synonyms Write the following selection words on the board: *morass, quagmire, mire, slough*. Explain that all of these are synonyms for another selection word, *swamp*. The words have the following figurative meanings: *morass* (something that traps, confuses, or impedes); *quagmire* (a difficult position); *slough* (a state of moral degradation or spiritual dejection). Discuss these meanings with students. Have students record each word and its meaning into their vocabulary logs or journals. After they read the story, ask students to consider what makes the words particularly well suited to the story. (*All could be applied to Tom Walker's moral situation.*)

Setting a Purpose for Reading Encourage students to read the story to find out what changes in traditional Puritan values were taking place during this period in America, according to the author.

During Reading

Analyzing Characterization Ask students what is meant by characterization. (***Characterization** is the method an author uses to reveal the personalities of characters in a story.*) Remind students that authors can reveal characters directly and indirectly. Ask students to define *direct* and *indirect characterization*. Elicit from students that, when using **direct characterization,** the author makes explicit statements about characters. In **indirect characterization,** the author reveals a character through what the character says, thinks, and does, as well as through the reactions of others to the character. **Ask a volunteer to read aloud the second paragraph, which begins "About the year 1727 . . . "** Then ask: *What personality trait of Tom Walker does the narrator state directly?* (Tom Walker is "miserly.") Explain that this statement demonstrates direct characterization. Then ask students what they can infer about the characters of Tom Walker and his wife from their actions; for example, "they even conspired to cheat each other." (*Possible responses: Walker and his wife have no love between them. Both are selfish.*) Tell students that this conveying of a character trait through the action of the character is indirect characterization. As students read the selection, ask them to point out examples of indirect characterization. **Have students read the story silently.**

Using the Reading Guide Divide the reading of the story into two sections. (See the reading guide.) Ask students to add the missing information to their reading guides during or after reading each section of the story.

Identifying Conflict Remind students that the plot of a short story is usually built around an important conflict that affects the main character. Ask: *What is conflict in literature?* (**Conflict** is the central struggle between two opposing forces.) Ask students to identify the conflict that is introduced when Walker meets "Old Scratch" in the swamp. (*Tom Walker meets the devil, and the devil offers him a deal. The conflict here is a moral one.*) Minor internal conflicts follow: Walker wrestles with himself over whether to accept the devil's offer and whether to tell his wife about it. Explain that the main conflict emerges near the end of the story. **Read aloud three consecutive paragraphs—the first paragraph beginning "Thus Tom was the universal friend . . . "**—and model the process of identifying conflict in the story.

> ***Modeling*** From these paragraphs, I see that Walker has made money "hand over hand" and has become "a rich and mighty man." He has done this by "squeez[ing] his customers closer and closer and [sending] them at length, dry as a sponge, from his door." It is clear that he has profited in material ways from his arrangement with the devil. But now, as he gets older, Walker struggles with how to avoid "being damned" after selling his soul to the devil. He is so anxious that he becomes a religious zealot. Readers wonder whether the devil will "demand his due" and, if so, how. This unresolved conflict contributes to the building up of suspense.

After Reading

You may also use the selection questions and activities in *Glencoe Literature*.

Theme Remind students that **theme** is the central message of a work of literature. Have students recall the discussion of Puritan values that began the lesson. Then ask: *What is the theme?* (Possible theme: Greed endangers the soul.)

OBJECTIVES

- To analyze rhythm; to analyze imagery in a poem

To a Waterfowl and *Thanatopsis*

William Cullen Bryant

Before Reading

Building Background Have students read the Building Background notes in *Glencoe Literature*. Point out the word *romanticism* and ask students what they know about this literary movement. If necessary, explain that Romanticism was a movement in the early nineteenth century in art, music, and literature. Romanticism is characterized by spontaneous feelings and appreciation of nature. (Make clear that romanticism does not refer to romantic love.) Tell students that the poems they will read are about nature. Explain that the Romantic poets often used images of nature and explored the individual's connection to nature. Encourage students to describe a beautiful or interesting scene in nature, such as a sunset, a waterfall, a mountain, or a bird or an animal, and have them share their feelings about it.

Building Vocabulary On the board, write the following words, without definitions: *vainly* (uselessly), *illimitable* (measureless), *communion* (intimate fellowship), *eloquence* (the quality of forceful expressiveness), *blight* (something that impairs or destroys), *patriarchs* (men who are fathers or founders), *venerable* (impressive by reason of age), *sustained* (given support or relief). Have students locate these vocabulary words in the poems as they read and ask them to determine the meaning of each in context. Encourage students to look up the meanings of words they are unsure of in a dictionary. Have students write a sentence for each word in their vocabulary logs or journals, using each word as it is used in the selection.

Word Study: Connotation Point out that poetry achieves some of its effect by taking advantage of the subtle positive or negative emotions attached to words. Have students tell whether each of the vocabulary words has a positive, negative, or neutral connotation. Tell students to be sure of a word's **denotation** (dictionary definition) before determining its connotation. Encourage students to discuss any words on whose connotations they disagree. (*vainly*—negative; *illimitable*—neutral or positive; *communion*—positive; *eloquence*—positive; *blight*—negative; *patriarchs*—positive; *venerable*—positive; *sustained*—positive)

Setting a Purpose for Reading Encourage students to read the poems to find out how a poet influenced by Romanticism viewed nature.

During Reading

Questioning **Have partners take turns and read aloud four stanzas each of "To a Waterfowl."** Remind students to monitor their comprehension by **questioning**—asking themselves questions about parts of the text that are confusing. Give students the following example of questioning. Point to the word *whither* in the first stanza and say: *I wonder what the word* whither *means.* Ask a volunteer to clarify the meaning of the word (*whither* means "where") and have the volunteer paraphrase, or restate, what the poet is asking. (*Where are you going this evening?*)

Analyzing Rhythm **Ask partners each to read aloud half of "Thanatopsis."** Explain to students that rhythm is one important way in which poetry differs from prose. Like rhythm in music, rhythm in poetry can make a poem memorable. Help students learn how to recognize iambic pentameter. Write the first line of "Thanatopsis" on the board. Mark it as follows: "Tŏ hím/whŏ ín/thĕ lóve/ ŏf Ná/turĕ hólds/." **Read the line aloud, emphasizing the second syllable in each foot.** Model the process of analyzing rhythm in a poem.

> ***Modeling*** Each set of syllables with a stressed syllable is a **foot.** (Point to *Tŏ hím/* on the board.) An **iambic foot** has one unstressed syllable followed by a stressed syllable. As I read, I emphasize the second syllable in each foot. This line, with five feet, is called **pentameter,** and the pattern of stressed syllables indicate that this is **iambic pentameter.**

Then have students read chorally the line on the board. Encourage them to notice the rhythm of iambic pentameter. Ask what tone the use of iambic pentameter lends to "Thanatopsis." (*It lends a calm, rational, measured tone to the poem.*)

Interactive Reading Workbook
p. 25

Analyzing Imagery Remind students that **imagery** helps to create pictures in a reader's mind through descriptive writing. Images generally appeal to one or more of the five senses. Have students find images in the two poems that appeal to sight, hearing, and touch. Have several students read aloud lines that evoke vivid images. Then ask students to describe what they picture when they hear or read these lines and which senses the images appeal to. For example, in "To a Waterfowl" William Cullen Bryant describes (in line 18) "At that far height, the cold, thin atmosphere" and (in line 20) "the dark night." The first image appeals to the sense of touch and the second to sight. Ask: *What mood do the images help create?* (They help convey a lonely and melancholy mood.) *How do these types of images support the themes of the poems?* (The images are of nature. They emphasize the poet's belief in the power of nature and its importance in a person's life.) Have students complete Interacting with Text **Analyzing Imagery,** student workbook page 25.

After Reading

You may also use the selection questions and activities in *Glencoe Literature*.

Responding Lead a discussion about these poems by having students respond to the following questions.

1. Which poem did you like better? Why?
2. Which images helped you to enjoy or better understand the poem?
3. In "Thanatopsis" what does the poet say a person should do when he or she is frightened by thoughts of death? (*Go out into the open outdoors and listen to the teachings of Nature.*)

OBJECTIVES

- To analyze imagery; to identify figurative language

Old Ironsides and *The Chambered Nautilus*

Oliver Wendell Holmes

Before Reading

Activating Prior Knowledge Have students read the Building Background notes in *Glencoe Literature*. Point out that Oliver Wendell Holmes had a wide range of interests and often wrote about ideas or events that stirred strong feelings in him. Ask students whether there is any cause that has aroused their concern, such as saving the rain forests, protecting endangered animal populations, or stopping world hunger. Ask them to elaborate on their feelings about a particular cause and to discuss any actions they have taken on behalf of that cause.

Building Vocabulary On the board, write the following words, without their definitions: *victor* (one that defeats an enemy or opponent), *hulk* (the body of an old ship unfit for service), *wont* (accustomed), *crypt* (a chamber wholly or partly underground). Ask students to locate each word, as they read the poems, and to determine its meaning through context. Have them write the definitions that they formulate, along with the context clues in their vocabulary logs or journals.

Word Study: Greek Roots Write the word *nautilus* on the board. Explain that this word comes from the Greek words *nautilos*, meaning "sailor," and *naus*, meaning "ship." **Have a volunteer read aloud the information about the chambered nautilus** that is in the Building Background note in *Glencoe Literature*. (*A chambered nautilus is a sea creature that grows by expanding the number of "chambers" in its shell and moving into successive new chambers—and out of the old "chambers"—as it grows.*) Explain that the word *nautilus* derives from Greek roots because the sea creature was once thought to use its shell as a sail. It was viewed, in effect, as a "sailor" whose shell was its "ship."

Setting a Purpose for Reading Encourage students to read the poems to enjoy images of the sea.

During Reading

Analyzing Imagery **Have students in small groups read aloud "Old Ironsides."** Remind them that **imagery** helps to create pictures in readers' minds through the use of descriptive language. The imagery in literary works may evoke emotional responses in readers or listeners. Explain to students that imagery appeals to one or more of the five senses. Images contribute to the mood or feeling of a literary work. Challenge students in their small groups to find one or more images in the poem and the senses to which they appeal: sight, hearing, touch, taste, and smell. Have groups share their results with the class and explain how the images they found add to the mood of the poem. Possible responses follow.

Stanza 1: "the battle shout, / And burst the cannon's roar"; hearing; imagery helps create a violent, frightening mood.

Stanza 2: "Her deck, once red with heroes' blood"; sight; imagery helps create a militaristic, heroic mood.

Stanza 3: "Her thunders shook the mighty deep"; hearing and touch; imagery helps create a powerful, heroic mood.

Identifying Metaphor and Personification Ask students to define a metaphor. (*A **metaphor** is a figure of speech that presents an implied comparison between two seemingly unlike things.*) Point out line 7 of "Old Ironsides." Ask: *What is meant by "the meteor of the ocean air"?* (It is the ship's flag.) Point out that the poet does not say the flag is *like* a meteor. He simply calls the flag a meteor. Ask: *Why can the ship's flag be called "the meteor of the ocean air"? In what ways is the flag like a meteor?* (Possible response: The ship's flag can be compared to a meteor because it flashes through the air with the brightness or quickness of a meteor. Then remind students that **personification** is a figure of speech in which human traits are attributed to an animal, an object, a force of nature, or an idea. **Read aloud line 11** of "Old Ironsides" and ask students to explain what is being personified in it. (*The winds are said to be hurrying.*) Encourage students to point out examples of personification in the poem. (*Examples include referring to the ship as "her" and to the cannon as having a "roar."*)

Reading "The Chambered Nautilus" **Have partners read aloud alternating verses of "The Chambered Nautilus." Then read aloud to the class the last stanza** and model the process of identifying and determining the meaning of figurative language.

> ***Modeling*** In the last stanza, I know that the line "Build thee more stately mansions" is not a literal command to build elaborate homes because the speaker is addressing his soul. The speaker wants to change himself. He says to "leave thy low-vaulted past" and hopes that each "new temple" of his soul will be "nobler than the last." The speaker hopes to continue to grow spiritually until, in death, he can leave his "outgrown shell," as a chambered nautilus does, at the shore of life.

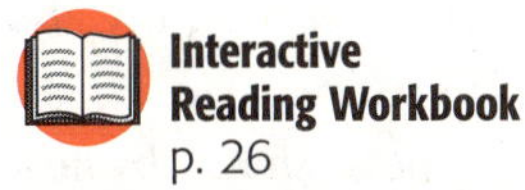
Interactive Reading Workbook
p. 26

Point out that the poet's idea about building stately mansions is a metaphor referring to the human need for spiritual growth. Have students complete Interacting with Text **Identifying Metaphor and Personification,** student workbook page 26.

After Reading

You may also use the selection questions and activities in *Glencoe Literature*.

Analyzing Have students analyze the poems by answering the following questions.

1. In the first stanza of "Old Ironsides," what does the speaker describe? (*He describes the tattered flag of the ship. He uses the flag to help him recall the ship's proud history and expresses sorrow because the flag will fly no more.*)
2. Which line in stanza 3 describes the action of the chambered nautilus? Did the chambered nautilus look toward the new or cling to the old? (*Line 18: "He left the past year's dwelling for the new." The creature "knew the old no more," so seemingly he did not look back at the old way of life.*)

OBJECTIVES

- To explore synonyms and connotation; to understand characterization

The First Snow-Fall

James Russell Lowell

Before Reading

Activating Prior Knowledge Let students know that this poem by James Russell Lowell is about a snowfall. Have them share experiences that they have had involving snow or anything they recall about snow from their reading. Ask: *What qualities does snow have? What does snow feel like underfoot? How heavy is snow? What is special about a first snowfall?*

Building Vocabulary On the board, write the following words, without their definitions: *muffled* (muted or subdued), *down* (young birds' feathers), *headstone* (memorial stone at the head of a grave), *leaden* (the color of lead; dull gray; oppressively heavy). Have students write a sentence for each vocabulary word. Then have them substitute into the sentence a synonym for the vocabulary word. (For example: The leaden sky hung over the city. The gray sky hung over the city.) Point out that the **connotation** of a word (the values or emotions associated with a word) affects the feeling conveyed by the sentence. After students have read the poem, have them share how the vocabulary words and their connotations affect the mood conveyed by the poem.

During Reading

Understanding Characterization **Call on volunteers to each read aloud a stanza of the poem.** Ask students what they know about the speaker of the poem. (*He is the father of two daughters, Mabel and another daughter who has died.*) Remind students that **characterization** refers to the methods a writer uses to reveal the personality of a character. Explain that poets may use characterization in a poem. Ask students to point out lines from the poem that reveal the personality of the speaker in "The First Snow-Fall." (*The speaker is sensitive to the beauty in nature; he observes, "Every pine and fir and hemlock / Wore ermine too dear for an earl, / And the poorest twig on the elm-tree / Was ridged inch deep with pearl."); the speaker is a loving father: he shows this by the endearing, gentle way he describes his daughter Mabel ("Up spoke our own little Mabel") and by his feelings for his child who has died ("I kissed [Mabel] . . . my kiss was given to her sister, / Folded close under deepening snow."); he is religious, as is shown by his attributing snowfall to "all-Father"; he has deep sadness, shown by his memories of his dead daughter ("I thought of a mound in sweet Auburn / Where a little headstone stood."*) Have students complete **Interacting with Text** **Characterizing a Speaker,** student workbook page 27.

Interactive Reading Workbook p. 27

After Reading

Vocabulary Follow-Up Ask students how the connotations of the vocabulary words and other words such as *muffled*, *scar*, and *deepening* affect the mood of the poem. Guide students to see that the melancholy mood and the idea of grief softened and blurred by the snow are conveyed by these words.

You may also use the selection questions and activities in *Glencoe Literature*.

OBJECTIVES

- To visualize; to analyze sound devices

The Tide Rises, the Tide Falls

Henry Wadsworth Longfellow

Before Reading

Building Background Tell students that this poem by Henry Wadsworth Longfellow is about tides and time. Invite students to describe the motion of the water and to tell what they know about ocean tides. (*The ocean rises and falls every twelve hours as a result of the gravitational pull of the Moon and the Sun.*)

Word Study: Rhyme Ask students: *What is rhyme?* (**Rhyme** is the repetition in two or more words of the same stressed vowel sounds and any successive sounds.) **Read aloud the following lines from the poem:** "Along the sea-sands damp and brown / The traveler hastens toward the town." Ask: *Which words rhyme?* (Brown *and* town *rhyme.*) Encourage students to note other rhyming words as they read "The Tide Rises, the Tide Falls."

During Reading

Visualizing **Have a volunteer read the poem aloud.** Ask students to **visualize**—to use the words in the poem to help them form mental pictures—the sea as it is described in the poem. Then ask: *What words help you to see and hear what happens?* Help students recognize that language such as "the sea-sands damp and brown," "darkness settles on roofs and walls," and "the little waves . . . efface the footprints in the sands" creates vivid images because the language includes specific details and these details appeal to the reader's senses.

Analyzing Sound Devices: Repetition and Alliteration Explain that poets use various devices to give a poem its unique sound. Sound devices include rhyme, repetition, and alliteration. Ask students: *Which words and phrases are repeated in the poem?* ("The tide rises, the tide falls," "darkness," "the sea") *How does the repetition affect the sound of the poem?* (The repetition gives the poem a soothing, rhythmic sound. The rhythm imitates the moving in and out of the tide.) Remind students that **alliteration** is the repetition of a series of initial consonant sounds. Ask: *What example of alliteration do you find in the first stanza?* ("curlew calls," "sea-sands") Have students complete Interacting with Text **Analyzing Sound Devices,** student workbook page 28.

Interactive Reading Workbook p. 28

After Reading

Synthesizing Invite students to discuss the traits that the poems of Oliver Wendell Holmes, James Russell Lowell, and Henry Wadsworth Longfellow have in common. Elicit from students that all contain much vivid natural imagery and that the poems of Holmes and Longfellow both use simple sentence structure and diction. Also, the poems of Holmes, Lowell, and Longfellow all make connections between a specific element of nature and an important lesson of life.

You may also use the selection questions and activities in *Glencoe Literature.*

OBJECTIVES

- To summarize; to connect with Emerson's philosophies of life

Concord Hymn, FROM *Nature*, and FROM *Self-Reliance*

Ralph Waldo Emerson

Before Reading

Building Background Have students read the Building Background notes in *Glencoe Literature*. Point out that Ralph Waldo Emerson was a philosopher as well as a poet and essayist. Explain to students that an individual's philosophy is a particular system of principles, concepts, attitudes, and conduct to which he or she subscribes. Tell students that the selections from "Nature" and from "Self-Reliance" express Emerson's ideas about nature and human nature. Invite them to discuss whether they think it is human nature for individuals to follow their own sense of what is right or whether they are more likely to follow the crowd.

Building Vocabulary On the board, write the following words, without their definitions: *reverence* (honor or respect either felt or shown), *exhilaration* (the state of being excessively cheerful; excitement), *egotism* (an exaggerated sense of self-importance), *temperance* (moderation in action, thought, or feeling), *contempt* (disdain; an attitude of superiority). Have students discuss their definitions. Instruct them to refer to a dictionary for definitions of words whose meanings they are unsure of. Ask students what all these words have in common. (*All describe human attitudes or traits.*) Ask students to watch for each word as they read the selections and to think about how each helps express Emerson's philosophies. Encourage students to record the words and their meanings in their vocabulary logs or journals.

Word Study: Latin Roots Write the word *ego* on the board. Explain that it is a Latin word meaning "I." Have students write on the board other words and phrases that use the root, such as *alter ego*, *egocentric*, *egoism*, and *egotist*. Ask students whether these words have a positive or negative connotation. (*positive for the first and negative for the others*) Point out that in psychological terms, having a strong ego is a positive trait. Encourage students to find out whether egotism is positive or negative in Emerson's writings.

Setting a Purpose for Reading Have students read the selections to find out about Emerson's attitudes toward the individual's connection with nature and toward self-reliance.

During Reading

Summarizing **Have students read the poem "Concord Hymn" chorally.** Invite volunteers to summarize the poem. Remind students that a **summary** briefly restates the main ideas of a passage. Ask: *What is the most important* *idea that Emerson is conveying in the poem?* (He is praising the courage, independence, and unselfishness of those who fought. Because of their actions, they have left a legacy of freedom.) Point out that in the last stanza Emerson is asking nature to spare the statue from erosion so that it will endure.

Next, **have students read the selection from "Nature" independently. Read aloud the first paragraph** and model the process of summarizing for students.

> ***Modeling*** **In the first three sentences, Emerson defines *solitude*. He says that a person is not in a state of solitude when he or she is alone reading and writing. To be truly alone, a person should look at the stars. Emerson sees the stars as a beautiful symbol of the sublime. I can summarize the paragraph by saying that the stars represent the ideal, sublime world to Emerson. Looking at them makes him feel a sense of solitude.**

Have students write a summary of each of the remaining paragraphs. Then ask them to discuss and compare their summaries and to determine what is the clearest expression of the main idea for each paragraph. **Have students read the selection from "Self-Reliance" independently,** following the same procedure to summarize each paragraph. Then have students complete Interacting with Text **Summarizing,** student workbook page 29.

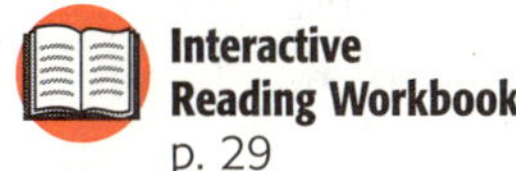
Interactive Reading Workbook
p. 29

Connecting In small groups, have students discuss examples or personal experiences that illustrate the following ideas from "*Self-Reliance*:"
(1) "To believe your own thought, to believe that what is true for you in your private heart, is true for all men,—that is genius."
(2) "In every work of genius we recognize our own rejected thoughts: they come back to us with a certain alienated majesty."
(3) "The virtue in most request is conformity."
Prompt discussion with the following: *Describe a time when you trusted your instincts. What happened? Have you ever dismissed your own idea only to hear someone else state it and discover that everyone thinks the idea is brilliant? How did you feel? What do you think about conformity? Describe the risks and benefits of nonconformity.*

After Reading

You may also use the selection questions and activities in *Glencoe Literature*.

Analyzing Ask students to recall Emerson's poem "Concord Hymn." Ask students how the ideas expressed in the poem relate to those in the essays. (*The poem honors common men who followed their consciences, risking their lives for freedom. Emerson would probably attach the virtues described in "Self-Reliance" to these "embattled farmers."*)

OBJECTIVES

- To analyze problems and solutions; to paraphrase

FROM

Walden and

FROM

Civil Disobedience

Henry David Thoreau

Before Reading

Activating Prior Knowledge Tell students that they will read a selection from *Walden*, by Henry David Thoreau. In *Walden* Thoreau describes his simple life in a ten-by-fifteen foot cabin located in the woods at Walden Pond. Have students read the Building Background notes preceding the selection, in *Glencoe Literature*. Suggest that they imagine themselves living as Thoreau did. Ask: *What would you miss most from your present way of life? What might you enjoy about living in the woods?* Have students discuss Thoreau's quotation "If a man does not keep pace with his companions, perhaps it is because he hears a different drummer." Ask them how this quotation may apply to their lives.

Building Vocabulary On the board, write the following words, without their definitions: *indispensable* (absolutely necessary), *institution* (an established practice in a society), *discerns* (detects; distinguishes), *insensibly* (unknowingly; unconsciously), *inexpedient* (not appropriate or advisable), *conscientious* (governed by the dictates of conscience), *condescended* (descended to a less dignified level), *enlightened* (insightful; informed spiritually or intellectually). Have partners discuss how prefixes, suffixes, and base words or word roots help them to determine the meaning of words. Tell them to write down their definitions and then to verify them by paying close attention to each word's use in context as they read the selections. Encourage students to record each word and its meaning in their vocabulary logs or journals.

Word Study: Latin Roots Write the words *conscious* and *conscience* on the board. Have students explain the meaning of each word. Explain that both words come from the same Latin root, *scire*, "to know." *Conscious*, an adjective, means "perceiving or noticing with a degree of controlled thought" and "having mental faculties not dulled by sleep, faintness, or stupor." *Conscience*, a noun, means "the sense of the moral goodness or blameworthiness of one's own conduct or character." Point out that the word *science* comes from the same Latin root. Have students use *conscious*, *conscience*, *consciousness*, and *conscientious* in sentences. Encourage students to notice the words in context as they read from "Civil Disobedience."

Setting a Purpose for Reading Encourage students to read the essays to discover ways in which Thoreau "marched to the beat of a different drummer."

During Reading

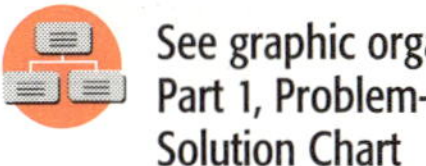

See graphic organizers, Part 1, Problem-Solution Chart p. T30

Analyzing Problem-Solution **Have students read the selection from *Walden* independently.** After they have completed their reading, explain that, by analyzing the problems and solutions presented in the essay, they can better understand the ideas that Thoreau expresses. Display on the overhead projector a transparency of the Problem-Solution Chart from graphic organizers, Part 1. Complete the chart as students offer their responses. Ask students: *What bothers Thoreau about modern life?* (People waste their lives worrying about petty and materialistic concerns.) *What actions does Thoreau take to solve this problem for himself?* (He moves to a tiny cabin in the woods, giving up material comforts and distractions.) *What is Thoreau's final solution to his problem?* (Simplify. Success, he believes, is based on stripping life to its essentials.)

Have students independently read the selection from "Civil Disobedience." Repeat the process of analyzing a problem and its solution in "Civil Disobedience." (*Problem: The American government makes decisions and takes actions that are morally objectionable to individuals. Actions: Thoreau refuses to pay a tax. He is therefore sent to jail. Solution: Each individual should remain steadfast in his or her convictions about specific issues, as Thoreau does. Then the government will evolve into one that treats the individual with respect.*)

Paraphrasing Point out that some of Thoreau's statements in "Civil Disobedience" are clear and easy to understand. Others, those that deal with the abstract, are more challenging. Suggest that students **paraphrase,** express a difficult sentence or passage in their own words. **Read aloud the second paragraph from "Civil Disobedience."** Model the process of paraphrasing for students.

> ***Modeling*** As I read the first sentence, I have a hard time understanding Thoreau's language and sentence structure. I reread it and put the question into statement form: "American government is a tradition. . . . " Then I substitute the word *trying* for "endeavouring," *continue* for "transmit itself," *undamaged* for "unimpaired," *future generations* for "posterity," and *honor* for "integrity." I can now paraphrase the sentence: *American government is a tradition that tries to continue undamaged for future generations but continuously becomes less honorable.*

Interactive Reading Workbook p. 30

Call on students to paraphrase sentences from "Civil Disobedience." Have students complete Interacting with Text **Paraphrasing,** student workbook page 30.

After Reading

You may also use the selection questions and activities in *Glencoe Literature.*

Analyzing Ask students to brainstorm about what effects Thoreau's beliefs and actions have had on society. Ask: *What specific people and groups do you think have been influenced by "Civil Disobedience" since Thoreau's time?* (Mahatma Gandhi acknowledged the influence of Thoreau's "Civil Disobedience" on his course of action to achieve independence for India from British rule. In addition, many leaders of the American Civil Rights movement of the 1950s and 1960s, as well as those who protested against the Vietnam War in the 1960s and 1970s, were influenced by Thoreau's concept of passive resistance.)

OBJECTIVES

- To analyze mood; to identify symbolism in a short story

The Minister's Black Veil: A Parable

Nathaniel Hawthorne

Before Reading

Activating Prior Knowledge Tell students that "The Minister's Black Veil" is a story about a minister who provokes reactions from his congregation because of something he wears. Invite students to discuss how a person's attire affects people's attitudes toward that person. Ask: *Have you ever been surprised by something a friend of yours wore—an accessory or an outfit? How do appearances influence your opinion of others?* Guide students to understand that sometimes people react negatively when they are faced with something they do not understand or expect.

Building Vocabulary Have students turn to Interactive Reading **Reading Guide,** student workbook pages 31–32. Review with them the Key Vocabulary and Terms for the first section of the story. Before students read the next section of the story, have them review the vocabulary for that section.

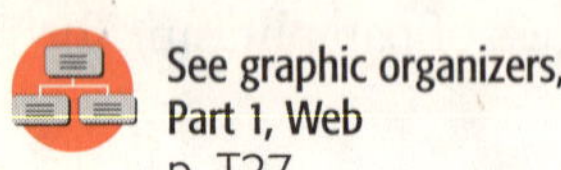

Word Study: Specialized Vocabulary Point out that the story has words that pertain to church and people associated with a church. Write the following words on the board: *sexton*, *pulpit*, *parson*, *clergyman*, *clerical*, *preacher*, *parishioners*, *congregation*, *minister*, *pastor*, *sermon*, and *deacons*. Create a transparency of a web and display it on the overhead projector. Have students organize their vocabulary words around a concept and suggest a concept to write in the center circle of the web. Two possible categories are "religious leaders and officials" (parson, clergyman, preacher, minister, pastor, sexton, deacons) and "people who attend church" (congregation *and* parishioners). The *pulpit*, a podium, is the place where a minister stands to give a *sermon*, a lecture or homily, in church. Explain that these words relate to most Christian churches; some other religions use the terms, but some may have their own terms to describe comparable elements.

Setting a Purpose for Reading Have students read the story to find out why the minister wears a black veil and how it affects his congregation.

During Reading

Analyzing Mood **Have students read the "The Minister's Black Veil" independently.** After students have finished reading, ask them to define the term *mood* and to explain how readers determine the mood of a story. (***Mood*** *is the emotional quality or atmosphere of a story.*) Explain that one element that creates a particular mood is the author's **diction,** or word choice. Have students point out several words and phrases that they think contribute to the mood of "The Minister's Black Veil." If necessary, **read aloud the following examples,** emphasizing the underlined words: when the minister's veil is first described, Hawthorne writes that the veil lends "a darkened aspect to all living and inanimate things," and he calls it a "gloomy shade." Later in the story, the author writes that "a cloud seemed to have rolled duskily from beneath the black crepe." He describes the veil as a "dismal shade." Near the end of the story (at the end of the paragraph that begins "Several persons were visible . . . "), the author describes the veil as it lay on the minister's face, "as if to deepen the gloom of his darksome chamber, and shade him from the sunshine of eternity." Point out that Hawthorne also uses the phrases "deathlike paleness" and "miserable obscurity" and repeats the word "melancholy" several times. Invite students to describe the mood of the story. (*All of these words and phrases help to create a mood of darkness and melancholy.*)

Using the Reading Guide Divide the story into two sections to correspond with the organization of the reading guide.

- The first section extends through the paragraph that begins "That night, the handsomest couple in Milford village . . . "
- The second section begins "The next day, the whole village of Milford talked of little else than Parson Hooper's black veil."

Have students fill in information to complete their reading guides, student workbook pages 31–32, after they have read each section of the story.

Identifying Symbolism Tell students that a **symbol** is an object, a person, a place, or an experience that stands for something else. For example, explain that a flag is a symbol for a country. Point out that in the story, Mr. Hooper says, "This veil is a type and a symbol." Discuss the symbolism of the veil: point out that the veil is a tangible object with a use—a veil may cover the face of a bride, for example. However, a veil also has a symbolic meaning. Ask: *What does the veil in this story symbolize?* (Possible response: The veil may symbolize guilt or sin.) *What might the color of the veil symbolize?* (Black usually symbolizes death or mourning.) *What other objects in the story might be symbols?* (Possible response: The pulpit could be a symbol of Mr. Hooper's high position in the community and his role of moral leadership.)

After Reading

You may also use the selection questions and activities in *Glencoe Literature*.

Analyzing Theme Remind students that the **theme** of a story is its central message, its underlying meaning. Explain that a literary work may have more than one theme. To analyze the theme of this story, review the meaning of the veil and its effect on Mr. Hooper and others. Ask: *What does the veil symbolize?* (At the end of the story, the minister reveals that the veil stands for the secret sins that separate a person from God and others.) *Do you think that Mr. Hooper's veil has made his life better? Do you think that it has helped the members of his congregation to become better people?* (Possible response: While the veil kept Mr. Hooper apart from friendship and closeness with others, it gave him a certain mystery and made him "an efficient clergyman.") *How would you state the theme of the story?* (Possible responses: Guilt over secret sin separates a person from others and from God; forcing others to confront their sins leads one further away from God; hanging onto guilt instead of forgiving oneself can ruin one's life.)

OBJECTIVES

- To use summarizing, questioning, clarifying, and predicting for understanding literature

The Three-Piece Suit

Ali Deb

Translated by Alice Copple-Tošić

Before Reading

Activating Prior Knowledge Tell students that "The Three-Piece Suit" is a story about a man who splurges by buying an expensive suit. Ask students what it means to "splurge." They may say that splurging involves spending more than one can generally afford on an item that one does not need. Point out that spending a large amount of money may initially cause feelings of happiness and excitement but may eventually cause "buyer's remorse," or regret.

Building Vocabulary Write the following words, without definitions, on the board: *glib* (marked by ease and informality showing little thought), *austerity* (a state of offering little or no scope for pleasure), *prudently* (cautiously), *supplementary* (additional), *consequence* (power to produce an effect). Ask students to guess at the meanings of the words. Have them use the words in sentences. Encourage students to look up in a dictionary definitions for the words they do not know. As they read the story, tell students to notice the way each word is used in context. Have students record these words and their definitions in their vocabulary logs or journals.

Word Study: Related Forms of Words Explain to students that if they know the meaning of *literal* (an adjective meaning "actual"), they will be able to discern the meaning of *literally* (an adverb meaning "actually"). Tell students that knowing the meaning of one form of a word usually can enable readers to deduce the meaning of its other forms. Write the following words on the board but do not write the definition of the adverbs: *abominable* (extremely unpleasant—adjective), *abominably* (in an extremely unpleasant manner—adverb); *prudent* (cautious—adjective), *prudently* (in a cautious manner—adverb). Have students determine the meanings of the adverbs on the board.

Setting a Purpose for Reading Have students read the story to find out the unexpected results of one man's splurging.

During Reading

Using Reading Strategies Write the names of the following four reading strategies on the board: summarizing, questioning, clarifying, and predicting. Remind students that readers often use these reading strategies without being aware of it. Ask students to define **summarizing** (briefly *stating the main ideas of a passage in one's own words*); **questioning** (*asking questions during reading about things that are confusing*); **clarifying** (*rereading to eliminate confusion about what has been read*); and **predicting** (*making a guess, on the basis of what has happened so far, about what will happen next*). **Read aloud the first five paragraphs of the story.** Then model the process of using these reading strategies.

Modeling I can **summarize** what I have read so far. The narrator spends too much money on a beautiful new suit, and his friends make a big fuss. He pays for drinks—because he looks so prosperous, it is expected of him. I **question** why the narrator has spent so much money on a suit. And I am not sure what the narrator means about "ordinary cigarettes." To **clarify,** I reread. I realize that the narrator must have bought cigarettes that do not have tar and nicotine or that are imported. I suspect that he has done so not for health reasons but for the same reason he bought the suit. Finally, I **predict** what the narrator will do next. I think that he will find it will cost him even more money to keep up appearances.

Monitoring Comprehension **Have students take turns reading paragraphs of the story aloud in small groups.** Write the following chart on the board. After groups read aloud each segment of text, have them follow the procedure described in the chart. Review the strategies, the role of the leader, and how the group is to interact with the leader. Designate a leader for each group. Circulate in the room, as student discussions are taking place, to guide the groups' efforts.

Strategy	How Student Leader Helps	The Group's Responses
Summarize	The leader gives a summary of the segment of text that may answer the questions *who? what? where? why?* and *when?*	The group offers ideas for additions to and clarifications of the leader's summary.
Question	Then the leader identifies questions about what was just read.	Group members try to answer the questions. They propose additional questions.
Clarify	The leader guides the group to answer the questions and rereads confusing passages aloud.	Group members also seek answers and ask for clarification when information is unclear.
Predict	The leader predicts what may happen in the next reading segment.	Group members offer their own predictions about what may happen next.

Have students complete Interacting with Text **Questioning,** student workbook page 33.

After Reading

You may also use the selection questions and activities in *Glencoe Literature.*

Analyzing Remind students that there can be more than one theme for a story. Ask: *What is the theme of the selection?* (Possible responses: Living beyond one's means may bring unexpected problems; one can't judge a person by his or her appearance; trying to be someone other than oneself may backfire.) On the board, write the themes that students suggest and encourage discussion. Ask students to point out parts of the story that support the main themes.

OBJECTIVE

- To analyze narrative point of view

To Helen, The Raven, and *The Pit and the Pendulum*

Edgar Allan Poe

Before Reading

Activating Prior Knowledge Have students read "Meet Edgar Allan Poe" in *Glencoe Literature*. Point out that Poe is credited with being "a master of horror." Tell students that "The Pit and the Pendulum" is a horror story. Invite students to discuss the differences between horror films and horror stories in print. Write students ideas on the board, under the appropriate headings. (*Horror films: Special effects can help make monsters appear frightening; horror movies often have helpless victims, gory violence, atmospheric lighting, and suspenseful music. Horror stories, print: Images of monsters and other characters are based on the writer's descriptions and the reader's imagination; gore is described; no music or lighting contributes to the atmosphere.*) Encourage students to discuss what they like about horror stories conveyed through each medium.

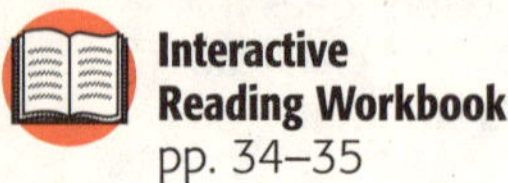

Interactive Reading Workbook
pp. 34–35

Building Vocabulary Have students turn to Interactive Reading **Reading Guide,** student workbook pages 34–35. Review with them the Key Vocabulary and Terms for the first section of the story "The Pit and the Pendulum." Before students read the next section of the story, have them review the vocabulary for that section.

Word Study: Connotation Explain that writers choose words carefully to create a particular mood and also to build a feeling of suspense or horror. Ask students in pairs to scan "The Raven" for words that help create the mood of the poem and to write them down. (*"dreary," "weak," "weary," "bleak," "ghost," "sorrow," "terrors," "darkness," "dreaming," "echo," "mystery," "ghastly," "grim," "grave," "unmerciful," "melancholy," "burden," "ominous," "grim," "gaunt," "desolate," "haunted," "evil"*) Ask students whether the connotations of these words are basically positive or negative and what the words suggest about the mood of the poem. (*Most have negative connotations that suggest a mood of darkness, mystery, or terror.*) As students read, have them notice how these words work in context to help create the poem's mood.

Setting a Purpose for Reading Encourage students to read the poems and the short story to find out how one of the most influential authors of gothic horror achieved his effects.

During Reading

Analyzing Point of View Ask students: *What does the term* point of view *mean?* (**Point of view** is the relationship of the narrator to the story.) Remind students that the narrator in a story with a first-person point of view is a character in the story who is referred to as "I." The narrator in a story with a limited third-person point of view is a character in the story who is referred to as "he" or "she." The narrator in a story told from an omniscient point of view is outside the story. An omniscient narrator may reveal the thoughts of more than one character and may provide information that is beyond what any one character would know.

Remind students that the **speaker** of a poem is the narrator. **Have students read "To Helen" and "The Raven" aloud with a partner, with partners alternating stanzas.** Have students identify the point of view from which each poem is told. (The "story" in both poems is told from the first-person point of view.)

Have students read "The Pit and the Pendulum" independently. Ask: *From which point of view is "The Pit and the Pendulum" told?* (The story is written from the first-person point of view.) *What effect does the first-person point of view have on the suspense created in the story?* (The first-person point of view makes the narrator's problems seem more immediate.) **Read aloud the first four paragraphs of the story** and model the process of determining point of view.

> ***Modeling*** The first word of the story is "I," and the word is not in quotation marks as it would be if it were dialogue spoken by a character. The word *I* indicates that the story has a first-person narrator. I learn that the narrator, imprisoned in a dark chamber, is drifting in and out of consciousness. As I read further, I get a sense of his emotions in these circumstances. I notice the unusual diction and sentence structure the narrator uses. He says, "In the deepest slumber–no! In delirium–no! In a swoon–no! In death–no! even in the grave all *is not* lost." I feel that I'm inside the narrator's mind. I can tell that he is so frightened that he is thinking in excited fragments. Clearly, having this character tell his story will create suspense and impact in the story.

Call on volunteers to choose passages they find effective or powerful. Ask students to read the passages aloud. Encourage students to explain how the first-person narration helps the author achieve the effect of horror.

Using the Reading Guide Divide the story into two reading sections, as indicated in the reading guide. (The second section begins "Looking upward I surveyed . . . ") Remind students to add the missing information to their reading guides after they read each section of the story. Have students work independently or in groups to complete their reading guides.

After Reading

You may also use the selection questions and activities in *Glencoe Literature*.

Evaluating Help students evaluate the author's technique in "The Pit and the Pendulum."

1. Was the author effective at building suspense? Explain. (*Yes, the author was effective at building suspense. Examples of close calls that the narrator has: almost falling into the pit, almost being sliced by the pendulum, and having the walls close in on him.*)
2. Do you think the narrator's attempts at escape were well reasoned out and realistic? (*Possible answer: Although the narrator was in surrealistic, unlikely situations, his actions in the circumstances were believable, and the emotions he felt were reasonable.*)

OBJECTIVES

- To draw conclusions; to recognize figurative language

FROM

My Bondage and My Freedom

Frederick Douglass

Before Reading

Activating Prior Knowledge Have students read "Meet Frederick Douglass" and the Building Background notes in *Glencoe Literature*. Point out that the autobiography *My Bondage and My Freedom* was written by a formerly enslaved person. Invite students to discuss books or stories about slavery in the United States. (*Examples:* Uncle Tom's Cabin *and* Roots.) Ask students whether they found the accounts in the selections realistic and have them explain why or why not.

Building Vocabulary On the board, write the following words, without their definitions: *congenial* (agreeably suited to one's nature, taste, or outlook), *stringency* (a state marked by strictness or severity), *prerogative* (right, power, or privilege) *destitute* (lacking something necessary or desirable), *abode* (home), *divest* (to take away from), *consternation* (distress or dismay leading to confusion), *avail* (to be of use or advantage), *recapitulates* (summarizes), *redolent* (reminiscent, suggestive). Tell students to check a dictionary if they are unsure of a word's meaning. Encourage students to write each word and its definition in their vocabulary logs or journals.

Word Study: Latin Root *bene* On the board, write the selection words *benevolent* and *benevolence*. Explain that they are based on the Latin root *bene*, which means "well." In *benevolent*, the root is combined with another Latin root *volēns*, meaning "to wish." Ask students to brainstorm for (or to find in a dictionary) other words that have the root *bene*. Then have students find out the meaning of the word it combines with. (*Examples:* benediction, dicere—*to say;* benefactor, facere—*to do;* benefit, facere—*to do.*)

Setting a Purpose for Reading Have students read the selection to find out about Frederick Douglass's experiences and his thoughts about slavery.

During Reading

Drawing Conclusions **Have students read the selection independently.** After they have read, remind students that **drawing conclusions** is using one's own reasoning to make broad statements that are based on several details from a text. Ask students what conclusions they can draw from the following details from the text: "*Nature has done almost nothing to prepare men and women to be either slaves or slaveholders. Nothing but rigid training, long persisted in, can perfect the character of the one or the other.*" (Being enslaved or holding slaves is unnatural because slavery goes against human nature.) Write the following details from the text on the board and have students draw conclusions from the statements.

1. Slave holders did not want enslaved persons to learn to read.
2. Douglass learned to read.
3. In a schoolbook, he read a dialogue that greatly influenced him; it was a discussion between a master and an enslaved person.
4. The more materials he read, the angrier he became. He also became depressed.

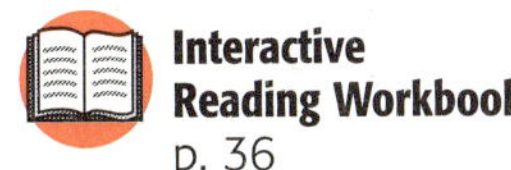
Interactive Reading Workbook
p. 36

Students may conclude the following: Slave holders feared education for enslaved persons, because enslaved persons, once given a broader view of life, would be angered about the life they were forced to lead. Douglass proved that knowledge leads to awareness and to rejection of unfair circumstances. Have students complete Interacting with Text **Drawing Conclusions,** student workbook page 36.

Recognizing Figurative Language Ask students why authors use **figurative language.** (*It is used for descriptive effect, in order to convey ideas or emotions.*) Remind students that figurative expressions are not literally true but express some truth beyond the literal level. Also remind students that a **figure of speech** is a device such as metaphor, simile, or symbol. Model the process of recognizing and interpreting figurative language.

> ***Modeling*** Douglass writes, "Knowledge had come; light had penetrated the moral dungeon where I dwelt; and, behold! there lay the bloody whip, for my back, and here was the iron chain. . . . This knowledge opened my eyes to the horrible pit, and revealed the teeth of the frightful dragon that was ready to pounce upon me." I know that Douglass is using figures of speech to discuss slavery and its impact. He makes a comparison between slavery and a dungeon and a pit. Slavery, like a pit and a dungeon, is something that one doesn't easily escape from. The "bloody whip" and the "iron chain" are symbols of slavery. The "frightful dragon" is the force that is used to keep persons enslaved. Douglass makes the horror of slavery vivid by using figurative language.

Ask students to identify additional figures of speech from the selection and to interpret them for the class.

After Reading

You may also use the selection questions and activities in *Glencoe Literature*.

Connecting Remind students that Douglass shows how knowledge—and, in particular, a reading about slavery in a schoolbook—changed his life. Ask students to name any books or stories they have read that had a profound influence on their lives. Invite students to share the impact the stories had on them.

OBJECTIVES

- To analyze rhythm; to make inferences; to analyze imagery

Swing Low, Sweet Chariot, Go Down, Moses, and *Follow the Drinking Gourd*

Before Reading

Activating Prior Knowledge Have students read the Building Background notes in *Glencoe Literature*. Point out that African American spirituals are part folk song, part hymn, and part work song. Ask students to name any spirituals they are familiar with or possibly to sing a few lines of one. What topics are presented in spirituals? Have students discuss how certain present-day music (such as folk, blues, or rap) compares to spirituals.

Building Vocabulary On the board, write the following words, without their definitions: *chariot* (a light four-wheeled pleasure carriage or a two-wheeled horse-drawn battle car of ancient times used in processions and races), *pharaoh* (a ruler of ancient Egypt), *oppressed* (crushed or burdened by abuse of power or authority), *spoil* (plunder taken from an enemy in war), *quail* (a migratory game bird). Ask students to guess at the meaning of each word and to use the words in sentences. Then discuss the words and their meanings with students. Encourage students to record each word and its definition in their vocabulary logs or journals.

Word Study: Dialect On the board, write the following words from the spirituals, without their standard forms: *'way*—away; *ole*—old; *thro'*—through; *o'er*—over; *a-waiting*—waiting. Ask students what the standard form of each word is. Ask what all of the words have in common. (*They are the contracted forms of words or the spellings that show how the words are pronounced. All are examples of informal speech.*) Ask students to note the words when they read the spirituals and to determine why these forms of the words were used. (*The contracted forms of words were used to make the song lines rhythmic or to make them rhyme with other lines.*)

Setting a Purpose for Reading Encourage students to think about the meaning that the spirituals may have had to enslaved persons.

During Reading

Analyzing Rhythm **Have students read chorally "Swing Low, Sweet Chariot."** After they have read, explain to students that **rhythm** is the pattern of beats created by the arrangement of stressed and unstressed syllables in a poem or song. Rhythm is pleasing to the ear and makes the song or poem, and its ideas, memorable. Explain that in spirituals, as in other songs, the rhythm can be regular, with a predictable pattern or meter, or it can be irregular. **Reread aloud the first two verses of "Swing Low, Sweet Chariot"** and model the process of identifying rhythm.

Modeling As I read, I notice that the **refrain,** the regularly repeated line "Coming for to carry me home," is important, both because it is repeated and because of its insistent rhythm. When I write the line and then say it, I notice which syllables are stressed. The line has this rhythm: *Cóming / fór tŏ / cárrў / mé hóme.* The line has three metrical feet that each have one accented syllable followed by one unaccented syllable and then one foot that contains two accented syllables. The rhythm and repetition help emphasize an important theme in the song.

Making Inferences **Have students read "Go Down, Moses" chorally.** Remind students that making an **inference** involves using reasoning and experience as tools for recognizing what the text implies or suggests but does not directly state. Explain to students that as with other spirituals, the composer (or composers) of "Go Down, Moses" is unknown. However, students can infer some attributes of the composer by reading the spiritual. Ask students what they infer about the composer of "Go Down Moses" and have them provide evidence from the song that supports their inferences. (*Possible responses: The composer was knowledgeable about the Bible, as is shown by allusions to Moses and Egypt. The composer had strong yearnings for freedom, as is shown by the refrain "Let my people go." The composer respected those who led others to freedom, as is shown by referring to Moses as "bold."*)

Analyzing Imagery Remind students that **imagery** refers to word pictures that writers create to evoke an emotional response in readers or listeners. Ask students how writers create effective images. (*Writers use sensory details, or descriptions that appeal to one or more of the five senses: sight, hearing, touch, taste, and smell.*) Have students point out examples of imagery in "Go Down, Moses" and name the sense to which each image appeals. (*Example: "They sang a song of triumph" appeals to the sense of hearing.*) Ask students how the imagery adds to the power of the songs. Explain that images in "Go Down, Moses" focus mainly on Old Testament earthly images. The images in "Swing Low, Sweet Chariot" focus mainly on heavenly images of a chariot and angels. **Now have students read "Follow the Drinking Gourd" chorally in small groups.** Ask students what the focus of the imagery is in "Follow the Drinking Gourd." (*The focus is nature imagery.*) Encourage students to point out examples in the poem that support their answer. Have students complete **Interacting with Text** **Analyzing Imagery,** student workbook page 37.

Interactive Reading Workbook
p. 37

After Reading

You may also use the selection questions and activities in *Glencoe Literature*.

Responding Help students respond to the spirituals by discussing together the following questions.

1. Which spiritual did you like best? Why?
2. What new insights into slavery did you gain as a result of reading or listening to the spirituals?
3. What modern-day songs compare with these spirituals? In what ways?

OBJECTIVE

▸ To analyze style

And Ain't I a Woman?

Sojourner Truth

Before Reading

Building Background Have students read "Meet Sojourner Truth" and the Building Background notes in *Glencoe Literature*. Ask students to summarize the positions in society of African Americans and of women in the 1850s. (*African Americans were enslaved in the South; no women in the United States could vote.*) Have students suggest, on the basis of what they have read on the Before You Read page of *Glencoe Literature*, character traits to describe Sojourner Truth. (*Possible responses: Sojourner Truth was witty and outspoken. She had common sense and courage.*)

Building Vocabulary On the board, write the following idioms, without their meanings: "out of kilter" (*out of order*) and "in a fix" (*in a predicament*). Have students provide meanings for the idioms and then use each in a sentence. Explain that both phrases are **idioms,** expressions or sayings that are peculiar grammatically or that have a meaning that cannot be determined by examining the individual words. Have students write these idiomatic expressions and the meaning of each on a page for idioms in their vocabulary logs or journals. Encourage students to add to the list as they find other idioms in their reading.

Word Study: Verb *to bear* Point out to students the last sentence in the first paragraph, which begins "I have borne thirteen children." On the board, write the word *borne* and tell students that it is the past participle of the verb *to bear*. Ask students what *to bear* means. (*to give birth to*) On the board, write the infinitive and its definition. Explain that *bore* is the past tense of *to bear*. On the board, write the word *bore*.

Setting a Purpose for Reading Encourage students to read the selection to find out the techniques Sojourner Truth used to argue for women's rights.

During Reading

Analyzing Style and Technique **Call on volunteers to read the selection aloud.** Remind students that **style** consists of the qualities that distinguish an author's work. Elements such as diction, sentence style and length, and the use of figures of speech and imagery all help create a distinctive style. Point out that Sojourner Truth's real words, according to the note "The Real Words?" in Building Background, were not recorded. For example, it is known that she spoke standard English. However, have students analyze the style of the writing of "And Ain't I a Woman?" by asking them the following questions: *What are some examples of Truth's unique diction? How would you describe the diction?* (Words and phrases such as "out of kilter," "ain't," "twixt," "in a fix," and "'cause" are folksy and down-to-earth.) *What interesting sentence structures does Truth use? What flavor do they lend the speech?* (She uses structures such as "all this here talking" and "as much rights as men" that lend a simple, informal tone.) Ask: *What techniques does she use to emphasize her ideas?* (She inserts short, dramatic sentences such as "Look at me!" She repeats the same question—"and ain't I a woman?"—to emphasize her ideas and to belittle indirectly the thoughts of her opponents.) *What images and figures of speech does Truth use? How do they affect the speech's style?* (She presents the image of women being helped into carriages and over ditches and the metaphor "if my cup won't hold but a pint." The images convey her ideas vividly.) **Reread aloud the second paragraph** and model the process of analyzing style.

> ***Modeling*** Sojourner Truth says, "Then they talk about this thing in the head; what's this they call it? [Intellect, someone whispers.] That's it, honey." I think it is unusual for a speaker to admit to a lack of knowledge and also to address the audience with a familiar term like "honey." I think Truth uses this style to instill confidence in her audience and to suggest her own humility so that people are more willing to listen to her message.

p. 38

Have students complete **Interacting with Text** **Analyzing Style,** student workbook page 38.

After Reading

You may also use the selection questions and activities in *Glencoe Literature*.

Building Background Follow-Up Have students add to the characterization of Sojourner Truth that they began before reading. Ask them to point out parts of the text that support their characterizations. (*Possible response: Sojourner Truth is a wise, intelligent, and passionate advocate for women.*)

Analyzing Help students analyze the selection by asking them the following questions.

1. What emotions does Sojourner Truth exhibit in the speech? Do these help or hurt her argument? (*She is indignant and shows anger and grief. These emotions lend passion to her argument. Her grief and hardships make her a sympathetic figure to her audience.*)
2. Do you think Sojourner Truth's primary purpose in speaking is to gain rights for women? Or does she have another primary purpose? Explain. (*Possible response: In this speech, Truth identifies herself with white women, yet her life is far removed from the life of the women she addresses. Through this technique, she establishes commonality with them, indirectly pointing out inequities between treatment of African Americans and that of white people. Secondarily, she makes clear the strength of women.*)
3. Who is the audience Sojourner Truth is trying most to reach? (*Possible responses: In particular, Truth is trying to change the minds of the opponents of women's rights. She may be trying to reach all people with her message of the power of women and the inequities between the life of white people and that of African American people.*)
4. In what ways do you think Truth's speech is effective? (*Possible response: Truth's speech is effective in that she is forceful and convincing. She gives examples of the strength of women in comparison to men—"I have ploughed and planted, and gathered into barns." She argues against specific points that her critics have raised—"Christ wasn't a woman!"*)

OBJECTIVES

- To analyze characterization; to analyze imagery; to recognize author's purpose

FROM

His Promised Land

John P. Parker

Before Reading

Activating Prior Knowledge Have students read "Meet John P. Parker" and the Building Background note in *Glencoe Literature*. Point out that Parker was an enslaved person who bought his own freedom. After moving north, he became active in helping other enslaved people escape to freedom. Invite students to describe ways in which those who were enslaved became free before the Civil War. Help students recall that some escaped with help from the Underground Railroad, some were able to buy their freedom, some were set free by their owners, and some ran away on their own. Discuss with students the risks or hardships associated with each method of attaining freedom.

Building Vocabulary On the board, write the following words, without their definitions: *epoch* (a notable event that marks the beginning of a period of history), *mulatto* (a person of mixed white and Negro ancestry), *overseer* (supervisor, task master), *flight* (an act of running away), *disheartened* (having lost spirit or morale), *confiscated* (seized by authority). Have students identify each word as a noun, a verb, or an adjective and then ask them to use each word in a sentence. (*All are nouns except* disheartened, *an adjective*, *and* confiscated, *a verb*.) Point out that *flight* is a multiple-meaning word. Have students find out, when they read, which meaning it has in this selection. Encourage students to record the words and their definitions in their vocabulary logs or journals.

Word Study: Abolitionist Explain to students that abolitionists were people committed to ending the practice of slavery, which they considered immoral as well as inhumane. The word *abolitionist* comes from the verb *abolish*, which means "to put an end to." The action of abolishing is called *abolition*. Let students know that *abolition* is used in other contexts as well as in reference to slavery. Give an example such as the following: *Our political party seeks the abolition of sales tax.*

During Reading

Analyzing Characterization **Have students read the selection independently.** Remind students that a **main character** in a literary work is central to the story and is typically characterized in depth. Also remind them that **characterization** refers to the methods an author uses to reveal the personality of a character. Then distribute copies of the Web graphic organizer (see Part 1) and have pairs of students prepare a character web for Eliza. Each circle of the web should contain a character trait of Eliza and an example from the text that supports the suggested trait. **Read aloud the paragraph that begins with "I have the story directly from Rev. John Rankin."** Model the process of analyzing the character Eliza.

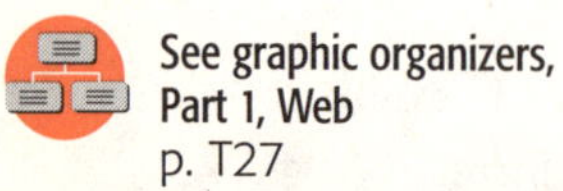
See graphic organizers, Part 1, Web p. T27

Modeling Eliza learned that she might be "sold down the river." The author writes, "This alarmed her to the point she decided she would run away with her baby." The word "alarmed" and the suddenness of Eliza's action makes me think that she was extremely frightened. In response to her fear, she took action—she ran away. In the character web, I'll write "took action—ran away when she heard bad news."

When students have completed their webs, have several share what they have written. (*Possible traits and supporting information: bravery—Eliza starts across the river despite repeated warnings, barking dogs, and men shooting; maternalism—she takes her baby with her, she tries to keep her baby warm, and she throws her baby to safety three times; persistent—Eliza continues across the river despite falling through the ice three times.*) Have students complete **Interacting with Text** **Analyzing Characters,** student workbook page 39.

Interactive Reading Workbook
p. 39

Analyzing Imagery Point out to students that the author creates many **images,** or mental pictures derived from descriptive or detailed writing and the reader's own imagination, to tell the story of Eliza. Have students find descriptive passages that present images which appeal to the senses of sight, hearing, and touch. (*Possible responses: hearing—"the baying of the dogs," "they yelled for her to come back and then began firing their pistols over her head," "the dogs on the bank kept up a fearful noise"; touch—"soft ice" and "cold, wet, and weary"; sight—"she went through the soft ice into the river," "throwing the baby from her," "the Rankin beacon light, which shone every night in the window."*) Ask students what the vivid images contribute to the story. (*The images add suspense and emphasize the danger that Eliza faces and the misery that she endures.*)

Recognizing Author's Purpose Remind students that **author's purpose** refers to an author's intent in writing a piece of literature. Typically, authors write to accomplish one or more of the following purposes: to persuade, to inform, to explain, to entertain, or to describe. Ask students to describe the author's purpose in relating Eliza's story. Help them see that the author has several purposes: He persuades by illustrating the horrors of slavery; he describes by showing Eliza's courage; he informs by presenting the dilemmas of those who are trying to help enslaved persons and the background information for an episode of *Uncle Tom's Cabin;* and he entertains by telling an exciting story. Ask what Parker's main purpose was. (*to persuade people to abolish slavery*)

After Reading

You may also use the selection questions and activities in *Glencoe Literature*.

Reviewing and Analyzing Help students review and analyze the selection. Ask: *How does the man who lives near the river help Eliza? Does he do all he can to help her?* (The man lets Eliza in, puts her by the fire, prepares food, gives her advice and a shawl, leads her to the river, and gives her a rail to keep her from drowning. Then he leaves her at the river to cross by herself. Students may think that the man does all that one could expect, considering the punishment for helping a runaway; or they may think that the man is irresponsible to let Eliza attempt such a dangerous journey, especially with a child.)

OBJECTIVES

- To use summarizing, questioning, clarifying, and predicting; to monitor comprehension

FROM

Mary Chesnut's Civil War

Mary Chesnut

Before Reading

Building Background Have students read "Meet Mary Chesnut" and the Building Background note in *Glencoe Literature*. Point out that Mary Chesnut presents a unique perspective of the Civil War because her husband was a leading figure of the Confederacy. Explain that Chesnut's husband plays an important part in the events she describes in her journal.

Building Vocabulary On the board, write the following words, without their definitions: *fleet* (a number of warships under a single command), *row* (a noisy disturbance or quarrel), *ensue* (to take place afterward, to result), *foreboding* (a premonition of coming evil), *envoy* (messenger, representative). Ask students to explain how each word might relate to war and to consult a dictionary for any words whose meaning they do not know. Encourage students to record each word and its definition in their vocabulary logs or journals.

Word Study: Homographs Write the selection word *row* on the board and explain that it has two distinct meanings and two distinct pronunciations. *Row* (which rhymes with *so*) means "a number of objects arranged in a straight line." *Row* (which rhymes with *cow*) means "a noisy disturbance or quarrel." Explain that these words are **homographs,** words that are spelled the same way but have different meanings; some homographs have different pronunciations. On the board, write the following words, without their definitions.

bow—to bend the head, body, or knee; something bent into a simple curve

lead—to guide on a way; a silver-gray metallic element

bass—deep or grave in tone; a kind of fish

Have students pronounce each word according to its meaning. As they read the selection, ask them to notice any homographs, to check their pronunciation of the word, and to verify that they know the meaning of each.

Setting a Purpose for Reading Encourage students to read the selection to find out how a Southern woman in an influential family experiences the start of the Civil War.

During Reading

Using Reading Strategies On the board, write the following terms: *summarizing, questioning, clarifying,* and *predicting*. Then **read aloud the first journal entry up to "And now, patience—we must wait."** Model the process of using the four strategies to help understand the passage.

> ***Modeling*** I can **summarize** this passage by telling *who was involved and what, when, where,* and *why the events took place.* Mary Chesnut,

the wife of a South Carolina senator, is waiting as Confederate troops prepare to attack Federal troops at Fort Sumter in April 1861. Next, I **question** some of the details of the passage. I wonder who Anderson is and what the significance is of his blue lights. I reread to **clarify.** I infer that he is heading the Federal troops at the fort and that the Southerners are carefully watching everything he is doing there. Finally, I **predict** what will happen next. I notice that Mary Chesnut talks about "intense excitement" and says that the men talk "delightfully." I predict that there will be much more excitement when the fort is attacked.

Interactive Reading Workbook
p. 40

Monitoring Comprehension **Have students take turns reading the selection aloud in small groups.** Divide the selection into three sections: section 1, from the beginning to the paragraph that begins "Yesterday was the merriest "; section 2, to the journal entry dated "April 13, 1861"; section 3, to the end of the selection. Draw on the board the chart that follows. Explain that, after reading each section of text, groups are to follow the procedure described in the chart. Designate a leader for each group. Circulate in the room as student discussions are taking place to guide the groups' efforts. After students have read section 2, have them complete **Interacting with Text** **Summarizing and Questioning,** student workbook page 40.

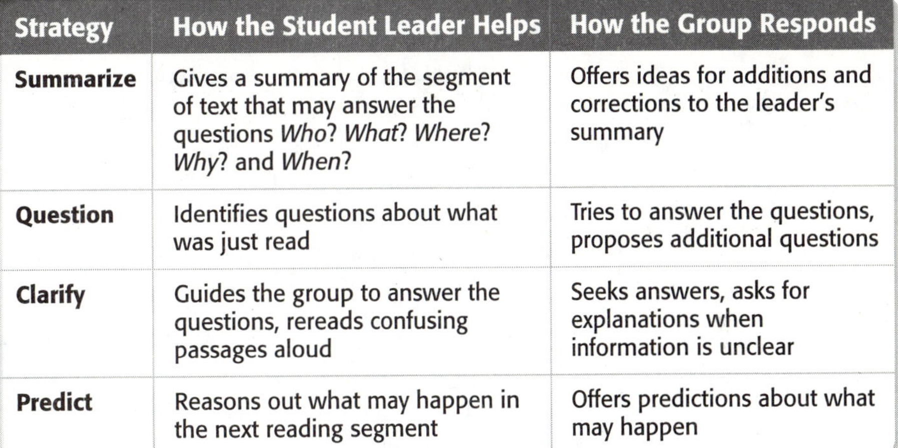

Strategy	How the Student Leader Helps	How the Group Responds
Summarize	Gives a summary of the segment of text that may answer the questions *Who*? *What*? *Where*? *Why*? and *When*?	Offers ideas for additions and corrections to the leader's summary
Question	Identifies questions about what was just read	Tries to answer the questions, proposes additional questions
Clarify	Guides the group to answer the questions, rereads confusing passages aloud	Seeks answers, asks for explanations when information is unclear
Predict	Reasons out what may happen in the next reading segment	Offers predictions about what may happen

After Reading

You may also use the selection questions and activities in *Glencoe Literature*.

Evaluating Help students evaluate the selection by discussing together the following questions.

1. Are Mary Chesnut's journal entries effective in making vivid the firing on Fort Sumter? Explain. (*Possible response: Yes. Mary Chesnut's thoughts and observations reveal a personal view of what was going on among the Southerners at the time of the firing on Fort Sumter.*)
2. What personality traits of Chesnut are revealed by her journal entries? (*Possible response: Chesnut is a good observer. She is dramatic and excitable, enthusiastic about being able to participate on some level. She is a devoted wife, proud of her husband's role. Her descriptions of social gatherings reveal her as somewhat gossipy and flighty.*)

OBJECTIVES

- To determine fact and opinion; to analyze tone

Letters to His Family

Robert E. Lee

Before Reading

Building Background Explain that people communicated with distant friends and family members by letter during the Civil War. Today such letters that contain interesting information about historical events are highly valued by scholars. Ask: *What kind of information about historical events might such letters provide? How is this information different from what might appear in other documents?* (Letters contain more personal information, such as how decisions are made, as well as personal thoughts and feelings about events.) Have students read "Meet Robert E. Lee" and the Building Background note in *Glencoe Literature*. Invite students to discuss the kind of information they might look for in Lee's letters if they were historians researching the Civil War.

Building Vocabulary On the board, write the following words, without their definitions: *aggrieved* (suffered from an infringement or denial of legal rights), *dissolution* (a separation into component parts), *secession* (formal withdrawal from an organization), *forbearance* (patience), *preamble* (an introductory statement; here, the introduction to the U.S. Constitution), *compact* (an agreement or covenant), *idle* (lacking worthwhile purpose). Have students explain the meaning of each word. Point out that *idle* and *compact* have several meanings. Have students determine each word's meaning from context. Encourage students to write the words and definitions in their vocabulary logs or journals.

Word Study: Greek Roots On the board, write the selection word *anarchy*. Explain that it comes from the Greek word *archos* meaning "ruler" and the prefix *an-* meaning "not" or "without." On the board, write the following words that contain the root *archos* and have students find in a dictionary the meaning of each prefix and of each word: *monarchy* (*mon*—one; rule by a single person); *oligarchy* (*olig*—a few; rule by a group); *patriarchy* (*patri*—lineage or father; social organization marked by the supremacy of the father); *hierarchy* (*hieros*—sacred; a ruling body of clergy or the classification of a group of people according to ability or to social, economic, or professional standing). Discuss the meanings of the words with students. As students read the selection, have them look for the word *anarchy* and ask them to note its meaning ("the absence of government") in context.

Setting a Purpose for Reading Have students read the selection to find out how the leader of the Confederate troops felt about the possibility of a civil war.

During Reading

Determining Fact and Opinion **Have students read the selection aloud in small groups.** After students have read the selection, remind them that a **fact** is a statement that can be proved and an **opinion** is a statement of belief that cannot be proved or disproved. Explain that writers can often lend validity to their opinions by assembling support from experts and by supporting opinions with facts. Point out that Lee expresses a strong opinion in his letters. Have students identify the most important opinion Lee expresses and the evidence with which he supports his opinion. (*Opinion: Dissolving the Union would be the greatest catastrophe possible for the country. Evidence: Washington, Hamilton, Jefferson, Madison, and the other founding fathers envisioned a government, not anarchy.*) Ask students whether Lee's opinion is convincing and have them explain why it is or is not convincing. (*Lee's argument is convincing because he backs up his ideas with references to the ideas of the framers of the Constitution and the ideology of the patriots who founded the country.*)

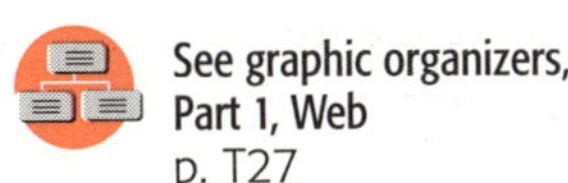
See graphic organizers, Part 1, Web p. T27

Analyzing Tone Remind students that **tone** is a reflection of an author's attitude toward the subject matter. Explain that tone of a literary work may be conveyed through elements such as word choice, sentence structure, figures of speech, and even punctuation. Tone expresses attitudes as well as content. Create a transparency of the Web graphic organizer and display it on the overhead projector. Write *tone* in the center circle. **Reread aloud the first letter up to "May God avert both of these evils from us."** Model the process of analyzing tone.

> ***Modeling*** Before I began reading Lee's letters, I wasn't sure what to expect. Since the letters are to family members, I thought that they might speak of everyday matters and have an informal tone. From the beginning of the first letter, though, I can see that Lee's tone is not informal. He says of George Washington, "How his spirit would be grieved." I would describe Lee's tone as solemn. He talks about a grave issue in a serious way.

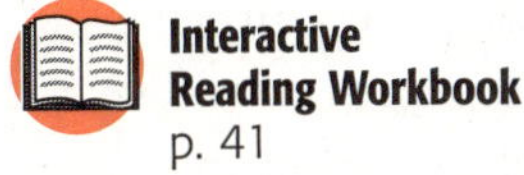
Interactive Reading Workbook p. 41

Have students suggest words that describe Lee's tone and give examples that support each adjective. On the web, write the words that students suggest. (*Possible responses: (1) The tone is serious: Lee uses formal language such as "perusal," "permit myself to believe," and "the fruit of his noble deeds." (2) The tone is concerned: "I fear that mankind will not for years be sufficiently Christianized to bear the absence of restraint and force." (3) The tone is sad: "A Union that can only be maintained by swords and bayonets . . . has no charm for me."*) Have students complete Interacting with Text **Analyzing Tone,** student workbook page 41.

After Reading

You may also use the selection questions and activities in *Glencoe Literature*.

Analyzing Ask the following questions to help students analyze Lee's letters.

1. Lee says that he is "willing to sacrifice everything but honor" to preserve the Union. Within a short time he accepts the command of Virginia's troops. What conclusion can you draw about how Lee feels when Virginia secedes from the Union? (*Because Lee believes that the country should stay united, he must be greatly saddened when the Southern states secede. Nonetheless, his sense of personal honor requires that he fight for the Confederacy, which represents his home state.*)
2. What do Washington, Hamilton, Jefferson, and Madison symbolize to Lee? (*They symbolize the foundation of the country and the patriotism, wisdom, and loyalty to the Union that went into creating the Constitution.*)

OBJECTIVES

- To visualize events; to analyze plot; to understand flashback

An Occurrence at Owl Creek Bridge

Ambrose Bierce

Before Reading

Activating Prior Knowledge On the board, write the saying *All is fair in love and war*. Ask students to explain the saying and to share ideas about whether they agree with the saying. (*Possible response: Extreme situations demand extreme solutions. Anything a person does to help the cause during a war—from stealing, to spying, to murder—is justifiable.*) Discuss whether war is an excuse for criminal behavior. Have students read "Meet Ambrose Bierce" and the Building Background note in *Glencoe Literature*. Encourage students to decide, as they read the story, whether Bierce would agree with the saying.

Building Vocabulary On the board, write the following words, without their definitions: *spectators* (those who look on or watch), *infantry* (soldiers armed, trained, and equipped to fight on foot), *subordinates* (soldiers of lower rank), *dignitary* (one who holds a position of dignity or honor), *manifestations* (demonstrations, displays), *vulgar* (common), *gallant* (spirited, brave), *rustic* (appropriate to the country in plainness and sturdiness), *apprised* (informed), *gesticulated* (made gestures). Have students identify the words that name people. Then, on the board, write the following sentences with underscores shown. Have students fill in each blank with a word that completes the definition. Possible answers are shown.

People who watch are spectators.

People who occupy a lower rank are subordinates.

A person who is highly honored is a dignitary.

Soldiers who fight on foot are members of the infantry.

Encourage students to record the vocabulary words and definitions in their vocabulary logs or journals.

Word Study: Suffixes *-ance* and *-ence* Point out the word *occurrence* in the title. Explain that the suffixes *-ance* and *-ence* mean "an action or process" or "a quality or state." Either of these suffixes, when added to a verb, makes a noun. Therefore, *occurrence* means "the action of occurring." Have students add the correct suffix to each of the following words: *perform* (performance), *import* (importance), *differ* (difference), *prefer* (preference), *defer* (deference), *disturb* (disturbance), *recur* (recurrence). Ask students to consult the dictionary when they are unsure about the spelling of the suffixed word.

Setting a Purpose for Reading Have students read the story to find out what happened at Owl Creek Bridge.

During Reading

Visualizing Tell students that **visualizing** during reading is creating pictures in their minds that are based on the words in the text and their own imaginations. Suggest that students visualize each scene as they read the story. **Have students read the story silently.** After they read, have partners skim the story and list the scenes that they found particularly vivid. Have student pairs locate the details that made the scene vivid and helped them to visualize it. When student pairs are finished, ask volunteers to describe the scenes and details they have noted. (*Examples of vivid scenes: Farquhar's standing on the bridge with the enemy soldiers—"a single company of infantry in line, at 'parade rest,' the butts of the rifles on the ground"; Farquhar's struggling in the water—"He felt his head emerge; his eyes were blinded by the sunlight; his chest expanded convulsively"; Farquhar's being shot at in the water—"rising again toward the surface, met shining bits of metal, singularly flattened, oscillating slowly downward"; Farquhar's meeting his wife—"his wife, looking fresh and cool and sweet"; and Farquhar's hanging from the bridge—"his body, with a broken neck, swung gently from side to side."*)

Analyzing Plot: Rising Action Remind students that a typical plot is composed of several events that lead toward the **climax,** the point in the story of highest tension or suspense. Almost every event in the plot leads to the climax. These events are called the **rising action** of the story. In a suspenseful plot, the reader's concern and involvement increases with each event. Have students list events from the selection that form the rising action of the plot. (*1. Farquhar is being prepared for hanging at Owl Creek Bridge. 2. He looks down at the water and thinks of his wife and children. 3. During the hanging, Farquhar falls through the bridge, and the rope breaks; he falls into the water. 4. Farquhar loosens the noose and swims; soldiers on the bridge shoot at him. 5. Farquhar comes on shore; he hurries home. 6. At last he sees his wife.*)

Analyzing Plot: Flashback Explain to students that the events in most stories are presented in **chronological order**—the order in which they occur in time. When the order of events is interrupted by an event that occurred earlier, the narrator is using a **flashback.** A flashback gives readers information that may help explain the main events of the story. Ask students to locate the flashback in "An Occurrence at Owl Creek Bridge." (*Section II is a flashback.*) Ask: *How does this flashback help you understand the events in the story?* (In the flashback, the narrator explains who Farquhar is, what his life is like, and how he came to be arrested by Union soldiers.) Discuss with students what effect the flashback has on the suspense of the story. Have students complete Interacting with Text **Analyzing Plot,** student workbook page 42.

After Reading

You may also use the selection questions and activities in *Glencoe Literature.*

Responding Tell students that when they react to what they have read, they are **responding.** Ask them to describe their feelings about Farquhar. Are they sympathetic? If so, what elements make Farquhar a sympathetic character? (*Students may feel sympathy for Farquhar because readers see most of the action through Farquhar's eyes. They share his hope to see his wife and his struggle to survive.*)

OBJECTIVES

- To analyze imagery; to recognize irony

Shiloh

Herman Melville

Before Reading

Building Background Ask students what they know about the Battle of Shiloh. Let them know that the Battle of Shiloh took place in April of 1862 near the shore of the Tennessee River at Pittsburg Landing, Tennessee. The Confederate army engaged the Federal army, each group with about 40,000 men. The Confederates were winning the battle until their leader, Albert Sidney Johnston, was shot and killed. Then the Federals resurged and won the battle. Both sides suffered terrible losses—the Federals lost 13,047 men, and the Confederates lost 10,694. Have students read "Meet Herman Melville" and the Building Background notes in *Glencoe Literature*. Point out that Melville wrote "Shiloh" after visiting a cousin during the war and being shocked by the horrors and violence of battle.

Building Vocabulary On the board, write the following words and definitions from the poem: *parched* (dried out), *groan* (to utter a deep moan expressing pain or grief), *hushed* (quiet). Ask volunteers to give a synonym for each word. (*Examples: parched—arid; groan—moan; hushed—quieted.*) Point out that all three vocabulary words are vivid descriptive words. Ask volunteers to use each word in a sentence and to say the sentence dramatically to emphasize the word's meaning. Encourage students to record each word and its synonym in their vocabulary logs or journals.

During Reading

Recognizing Irony **Have a volunteer read the poem aloud to the class.** Remind students that **irony** is a contrast or discrepancy between appearance and reality. Ask students to describe the setting of the poem and to explain why it is ironic. (*The setting is a "hushed," peaceful field near a church. The only activity is that of the swallows. This calmness contrasts with the horrible violence that has recently occurred in the field. Irony is presented through the contrast of the battle with the peacefulness of the surroundings.*) Have students complete **Interacting with Text** **Recognizing Irony,** student workbook page 43.

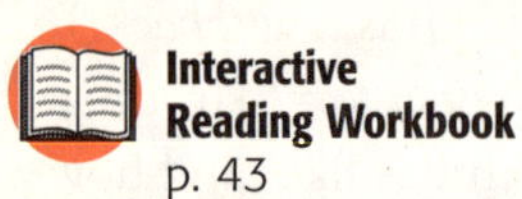
Interactive Reading Workbook p. 43

After Reading

You may also use the selection questions and activities in *Glencoe Literature.*

Analyzing Theme Remind students that the **theme** of a literary work is the author's central message. Help students analyze the theme of the poem. Ask them to paraphrase lines 15 and 16. (*The soldiers did not care at all about fame or patriotism as they were dying.*) Have students explain the idea that they think the poet conveys. (*Dying makes clear to people what is really important. People may have illusions of courage and glory before fighting in a war, but war's ugly reality soon becomes clear.*) Ask students to tell what they think the theme of the poem might be. (*War is tragic.*)

OBJECTIVES

- To paraphrase a speech; to analyze diction in a speech

The Gettysburg Address

Abraham Lincoln

Before Reading

See graphic organizers, Part 1, Web p. T27

Activating Prior Knowledge Invite students to recall speeches that they have heard by politicians or political candidates. Distribute copies of the Web graphic organizer and create a transparency of it for display on the overhead projector. In the center circle, write *political speeches*. Ask students to complete the web by naming characteristics of political speeches. (*Possible responses: long-winded, filled with slogans, slanted.*)

Building Vocabulary On the board, write the following words, with their definitions: *conceived* (originated), *proposition* (theory, assumption), *nobly* (in a way that demonstrates superior ideals). Discuss the meanings of the words with students. Encourage students to record each word and its definition in their vocabulary logs or journals.

During Reading

Interactive Reading Workbook p. 44

Paraphrasing **Call on volunteers to read the speech aloud as other students follow along in the textbook.** After students have read, remind them that **paraphrasing** is restating a passage in one's own words. Explain that an easy way to paraphrase is to substitute simple words for complex ones and to simplify sentence structure. Point to the first sentence in the speech. Remind students that *score* means "a set of twenty." Ask: *How would you paraphrase the first sentence of the speech?* (Eighty-seven years ago, our founders created a country based on democratic principles.) Have students complete Interacting with Text **Paraphrasing**, student workbook page 44.

Analyzing Diction Remind students that **diction** is a writer's choice of words. Ask students why writers struggle to choose exactly the right words for a piece of writing. (*Using the "right words" helps the writer convey the desired tone and meaning.*) Have students analyze how Lincoln's word choice succeeds in conveying his message. **Read aloud the following sentence:** "But in a larger sense, we can not dedicate—we can not consecrate—we can not hallow—this ground." Have students discuss Lincoln's word choice and grammatical form in the sentence. Lead students to conclude that Lincoln's diction is formal, yet simple and straightforward; his word choice conveys a somber tone that is appropriate for the occasion.

After Reading

You may also use the selection questions and activities in *Glencoe Literature*.

Evaluating Ask students to review their webs and then to evaluate Lincoln's speech. What characteristics make it memorable? (*The characteristics that make the Gettysburg Address memorable are a formal, somber tone that conveys respect for the occasion; simplicity, clarity, and a logical pattern of organization; parallelism and repetition to stress key ideas; and a dominant sense of purpose—to honor the soldiers who have died and to recall the goals of the nation.*)

OBJECTIVES

▶ To analyze organization; to recognize symbolism

The Gift in Wartime

Tran Mong Tu

Translated by Vann Phan

Before Reading

Building Background Invite students to share what they know about the attitudes of U.S. citizens during the Vietnam War. If necessary, tell students that public opinion about the war was divided. Many people protested against the war, considering it unjust and unjustifiable. Other citizens thought that the United States should strive for victory at any cost. Explain that "The Gift in Wartime" is a poem about a loss that occurred during the Vietnam War.

Building Vocabulary Point out that the words *grave* and *tomb* are synonyms. Both are places to be buried in. A grave is dug in the ground. One meaning of *tomb* is "a grave"—an excavation for burial in the ground. However, a tomb can also be aboveground. For example, a mausoleum is a tomb. Explain that both words—*tomb* and *grave*—have symbolic value in poetry.

During Reading

Noting Organization **Ask two volunteers to read alternating stanzas of the poem aloud as other students follow along in the textbook.** After the reading, ask students what they notice about the organization of the poem. (The first, third, and fifth stanzas begin with "I" and refer to beautiful objects—roses and a wedding grown—and to images of youth, love, days, and seasons. The second, fourth, and sixth stanzas are addressed to "you"—a soldier, the speaker's beloved—and include images of war: military medals, blood, "war dress," enemy, and death.)

Recognizing Symbolism Explain that a **symbol** is something that has a meaning that goes beyond the literal. Point out that the poem describes several real objects that also have symbolic meanings. Have students explain what the following symbolize in the poem: roses (*love and beauty*); wedding gown (*love and marriage*); tomb (*death*); medals, badge (*military service, war*); blood, war dress (*death in war*); summer days, cold winters, springtime (*the passage of time, life*); shrapnel (*war, death*). Have students complete **Interacting with Text** **Recognizing Symbolism,** student workbook page 45.

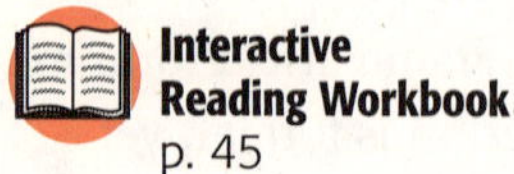
Interactive Reading Workbook
p. 45

After Reading

You may also use the selection questions and activities in *Glencoe Literature.*

Interpreting Ask the following questions to help students interpret the poem.

1. What is the theme of the poem? (*Possible theme: War changes the lives of people forever.*)
2. Do you think the poem is an effective argument against war? Explain why or why not. (*Possible response: The poem is an effective argument against war in that it communicates how war hurts more than those who fight in it.*)

OBJECTIVES

- To interpret; to identify sound devices; to synthesize

Whitman's Poetry

Walt Whitman

Before Reading

Activating Prior Knowledge Have students read "Meet Walt Whitman" and the Building Background notes in *Glencoe Literature.* Point out that Walt Whitman is remembered for creating a new form and new subject matter for poetry that captures the personality of the nation and its people. Ask students to imagine that they are creating a new style of poetry to capture the personality of the United States in the twenty-first century. Have them brainstorm about the styles of writing they might use and the important ideas that they would want to present.

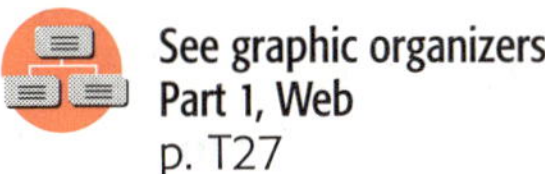

See graphic organizers, Part 1, Web p. T27

Building Vocabulary On the board, write the following words, without definitions: *mason* (a skilled worker who builds by laying units of stone or brick), *ploughboy* (a farm worker whose job is to operate the plow), *astronomer* (one who studies objects and matter outside the earth's atmosphere), *brokers* (agents who negotiate contracts of purchase and sale). Ask students to make a word web in their vocabulary logs or journals. Have students arrange in their word webs the words on the board. Then have them define the words. Tell them to add other appropriate words to the web as they read Whitman's poems. Ask students to notice, as they read the poems, how the words are used in context. Encourage students to record each word and its definition in their vocabulary logs or journals.

Word Study: Synonyms and Antonyms Ask students to define *synonym* and *antonym.* If necessary, remind them that **synonyms** are words that have the same or nearly the same meanings. **Antonyms** are words that have opposite meanings. Explain that knowing a word's synonym or its antonym can help readers understand and remember the meaning of the word itself. On the board, write the words *blithe*, *robust*, *unaccountable*, *divine*, and *ruthless.* Ask students what all the words have in common. (*All are adjectives.*) Have students write a synonym and an antonym for each word. (*Examples: blithe—cheerful/melancholy; robust—strong/weak; unaccountable—unexplainable/explicable; divine—heavenly/earthly; ruthless—cruel/merciful.*)

Setting a Purpose for Reading Have students read the poems to find out how Whitman interprets several American experiences.

During Reading

Interpreting Remind students that **interpreting** is attaching meaning to what is read, by using their own knowledge and experience. Tell students that interpreting requires first understanding what is read. Tell students that **you will read aloud "I Hear America Singing."** Suggest that they listen for key ideas. Then model the process of interpreting ideas.

Modeling In "I Hear America Singing," Whitman seems simply to be listing the names of occupations and describing the work of each worker. The workers Whitman describes are confident about their skills and pleased with themselves. They enjoy what they do. I think that each worker listed represents a group of workers who do the same work and that, by listing the different types of workers, Whitman is creating a "mosaic" of America. I can see that he is making a point about what gives America its vitality—its varied people. Whitman sees Americans as cheerful, hard-working, and optimistic.

Have students read the other poems aloud in small groups. Invite them to interpret what they have read.

Identifying Sound Devices Point out that Whitman wrote in **free verse,** poetry that has no fixed pattern of meter, rhyme, line length, or stanza arrangement. Explain that his poems do not rhyme but that Whitman's poems include other sound devices that make the poems musical. Define **onomatopoeia** (a word that imitates the sound it describes), **repetition** (the recurrence of sounds, words, phrases, lines, or stanzas in a piece of writing), **rhythm** (the pattern of stressed and unstressed syllables), and **alliteration** (the repetition of initial consonant sounds in words in close proximity). Guide students to analyze sound devices by asking the following questions.

1. What is the theme of "I Hear America Singing"? (*The theme is that America's vitality comes from its people—confident, robust workers who enjoy their work.*) How is repetition used to emphasize this theme? (*The word* singing *is repeated in almost every line; it emphasizes the concepts of the individuality of Americans, their enthusiasm, and their work ethic.*)
2. Find an example of alliteration in the first line of "Beat! Beat! Drums!" (*Repetition of the word* beat *and of the* b *sound in* beat, bugles, *and* blow.)
3. What does the repetition of this sound and the rhythm of the first line suggest? (*These create a staccato rhythm that imitates the beat of a drum.*)

Interactive Reading Workbook
p. 46

Have students complete **Interacting with Text** **Identifying Sound Devices,** student workbook page 46.

After Reading

You may also use the selection questions and activities in *Glencoe Literature*.

Synthesizing Tell students that **synthesizing** is combining information in a new way, so as to formulate new understanding or new knowledge. Ask the following questions to help students synthesize information.

1. What is the theme of each poem? (*"I Hear America Singing"—America's vitality comes from its people; "When I Heard the Learn'd Astronomer"—experiences may bring one closer to understanding than a scholarly analysis; "A Sight in Camp in the Daybreak Gray and Dim"—war is tragic, marked by suffering and death; "Beat! Beat! Drums!"—war is a ruthless force that overpowers peaceful life.*)
2. What do these themes reveal about the attitudes and viewpoints of Walt Whitman? (*Possible response: Through these poems, Whitman presents ideas about the joy of life and the tragedy of war.*)

OBJECTIVES

- To analyze imagery; to respond; to interpret

FROM

Song of Myself

Walt Whitman

Before Reading

Building Background Invite students to look over the paintings in *Glencoe Literature* that accompany the selection from *Song of Myself*. Ask what they think the poem might be about. Encourage students to discuss what they already know about Walt Whitman and his poetry. Explain that the selection from *Song of Myself* in the textbook expresses wide-ranging themes and ideas about humanity and nature. Point out that the poem is filled with **paradoxes,** statements that seem to be contradictory but that may nonetheless contain truth.

Building Vocabulary On the board, write the following words, without definitions: *creeds* (sets of fundamental beliefs), *comrade* (intimate friend or associate), *novice* (beginner), *myriads* (great numbers), *caste* (division of society based on wealth, rank, or occupation), *contemptible* (worthy of disdain), *barbaric* (marked by a lack of restraint), *bequeath* (to hand down). Have students write definitions for the words with which they are familiar. Then have them find definitions in a dictionary for the remaining words. Encourage students to record each word and its definition in their vocabulary logs or journals.

Word Study: Antonyms Explain that Whitman uses many sets of **antonyms,** words that have opposite meanings. Point out the antonyms in line 28: "old"/"young," "foolish"/"wise." As students read the poem, have them record in their vocabulary logs or journals other pairs of antonyms.

Setting a Purpose for Reading Encourage students to read the poem to discover how the speaker asserts his connection with others.

During Reading

Analyzing Imagery Ask students to define *imagery*. (***Imagery*** *consists of "word pictures" that writers create with descriptive words and details.*) Read the following lines from the poem in which the speaker addresses his son.

> "Long have you timidly waded holding a plank by the shore, / Now I will you to be a bold swimmer, / To jump off in the midst of the sea, rise again, nod to me, shout, and laughingly dash with your hair."

Invite students to share what they picture and which words help them form images in their minds. (*Possible responses: The language "timidly waded," "holding a plank," "bold swimmer," "jump off in the midst of the sea, rise again, nod to me, shout, and laughingly dash with your hair" helps me picture a young man just learning to swim, clinging to a plank that anchors him to shore. His father urges him to release the plank, to jump boldly in and let the sea wash over him. The son is asked to wave confidently, his hair washed back from his face, to his father on the shore.*) **Ask students to read the poem independently in small groups. Then have them take turns reading aloud passages that they find particularly vivid. Then reread aloud lines 35–39.** Ask: *What view of our nation do the images create? Do the images present stereotypes of people? Explain your answer.* (Possible response: The images show the diversity of people and lifestyles created by the geographical variations within our country. Kentuckians and "Kanadians" are stereotypical, but these are also broad-stroked representative "word portraits" of Americans in Whitman's time. Have students complete **Interacting with Text** **Analyzing Imagery,** student workbook page 47.

Interactive Reading Workbook
p. 47

Responding Tell students that responding is reacting to what they have read. Responding includes the spontaneous thoughts and feelings that the reader experiences while reading. **Read aloud lines 97–99** and model the process of responding.

> ***Modeling*** When I read "I celebrate myself, and sing myself," I almost feel the enthusiasm of the speaker. Whitman writes in line 3: "For every atom belonging to me as good belongs to you." He says that we share the same atoms–we are made of the same material, "cut from the same cloth." I read in line 28 "I am of old and young, of the foolish as much as the wise." The speaker seems to feel himself a part of all. I know that feeling–it's like that of shared experiences, such as playing a piece of music with other musicians. I find myself smiling at lines 97–99: "Do I contradict myself? / Very well then I contradict myself, / (I am large, I contain multitudes.)" I've heard people anticipate and overrule objections because it's important to make a point. Also, I find thinking of a person's "containing multitudes" a funny idea.

Have students work with partners or in small groups to respond to short passages that they found vivid and interesting. If students have difficulty, point out that lines 26–27 and 68–69 express compelling ideas that relate to many lives.

After Reading

You may also use the selection questions and activities in *Glencoe Literature*.

Interpreting Tell students that **interpreting** is attaching meaning to what is read, by using personal experience and knowledge. Explain that the speaker refers to several "impalpable," or intangible, issues, such as spiritual fulfillment. Ask students to interpret the speaker's views from lines 78–80. (*Possible interpretation: The speaker strives to become part of the universe—"enfolders of these orbs"—and to gain all available knowledge. He wonders whether, were that to happen, he would be satisfied. His spirit answers that even achieving the goal of understanding everything would not give him satisfaction but would instead make him reach for more.*)

OBJECTIVES

- To summarize; to analyze dialogue; to analyze analogy

The Useless and The Butterfly Dream

Chuang Tzu

Translated by Martin Palmer

Before Reading

Building Background Have students read "Meet Chuang Tzu" and the Building Background notes in *Glencoe Literature*. Point out that the author of the selections was a philosopher who, along with Lieh Tzu and Lao Tzu, founded Taoism, a philosophy based on the concept that peace and happiness come from understanding and accepting one's true nature. Have students brainstorm for names of philosophers (examples: Confucius, Socrates, Aristotle, Plato, Augustine, Descartes, Locke, Kant). Invite students to share the high points that they know of any particular philosophy. Ask what kinds of issues philosophers ponder and why. (*Possible responses: Philosophers seek to understand the meaning of life. They reflect on such ideas as how best to live, the nature of reality, the existence of God, the morality of certain behaviors, and the nature of knowledge and of beauty.*)

Building Vocabulary On the board, write the word *void*. Explain that this word as a noun means "a gap" or "an empty space." Explain that the word *void* comes from the Latin word *vacīvus*, meaning "empty." Encourage students to name other words related to *void* in etymology and meaning. (*Examples: vacuum, vacant, vacate, vacation, vacuous, avoid.*) Ask students to note the word *void* when they read the selection and to determine why it is capitalized.

Word Study: Past Tense Explain that the word *dreamt* is one form of the past tense of *dream*. The other form of the past tense is *dreamed*. Explain that the past-tense form *dreamt* is modeled on that of words such as *mean*, *sleep*, *keep*, *leap*, and *creep*. Ask: *What do all these words have in common?* (All have a long *e* sound spelled *ea* or *ee*.) *What is the past tense of each word? If there is more than one way to form the past tense of a word, give both forms.* (meant, slept, kept, leapt *or* leaped, crept)

Setting a Purpose for Reading Have students read the selection to find out what philosophical issues concern Chuang Tzu.

During Reading

Summarizing **Have students read the selections aloud in pairs.** Remind students that **summarizing** is a cohesive retelling in their own words of the most important ideas in a passage or a literary work. Ask one student from each pair to summarize "The Useless" and ask the student's partner to summarize "The Butterfly Dream." (*In "The Useless," Hui Tzu questions Chuang Tzu's teaching of "useless" knowledge. Chuang Tzu answers through the use of an analogy that we need what is "useless" in order to give meaning to what is "useful."*

In "The Butterfly Dream," Chuang Tzu retells a dream in which he was a butterfly and woke up wondering whether reality was his life as Chuang Tzu or as a butterfly.)

Analyzing Dialogue Remind students that **dialogue** is the exact words spoken by characters in a literary work. Explain that dialogue in fiction helps move the plot along and also can be used to reveal the personalities of the characters. Dialogue is also used in nonfiction and poetry. Ask students why they think "The Useless" was written in the format of a dialogue between two characters. Then model the process of analyzing dialogue.

> ***Modeling*** **The poet's technique of using dialogue as a format for the poem immediately gets my attention. I notice Hui Tzu's condemnation of or disdain for Chuang Tzu's views in the first statement of dialogue in the poem. I want to know Chuang Tzu's response. As I read on, I hear the voice of Chuang Tzu explaining his own philosophy: All knowledge is connected and important. Since the poet is Chuang Tzu, his "answer" within the poem provides an opportunity for the poet to express his own philosophic views.**

Have students suggest likely traits of Chuang Tzu's character that are revealed through his words. (*wisdom, patience, and imagination*)

Analyzing Analogy Tell students that an **analogy** is a comparison used to show similarities between ideas or things that are otherwise dissimilar. Point out that, by using an analogy, an author may help readers understand an unfamiliar or complicated idea by comparing that idea to something familiar. Have students identify the analogy in "The Useless." (*Philosophical thoughts are to practical knowledge as the broad expanse of the earth is to the small space one human being needs.*) Ask students what Chuang Tzu is explaining with this analogy. (*He uses the analogy to expound on what is "useful."*) Then ask students to define personification. (***Personification*** *is a figure of speech in which an animal, object, force of nature, or idea is assigned human characteristics.*) Ask a volunteer to point out an example of personification in "The Butterfly Dream." (*The author assigns to a butterfly the human ability to dream. He says, "But I could not tell, had I been Chuang Tzu dreaming I was a butterfly, or a butterfly dreaming I was now Chuang Tzu?"*) Have students complete **Interacting with Text** **Analyzing Analogy,** student workbook page 48.

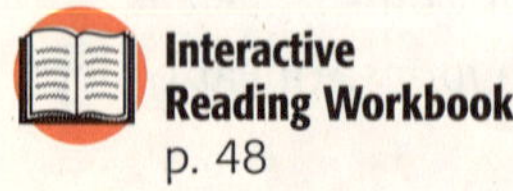
Interactive Reading Workbook
p. 48

After Reading

You may also use the selection questions and activities in *Glencoe Literature*.

Vocabulary Follow-Up **Have a volunteer reread lines 9–13.** Ask students why they think Chuang Tzu capitalizes the word "Void." (*Students may say that "Void" describes the emptiness as though it were an actual place into which we would fall without the purpose of life that gives us our bearings.*)

Purpose for Reading Follow-Up Ask: *With what philosophical issues is Chuang Tzu concerned in the selections?* (He is concerned with the meaning of life, the nature of knowledge, and the nature of reality.) Encourage students to point out parts of the selections that support the issues they suggest.

OBJECTIVES

- To interpret; to analyze style

Dickinson's Poetry

Emily Dickinson

Before Reading

Building Background Tell students that *Glencoe Literature* contains several poems by Emily Dickinson. Ask students what they know about this poet, her poetry, and her life. Explain that Dickinson was a recluse for much of her adult life. Ask: *What disadvantages would a writer who rarely left home have?* (He or she would miss observing people, places, and events that might be sources of subject matter or that would lend insight.) *What advantages do you think the writer might have?* (He or she would be able to focus entirely on reading and writing without the distractions of work or social obligations; he or she would rely on inner resources to find value in life.) Have students read "Meet Emily Dickinson" and the Building Background notes in *Glencoe Literature*.

Building Vocabulary On the board, write the following words, without definitions: *spurn* (contemptuous treatment), *goads* (urges or stimulates into action), *discerning* (showing insight and understanding), *starkest* (most extreme; absolute), *stillness* (quietness), *assignable* (able to be transferred to another), *interposed* (came between), *surmised* (imagined or inferred on slight grounds), *oppresses* (burdens spiritually or mentally). Have students provide definitions for all of the words, referring to a dictionary as needed. Ask students to note the meanings of the words in the context of the poems as they read. Encourage students to record each word and its definition in their vocabulary logs or journals.

Word Study: Multiple-Meaning Words On the board, write the selection words *madness*, *sense*, *comprehend*, *stillness*, and *assignable*. Explain that each word has at least two meanings; choosing the correct meaning, based on the word's context in the poem, will help them understand the poem. However, make the point that in poetry, in particular, attributing more than one meaning to a word often enriches the poem's meaning. Have students write on paper the meaning with which they are most familiar for each word on the board. As they read, have students analyze how the word is used in the poem.

Setting a Purpose for Reading Have students apply what they have learned about Emily Dickinson's life to understanding the insights in her poetry.

During Reading

Interpreting Explain that reading poetry is a personal experience that requires the reader to **interpret** (attach meaning to what is read, drawing on personal knowledge and experience) language use as well as complex or ambiguous ideas. Remind students that interpreting a passage is almost like translating it. **Read aloud "My life closed twice before its close"** and model the process of interpreting.

Modeling I'm not clear about how the speaker's life "closed twice before its close." Reading on, I notice that the speaker presents the idea of "parting." I'll try to use my understanding of parting as the closing of life to clarify the meaning of the rest of the poem. In the last two lines, the concept of "parting" is presented as a **paradox**–a statement that seems contradictory. I can see why parting is "all we need of hell," because parting from a loved one is painful. What is the heavenly aspect of parting? I think the state of being in love or loving someone is heavenly. If the speaker is telling of separation from a loved one, then her earlier statements of "life closing" may refer to previous relationships or previous partings from the beloved.

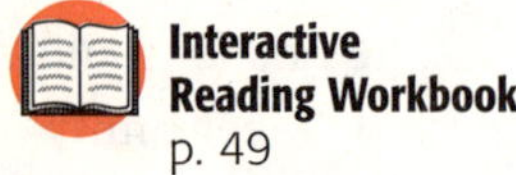
Interactive Reading Workbook p. 49

Ask students to propose their own interpretations of the poem. **Then call on volunteers to read aloud the other Dickinson poems.** Encourage students to suggest interpretations of the poems. Have students independently complete Interacting with Text **Interpreting,** student workbook page 49.

Analyzing Style Remind students that an author's **style** is his or her own unique way of communicating ideas. Word choice and the length and arrangement of sentences help reveal an author's style. For example, an author's style may be to write in short, direct sentences or to pose rhetorical questions and then answer them. Explain that Dickinson has a highly recognizable style. Ask students:

1. *What unusual elements do you notice in Emily Dickinson's poems?* (Dickinson's use of dashes and the capitalization of many common nouns)
2. *How does the punctuation affect the sound of the poems?* (Dashes may make the poems sound as if they were written in a rush or just jotted down.)
3. *What is the effect of her unusual use of capitalization?* (Capitalization serves to emphasize words and ideas.)
4. *What is the typical line length of these poems?* (The length of the lines is short.)
5. *Are the poet's statements direct or indirect?* (They are direct but often have more than one level of meaning.)
6. *Identify at least five words that Dickinson uses as topics in more than one of these poems*. (The words *life*, *eternity*, *divine/divinest*, *immortality*, *majority*, and *death/dying/died* are used in more than one of the poems.)
7. *What tone do these words help convey?* (The words help convey a serious tone.)

After Reading

You may also use the selection questions and activities in *Glencoe Literature*.

Word Study Follow-Up Review the multiple-meaning words with students. In the following list of words, the first meaning is the one used in the poems: *madness* (insanity; anger), *sense* (sanity; the faculty of perceiving through the sense organs), *comprehend* (to grasp the meaning of; contain or hold—both meanings may be meant), *stillness* (quietness; motionlessness—both may be meant), *assignable* (able to be transferred to another; able to be appointed as a duty or task).

OBJECTIVES

- To understand dialect and the author's purpose for using it; to monitor comprehension

The Celebrated Jumping Frog of Calaveras County

Mark Twain

Before Reading

Building Background Explain to students that they are about to read a humorous story by a well-known American writer, Mark Twain. Ask students to share what they know about Mark Twain and his most famous books, *The Adventures of Tom Sawyer* and *The Adventures of Huckleberry Finn*. Have students read "Meet Mark Twain" as well as the Building Background notes in *Glencoe Literature*. Have volunteers discuss anything they know about the California Gold Rush and mining towns. Ask: *Why did mining towns have little entertainment during the Gold Rush?* Help students realize that, at that time, there were no television sets or radios. Transportation was difficult, so even newspapers from big towns or cities were not usually available. People had to make their own entertainment.

Building Vocabulary Explain to students that the story has two parts: a rather formally written introduction, and a story that a character tells about a famous jumping frog. Write on the board the following words, without their definitions: *celebrated* (famous), *cherished* (treated with affection), *compliance* (accordance), *lurking* (sneaking), *infamous* (widely known for wrongdoing), *personage* (a noted person), *monotonous* (boring). Invite students to tell what they know about these words and their meanings. If necessary, have them check their definitions in a dictionary. Encourage students to record each word and its meaning in their vocabulary logs or journals.

Word Study: Dialect Tell students that the storyteller character, in the second part of the selection, uses **informal language,** the kind that people use in everyday conversation. Explain that Mark Twain writes the character's speech in the narrating style of a storyteller. Write on the board the following words from the selection, without their definitions: *curiosest* (dialect for *most curious*), *warn't* (dialect for *weren't*), *jest* (dialect for *just*). Invite students to speculate on each word's meaning. Then provide the definitions. Explain that a **dialect** is a form of language used by a group of people in a specific time or region. Point out to students that the story has many examples of dialect. **Read aloud the first paragraph of Simon Wheeler's story,** beginning "There was a feller here once by the name of *Jim* Smiley. . . ." Ask students to follow along in their books and to notice how Simon Wheeler's dialect becomes more easily understood when they hear his story read aloud.

Setting a Purpose for Reading Have students read the selection to enjoy a humorous story and to find out what is so special about the "celebrated jumping frog of Calaveras County."

During Reading

Monitoring Comprehension **Have students read the story independently.** Before they begin, remind them to monitor their comprehension as they read by stopping occasionally to ask themselves whether they understand what they are reading. Explain that often when reading a story that includes dialect, readers miss the meaning of a sentence the first time they read it. Suggest that one good way to **clarify** the meaning of any sentence is to reread the sentence aloud. Reading aloud often helps the reader understand the character's "speech" and thus the meaning of a passage. Ask students to identify other reading strategies, besides clarifying, that they use to monitor their comprehension. (*Possible responses:* ***summarizing*** *by answering* who, what, where, why, *and* when *questions about their reading;* ***questioning*** *important ideas.*) Then have students complete Interacting with Text **Monitoring Comprehension,** student workbook page 50.

Interactive Reading Workbook
p. 50

Reading Footnotes Point out the notes at the bottom of the selection pages. Remind students that **footnotes** support comprehension by explaining unfamiliar references or by clarifying difficult passages in the text. Footnotes also supply pronunciations for names of people and places and for words from other languages. **Read aloud the first sentence of the second paragraph of Wheeler's story starting with "*Thish-yer*"** and then model the process of using footnotes.

> ***Modeling*** As I read, I wonder right away what that first word—*Thish-yer*—means. I see that it has a footnote number, so I check footnote 13 at the bottom of the page. I read that *Thish-yer* is dialect for "this here." Reading on, I'm not quite sure what the word *consumption* means. I read footnote 14 and see that it means "tuberculosis," which I know is an infectious disease. The phrases "Thish-yer Smiley" and "the consumption" show Simon Wheeler's way of speaking, or dialect. The footnotes help me to understand this unfamiliar use of language.

Recognizing Author's Purpose Remind students that an author may write for any one or more of several purposes: to persuade, to inform, to explain, to entertain, or to describe. Ask students why they think that Mark Twain may have written such a story in dialect. (*Mark Twain wrote the story to entertain. The way in which Wheeler relates events is a great part of the fun of the story.*)

After Reading

You may also use the selection questions and activities in *Glencoe Literature.*

Retelling and Responding Ask volunteers to retell the story in their own words. Let listeners compare the students' retold versions to Mark Twain's original. Ask: *In the retelling, is there a difference in the sound of the story? Which version do you like better—the retold version or the written story? Why?*

OBJECTIVE

- To recognize foreshadowing

The Outcasts of Poker Flat

Bret Harte

Before Reading

Building Background Tell students that the story they are about to read takes place in the mountains of California soon after the Gold Rush of 1848 has begun. Invite students to tell what they know about the Gold Rush. Explain that many mining towns sprang up during this period and were populated by some rough characters. Explain that townspeople often wanted their towns to become more respectable, so they discouraged "unsavory characters" from staying in their towns. This story is about a group of those outcasts—people who were thrown out of the town of Poker Flat.

Building Vocabulary Write on the board the following words, without their definitions: *outcasts* (those who are forced out of a group), *ominous* (threatening), *predisposing* (presumed or prejudiced), *conjecture* (a guess), *equity* (fairness), *intimidation* (the act of making fearful, of compelling, or of deterring), *expletives* (swear words), *emigrant* (a person who moves away from a place), *remonstrances* (verbal warnings). Ask students to suggest the definition for any word they are familiar with. Have them check a dictionary for the meanings of words they do not know. Encourage students to record the words and their meanings in their vocabulary logs or journals.

Word Study: Prefixes Remind students that breaking a word into parts can sometimes help them figure out the meaning of an unfamiliar word. Write on the board the words *unused* and *uncertain*. Ask students to point out the prefix and to tell what the prefix means in both words. (*Un-* in both words means "not.") Ask for examples of other prefixes and list them on the board in a chart such as the one shown. Work with students to add the meanings of the prefixes and some examples of words that include those prefixes. Then add the words from the following chart if students have not already suggested them. Encourage students to look for other words with these prefixes as they read the story.

Prefix	Meaning	Examples
un-	not	ungovernable
im-	not	improper
re-	again, back	reimbursing

Setting a Purpose for Reading Have students read the story to find out who the outcasts of Poker Flat are and what happens to them.

Developing the Plot Write the word *foreshadowing* on the board and ask students what they think it means. Explain that **foreshadowing** is a technique that gives readers hints about what is going to happen. In this way, authors build up suspense and inspire readers to read on quickly. **Read the story aloud to students through the eighth paragraph,** which begins "The road to Sandy Bar—a camp that . . . " Ask students what they think is likely to happen and why they think so. Then model the process of recognizing foreshadowing, on the basis of the last paragraph you read aloud.

> ***Modeling*** As I read this last paragraph, I realize that the author has given some hints about trouble ahead. For one thing, the way to Sandy Bar is over a steep mountain range, and the characters are traveling on a mule and horses. The journey is described as "a day's severe travel," and the trail is "narrow and difficult." These details hint that whatever comes next in the story is going to be difficult for these characters.

Interactive Reading Workbook p. 51

Have them complete  **Recognizing Foreshadowing,** student workbook page 51. After students have completed workbook page 51, **have them finish reading the story independently.** As they read, encourage them to look for the author's use of foreshadowing: they should note clues that hint of events to come.

Monitoring Comprehension Encourage students to monitor their comprehension by asking themselves the following questions during reading: *Do I understand what I'm reading? What don't I understand?* If students realize they do not understand an idea in the text, one strategy that they might use is **reading on.** Tell them to reread the sentence that they do not understand but then to continue reading. Sometimes the meaning of the troublesome sentence becomes clear after reading and understanding subsequent sentences that develop ideas and extend events.

After Reading

You may also use the selection questions and activities in *Glencoe Literature*.

Reviewing and Analyzing Help students review and analyze the story by asking them the following questions.

1. After Uncle Billy steals the mules, the outcasts regroup and seem content. What clues does the author provide to prepare readers for what is to come? (*Even when the mood of the outcasts is happy, Bret Harte presents a stormy setting, with violent images that foreshadow the hardships to come.*)
2. Were you surprised by Mr. Oakhurst's final action? Why or why not? (*Possible response: No, I was not surprised by Oakhurst's final action. He had consistently taken control of the situations he found himself in. When he realized his fate, he again took control and ended his life on his own terms.*)

OBJECTIVES

- To compare and contrast; to differentiate between fact and opinion

Chief Sekoto Holds Court

Bessie Head

Before Reading

Activating Prior Knowledge Explain to students that the story they will read takes place in Botswana, a small country in southern Africa. Display a map of Africa and point out Botswana. Explain that "Chief Sekoto Holds Court" is about justice. The story presents a modern court case that must be settled by a tribal chief. Invite students to discuss things that they think are unique about the court system in the United States. Have students suggest qualities that they think are essential for a judge. (*Possible responses include objectivity, intelligence, lack of prejudice, sense of fairness.*)

Building Vocabulary On the board, write the following words, without their definitions: *wrath* (extreme anger), *rowdy* (loud and disorderly), *mankind* (all human beings), *rowdiness* (condition of being rowdy), *practising* (British spelling for *practicing*), *bewildered* (confused), *pneumonia* (disease of the lungs), *judgement* (British spelling for *judgment*). Ask which two words appear to be misspelled. Lead students to identify *practising* and *judgement*. Point out that the author of this story wrote in British English, which most African writers use when they write in the English language. One difference between the two forms of English is the spelling of some words. Write on the board the correct American English spellings *practicing* and *judgment* for students to compare. Work with students to define the other words listed. Have students record the new vocabulary words in their vocabulary logs or journals. You may want to have students begin a special section for British spellings of familiar words.

Word Study: Compound Words Remind students that two words are sometimes written together to make a **compound word.** Write the following compound words on the board: *outlook*, *mankind*, and *far-off*. Ask students to identify the two words that make up each compound word. Draw attention to the hyphen in *far-off* and point out that although most compound words are written together as one word, some are connected by hyphens. (Note for students that some compound words, such as *ice cream*, are written as separate words.) Suggest that students write in their vocabulary logs or journals any other compounds they find as they read the story. (Examples of compound words in the selection: *weekday*, *afternoon*, *outlying*, *witchcraft*, *themselves*, *yourself*, *throughout*, *household*, and *courtyard*.)

Setting a Purpose for Reading Have students read the story to find out how Chief Sekoto decides a case that has come to his court.

During Reading

Comparing and Contrasting **Have students read the story independently.** Explain to them that by comparing and contrasting what they read to what they already know, they can better understand new ideas. Remind students that **comparing** is thinking about how two ideas, characters, or events are alike. **Contrasting** is thinking about how two ideas, characters, or events are different. **Read aloud the paragraph that begins "I would like to see the contents"** and model the process of comparing and contrasting.

> ***Modeling*** As I read, I see that the judge examines the evidence. This part of the process is somewhat similar to the way evidence is presented to a judge in a courtroom in the United States. Therefore, I can say that a trial in Botswana is like a trial in the United States in that evidence is introduced. I notice, however, that Mma-Baloi doesn't have a defense attorney. That is definitely different from the trial procedures used in the United States.

Determining Fact and Opinion Ask students to define *fact* and to explain how a fact is different from an opinion. (*A **fact** is something that can be proved, and an **opinion** is a judgment, belief, or conclusion; it cannot be proved.*) **Read aloud the paragraph that begins "Evidence was that Mma-Baloi had always lived . . . ."** Then ask students to consider the villagers' accusations against Mma-Baloi. Ask: *Are the villagers stating facts or opinions about Mma-Baloi? What makes you think so?* (They are stating opinions. Because she was different from the villagers, and not because the prosecutors had any evidence that could be proved linking her to the crime, Mma-Baloi was accused of killing a number of children who had died suddenly.) **Then have a volunteer read aloud the paragraph that begins "It was near noon."** Ask students:

- *Are the doctor's statements about the case facts or opinions? How do you know?* (The doctor's statements are facts: A postmortem examination provides scientific proof that the cause of the children's deaths is pneumonia and that the cause of the woman's death is "the septic condition of the womb.")
- *Do you think Chief Sekoto is interested in finding out the facts of the case? What makes you think so?* (Yes, the chief wants to find out the facts. He calls for the doctor who he knows will present scientific evidence.)

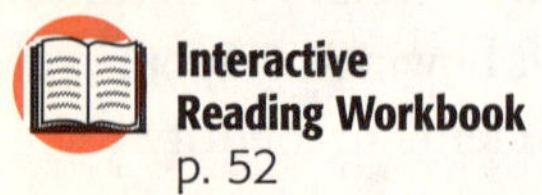
Interactive Reading Workbook
p. 52

Have students complete Interacting with Text **Determining Fact and Opinion,** student workbook page 52.

After Reading

You may also use the selection questions and activities in *Glencoe Literature.*

Making Judgments Remind students that **making judgments** is forming opinions about a character: Did he or she act fairly or unfairly? Is the character good or bad? Is the character right or wrong? Ask: *What kind of person do you think Chief Sekoto is? Why do you think so? Do you think he does the right thing in deciding this case? Why or why not?* Help students to judge other characters in the story by asking: *What do you think of the villagers? Do you think Mma-Baloi does the right thing by trying to help the ill woman who dies? Why or why not?*

OBJECTIVE

▸ To predict outcomes

To Build a Fire

Jack London

Before Reading

Building Background Have students read "Meet Jack London" and the Building Background notes in *Glencoe Literature*. Ask students to tell about experiences they have had or heard about in which people have been exposed to extremely cold temperatures. Ask: *What are the effects on the human body of extreme cold?* Lead students to conclude that extremely cold temperatures can be fatal. Then invite discussion. Ask: *What would you do if you were going to be outside in very cold weather?*

Interactive Reading Workbook pp. 53–54

Building Vocabulary Refer students to the Interactive Reading **Reading Guide** on student workbook pages 53–54. Explain that one use of this reading guide is to help them keep track of important new words and expressions. Read with students through the vocabulary for "To Build a Fire." If necessary help clarify the meaning of words by providing examples.

Word Study: Verb Forms Write the following words on the board: *spit/spat; smite/smote*. Point to *spat* and *smote* and explain that the words are past-tense forms of the verbs *spit* and *smite*. Explain to students that many modern English words that come from old English form their past tense by a change in a vowel in the middle of the word. Then ask students how most verbs form the past tense. Help them recall that most past-tense verbs are formed through the addition of *-ed* to the end of the word. Explain that verbs such as *spit* and *smite* are called **irregular verbs** because their tenses are not formed in the same way as the tenses of regular verbs are formed. Provide several examples of regular and irregular verbs, including those on the vocabulary list (*mediate/mediated, freeze/froze*). Have students begin a list of such verbs that they find as they read the selection. Students can write the verbs in their vocabulary logs or journals. Start by presenting on the board a chart like the following.

Verb Forms

Verb Type	Infinitive	Past	Past Participle
Regular	(to) turn (to) pause (to) seem	turned paused seemed	(has, have) turned (has, have) paused (has, have) seemed
Irregular	(to) be (to) hide (to) fling	was, were hid flung	(has, have) been (has, have) hidden (has, have) flung

Setting a Purpose for Reading Read aloud the title of the story and ask: *What could be important about building a fire?* Suggest that students read the story to find out.

During Reading

Visualizing **Read aloud the title and the first three paragraphs of the story,** as students follow along in their textbooks. Ask students to think about the man and his surroundings as you read and to try to picture him in their minds. Then encourage students to discuss how they **visualize** the scene. **Have students read the rest of the story aloud in small groups.**

Making Predictions Remind students that they should stop frequently as they read to **make predictions,** or make statements about what might happen next. **Read aloud the paragraph that begins "At twelve o'clock . . ."** and model predicting.

> ***Modeling*** I want to think about some clues I've read so that I can predict what I think will happen. I've read that it is extremely cold, and the man's fingers and toes are getting numb. I know that such severe low temperatures can be dangerous. I wonder what he will do next. I know the title of the story is "To Build a Fire," and I read that the man forgot to build a fire to thaw out. I predict he's probably going to try to build a fire to warm himself up. I'll continue reading to see whether what happens matches my prediction.

Encourage reading groups to stop from time to time to make predictions about what they think might happen next. Suggest that students write down their predictions so that they can check to see whether their predictions came true. Have students follow the story sections in their reading guides, stopping at the end of each section to make predictions.

- first section – stop reading at the end of the paragraph that begins "When the man had finished . . . "
- second section – stop reading at the end of the paragraph that begins "At last, when he could endure no more . . . "
- third section – read from the beginning of the paragraph that begins "The sight of the dog . . . " to the end of the story.

Using the Reading Guide Make sure that students understand that as they read, they should add information to their reading guides on student workbook pages 53–54. You may wish to have students work on their reading guides in small groups.

After Reading

> You may also use the selection questions and activities in *Glencoe Literature*.

Making Predictions Follow-Up Ask students: *Did the end of the story surprise you? Why or why not?* Discuss whether students predicted the ending. Ask: *What clues did you find throughout the story that hinted at the ending? How does knowing the kind of person the main character is help you to predict what happens to him?*

Analyzing and Connecting Point out that the man in the story simply does not realize from the beginning the extreme danger he may be in. Ask: *Does that kind of thinking happen in real life? How might you protect yourself and others from thinking this way?* Have students write their answers in their journals.

OBJECTIVE

▶ To draw conclusions about a speech

I Will Fight No More Forever

Chief Joseph

Before Reading

Building Background Explain to students that the selection they will read is a short speech given by Chief Joseph, head of the Nez Percé nation. Have students read "Meet Chief Joseph" and the Building Background note in *Glencoe Literature*. Invite students to share what they know about fighting between Native Americans and settlers in the 1800s. (*Many native people lost their lives. Most of those who survived lost their land and ultimately their way of life.*)

Word Study: Native American Names Write on the board the names *Nez Percé*, *Hinmaton Yalaktit*, and *Too Hul Hul Suit*. Explain that some Native American groups, in the early 1800s, did not have writing systems. Europeans wrote Native American names the way they thought the names sounded. In some cases, Europeans assigned names to Native Americans. Point out *Nez Percé* and explain that French explorers gave this French name, meaning "pierced nose," to a group of Native Americans because members of the group had pierced noses.

During Reading

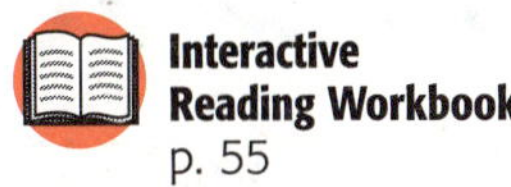

Interactive Reading Workbook p. 55

Drawing Conclusions Ask students: *What does it mean to draw conclusions?* (**Drawing conclusions** about a character or a situation is making general statements based on the information presented in a selection as well as one's own knowledge and experience.) Then **ask a volunteer to read the speech aloud** as students follow along in their textbooks. Have students discuss what they think motivated Chief Joseph to make the speech "I Will Fight No More Forever." Ask: *How do you think the chief was feeling as he gave this speech? What phrases in the speech help you to draw a conclusion about the way the chief was feeling?* (The chief was feeling worn out and defeated. This is evident in his repeated use of the phrase "I am tired," and his stating "my heart is sick and sad.") **Ask the class to reread the speech aloud together with expression,** speaking in the way they think Chief Joseph may have spoken. Then have them complete Interacting with Text **Drawing Conclusions,** student workbook page 55.

After Reading

You may also use the selection questions and activities in *Glencoe Literature*.

Reviewing and Analyzing Help students review and analyze the selection with the following questions.

1. Why does Chief Joseph want to stop fighting? (*After years of fighting, he realizes that his people have been devastated—too many have died, too much has been lost. He wants to save those who are left.*)
2. Do you think Chief Joseph's decision to stop fighting is wise or cowardly? Explain. (*Students may say he is wise and he accepts defeat with dignity.*)

OBJECTIVES

- To recognize tone; to identify the main idea

Let Us Examine the Facts

Corn Tassel

Before Reading

Activating Prior Knowledge Have students read "Meet the Cherokee of Corn Tassel's Era." Also encourage them to read the Building Background note in *Glencoe Literature*. Then invite students to suggest reasons for the United States government to have fought Native American groups in the 1700s. (*Possible response: The U.S. government wanted the land that was occupied by many groups of Native Americans. In addition, settlers of European descent were probably suspicious and fearful of people who looked different from them and who lived in a different manner.*) Have students discuss their views on the settlers' claiming the land where Native Americans lived, hunted, and fished. Ask: *Why did the settlers think they could claim land that did not belong to them?*

Building Vocabulary Write on the board the following words, without their definitions: *retort* (answer), *transposing* (reversing), *relinquishing* (giving up), *maneuvers* (movements), *desolation* (ruin, destruction), *reformation* (cultural change), *livelihood* (means of making a living), *equivalent* (of equal value). Invite students to suggest meanings for the words and have them check their definitions against those in a dictionary. Ask volunteers to use the words in sentences. Encourage students to record the words and their meaning in their vocabulary logs or journals.

Word Study: Latin Roots Tell students that many words in the English language have Latin roots. Explain that knowing something about common Latin roots can help them figure out the meanings of unfamiliar words. Copy on the board the following chart. Point out the words from the selection and the prefixes and Latin roots and their meanings. Then brainstorm with students for other English words that have Latin roots. Have students check a dictionary to make sure that their examples come from the Latin root given.

Word from Selection	Prefix and Latin Root	Meaning of Prefix and Root
receive	re- + cipere	back, again + to take, seize
transpose	trāns- + pōnere	across, from one place to another + to place
reject	re- + jectus	back, away + to throw

Setting a Purpose for Reading Have students read the selection to find out what facts Corn Tassel wants to examine and what the facts will prove.

During Reading

Recognizing Tone **Have a volunteer read aloud the first two paragraphs of the selection and have students follow along in their textbooks.** Then remind students that **tone** is the attitude toward a subject that is expressed by the author or speaker. Tone many be communicated through particular words and details that express emotions. For example, word choice or phrasing may convey humor, sarcasm, respect, dread, or lightheartedness. Have students discuss Corn Tassel's tone. Encourage them to identify words, details, or phrasing that suggest tone. Ask:

- *How does Corn Tassel communicate disgust with the treaties of the whites?* (Example: "It is a little surprising . . . their whole cry is *more land!*")
- *How does he communicate sarcasm?* (Example: Corn Tassel calls whites "my brother warriors.")

Identifying Main Ideas **Have students finish reading the selection silently.** Ask students: *What is the most important idea in a paragraph called?* (**the main idea**) *What are the examples or ideas that further explain the main idea called?* (**supporting details**) Remind students that many times, but not always, the main idea is the first sentence of a paragraph. Explain that a main idea may be anywhere in a paragraph; or it may not be stated at all—it may be implied. To model identifying an implied main idea for students, **read aloud the paragraph that begins "Indeed, much has been advanced on the want of what you term civilization among the Indians."**

> ***Modeling*** In the first sentence, Corn Tassel reviews that whites want the Indians to adopt unfamiliar laws, religion, manners, and customs. The next sentence tells how Corn Tassel and his people do not see that any of the white people's ways have had a good effect, so they wonder why they would want to adopt the whites' customs. The implied main idea is that the way of life of Corn Tassel's people is as valid as the settlers' way of life.

Have students ask themselves questions as they read each paragraph: *What is each sentence about? Is there one sentence that tells about the whole passage? What main idea do the supporting details point out?* Have students complete Interacting with Text **Identifying Main Ideas,** student workbook page 56.

After Reading

You may also use the selection questions and activities in *Glencoe Literature*.

Purpose for Reading Follow-Up Remind students of their purpose for reading the selection. Ask: *What are some of the facts that Corn Tassel wants to examine?* (The claiming of land occupied by Native Americans seems to be a pattern of the peace treaties; the whites march into these territories, destroy, and conquer; they did not secure the junction at the Holstin and Tennessee Rivers, however, so they did not conquer all rivers "above them"; the whites want Native Americans to adopt European ways, yet whites do not act in a civilized way.)

OBJECTIVES

- To understand characterization; to recognize figurative language

The Story of an Hour

Kate Chopin

Before Reading

Activating Prior Knowledge Tell students that "The Story of an Hour" is about one hour in a woman's life during which she receives overwhelming bad news. Encourage students to discuss the way people usually respond to bad or tragic news. Ask: *How do you think people usually react when they hear bad news? Under what circumstances might they act differently?*

Building Vocabulary Write on the board the following words from the story, without their definitions: *afflicted* (distressed), *intelligence* (news), *aquiver* (quivering, trembling), *eaves* (the part of a house that lies just under the edge of the roof), *bespoke* (spoke, demonstrated), *subtle* (not obvious), *monstrous* (ugly, terrible), *imploring* (begging). Tell students that writers sometimes use a word to convey something slightly different from its most familiar meaning. Point to the word *intelligence*. Ask: *What do you think this word usually means?* (intellectual capability, aptitude; wisdom) Explain that another of its meanings is "news." Point out that this meaning sometimes has a variation: "secret information." It is this last meaning that is intended when one refers to some governments' gathering "intelligence." Write the meaning "news" next to *intelligence* on the board. Then ask students to suggest meanings for the remaining words on the board. Have students refer to a dictionary if necessary. Suggest that students record the vocabulary words and their meaning in their vocabulary logs or journals.

Word Study: Multiple-Meaning Words Recall with students the different meanings of the word *intelligence*. Remind them that when a familiar word does not seem to make sense in a sentence, the word probably has more than one meaning. Encourage them to use context clues to help them figure out a different meaning for the word. Students may also consult a dictionary to check all possible meanings of the word and to select the one that fits the context. On the board, write the following phrases from the story. Include the underlining but omit the meanings in parentheses. Point to the underlined word in each phrase and ask students what the most common meaning of the word is. Then let students brainstorm to interpret the meaning of the word as it is used in the phrase. The definition in parentheses reflects the meaning of the word as used in each phrase listed.

1. to break to her as gently as possible the news **(make known, tell)**
2. in broken sentences **(disjointed, incomplete)**
3. when the storm of grief had spent itself **(exhausted)**
4. had never looked save with love upon her **(except, but)**

Setting a Purpose for Reading Have students read the Building Background notes in *Glencoe Literature*. Point out that a common notion at the time this story was written was that women were suited only to being wives and mothers and that their place was in a role subservient to men. Suggest that students read the story to see how these attitudes affect the main character of the story.

During Reading

Understanding Characterization **Have students read the story silently.** Ask them to stop reading at the end of the seventh paragraph, which begins "She was young . . . " Briefly discuss the character of Mrs. Mallard with students. Ask: *How does Mrs. Mallard react to the news that her husband is dead? Do you think that her reaction is one most people might have under the same circumstances? Why or why not?* **Have students continue reading as before through the paragraph that begins "Free! Body and soul free!"** Then model the process of understanding characterization.

> *Modeling* As I read further, I see Mrs. Mallard in a little different light. When she first hears the bad news, she reacts as anyone would expect her to, with great grief. But now I learn more about her. Her reactions begin to change. She is not so sad about the loss of her husband, after all. When she says, "Free! Body and soul free!" her exultant words and actions indicate that she is beginning to think of herself as an independent woman.

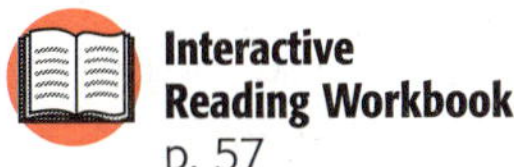
Interactive Reading Workbook p. 57

Have students finish reading the story. Engage them in a discussion about the personality of Mrs. Mallard. Have them explain what they like or do not like about her. Then have students complete Interacting with Text **Understanding Characterization,** student workbook page 57.

Recognizing Figurative Language Tell students that **figurative language** refers to words and phrases that are not intended literally. Write *metaphor* and *personification* on the board. Ask students what they know about these types of figurative language. If necessary, explain that a **metaphor** is a comparison of two things that are not basically alike. A metaphor does not include the words *like* or *as*. Ask volunteers for examples of metaphors. (One example: *The stars are diamonds in the sky*.) Explain that **personification** is ascribing human attributes to an object, idea, or animal. Invite students to suggest examples of personification. Ask students to find in the story one example of metaphor and one of personification. List their responses on the board. (*Metaphor: "the storm of grief," "a long procession of years"; personification: "she felt it, creeping out of the sky, reaching toward her," "blind persistence,"* and *"monstrous joy that held her," "joy that kills."*)

After Reading

You may also use the selection questions and activities in *Glencoe Literature*.

Analyzing Character Discuss the ending of the story. Ask: *Was the ending shocking or surprising? With what you know about Mrs. Mallard's personality and circumstances, does the ending follow logically? Why or why not?* (Possible response: The ending follows logically. Mrs. Mallard is emotional and vulnerable. She has just received a shock—news that her husband died in a train accident; then she is shocked again—her husband is not dead after all. Also, Mrs. Mallard's heart disease is referred to at the beginning of the story.)

OBJECTIVES

- To analyze cause-and-effect relationships; to connect

A Wagner Matinée

Willa Cather

Before Reading

Activating Prior Knowledge Tell students that "A Wagner Matinée" is about a woman who really enjoys listening to music. Ask students to discuss the importance of music in their lives. Ask: *How often do you listen to or play music? How important is music to you? How might you feel if circumstances prevented you from hearing music for a long time?*

Building Vocabulary On the board, write the following words, without their definitions: *matinée* (an afternoon performance), *altogether* (completely), *gangling* (awkward and tall), *alight* (to step down), *boardinghouse* (a place providing rooms for rent and three meals daily), *sixties* (the 1860s), *reverted* (changed back to), *lest* (for fear that), *kinswoman* (woman related by birth or marriage). Discuss the origin of the word *matinée*. Tell students that *matinée* is in fact a French word; it literally means "morning event" but is used now to mean a daytime performance—usually an afternoon performance. The preferred English spelling of *matinee* today is without the accent mark. Ask students to brainstorm for the meanings of the other words, referring to dictionaries as necessary. You may have to provide the meaning of *sixties* as it is used in the story. Suggest that students record the vocabulary words and meanings in their vocabulary logs or journals.

Word Study: Suffixes Remind students that a **suffix** is a word part added to the end of a word that changes the meaning and the part of speech of the word. Write *appear* and *appearance* on the board and have a volunteer point out the suffix in *appearance*. (*-ance*) Tell students that verbs often are made into nouns by adding suffixes. Write the following suffixes on the board: *-ion*, *-tion*, *-ance*, *-ing* and *-ment*. Referring to the suffixes on the board, ask students to suggest examples of verbs that are changed to nouns when a suffix is added. Write students' suggestions on the board. Invite students to find examples in the story of nouns that are formed by adding a suffix to a verb. (*Examples:* communication, recollection, appearance, dwellings, conjugations, performance, enjoyment, instructions, surroundings.)

Setting a Purpose for Reading Suggest that students read the selection to discover how one woman reacts to a concert.

During Reading

Analyzing Cause-and-Effect Relationships Remind students that a **cause** is a situation or event that makes something else happen. The **effect** is what happens. Distribute to students copies of the Cause-and-Effect Chart in Part 1. Then **read aloud the first two paragraphs of the selection** and model the process of analyzing cause-and-effect relationships.

Modeling **I read that the narrator receives a letter from an uncle. He reacts to the letter emotionally. His reaction is the effect. The letter from his uncle is the cause of his emotional reaction.**

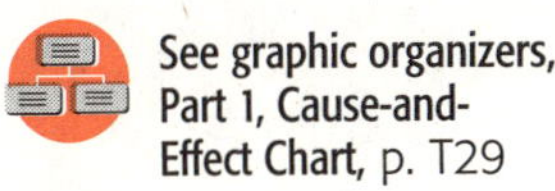
See graphic organizers, Part 1, Cause-and-Effect Chart, p. T29

Create a transparency of a cause-and-effect chart and display it on the overhead projector. Enter *a letter from an uncle* in the top lefthand box as the cause that leads to—indicate the arrow pointing to the box on the right—the effect: *The narrator is mentally taken back to his youth, while growing up with his aunt.*

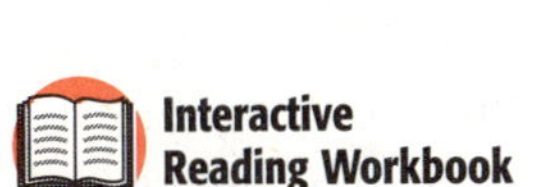
Interactive Reading Workbook p. 58

Tell students that, in order to discover whether there really is a cause-and-effect relationship between two situations, they should ask themselves why a certain event or situation took place or came about. If it was a result of another event, the two events or situations are connected by a cause-and-effect relationship. **Have students read the story silently.** Suggest that students continue to enter on their charts the cause-and-effect relationships they notice as they read the story. Have students complete **Interacting with Text** **Analyzing Cause-and-Effect Relationships,** student workbook page 58.

After Reading

You may also use the selection questions and activities in *Glencoe Literature.*

Analyzing Help students analyze the story with the following questions.

1. Why has Aunt Georgiana been deprived of music for so long? (*At the time the story takes place, there are no radios, television sets, or CD players. Settlers such as Georgiana and Howard live far from cities where live music concerts are held. Georgiana has lived on the frontier for thirty years.*)
2. What details from Aunt Georgiana's life help you to understand the character? What do you think Aunt Georgiana is like? (*Before her marriage, Georgiana was a music teacher at the Boston Conservatory. Georgiana is an accomplished woman and a hard worker—"after cooking three meals [she] would often stand until midnight at her ironing board." She is emotional—"She burst into tears and sobbed pleadingly."*)

Cause-and-Effect Relationships Follow-Up Review with students the cause-and-effect relationships they entered on their charts. Make students aware of several basic cause-and-effect relationships in the story: Aunt Georgiana's mothering of Clark causes his affection and protective feelings toward her; Aunt Georgiana's marriage causes her to live on the frontier far away from access to classical music; and the long deprivation of music causes Aunt Georgiana's emotional reaction at the concert.

Connecting Remind students that when they **connect,** they think about how what they have read relates to their own lives. Encourage students to discuss the power music has to influence emotions. Ask whether they have ever been at a concert listening to a powerful song that stirred their emotions. Ask: *How did you feel as you listened to the music?*

OBJECTIVES

- To paraphrase a poem; to connect to the meaning of a poem

Douglass and *We Wear the Mask*

Paul Laurence Dunbar

Before Reading

Building Background Tell students that they will read two poems by Paul Laurence Dunbar. Have students read "Meet Paul Laurence Dunbar" in *Glencoe Literature*. Invite students to anticipate what poems titled "Douglass" and "We Wear the Mask" might be about. Explain that the poem "Douglass" is directed to Frederick Douglass, who had formerly been enslaved but ultimately became a famous abolitionist speaker. You may want to review briefly the biographical information about Douglass, which is presented in Theme Four of *Glencoe Literature*.

Building Vocabulary Lead a discussion with students about the language of poetry. Ask them what they have noticed about the ways in which poets present words that give words a unique appearance. Write on the board the following words from the poems, omitting their meanings: from "Douglass"—*fall'n* (fallen), *thou* (you), *didst* (did), *thee* (the singular form of *you*, used as the object of a verb or preposition), *amaze* (amazement), *fro* (from), *lieth* (lies: is in a certain condition), *thy* (your), *o'er* (over); from "We Wear the Mask"—*mouth* (speak), *overwise* (too wise). Invite students to speculate on the meanings of these words. You may want to point out that the words *thou*, *thee*, *thy*, *didst*, and *lieth* are old-fashioned forms of words we use today. Tell students the meanings (provided in parentheses) for the words. Ask them to record the words and their meaning in their vocabulary logs or journals.

Word Study: Poetic Language Ask students: *What is the meaning of* ***rhyme?*** (the repetition of the same stressed vowel sounds and any succeeding sounds in two or more words) *What is the meaning of* ***rhythm?*** (the pattern of beats created by the arrangement of stressed and unstressed syllables, especially in poetry) Explain that rhythm gives poetry a musical quality and that rhyme and rhythm are both characteristics of many poems. Point out that poets may change words slightly in order to fit into a certain rhythm or rhyme scheme. Explain that many of the vocabulary words are those that the poet may have altered for this reason. Have students explain how the words are changed. Also have them scan "Douglass" to recognize how the changed words fit in the poem. (*The words* fallen *and* over *are shortened and changed to* fall'n *and* o'er *so as to fit the rhythm; the word* amaze *is used instead of* amazement*—the suffix* -ment *being removed so that* amaze *fits the rhyme scheme.*)

Setting a Purpose for Reading Suggest that students read the poem "Douglass" to find out what the speaker has to say to Frederick Douglass. Have them read "We Wear the Mask" to find out who wears the mask.

During Reading

Paraphrasing **Have partners read the poem "Douglass" aloud, with each partner reading one stanza.** Bring the class together and ask volunteers to tell the group what *paraphrasing* means. Lead students to understand that **paraphrasing** is retelling a story or poem in one's own words. Have students discuss the value of paraphrasing: it can help readers to understand the author's meaning and to reconsider and review the ideas in the selection. **Read the second stanza aloud to students.** Ask them what situation they picture as they listen to the words of the poem. Help them realize that the poet has used the metaphor of people in a boat ("shivering bark") during a storm ("o'er the storm") in making his points. (Much of the imagery relates to being endangered at sea.) Then model the process of paraphrasing.

> ***Modeling*** I read, in the first line, "the waves of swift dissension swarm." I know that a wave is a powerful force, that *dissension* means "disagreement," and that *swarm* can mean "overwhelm." This line, therefore, must mean *There is overwhelming disagreement.* The poem's second line speaks of "Honor" (which means integrity, respect, or responsibility) as a "strong pilot," which should guide actions but instead lies "stark," or stiff and rigid. I paraphrase this as *People no longer act honorably* or *A Sense of honor doesn't motivate people to act in the right way anymore.*

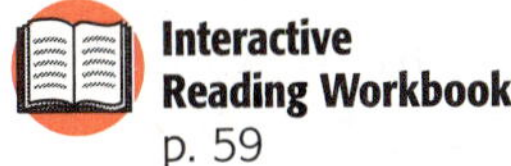
Interactive Reading Workbook
p. 59

Encourage students to paraphrase lines of the poem that they have trouble understanding. Ask them to complete Interacting with Text **Paraphrasing,** student workbook page 59.

Connecting **Have students read "We Wear the Mask" chorally.** Then ask: *What do you think "the mask" is?* (The mask is any expression that covers up real feelings.) *Who wears the mask, according to poet Paul Laurence Dunbar?* (African Americans collectively wear the mask.) *Why do they wear it?* (African Americans wear the mask to hide their true feelings and their suffering.) Ask students to consider how "wearing the mask" might apply to their own lives. Ask: *How do you think the people referred to in the poem—"we"— feel about themselves and their situation? How do you think they feel about the others who see them "wearing the mask"? Are there situations in your life when you "wear a mask"?*

After Reading

You may also use the selection questions and activities in *Glencoe Literature*.

Responding Help students respond to the poems by asking them the following questions.

1. Which poem did you prefer? Why? What is your favorite line in the poem? What does the line mean to you?
2. What is the overall theme expressed in "Douglass"? (*Strong leadership, like Frederick Douglass's, is needed to guide the movement toward increasing rights for African Americans.*)
3. What does the repetition of the words "we wear the mask" emphasize in the poem? (*This repetition reinforces the overall message of the poem, which is that people, particularly African Americans, wear a mask to hide their anguish.*)

OBJECTIVES

- To draw conclusions; to make inferences

Lucinda Matlock and *Fiddler Jones*

Edgar Lee Masters

Before Reading

Building Background Ask students what a *portrait* is. (*A portrait is "a painting, photograph, or other representation of a person or group of persons."*) Explain that besides visual representations, there are "word portraits," verbal representations of characters in stories or poems that capture personality or appearance. Tell students that they will read two poems, each one a word portrait of a character. Have students read "Meet Edgar Lee Masters" and the Building Background notes in *Glencoe Literature*.

Building Vocabulary Write on the board the following vocabulary words, omitting the meanings in parentheses: from "Lucinda Matlock"—*ere* (before), *drooping* (failing); from "Fiddler Jones"—*vibration* (quivering motion), *clover* (a plant that, according to legend, brings good luck), *hereafter* (after this time), *ruinous* (causing ruin and destruction), *medley* (combination). Ask students to suggest a meaning for each word. Let students know the definitions of the words as provided in parentheses above. Encourage students to record the vocabulary words and their meaning in their vocabulary logs or journals.

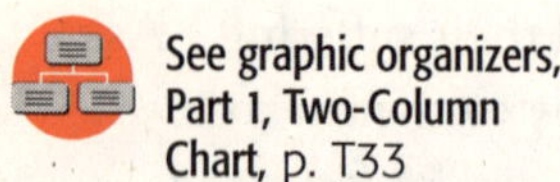
See graphic organizers, Part 1, Two-Column Chart, p. T33

Word Study: Homophones Write on the board the word *homophone* and ask students to provide its meaning. (**Homophones** are words that sound the same but have different meanings and usually different spellings.) Create an overhead transparency of a two-column chart and display it on the overhead projector. **Then read aloud the first three lines of "Lucinda Matlock."** Point out the word *one* in line 3 and ask students to provide a homophone for it. (*won*) Record this information on the class chart. After they have finished reading the poem, work with students to complete the chart by using words from the poem.

Word from the Poem	Homophone
for	four
eight	ate
made	maid
weed	we'd
passed	past
to	too, two
hear	here
son	sun

Setting a Purpose for Reading Have students read the poems to find out how the poet describes two people and their lives.

During Reading

Drawing Conclusions Ask students: *What is the process of drawing conclusions?* (**Drawing conclusions** is pulling together the details in what is read and using the details and reasoning to make general statements about a character or situation.) **Have students read "Lucinda Matlock" silently. Then reread the poem aloud** as students follow along in their books. Encourage students to note details about Lucinda Matlock's personality. Ask: According to the details in lines 10 through 15, what kind of person is Lucinda? (*energetic, nurturing, hard working, busy, appreciative of nature, happy, positive*) Then **read "Fiddler Jones" aloud to students as they follow along in their books.** Model drawing conclusions about the personality of Fiddler Jones, using the details provided in the poem.

> ***Modeling*** The first four lines of the poem, ending with "Why, fiddle you must, for all your life," tell me that Fiddler Jones is a friendly, happy man with a positive outlook. He says, in lines 20–23, "And I never started to plow in my life / That some one did not stop in the road / And take me away to a dance or picnic." This tells me that the man enjoys music, dancing, eating, and being with others. At the end of the poem, Fiddler Jones says that he doesn't have "a single regret." Although Fiddler Jones may have neglected his farm when people stopped him to play his fiddle, I draw this conclusion about him: Fiddler Jones is a man with a pleasant disposition who has enjoyed his life.

Making Inferences Explain to students that making inferences is a skill that is similar to drawing conclusions. Drawing conclusions requires pulling together many details to make a general statement about a character or event. Making inferences requires understanding a detail or fact that is not written but is implied. In "Fiddler Jones," lines 7–8, read, "you rub your hands / For beeves [beef] hereafter made ready for market." The reader might infer that "you," the audience addressed by the speaker, is the people in Fiddler Jones's community—in particular, he seems to be addressing the farmers. The reader might infer from "rub your hands" that the speaker is describing farmers who are eager to sell their beef, probably for the money that they will gain. Point out that the poet does not *state* that farmers are eager to sell their beef—he *implies* it by stating that the farmers "rub their hands." Encourage students to point out other inferences that they can draw from "Fiddler Jones." Then have them review the poem "Lucinda Matlock," thinking about the inferences they make as they read. Have students complete Interacting with Text **Making Inferences,** student workbook page 60.

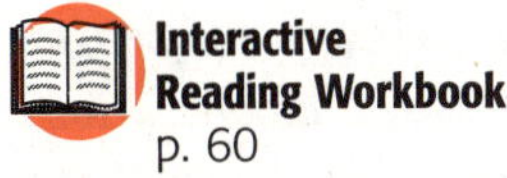

p. 60

After Reading

You may also use the selection questions and activities in *Glencoe Literature*.

Analyzing Character Discuss with students the kinds of people Lucinda Matlock and Fiddler Jones are. Ask: *What is special about Lucinda Matlock? About Fiddler Jones? How do you know?* Encourage students to point out details in the text to support their analyses.

OBJECTIVES

- To identify rhyme; to visualize; to draw conclusions

Richard Cory and *Miniver Cheevy*

Edwin Arlington Robinson

Before Reading

Building Background Explain to students that "Richard Cory" and "Miniver Cheevy" are both poems about fictional individuals. The poet is Edwin Arlington Robinson, who, like Edgar Lee Masters, wrote poetry centered on his memories of his hometown. Have students read the Building Background note in *Glencoe Literature*. Prepare students to read the poems by asking them to discuss the adage "You can't tell a book by its cover." Suggest that they keep the adage in mind as they read the poems.

Building Vocabulary Write on the board the following words, without their meanings: from "Richard Cory"—*crown* (top of the head); from "Miniver Cheevy"—*assailed* (attacked with arguments), *renown* (fame), *vagrant* (a homeless wanderer), *albeit* (although), *mediaeval* (during the Middle Ages). Point to the word *mediaeval* on line 23 in the poem and point out that the letters *a* and *e* are joined together in the word. Explain that in printing terminology, these joined letters are called a *ligature*. A ligature was often used in old-fashioned printing. Words that sometimes were once written with *ae* joined, such as *encyclopaedia*, are now usually spelled with the letter *e* replacing the ligature of *a* and *e*. Tell students that knowing Latin roots may help them figure out the word *mediaeval*. Explain that the Latin word *medius* means "mid," as in the word *medium*. Point out that Latin *aevum* means "age." Help students suggest meanings of the other vocabulary words. Encourage them to enter the words and their meanings in their vocabulary logs or journals.

Word Study: Rhyme Invite students to discuss rhyme. Ask: *What is rhyme? How can we tell that certain words rhyme?* Make sure that students understand that words that have true **rhyme** have the same last stressed vowel or vowel-plus-consonant sounds. Emphasize that the sounds make the rhymes, not the spellings of the words. Ask volunteers to provide examples such as *cow, plough, now,* which all have the same final vowel sound; and *moon, soon, croon,* which all have the same final vowel-plus-consonant sounds. Write on the board the words *sleigh* and *way* and point out that these two words rhyme because they have the same final vowel sound, even though that sound is spelled differently. Point out that some words rhyme when several syllables have the same final sounds, as in *measure* and *pleasure*. Remind students that many poems include rhyming words, usually at the ends of lines. As they read the poems, encourage students to watch for rhyming words and to notice where the rhyming words occur in the poems.

Setting a Purpose for Reading Suggest that students read the poems to find how the characters Richard Cory and Miniver Cheevy are alike, as well as how they are different from one another.

During Reading

Visualizing Ask students what they do when they visualize something as they read. Make sure they realize that **visualizing** means using the words they have read to help them picture something in their minds. Point out that visualizing is a strategy that can help readers better understand what they read. Ask students to visualize the title character as **you read aloud the first two stanzas of "Richard Cory."** Model visualizing how Richard Cory looked and acted.

> ***Modeling*** As I read the poem, I begin to visualize Richard Cory. I see a picture in my mind's eye of a man who is neat and slender. His clothes are neat but understated, not loud or flashy. In fact, I imagine him in a conservative dark suit. This suit isn't mentioned in the poem, but I know that when I visualize, I can draw on my own experience and imagination as well as the details the writer provides. I picture Richard Cory's bearing as very much that of a gentleman as he walks down the sidewalk, with a regal bearing and good manners that impress everyone.

Interactive Reading Workbook
p. 61

Call on a volunteer to finish reading the poem aloud, as students follow along in their textbooks. Have students complete **Interacting with Text** **Visualizing,** student workbook page 61, either during or after reading.

Drawing Conclusions **Have partners read aloud "Miniver Cheevy," progressing through an oral reading by taking turns and each reading aloud a verse.** Remind students that good readers draw conclusions while reading. Ask what **drawing conclusions** means. Help students realize that readers draw conclusions when they make a general statement about a character or a situation based on several bits of information they have read, combined with what they already know from their own experience. Conclusions are also the result of logic. Ask: *What conclusions can you draw about Miniver Cheevy's personality?* (Possible response: Miniver Cheevy is an unhappy, miserable person who complains constantly.) *How does he spend most of his time?* (He spends his time dreaming of the time of knights and kingdoms.) *What does he not do that he might be expected to do?* (He does not work.) Ask students to draw conclusions about the characters in the two poems and share how Richard Cory and Miniver Cheevy are alike. (*Possible response: Both characters seem to live in private worlds; both are unhappy.*)

After Reading

> You may also use the selection questions and activities in *Glencoe Literature*.

Connecting Remind students of their discussion of the adage at the beginning of the lesson. Point out that in the poem "Richard Cory" the title character is greatly admired and appears to have everything he wants in life. Ask: *How are appearances deceiving here?* Have students write in their journals about what the poem means and how they might apply this information to their own lives.

OBJECTIVE

▶ To use the reading strategies of summarizing, questioning, clarifying, and predicting

The Open Boat

Stephen Crane

Before Reading

Activating Prior Knowledge Tell students that they will read a story about four men in a small boat on the open sea. Ask them to discuss what they know about boats, sailing, and the power of the sea. Have them read "Meet Stephen Crane" and the Building Background notes in *Glencoe Literature*.

Interactive Reading Workbook pp. 62–63

Building Vocabulary Refer students to the Interactive Reading **Reading Guide,** student workbook pages 62–63. Remind them that one use of this reading guide is to help them keep track of important new words and expressions. Read through the Key Vocabulary and Terms for "The Open Boat" with students. If necessary, help clarify the meaning of these vocabulary words by providing examples.

Word Study: Idioms and Expressions Tell students that an expression does not always reflect the literal meaning of the words in it. Offer *catch a cold* as an example. Explain that when one becomes ill with a cold, he or she does not literally "catch" the cold as a catcher at a ballgame catches a ball. *Catching a cold* is understood to mean "becoming ill with a cold virus." Ask volunteers to suggest other common expressions. (Examples are *in the doghouse* and *play by ear.*) Explain to students that they will find expressions in the story they will read. Write the following expressions on the board, omitting their meanings: *by the same token* (similarly), *willy nilly* (whether one likes it or not; haphazardly), *to and fro* (back and forth), and *hemming and hawing* (making hesitating sounds). Have students brainstorm about what the expressions might mean. Encourage them to notice idioms and expressions in context as they read the selection.

Setting a Purpose for Reading Have students read this suspenseful adventure story for enjoyment and to find out what happens to the men in the boat.

During Reading

Using Reading Strategies Provide each student with a copy of the following chart of reading strategies. Review the following strategies with students: **summarizing**—retelling in one's own words the most important ideas in what one has read; **questioning**—asking questions during reading about things that are hard to understand; **clarifying**—finding answers to those questions and rereading to make sure that ideas in the text are expressed clearly; and **predicting**—making a good guess, based on the text, about what is likely to happen next. Review the second and third columns of the chart with students.

Strategy	How Student Leader Helps	The Group's Responses
Summarize	The leader gives a summary of the segment of text that may answer the questions *who*, *what*, *where*, *why*, and *when*.	The group offers ideas for additions and corrections to the leader's summary.
Question	Then the leader identifies questions about what was just read.	Group members try to answer the questions. They propose additional questions.
Clarify	The leader guides the group to answer unresolved questions and to seek clarification of difficult passages.	Group members seek answers for questions, clarify information, and ask for any needed help with understanding confusing passages.
Predict	The leader predicts what may happen in the next reading segment.	Group members offer their own predictions about what may happen.

Read aloud the first six paragraphs of "The Open Boat." Model the process of using these four reading strategies.

> ***Modeling*** As I read, I stop to **summarize.** Four men are in a small boat on the sea. I **question** how all four men fit into a boat that has been compared in size to a bathtub. In order to **clarify,** I reread the descriptions of the men and what they are doing. (*Reread paragraphs 3–6.*) It's clear that these men have been thrown together as survivors of a shipwreck. I **predict** that the story will deal with what they do to survive.

Monitoring Comprehension **Have small groups of students read the story aloud.** Have each group select a leader. Divide the story into three sections, following the divisions in the reading guide: section 1—parts i, ii, and iii; section 2—parts iv and v; section 3—parts vi and vii. **When the groups have read the first section, have them complete the activities on the reading-strategy chart.** Remind students that, as they read, they should refer to their reading guides, student workbook pages 62 and 63, and add the missing information before they read each subsequent section.

After Reading

> You may also use the selection questions and activities in *Glencoe Literature*.

Evaluating Have students respond to the story by asking the following question. Is the author successful at building suspense? Explain. (*Possible response: Yes. Stephan Crane builds suspense by describing the emotional turbulence of the men in the boat. He describes the men's sense of relief when they think they will be rescued. Then he describes their profound disappointment when they realize that no one is coming for them. Crane also creates suspense by describing the danger the men face as the waves lift the boat and then slam it down again.*)

OBJECTIVE

- To recognize author's viewpoint

In a Station of the Metro and *A Pact*

Ezra Pound

Before Reading

Building Background Have volunteers read aloud the information about Imagist poetry in the Literature Focus section preceding these selections in *Glencoe Literature*. Draw a web on the board and write *Imagist Poetry* in the center circle. Have students suggest adjectives that describe Imagist poems. (*brief, concrete, precise, everyday, free-form, image-filled*) Record students' suggestions on the web.

Building Vocabulary On the board, write the following words from "A Pact," without their definitions: *pact* (truce), *detested* (hated), *pig-headed* (stubborn). Ask students to share what they know about each word. Provide students with definitions as necessary. Have them write these words and their definitions in their vocabulary logs or journals.

During Reading

Understanding Metaphor **Have a volunteer read aloud "In a Station of the Metro."** Ask students to find the metaphor in the poem. (*People's faces on the train are described as petals on a branch.*)

Recognizing Author's Viewpoint Remind students that the **author's viewpoint** is the author's personal attitude or belief that underlies and often influences his or her writing. Both word choice and tone tell a great deal about an author's viewpoint about a subject. **Have a student read "A Pact" aloud.** Ask: *Who is the subject of this poem?* (Walt Whitman) *What words suggest Pound's attitude toward Whitman?* (*detested, pig-headed, father, son*) Then have students complete Interacting with Text **Analyzing Author's Viewpoint,** student workbook page 64.

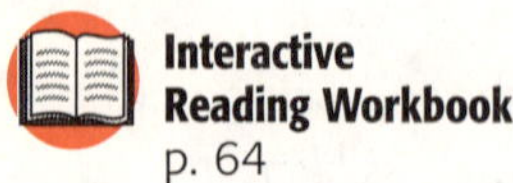
Interactive Reading Workbook
p. 64

After Reading

You may also use the selection questions and activities in *Glencoe Literature.*

Reviewing and Analyzing Ask the following questions to help students review and analyze "A Pact."

1. How are the speaker's feelings about Whitman like a son's attitude toward his father? (*A son may go through a time of resenting his father as the son struggles to be independent of the father; once a young man matures, he may be more able to accept and acknowledge how his father has influenced him.*)
2. What is the "pact" that the speaker suggests? (*The "pact" is an agreement the speaker wishes for: that he and Whitman will have a creative exchange of ideas.*)

OBJECTIVES

- To understand figurative language; to infer character from statements

The Love Song of J. Alfred Prufrock

T. S. Eliot

Before Reading

Activating Prior Knowledge Explain to students that the speaker in the "The Love Song of J. Alfred Prufrock" is a man who sees weaknesses in his life but lacks the confidence and courage to change. Ask students to recall a time when they wanted to act or speak up about an important matter but felt too self-conscious to do so. Ask them to think about how their self-consciousness made them feel. Suggest that they pay attention, as they read or listen to the poem, to how Prufrock sees and judges himself.

Building Vocabulary On the board, write the following words from the poem, without definitions: *indecision* (wavering; inability to decide), *revisions* (changes), *scuttling* (moving with a quick, shuffling gait), *marmalade* (a jelly made with citrus fruit and rind), *porcelain* (hard, fine, white ceramicware), *overwhelming* (overpowering), *attendant* (waiting upon in order to serve), *meticulous* (very careful about details). Ask students to share what they know about each word. As a class, develop a definition for each word. Then ask students to verify their definitions in a dictionary and to record these words and definitions in their vocabulary logs or journals.

Word Study: Multiple-Meaning Words Remind students that many words have more than one meaning. Readers must consider a word's **context**—the surrounding words or the sentence in which a word is used—to decide which meaning is appropriate. If necessary, they should refer to a dictionary for the possible definitions of the word in question. **Read aloud the following sentences that include words from the poem, emphasizing the word in boldface type.** Have students choose which meaning of the word is intended. The correct answer is underscored.

1. The storm was **dying** down now.
   - a. losing life
   - b. longing keenly
   - c. ceasing to function
   - d. <u>subsiding</u>
2. The bride's train was long enough to **trail** along the ground.
   - a. <u>hang down so as to drag</u>
   - b. straggle
   - c. track
   - d. pursue

Setting a Purpose for Reading Invite students to read to find the clues that reveal what sort of man J. Alfred Prufrock is and why it is so hard for him to "sing" or declare love to anyone.

During Reading

Understanding Figurative Language Call on volunteers to read the poem aloud. **Then have a volunteer read aloud the first three lines below the epigraph in the poem.** Ask students to explain what these lines mean. If necessary, point out that the comparison is a **simile,** a type of figurative language in which words such as *like* or *as* are used in the comparison of seemingly unlike things. Have students tell what two things are compared. (*The evening is compared to an unconscious patient in surgery.*) Ask why students think Eliot made this comparison and how it affects the way readers visualize the scene. (*The comparison makes the evening seem sickly and still. It suggests lifelessness and the inability to move. Eliot may have made this comparison to set the tone for the rest of the poem.*) **Have students read on through the stanza to find another simile.** (*"Streets that follow like a tedious argument"*) Ask them to explain its meaning. Then have students complete Interacting with Text **Analyzing Figurative Language,** student workbook page 65.

Interactive Reading Workbook
p. 65

Making Inferences **Ask students to reread lines 37–48 and to suggest a specific adjective to describe the tone of voice that Prufrock might use to deliver these lines.** (*agonized, fearful*) Remind students that many selections require them to **make inferences,** or to discover unstated meanings that are suggested by a passage. Then model the process of inferring based on this passage.

> ***Modeling*** As I listen to these lines, I hear the frustration and fear in Prufrock's voice. I can tell that he is self-conscious because he is painfully aware of how people talk about his aging body. He wants to do something daring, but he is afraid. He repeatedly asks himself, "Do I dare?" From the title of the poem, I reason that he wants to declare his love to one of the women in the drawing room. He is uncertain and keeps changing his mind from moment to moment ("decisions and revisions which a minute will reverse"). From his behavior and words, I can infer that Prufrock is a timid man who feels inadequate.

Call on volunteers to read aloud other passages (lines 49–54, 55–61, and 111–119) and infer what they show about Prufrock's mood and character.

After Reading

You may also use the selection questions and activities in *Glencoe Literature*.

Reviewing and Interpreting Ask the following questions to help students review and interpret the poem.

1. Who are the people with whom Prufrock associates? What are they like? How do they regard him? (*Prufrock focuses on sophisticated women who have the poise that he lacks. They appear to be confident and entertain themselves with tea and trivial conversations. He believes they think him foolish, inadequate, and insignificant.*)
2. When does Prufrock speak about the sea? What do you think the sea symbolizes, or represents, to him? (*In lines 73–74, he states his belief that he "should have been a pair of ragged claws / Scuttling across the floors of silent seas." In lines 124–131, he describes mermaids who sing and ride the waves. The sea appears to represent a natural and vital state that is the opposite of his confined world; such freedom he cannot hope to attain.*)

OBJECTIVE

- To analyze sensory language

The Red Wheelbarrow and This Is Just to Say

William Carlos Williams

Before Reading

Building Background Have students read the information in the Before You Read notes in *Glencoe Literature*. Point out the connection between William Carlos Williams and Ezra Pound. Ask students what they expect Williams's poems to be like. (*Students may suggest that the poems will contain images of everyday things that are described in simple language.*)

Word Study: Compound Words Have students find compound words in "This Is Just to Say." (*breakfast, icebox)* Explain that the term *icebox* was coined in 1854; it was a wooden box into which a block of ice was placed, along with food to be kept fresh. Later, the term *icebox* came to refer to the electric version of an icebox—a refrigerator. *Breakfast* names the first meal eaten upon waking, upon breaking the "fast" of the night.

During Reading

Analyzing Sensory Language Call on a volunteer to read "The Red Wheelbarrow" aloud. Ask: *What sense does this poem relate to?* (sight) *What words make the scene vivid?* ("red," "glazed," "rain water," "white")

Have students silently read "This Is Just to Say" and ask them to name the senses the poem appeals to. (*taste, smell, touch*) Then have students complete Interacting with Text **Analyzing Sensory Language,** student workbook page 66.

Interactive Reading Workbook p. 66

Rereading Have volunteers read "This Is Just to Say" aloud, using tone of voice to communicate their interpretation of the speaker's intended meaning.

After Reading

You may also use the selection questions and activities in *Glencoe Literature*.

Analyzing Ask students the following questions to help them analyze the poems.

1. Why do you think Williams left out most punctuation and capital letters in "The Red Wheelbarrow"? (*Doing so emphasizes the simplicity of the language and the images, and calls more attention to the line structure, all of which contribute to the poem's overall effect.*)
2. Why do you think these poems have such short lines? (*The short lines isolate and emphasize words so that the words are considered singly and slowly. The short lines thus encourage visualization of each object or experience described.*)

OBJECTIVES

- To compare and contrast; to interpret underlying meaning

Anecdote of the Jar

Wallace Stevens

Before Reading

Activating Prior Knowledge Ask students to recall a time when they visited a wilderness area, such as a national park. Ask: *What objects did you bring with you into the wilderness? How did these objects contrast with the natural setting? Did the contrast enable you to see the objects in a new light?* Tell students that the poem they will read is about a natural setting and a simple object, a jar.

Building Vocabulary Write the following words from the poem on the board, without definitions: *anecdote* (a brief, interesting story), *slovenly* (disorganized, untidy), *sprawled* (spread out awkwardly), *dominion* (the authority to rule). Have students use a dictionary to find definitions and pronunciations of unknown words. Invite students to share their definitions before they enter them in their vocabulary logs or journals.

During Reading

Comparing and Contrasting Remind students that **contrasting** is examining how two things are different. **Ask students to read the poem silently.** Then ask these questions: *What two things are being contrasted in the poem?* (a jar and the wild area around it) *Why might Stevens have chosen to contrast them?* (He may have wanted to show how the synthetic world differs from the natural world.) *What words does the poet use to describe each?* (wilderness—"slovenly," "sprawled"; jar—"round," "tall," "of a port in the air," "gray," "bare")

Interactive Reading Workbook p. 67

Have students complete Interacting with Text **Comparing and Contrasting,** student workbook page 67.

After Reading

You may also use the selection questions and activities in *Glencoe Literature*.

Interpreting Explain that poems call on readers to interpret an underlying meaning, or a deeper meaning than the words first suggest. **Reread the first stanza aloud** and then model your thinking processes as you interpret the poem's deeper meaning.

> ***Modeling*** I wonder what the poet means by writing that the jar "made the slovenly wilderness surround that hill." The wilderness didn't change or move. The poet must be talking about his own way of seeing his surroundings. I think he means that the jar, which is something created by a person, made him notice the disorder of the wilderness. It may have made the speaker think of how people carve out a place in nature that is quite different from nature.

Then use these questions to help students interpret Stevens's ideas in the poem. *What is the meaning of the jar's taking "dominion"?* (The jar suggests control and order over the wild surroundings.) *What do you think Stevens means when he says, "It did not give of bird or bush?"* (The artificially made jar is not the regenerative life source that nature is.)

OBJECTIVES

- To understand stream-of-consciousness narrative; to use summarizing, questioning, clarifying, and predicting

The Jilting of Granny Weatherall

Katherine Anne Porter

Before Reading

Building Background Ask students to consider the sequence or pattern of their thoughts. Do their thoughts run in chronological order, or do they seem to be scattered? Introduce the term *stream of consciousness*. Explain that in a stream-of-consciousness narrative, an author focuses on the flow of thoughts of one or more characters in a way that is intended to mimic the way people actually think. The result is a text that expresses free flow of thought rather than an organized narrative sequence.

Building Vocabulary On the board, write the following story words, without their definitions: *drowsed* (napped), *tonic* (medicine), *rummaging* (searching), *clammy* (cold), *notion* (idea), *scandal* (disgrace), *mingled* (mixed), *disputed* (argued), *hypodermic* (surgical needle), *gauze* (mesh dressing for wound). Have students use the words they know in sentences that suggest their meaning. Then ask students to find in a dictionary the definitions of words that they do not know. Have them record the words and their meanings in their vocabulary logs or journals.

Word Study: Specialized Vocabulary Let students know that this story includes terminology that is related to the Roman Catholic Church and other Christian denominations. Discuss the meaning of the following words, inviting students to share their understanding of the terms: *saint* (an officially recognized person of exceptional holiness), *Holy Communion* (the receiving of the Eucharistic elements of bread and wine), *Father* (a title of respect for a priest), *Sister* (a title of respect for a nun), *crucifix* (a cross on which the figure of Christ appears crucified), *Mass* (a religious celebration of Holy Communion).

Setting a Purpose for Reading Have students read the story to learn what sort of life Granny Weatherall has had and what her thoughts are as she faces her death.

During Reading

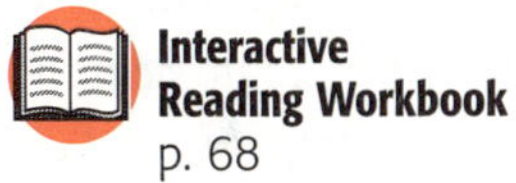

Understanding Stream of Consciousness **Read aloud the paragraph beginning "In her day . . ."** Ask students to identify things in the story that are happening in the present and things that have happened in the past. Remind students that a **stream-of-consciousness** narrative flows like a person's thoughts and is most likely not in chronological order. Have students complete Interactive Reading **Stream of Consciousness,** student workbook page 68.

Using Reading Strategies Discuss with students the following reading strategies:

- summarizing—putting the main points of a story into one's own words

- questioning—asking about things not understood during reading
- clarifying—finding answers to questions and making sure that all parts of the selection are understood
- predicting—making logical guesses about what might happen

Read aloud the first five paragraphs of "The Jilting of Granny Weatherall." Model the process of using these four reading strategies as a way to better understand the text.

Modeling As I read, I **summarize** what I've read. I know that an old woman lies in bed and is being tended by Doctor Harry. She dismisses him as too young to tell her what to do, while he warns that she must be "good"—or follow the doctor's orders. Next, I **question** a part that I do not understand. I wonder what the "forked green vein" is and why it makes the old woman's eyelids twitch. To **clarify** the passage, I reread. I see that the old woman is aware of her eyelids' twitching when the doctor puts a hand "like a cushion" on her forehead. This suggests that his hand gives her comfort from her pain. She must be very frail and ill. As I read on, I'll watch for more clues about her health.

Another question I have is why the doctor responds so agreeably even though the old woman is cross and short with him. His behavior suggests to me that he is used to this kind of crossness from her; I may find as I read that this abruptness is a trait of her personality. As I read, I'll learn more about this woman's character and how she interacts with others. From what I've read so far, I'll **predict** that she is a tough old woman who is at odds with her caregivers.

Have students, in groups of four, take turns reading the story aloud. Instruct groups to read three or four paragraphs at a time, taking turns in the role of leader. The leader should give a summary of the segment, identify questions, guide the group in finding answers to these questions, and then predict what will happen next and clarify what remains unclear. The group should offer additional ideas, questions, and predictions.

After Reading

You may also use the selection questions and activities in *Glencoe Literature*.

Reviewing and Analyzing Ask the following questions to help students review and analyze the story.

1. Recall the messages Granny has for John and George. In what tone of voice would she deliver each of these messages? (*She would speak with pride to her husband John about how well she managed the household and children; she would use a bitter, sharp tone to tell the man who jilted her that she had been better off without him.*)
2. What does religion mean to Granny? How does its meaning change as her death approaches? (*Granny is a woman of strong faith, and religion is a comfort to her. However, she expects a sign that she will be ushered into heaven. When only blackness greets her, she feels jilted once more and is bitterly disappointed.*)

OBJECTIVE

▶ To interpret a poem

Richness

Gabriela Mistral

Translated by Doris Dana

Before Reading

Activating Prior Knowledge Ask students to think of a joyful memory and to consider why they remember it. Then discuss memories that are not so pleasant and invite students to discuss whether these memories are as vivid as the happy ones. Explain to students that the speaker in the poem "Richness" expresses her ideas about memories. Suggest that students, as they listen to the poem, relate their own memories to the speaker's views.

Word Study: Spelling Let students know that three words that they will encounter in the poem are *rose*, *stolen*, and *sorrow*. Ask what they notice about the vowel sound in these words. (*All three words have the long* o *vowel sound.*) Ask students to suggest rules for spelling these and related words.

- *Rose:* The long vowel sound heard in *rose* is spelled by the vowel-consonant-silent-*e* pattern of letters at the end of a word. When a suffix is added to such a word, or when a compound word includes such a word, the word usually retains its long-vowel sound. (Related spelling words are *spokesman*, *notable*, *parole*.)
- *Stolen:* From the pronunciation of the word, it is clear that this word is divided after the *o*. The first syllable is open (ends with a vowel), indicating that this sound may be spelled simply *o*. (Related spelling words are *emotional*, *rosary*, *stoic*, *romantic poetry*.)
- *Sorrow:* In sorrow, *ow* is pronounced with the long *o* sound. (Not all words containing *ow* have the long *o* sound, however.) (Related spelling words are *shadows*, *swallow*, *callow*.)

During Reading

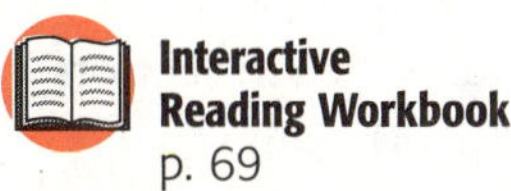
Interactive Reading Workbook p. 69

Interpreting a Poem **Ask a volunteer to read the poem aloud.** Then have students contrast the words *faithful* and *lost*. Ask them to think about their own experiences and to explain how both "faithful joys" and "lost joys" have enriched their lives. (*Having both suggests a full life and the experience of a range of emotions.*) Then have students complete Interacting with Text **Interpreting,** student workbook page 69.

After Reading

You may also use the selection questions and activities in *Glencoe Literature*.

Analyzing Ask students what they think the title is referring to. (*Possible answer: It refers to how all our emotional experiences—happy and sad—add to our lives.*) What does saying that the rose is loved and the thorn is loving suggest? (*A faithful joy is cherished, and a lost joy also enriches life.*)

OBJECTIVE

▶ To analyze the line structure of a poem

Ars Poetica

Archibald MacLeish

Before Reading

Activating Prior Knowledge Have students think of a poem they like. Ask what they like most about the poem. Is it the poem's rhyme and rhythm? Its imagery? Its message? Explain that the poem "Ars Poetica" outlines what Archibald MacLeish thinks a poem should be. Suggest that students read the poem to compare their ideas of what a poem should be to MacLeish's idea.

Building Vocabulary On the board, write the word *globed* and tell students that the word is an adjective. Ask what noun it is related to. (*globe*) Ask students to suggest what a globed fruit would look like. (*rounded*) Then write *medallions* (objects resembling medals) on the board and have a volunteer describe what a medallion looks like. Ask students to check their definitions against those in a dictionary.

Word Study: Two-Word Modifiers Point out the compound words *sleeve-worn* and *night-entangled* in the poem. Ask how the adjectives are alike. (*Both are hyphenated.*) Explain that the hyphen is necessary to clarify meaning. Without the hyphen in the phrase *sleeve-worn stone*, for example, the word *sleeve* could modify *stone*. Have students identify the noun that each hyphenated adjective modifies in the poem (*stone*, *trees*) and explain how the adjective alters their image of the noun.

During Reading

Analyzing Line Structure **Read the poem aloud.** Have students consider the construction of the stanzas. Model the process of analyzing stanza structure.

> ***Modeling*** **I see that the poem is organized in two-line stanzas, or couplets. In most of the stanzas, one line is much longer than the other. This draws my eye to the short lines. I think this technique emphasizes the words in the short line.**

Help students divide the poem into three parts: (1) Each third of the poem begins and ends with "A poem should be"; (2) in the middle of each section are two sets of images that illustrate the "bookend" *shoulds*; (3) each stanza ends with words that rhyme. Point out that the organization of stanzas helps convey a poem's meaning. Then have students complete Interacting with Text **Analyzing Line Structure,** student workbook page 70.

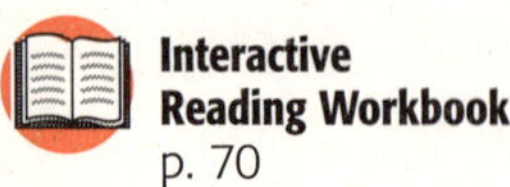
Interactive Reading Workbook p. 70

After Reading

Interpreting Ask students to read aloud lines that contain their favorite images from the poem and to tell in what sense the images are "wordless." (*They enable readers to "see" and "feel" what is being described; it is not the words themselves that are significant; it's what they evoke that is.*)

You may also use the selection questions and activities in *Glencoe Literature*.

OBJECTIVES

- To identify tone; to note the effect of inverted word order in sentences; to identify a rhyme scheme

Dirge Without Music and *Recuerdo*

Edna St. Vincent Millay

Before Reading

Building Background Tell students that they will read two poems—one about death and burial and a second about a treasured day. Have students read the Building Background notes that precede the selection in *Glencoe Literature.* Discuss with students the meaning of *repetition, rhyme,* and *rhythm* as they pertain to poetry.

Building Vocabulary On the board, write the following words: *crowned, fragment, formula, elegant, fragrant, approve, precious, ferry, fares.* Ask students to categorize the words they know according to part of speech (nouns—*fragment, formula, ferry, fares*; adjectives—*elegant, fragrant, precious*) and to give a definition for each. Then have students check their definitions against those in a dictionary. Students should write these words and definitions in their vocabulary logs or journals.

Word Study: Affixes Point out that a number of the words in the poems have prefixes and suffixes: *darkness, indiscriminate, gently, quietly, beautiful, bucketful.* Explain that the prefix *in-* expresses negation; the suffix *-ness* means "state or quality of"; *-ful* means "full of." Ask students to think of other examples of these affixes and to discuss how the affixes change the meaning of the base word.

Setting a Purpose for Reading Remind students that the **tone** of a literary work is a reflection of the writer's attitude toward his or her subject matter. Suggest to students that they read to identify the tone of each poem as well as the idea or theme each is communicating.

During Reading

Identifying Tone Point out the definition of *dirge* in the footnote of "Dirge Without Music." **Then read aloud the opening stanza** and have students describe the tone of the poem. (*solemn, formal*) Ask how the poem's formal language ("With lilies and with laurel," "I am not resigned") suits the subject of the poem. (*A death and a funeral are solemn and are usually accompanied by formal rituals, so the formal language fits this topic.*) **Have pairs of students read the rest of the poem aloud,** alternating stanzas and using the tone of voice they think is appropriate to the subject. **Then have pairs of students read "Recuerdo" aloud.** Ask how the tone of this poem differs from that of "Dirge Without Music" and why the tone suits the poem. ("Recuerdo" is light and positive in tone. The tone is appropriate because the poem describes a happy event.)

Noting Inverted Sentence Order Read aloud line 3 of "Dirge Without Music" and have a volunteer explain what is unusual about this sentence compared to most prose sentences one might read. (*Its subject and verb are placed at the end.*) Explain that this **syntax,** or word order, sounds formal or unusual because the subject and verb are not in their usual placement at the beginning of the sentence. Point out that this word order shift causes the reader to pay close attention and emphasizes the words that are in unexpected places. Then have students complete Interacting with Text **Inverted Word Order,** student workbook page 71.

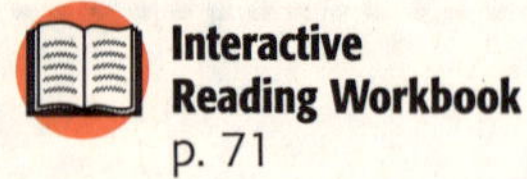

p. 71

Understanding Rhyme Scheme After they have read "Dirge Without Music" and "Recuerdo," have students look at the final words in each line to identify the rhyming words. Model the process of analyzing the **rhyme scheme,** or pattern of rhyme.

> ***Modeling*** **In "Dirge Without Music," I see that the first and third lines of a stanza have the same ending sounds. The second and fourth lines also rhyme. I know that letters are used to describe rhyme scheme, so the pattern of stanza 1 is *abab*; stanza 2 is *cdcd*, and so on. In "Recuerdo" the rhyming lines are in pairs, so the rhyme scheme in stanza 1 is *aabbcc*. The rhyme from the first two lines of stanza 1 is repeated in stanza 2, so it is *aaddee*. The regular pattern of rhyme gives a stabilizing and unifying effect to the poems. The repetition of *merry-ferry* throughout "Recuerdo" links the stanzas together.**

Have students use letters to determine the rhyme scheme of the remaining stanzas of the two poems.

Rereading Have volunteers reread each poem aloud to allow students to hear the effects of rhyme in the poems.

After Reading

You may also use the selection questions and activities in *Glencoe Literature*.

Reviewing and Analyzing Ask the following questions to help students review and analyze the poems.

1. What are some clues in the poem "Dirge Without Music" that reinforce the speaker's unwillingness to accept the death of those close to her? (*"the best is lost" and "I do not approve."*)
2. What references to money or wealth can you find in "Recuerdo"? What do these references convey about what the speaker values? (*The rising sun is compared to "a bucketful of gold"; the pair give away their fruit and money. These actions suggest that the speaker finds wealth in experiences, not in possessions or money.*)

OBJECTIVES

- To analyze an unconventional writing style; to analyze a sound device (repetition)

anyone lived in a pretty how town

E. E. Cummings

Before Reading

Building Background Have students read "Meet E. E. Cummings" and the Building Background notes in *Glencoe Literature*. Ask students to scan the poem and to share what they notice about it. (*They may point out that there are few capital letters and little punctuation.*) Ask students how the poem illustrates the poet's individuality. (*It does not conform to standard writing conventions and forces readers to look at things in new ways.*)

Building Vocabulary On the board, write the following words, without their definitions. Have students use the words in sentences that show their meaning: *sowed* (planted), *reaped* (harvested), *apt* (likely), *stooped* (bent). Provide those definitions that students do not know. Tell students to pay close attention to how the words are used in the poem. Then have them write the words and their definitions in their vocabulary logs or journals.

During Reading

Analyzing an Unconventional Style Have students read the poem silently. Point out that the lack of conventional punctuation and capitalization can make reading the poem challenging. Then copy the first stanza on the board and have students add the correct punctuation and capital letters. Ask students to describe in what ways the punctuated stanza achieves a different effect. Ask: What effect might the poet's unconventional style have on the reader? (*By using unconventional style, the poet is forcing the reader to pay closer attention to the content of the poem.*)

Analyzing Repetition Call on a volunteer to read the poem aloud, while students listen for repetition in lines. (*Repetition: the names of the seasons in lines 3, 11, and 34; "sun moon stars rain" in lines 8 and 36 and "stars rain sun moon" in line 21*) Then cover the lines in which repetition occurs and read the poem without those lines. Have students tell how the poem seems different without them. (*A unifying, harmonious quality is missing.*) Have them complete **Interacting with Text** **Analyzing Repetition,** student workbook page 72.

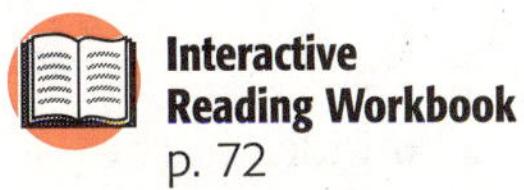

Interactive Reading Workbook p. 72

After Reading

Summarizing the Poem Have a volunteer summarize the life "anyone" and "noone" had together. Ask students what made "anyone" and "noone" special. (*They were an average man and woman living an ordinary life in a small town, but they loved each other deeply and shared life's joys and sorrows fully. Others seem uncaring and negative by comparison. The close relationship of these two gave their lives vitality.*)

You may also use the selection questions and activities in *Glencoe Literature*.

OBJECTIVES

- To summarize; to understand stanza pattern

Poetry

Marianne Moore

Before Reading

Building Background Explore students' expectations of poetry by asking them the following questions: *How do you feel about poetry? What do you expect from poems? What aspects of poetry can make it difficult to understand?* Explain that the selection, "Poetry," explores the problems many people have in understanding poetry. Suggest that students listen to the poem. Then ask them to think about whether the poet has addressed their specific concerns.

Building Vocabulary On the board, write the following selection words, without their definitions: *contempt* (scorn), *genuine* (real), *interpretation* (explanation), *unintelligible* (not understandable), *immovable* (steadfast), *statistician* (one who deals in numerical facts), *valid* (acceptable), *discriminate* (show prejudice), *triviality* (unimportance). Ask students to define the words they know and then to consult dictionaries to find definitions for unfamiliar words.

During Reading

Summarizing Explain to students that the speaker in "Poetry" freely admits that the problem with much poetry is that the language is difficult to interpret and seems unrelated to their experience. **Read the poem aloud to students,** having them listen for things that the poet dislikes and likes about poetry. After reading, point out the list in lines 11–18 and **have students read this section silently.** Ask: *How do these things differ from the usual notion of "poetic subjects"?* (These are details that are odd but engaging.) Ask what solution the poet suggests for creating poetry that is good. (*Present any subject that is interesting in an honest way.*)

Understanding Stanza Pattern Tell students that poems are arranged in **stanzas,** or groups of lines forming a unit within a poem. Number of lines, length of lines, use of rhyme, and other devices help create a pattern of organization that reinforces the poem's ideas.

After Reading

You may also use the selection questions and activities in *Glencoe Literature*.

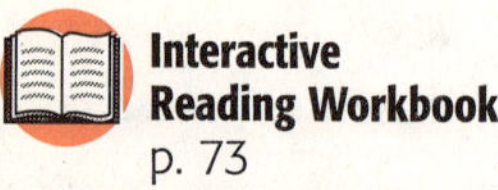

Interactive Reading Workbook p. 73

Summarizing Follow Up Encourage students to sum up the main idea in the poem. (*The speaker dislikes poetry that is obscure and trivial but is interested in sincere, honestly written poems.*) Then have students complete Interacting with Text **Summarizing,** student workbook page 73.

OBJECTIVES

- To infer character from details; to understand irony; to understand point of view in a story; to analyze plot

The Bridal Party

F. Scott Fitzgerald

Before Reading

Previewing the Selection Tell students that the "Bridal Party" is about a young man whose love is about to marry another, wealthier man. Have them page through the story, noting the illustrations and anything else that catches the eye. Ask them to suggest where and when the story takes place, on the basis of their previewing. Point out that the images of the paintings suggest that the story may be set in the 1930s. The characters in the story may be upper-class society people. Tell students that Fitzgerald knew this social scene well.

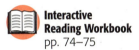

Interactive Reading Workbook pp. 74–75

Building Vocabulary Refer students to the Interactive Reading **Reading Guide,** student workbook pages 74 and 75. Point out the vocabulary words and the definitions in Part 1 of the reading guide. Explain that many of the words listed in each of the three parts of the reading guide describe characters in "The Bridal Party." List these words on the board: *pathetic*, *authoritative*, *brusque*, *square*, *sensitive*, *combative*, *assured*, *noncommittal*, *tragic*, *pleading*. Have students group words that describe similar or related traits. Then have them describe the kind of personality that each group of words suggests. How would such a person talk, walk, and treat others? For example, *authoritative*, *brusque*, *square*, *combative*, *assured*, and *noncommittal* might describe a controlling, unemotional person with a drive to accomplish. As they read, students should be alert to clues that suggest the personality of a particular character.

Word Study: Word Roots Write the following words and their meanings on the board: *charade* (an empty act or pretense), *hysterical* (exhibiting emotional, uncontrollable behavior), *proximity* (closeness, nearness). Then list these roots and meanings: *charrado* (Provençale French: chat, chatter); *hystera* (Greek: womb); *proximus* (Latin: nearest, next). Ask students to match each word with a root and to tell how the meaning of the root relates to the meaning of the entire word.

Setting a Purpose for Reading Have students read the story to learn why Michael cannot accept Caroline's decision to marry someone else.

During Reading

Using the Reading Guide Have students page through the selection and comment upon the organization of the story. (The story is divided into three parts.) **Suggest that students take turns reading the story aloud with partners.** When it is their turn to listen, the listening partners should follow along in the textbook. Remind students to refer to the footnotes in *Glencoe Literature* to find the meanings of unfamiliar words and phrases. Direct students to answer the questions in their reading guides as they read each story section. Have partners compare their answers before progressing to the next section of the story.

Making Inferences About Character Explain that authors reveal **character** by direct statements, by describing a character's actions and thoughts, and through the statements of a character. Remind students to infer what specific details reveal about a character as they read. **Call on a volunteer to read the paragraph in Section I beginning "Since his only support was that she loved him . . . "** Then model the process of making inferences about a character by focusing on the details in the paragraph.

> ***Modeling*** This paragraph tells me that Michael clings to the memory of Caroline's love. I see that, though he has lost her, Michael holds onto mementos and is nostalgic about a sentimental song. The language the author uses suggests that Michael is wallowing in self-pity. The phrase "leaned weakly" suggests weakness in his character. That he is washed ashore figuratively and is still holding onto to useless tokens of his former love makes him seem helpless, self-indulgent, and unable to get on with life.

Understanding Irony Explain that **irony** is the contrast between the expected result of an action and what actually happens or the saying of one thing when the opposite is intended. Ask how Michael's inheritance from his grandfather introduces irony. (*He could not marry Caroline because he was poor; now that she is about to marry someone else, he has money.*)

After Reading

You may also use the selection questions and activities in *Glencoe Literature*.

Understanding Point of View Explain that the story is told from the third-person limited point of view. (The writer presents the action as seen through the eyes of one character, and refers to that character as "he" or "she.") Ask students how the story is affected by being told as Michael sees it. (*The reader cannot know what characters other than Michael are thinking.*) Through discussion, guide students to understand that an omniscient narrator might have revealed that Caroline had favored Hamilton even while she professed to be in love with Michael.

Analyzing Plot Invite students to identify the **conflict** (struggle between opposing forces) and to trace the **rising action** (increasing tension), **climax** (the point of highest interest), **falling action** (what happens to the characters after the conflict), and **resolution** (the outcome) of the story. (*Michael struggles with Caroline and Hamilton to stop their marriage and win her back; he also struggles inwardly to accept losing her. The tension increases as the wedding grows closer and he cannot change her mind, as he learns that he is now rich and Hamilton is poor and has had a past romance. The climax occurs when both men plead their case and she decides to marry Hamilton. The wedding and reception provide the falling action, and the resolution is Michael's realization that he no longer loves Caroline.*)

Evaluating Character Ask students to describe briefly the personalities of Michael, Caroline, and Hamilton and then to tell which character they admire most and why. (*Students should see weaknesses and strengths in each character: Michael values money too highly and lacks confidence, but he also feels genuine love for Caroline; Caroline allows sympathy to be mistaken for love, but she is level-headed about her choice of a husband; Hamilton is able and self-confident, but he is very controlling.*)

OBJECTIVES

- To identify tone; to identify the use of apostrophe

Chicago

Carl Sandburg

Before Reading

Building Background Have students read "Meet Carl Sandburg" and the Building Background notes in *Glencoe Literature*. Point out Sandburg's love of the common people and his admiration for the energetic, rough city of Chicago. Ask students what impact they think these feelings may have had on the tone of the poem "Chicago." (*Students may say that the poem will be a song of praise.*) As students read the poem, encourage them to visualize the scenes the speaker describes.

Building Vocabulary On the board, write the following words, without their definitions, and explain that they help define the city described in "Chicago": *brawling* (fighting roughly), *brutal* (savage, unfeeling), *magnetic* (powerfully attracting), *slugger* (prize fighter), *destiny* (fate). Ask students to define these words, consulting a dictionary if necessary, and to use each word in a sentence. Have volunteers describe the character of the city suggested by these words.

During Reading

Analyzing Tone Remind students that the **tone** of a literary work reflects the author's attitude toward his or her subject matter, as conveyed by such elements as word choice, punctuation, sentence structure, and figures of speech. **Have students read the poem silently** and then ask them to describe the tone of voice with which it should be read. (*energetic, emphatic, proud*) **Call on several volunteers to read the poem aloud,** the first five lines and the repeated final two lines as a group and lines 6–21. Ask students to point out the images they found most effective and to describe how the lines contribute to the tone.

After Reading

You may also use the selection questions and activities in *Glencoe Literature*.

Identifying Apostrophe Explain that **apostrophe** is a device in which the poet speaks directly to an object, an idea, or an absent person. Have students reread the poem to identify the "you" to whom the poet is speaking. (*the city of Chicago*) Then have students complete Interacting with Text **Identifying Apostrophe,** student workbook page 76.

Analyzing Create a two-column chart transparency and display it on an overhead projector. Distribute copies of the Two-Column Chart to students. Ask students to return to the poem, noting the speaker's opinion of Chicago's negative and positive characteristics. (*positive: national center for railroad transport, industry, and meat processing, boldly energetic and aggressive, cunning, vital; negative: afflicted by crime, prostitution, poverty, ignorance.*) List these on the transparency and have students copy them onto their charts. Then have students identify the group of qualities—positive or negative—that matter the most to the speaker. (*the positive qualities*)

Interactive Reading Workbook p. 76

See graphic organizers, Part 1, Two-Column Chart, p. T33

OBJECTIVES

▸ To compare literal and figurative language; to identify theme

FROM

Songs of Gold Mountain

Anonymous

Before Reading

Building Background Have students read about the immigration of the Chinese people in the Before You Read notes in *Glencoe Literature*. Have students describe what they imagine the detention center at San Francisco Bay was like for the immigrants.

Building Vocabulary On the board, write the following words, without their definitions: *detention* (confinement), *officials* (people who hold office), *barrack* (military housing), *port* (harbor), *scarcity* (insufficiency of supply), *exceptional* (unusual), *deplorable* (wretched), *barbarians* (uncivilized people), *heroic* (valiant, fearless), *encompasses* (includes). Ask students to offer definitions for the words and to explain how each might relate to the treatment of the Chinese who immigrated to America. Ask students to use a dictionary to confirm their definitions.

During Reading

Responding Remind students that the men who wrote these poems were imprisoned without having committed any crime. **Call on volunteers to read each poem aloud,** using a tone that reflects how these men must have felt about their situation. Ask students to point out words and phrases that express their feelings. ("*How can I bear . . . ?*" "*misery,*" "*sadness,*" "*bows his head low,*" "*hearts ache in pain and shame,*" "*filled with rage*")

Comparing Literal and Figurative Language Remind students that **literal language** is language based on the definitions and standard usage of words. **Figurative language** is the use of words to express an idea beyond the literal definition of the words. Figurative language helps create images, or "figures," in a reader's mind. Explain that reading figurative language requires "translating" the words in order to understand their meaning. Write on the board *Arriving in America, I felt I had discovered great beauty and wealth.* Have students reread the first poem and find the figurative language that conveys this sentiment. ("*I have found precious pearls.*")Then have students complete **Interacting with Text** **Literal and Figurative Language,** student workbook page 77.

After Reading

Identifying Theme Explain that **theme** is the central idea stated or implied in a literary work. Ask students to explain the central message the Chinese poets express about their experience. (*They came seeking freedom and wealth but instead found indignity and misery.*)

You may also use the selection questions and activities in *Glencoe Literature*.

OBJECTIVES

- To analyze the writer's style; to identify cause and effect

In Another Country

Ernest Hemingway

Before Reading

Building Background Explain to students that the story "In Another Country" is set in Italy during World War I. Ask students what they know about World War I. Focus on the following ideas.

(1) Italy and the United States were allies in this war.

(2) The use of newly invented, potent killing weapons (poison gas, tanks, submarines, airplanes) made this war horrific in new ways.

(3) Trench warfare kept soldiers immobile and vulnerable for months on end, leading to a new type of casualty—the shell-shocked soldier. Immobilized by the terrible conditions and experiences endured, soldiers often suffered from severe depression.

Building Vocabulary On the board, write the following words, without definitions: *pavilions* (detached sections of a building), *fencer* (swordsman), *confidence* (belief), *rebuilt* (restored to its previous state), *lieutenant* (mid-level officer), *patriotic* (loyal to one's nation), *idiotic* (ridiculous), *utterly* (completely). Ask pairs of students to define the words they know. Each partner should take turns providing context sentences for the words and should have his or her partner use context to help in thinking of definitions. Then have students verify their definitions in a dictionary and enter the words and their definitions in their vocabulary logs or journals.

Word Study: Greek and Latin Roots The following words in the story are based on words from the Greek and Latin languages: *photograph* (from Greek *phōs*, meaning light, and *graphein*, meaning to write), *pneumonia* (from Greek *pneumōn*, meaning lung), and *invalid* (from Latin *invalidus*, meaning infirm). Explain the roots of these words and have students make connections to the words' meanings.

Setting a Purpose for Reading Remind students to pay attention to the author's style as they read and to assess how it suits the subject.

During Reading

Analyzing Style Explain that an author's **style,** or unique manner of writing, is created through many elements, including word choice, sentence structure, and tone. **Read aloud the opening paragraph of the story** and model the process of analyzing style.

> ***Modeling*** I see in the first sentence that the words are simple—they are mostly one-syllable words. Two simple clauses are joined by *but*. The second sentence uses the same types of words and joins clauses with *and*. In fact, as I look through the paragraph, I see that it consists entirely of simple ideas expressed in simple words. *And* is used nine times to join

these ideas. This sentence structure has the effect of piling ideas on top of each other without expressing much relationship between them. It is as though the speaker is able only to report simple, direct observations without thinking about how they make him feel. This technique creates a tone that is detached and objective.

Have students continue reading the story aloud, round-robin style. Pause as necessary to allow students to read the footnotes or to ask questions about passages they do not understand.

After Reading

You may also use the selection questions and activities in *Glencoe Literature*.

Identifying Cause and Effect Remind students that two events have a **cause-and-effect relationship** when one is the result of the other. **Call on a volunteer to reread aloud** the paragraph beginning "The boys at first were very polite." Then model the process of identifying a cause-and-effect relationship.

Modeling In this paragraph the author describes how the other wounded soldiers become aloof toward the narrator. This text makes me wonder what caused this reaction. I know that, in order to find a cause, I need to ask *Why? What caused the soldiers to feel aloof from the narrator?* An explanation can be found in the statement that he is "never really one of them" after the soldiers discover why he received his medals, that the narrator's medals were not given for brave actions. The paragraph tells me that the narrator feels "very much afraid to die." The author implies that the other soldiers with medals did act bravely and face death. I think they must believe that the narrator has not proved himself and does not deserve their respect. The differences in their understanding of obligation and courage have caused this rift between the narrator and the others.

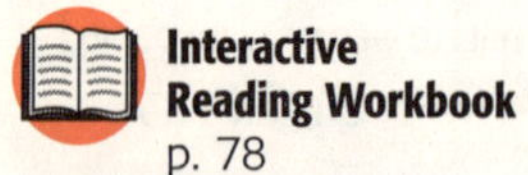
Interactive Reading Workbook p. 78

Now have students complete Interacting with Text **Analyzing Cause-and-Effect Relationships,** student workbook page 78.

Reviewing and Analyzing Ask the following questions to help students review and analyze the story.

1. What is the mood of this story? What communicates this mood? (*The mood is detached and rigid; the reporter-like style, images of dead animals and wounds or injuries without positive or negative comment, and the characters' deadpan reactions establish the mood.*)
2. The major is presented as an admirable man. What are his views on bravery and on love? What do his beliefs suggest about the theme of this story? (*The major does not "believe in bravery" and says of love that a man "should not place himself in a position to lose." He is cynical, having lost love and hope. His beliefs suggest that those who experience terrible losses, as in war, are physically and emotionally crippled and just go through the motions of living.*)

OBJECTIVE

- To make inferences about setting and character

Soldiers of the Republic and *Penelope*

Dorothy Parker

Before Reading

Building Background With students, read and review "Meet Dorothy Parker" and the Building Background notes in *Glencoe Literature*. Explain that many American and European volunteers supported the Republicans in the Spanish Civil War, while the Nazis and Fascists supported the Nationalists. The governments of France, Mexico, and the Soviet Union also supported the Republicans. Nonetheless, the Republicans were defeated in 1939, and World War II was about to begin. Author Dorothy Parker's support for the weary Republicans is evident in the tone of "Soldiers of the Republic."

Point out the lasting appeal of the *Odyssey* adventures, which were written thousands of years ago. Explain that the poem "Penelope" takes the viewpoint of Penelope, Odysseus's wife, not that of the adventurer. As they read the poem, students can think about how her viewpoint might differ from her warrior husband's.

Building Vocabulary On the board, write the following words, without definitions: *tolerant* (accepting), *ecstasy* (bliss), *adornment* (decoration), *calculated* (planned), *desperately* (frantically), *gingerly* (cautiously, carefully), *civilian* (nonmilitary), *igniting* (setting off, lighting), *appreciatively* (with thankfulness), *emphatically* (determinedly), *horde* (mob, swarm), *summon* (call). Ask volunteers to write definitions beside the words they know and to use the words in sentences. Provide definitions and contexts where necessary. Suggest that students watch for these words as they read the story and poem. Have students record the words and their definitions in their vocabulary logs or journals.

Word Study: Possessives Write the following possessives from the story on the board: *God's*, *officer's*. Explain that a singular word is made possessive by adding an apostrophe and an *s*. Then write these plural possessives: *children's* and *farmers'*. Ask students to compare the possessive form of each and then explain that, when a plural noun ends in *s*, only an apostrophe is added to make the plural possessive.

Setting a Purpose for Reading Have students read "Soldiers of the Republic" to learn how the war affected the Spanish people.

During Reading

Making Inferences **Have students read silently from the beginning of the story to the paragraph beginning "There were many soldiers . . . ."** Ask students to describe the atmosphere in the café and to point out details that helped them to visualize the scene. (*The atmosphere is shabby but cheerful and* *animated; clothing is worn and patched, and lights are dim, but families are gathered to chat and relax.*) Remind students that authors imply some ideas rather than directly stating them. Reason and experience will help readers determine what the author is implying. **Have a volunteer read aloud the opening paragraph of the story.** Then model the process of making inferences.

> ***Modeling*** The waiter is described as being very proud of the single ice cube he has put into each drink. This seems odd, for ice is usually available, in my experience. The waiter continues to look over his shoulder at the ice while he goes on with his work. This intensity suggests that ice is not only rare, but it is almost miraculous, to come by. I think the setting must be a very poor place or a place that does not have dependable electricity, which is needed to make ice cubes. I know that the story is set during a war, so I infer that the fighting and bombing may have interfered with utilities. From this paragraph I can tell that the circumstances are difficult.

Have a student read the second paragraph aloud and model the process of inferring what the author is suggesting by describing the darkness and the numerous babies in the café. Then have students complete Interacting with Text **Making Inferences,** student workbook page 79. When they have completed the workbook page, **have students read the rest of the story silently,** reasoning through passages they do not understand by making inferences based on clues in the text.

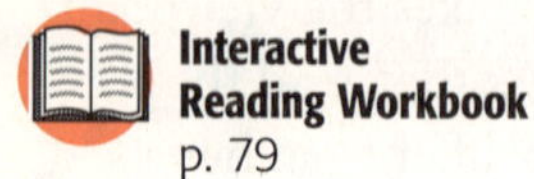
Interactive Reading Workbook
p. 79

Reading "Penelope" **Ask a volunteer to read the poem aloud.** After establishing the identities of the classical hero Ulysses (Roman name for Odysseus) and his wife Penelope, have small groups analyze each half of the poem and ask them to describe both scenes. (*Possible descriptions: at sea—sunny, breezy, open, silver, glittering, fast-moving, active, exciting; at home—quiet, slow-moving, confined, passive, routine*) Then ask students to tell how the details helped them to picture the speaker and "he." Ask groups to summarize in a sentence or two the different experiences of the speaker and "he." (*Odysseus explores the beautiful, boundless sea and has exciting adventures. Penelope waits at home and repeats her round of daily chores endlessly.*)

After Reading

You may also use the selection questions and activities in *Glencoe Literature.*

Analyzing Ask the following question: *Why do you think the soldiers in "Soldiers of the Republic" pay for the narrator's and her companions' drinks?* (Students may say that the soldiers are repaying the narrator for the cigarettes or are expressing their gratitude for a chance to have a normal, social occasion and forget the horrors of war for a short time.) Encourage students to share their thoughts about the nature of bravery in each selection.

OBJECTIVES

- To analyze blank verse; to notice characteristics of dramatic poetry; to describe diction in a poem; to analyze theme

Mending Wall, Birches, Stopping by Woods on a Snowy Evening, and *The Death of the Hired Man*

Robert Frost

Before Reading

Activating Prior Knowledge Have students read "Meet Robert Frost" and the Building Background notes in *Glencoe Literature*. Have students imagine or describe from their experience what life is like in "the country" (in rural areas). Ask them to share the sights, sounds, and feelings they associate with farms or to explain how they feel about nature when they walk through a field or a forest. Suggest that, as students read or listen to these poems, they remain aware of the sights, sounds, and feelings about nature that they recall.

Building Background Explain that the rural area where Frost lived in New Hampshire, which may have been the setting for many of his poems, consisted of poor, rocky soil and rugged forest. Farms were not large, and farming was not a prosperous vocation. As they read or listen to the poems, students should keep in mind both the beauty and the hardship that surround the speakers.

Building Vocabulary Write the following words and definitions on the board: *notion* (idea), *offence* (hurt feelings), *matter-of-fact* (plain-speaking), *fetch* (get and bring back), *conquer* (triumph over), *considerations* (reflections, issues), *pocket-money* (spending money), *grudge* (give with reluctance), *assurance* (confidence), *reference* (direction to some source of information), *appearances* (outward looks), *lounge* (sofa). Invite volunteers to make up sentences using each word in context so that its meaning as used in the poem is suggested.

Word Study: Contractions "The Death of the Hired Man," contains many contracted forms, most of which should be familiar to students. Two infrequently used contractions in the poem are *needn't* and *mustn't*. Have students use these contractions in sentences that demonstrate the words' meanings. Also ask students to notice the word "Harold's" as used in lines 81 and 82 and to determine which word is a contraction of "Harold is," rather than the possessive form, indicating ownership.

Setting a Purpose for Reading Have students read to notice the rhythms and language of the speakers' voices and how they harmonize with the setting.

During Reading

Dramatic Poetry Explain to students that "The Death of the Hired Man" is a **dramatic poem,** one that tells a story and reveals a character's personality through dialogue, monologue, and description. **Read aloud the first 10 lines of the poem.** Then have students repeat them with you, clapping on the stressed syllables in each line. Tell students that the poem is written in **blank verse**—unrhymed iambic pentameter, with each line having five pairs of syllables, each pair made up of an unstressed syllable followed by a stressed syllable. This meter suits a dramatic poem because it approximates the rhythms of natural speech. **Then have a volunteer read aloud through the end of Warren's speech ("I'm done").** Discuss whether the speech sounds natural.

Interactive Reading Workbook
p. 80

Then have students complete Interacting with Text **Analyzing Blank Verse,** student workbook page 80. After they complete the workbook page, **have students read the rest of the dramatic poem aloud in small groups.**

Describing Diction Explain that **diction** refers to the writer's choice of words. Ask students to reread a favorite passage of dialogue in "The Death of the Hired Man," noticing the way Frost's characters speak. (*For example,"Home is the place where, when you have to go there, / They have to take you in."*) Have students supply adjectives that describe Frost's diction. (*monosyllabic, spare, plainspoken, simple, direct*) Write the adjectives on the board. Then discuss how this diction adds to the mood and tone of the poem. Lead students to realize that the characters' simple but blunt way of talking suits the bare surroundings and honest emotions communicated in the poem.

Reading "Mending Wall," "Birches," and "Stopping by Woods on a Snowy Evening" Tell students that each of these three poems expresses a speaker's personal thoughts and feelings. **Have students read the poems silently to determine which use blank verse and to recognize the aspects of nature that are focused on.**

After Reading

You may also use the selection questions and activities in *Glencoe Literature.*

Analyzing Theme Remind students that **theme** is the underlying message in a literary work. Have students discuss their ideas about the theme of "Mending Wall." Point out that the speaker does not think the wall is necessary and that he finds his neighbor's attitude wrong-headed and "savage," or primitive. Help students form a statement of theme. (*Possible theme: The barriers we place between ourselves and others may be useless or contrary to what is natural.*) Then have students review details of the other Frost poems and ask them to form statements about the theme of each.

Appreciating Imagery Remind students that **images** are vivid pictures in a reader's mind that are created by the author's use of language. Ask students to choose one of the Frost poems, to point out images that they found most effective, and to identify the senses to which these images appeal. (*Example: the birches "click upon themselves / As the breeze rises, and turn many-colored / As the stir cracks and crazes their enamel." In these lines, the poet focuses on the ice-covered limbs through the senses of sound and sight. In the following lines, the poet focuses on the sense of touch to describe Silas's pathos: "He hurt my heart the way he lay / And rolled his old head on that sharp-edged chair-back."*)

OBJECTIVES

- To visualize; to identify a sonnet; to analyze rhyme scheme

My City

James Weldon Johnson

Before Reading

Activating Prior Knowledge Explain to students that the poem "My City" describes a country setting and the city of Manhattan. Ask students to recall times they have spent in each kind of place. Have them contrast the sights, sounds, and smells of each setting. Ask them to decide which setting they prefer. Suggest that students read the poem to compare their feelings about the countryside and the city with those of the speaker.

Building Vocabulary On the board, write the following words from the poem, without definitions. Ask students to share what they know about each: *threshold* (a starting place, beginning), *keenest* (sharpest), *throbbing* (pulsating with force), *spells* (compelling influences or attractions), *behold* (to see; observe). Supply definitions as necessary. Then ask students to write sentences using each word in context in their vocabulary logs or journals.

During Reading

Visualizing Remind students that they need to imagine the sights and sounds described in a poem in order to understand it fully. Invite students to make a mental sketch of each scene. **Call on a volunteer to read the first stanza of the poem aloud.** Ask students to describe what they picture and the senses that the images appeal to. Guide students in expressing how peaceful the setting is and how soothing the sensory impressions that describe it are. **Have another student read the second stanza aloud.** Invite students to tell what they visualize as they listen, pointing out specific words to which they respond. Then have students complete Interacting with Text **Visualizing,** student workbook page 81.

Interactive Reading Workbook
p. 81

Identifying Sonnet Form Explain that Johnson has written a **sonnet,** a traditional poetic form of fourteen lines with strict rhyme and rhythm requirements. Help students to analyze the sonnet's rhyme pattern. (*abbacddc efefgg*) Have them compare and contrast the structure and rhyme patterns of the poem's stanzas. (*The length of the stanzas and their pattern of rhyming are different.*) Explain that a sonnet may introduce a question and then answer it. Have students identify the central question posed in this sonnet and the way it is answered. (*When I die, what will I miss most? Manhattan.*)

After Reading

You may also use the selection questions and activities in *Glencoe Literature*.

Reviewing and Analyzing Ask these questions to help students understand the poem.

1. What words reveal the speaker's feelings about Manhattan? (*"Throbbing force," "thrill," and "shining towers" suggest his love for the city; "O God!" shows deep sadness at the thought of never being able to see Manhattan again.*)
2. What detail tells you that the speaker loves both the beauty and the ugliness of the city? (*He mentions "slums" as well as "shining towers."*)

OBJECTIVES

- To identify idioms; to analyze cause-and-effect relationships; to monitor comprehension

FROM

Dust Tracks on a Road

Zora Neale Hurston

Before Reading

Building Background Review with students "Meet Zora Neale Hurston" and the Building Background notes in *Glencoe Literature*. Point out that the selection is set in a period (about 1900) during which racial segregation and discrimination were common in the United States. Injustice for African American citizens was pervasive. Communities such as Eatonville (where author Zora Neale Hurston grew up), which offered African Americans a measure of freedom and self-government, were rare. As students read the selection, suggest that they keep in mind how this unusual situation may have affected Zora Neale Hurston's attitudes.

Building Vocabulary On the board, write the following words, without definitions: *self-assurance* (confidence), *squelcher* (something that curbs or subdues), *the duration* (time during which something lasts), *privilege* (a special right or benefit granted), *Greco-Roman* (from the civilizations of ancient Greece and Rome), *monarch* (king or queen), *gingham* (checkered cotton cloth), *profoundly* (deeply), *conceive of* (to imagine). Call on volunteers to supply definitions for words that they know. Provide sentences with context clues for unknown words and encourage students to determine the words' meanings. Have students check their definitions against those in a dictionary. Encourage students to record the words and their definitions in their vocabulary logs or journals.

Word Study: Idioms Explain to students that authors often use idioms to make their writing more vivid and to create the feeling of a certain time and place. An **idiom** is a group of words whose meaning as a unit is different from the dictionary definitions of the individual words. **Read aloud the following sentence** and ask students to identify the idiom: "'Don't you want me to go a piece of the way with you?'" Point out that "go a piece of the way" means "walk part of the distance." Have students use the footnotes that accompany the selection to define the following idioms: "cut one caper," "cut her eyes," and "lick the calf."

Setting a Purpose for Reading Have students read the selection to learn about Zora Neale Hurston's childhood and her developing talents.

During Reading

Analyzing Cause-and-Effect Relationships Remind students that, in a **cause-and-effect** relationship, one action or circumstance causes one or several other actions to take place. Explain that readers, by analyzing causes and effects, can better understand *what* happens in a story and *why* it happens. **Have a volunteer read aloud from the beginning of the excerpt to the paragraph**

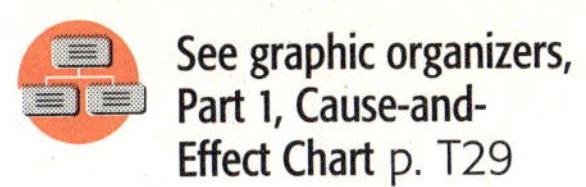
See graphic organizers, Part 1, Cause-and-Effect Chart p. T29

beginning "Perhaps a year before . . ." Tell students that Hurston's watching the passing traffic was a habit that had a number of effects. Create a cause-and-effect chart transparency and display it on the overhead projector. Write *watching passing traffic* in the "cause" box. Model the process of analyzing the effects of this cause for students, while you complete the graphic organizer.

> ***Modeling*** The first questions I ask to find the effects of Hurston's actions are *What happens?* and *What are the results?* I read in the fourth sentence that travelers often would hail Hurston. That is something that happens as a result of her sitting on the gatepost. I'll write *Travelers hailed her* in an effect box of the graphic organizer. Then I'll look to see what else happens when she sits on the gatepost.

Have students suggest the other effects of Hurston's action. (*The travelers are amused. Hurston is invited to ride along with the travelers.*) Have students complete Interacting with Text **Analyzing Cause-and-Effect Relationships,** student workbook page 82.

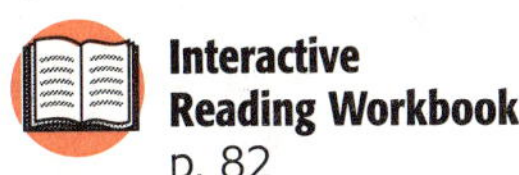
Interactive Reading Workbook p. 82

Monitoring Comprehension **Have students read silently through the paragraph that begins "That is how it was that my eyes . . ."** Tell students that asking themselves questions as they read can help ensure that they are understanding the selection. **Now read aloud the paragraph that begins "Yes, Jupiter had seen her . . ."** Model the process of monitoring comprehension.

> ***Modeling*** What is happening in this myth? Jupiter sees Persephone picking flowers. Then a chariot containing "the dark monarch" comes. Could that be the devil? I'll read on: "He had seen him when he seized Persephone." Will this sentence make sense if I substitute names for pronouns? "He [Jupiter] had seen him [the devil] when he [the devil] seized Persephone." Reading on, I see that Jupiter saw the black horses —of the devil's chariot?—go down Mount Aetna's throat. Mount Aetna is a volcano—they leaped down the opening of a volcano. "Persephone was now in Pluto's dark realm . . ." Oh yes, Pluto, not the devil, is the god of the underworld. Pluto has taken Persephone to the underworld.

Have students read the rest of the selection silently. Suggest that they pause after reading every few paragraphs to ask themselves questions about what they have read.

After Reading

You may also use the selection questions and activities in *Glencoe Literature.*

Analyzing Ask students how Zora Neale Hurston regards myths and Bible stories and which ones she likes best. (*Certain stories exalt and inspire her with their illustrations of strength, majesty, and wisdom. She especially likes the stories of Pluto and Persephone, of Thor and Odin, and of King David in the Bible.*) Ask students to characterize actions in these stories that Hurston admires. (*Hurston admires actions that are "larger than life," show fearlessness, and have a great impact on the world.*) Ask how Hurston's actions show that she has traits similar to those of the characters whom she admires.

OBJECTIVES

- To visualize; to interpret meaning; to identify tone; to compare and contrast

If We Must Die and *The Tropics in New York*

Claude McKay

Before Reading

Activating Prior Knowledge Have students read "Meet Claude McKay" and the Building Background notes in *Glencoe Literature*, paying particular attention to the note "The Time and Place." Have students recall a time when they felt discriminated against or observed racial prejudice in action. Have students record in their journals the emotions they felt and the actions they took or thought about taking. As they read the poem, students can compare their responses with those of the speaker.

Building Vocabulary On the board, write the following words from "If We Must Die" and "The Tropics of New York," without their definitions: *kinsmen* (persons of the same background), *foe* (enemy), *parish* (a local church with its field of activity), *rills* (brooks). Ask students to suggest definitions for the words. Provide meanings as necessary and have students copy the words and definitions in their vocabulary logs or journals.

Word Study: Multiple-Meaning Words Provide small groups of students with the following list of words, without definitions: *mad* (insane), *lot* (fate, fortune), *pack* (a group of animals that hunt or run together), *green* (not ripe), *hungry* (filled with longing). Have students jot down two or more meanings for each word. Write the following sentences on the board and have students select the appropriate meaning for each word, on the basis of its context.

- The scientist concocted a *mad* plan to destroy the world.
- It was her *lot* to remain at home and care for her ailing parents.
- One wolf establishes dominance in the *pack*.
- Eating the *green* persimmons made me sick.
- Talking with her cousin from her homeland made Stella *hungry* to see it again.

Setting a Purpose for Reading Have students read the poems to compare the tone of each with that of the others.

During Reading

Visualizing **Have students listen closely as you read aloud "If We Must Die."** Ask them to picture the actions described in the poem. Then invite them to describe the scenes they imagined as you read. (*Possible responses: vicious dogs attacking helpless hogs; fierce fighting; outnumbered soldiers backed to a wall but fighting bravely.*) Have volunteers explain how watching scenes like this on television or in a movie might make them feel. (*outraged, helpless*) Ask what mood and tone these images create in the poem. (*angry, proud*)

Interpreting Explain to students that thinking about the descriptions and comparisons in poetry in terms of what they already know will help them interpret what the poet is saying. **Have students reread the first four lines of "If We Must Die."** Then model the process of interpreting meaning.

> ***Modeling*** In the opening line, the speaker confronts the possibility that he and his comrades must die. This statement creates a sense of urgency. The description of hogs encircled by wild dogs contains violent imagery. Picturing the scene arouses fear and anger about the unfairness of the situation. How do the hogs relate to the "we" of the poem? I think the "we" is African American people. I know that African Americans in the past were abused and violently maltreated. In a way, African Americans were sometimes "penned" by laws and prejudices into subhuman conditions. Any attempt to gain equality met with violent countermeasures. I think the poet is saying that racists in America are like a pack of dogs and that racism viciously denies African Americans basic human rights.

Encourage volunteers to continue reading the poem and interpreting its meaning.

Identifying Tone Remind students that a writer creates **tone,** which often reflects the author's attitude toward the subject, through elements such as word choice, sentence structure, and figurative language. **Call on a volunteer to read aloud "The Tropics in New York."** Have students locate words or phrases that express admiration for the tropics. (*"fit for the highest prize," "mystical blue skies," "benediction," "nun-like hills"*) Then ask them to infer the tone suggested by the phrases "a wave of longing" and "turned aside and bowed my head and wept." (*sorrow, homesickness*)

After Reading

You may also use the selection questions and activities in *Glencoe Literature*.

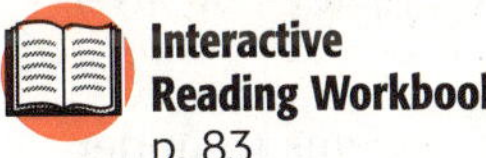

Interactive Reading Workbook
p. 83

Comparing and Contrasting Have students analyze the two poems to discern similarities and differences between them. (*Both poems rhyme and have regular metrical structure; they differ in tone, action, and type of imagery.*) Then have students complete Interacting with Text **Comparing and Contrasting,** student workbook page 83.

Analyzing Ask students these questions: *In "The Tropics in New York," where is the speaker? How do you know?* (The speaker is at a fruit market in New York City; the title names the city, and the first stanza describes the exotic fruits the speaker sees in a window.) *Why does the fruit make the speaker think of the tropics?* (He says that the sight brings memories, so he must at some time have been in the tropics. He also associates the tropics with a blessed or holy place, so students may infer that the tropics are significant to him, probably because he once lived there.) *What does the final stanza tell about the speaker?* (He is filled with longing for "familiar ways"; sorrow makes him turn away. This implies that New York is unfamiliar to him and that he does not think of it as home.)

OBJECTIVES

- To analyze diction; to identify the speaker; to summarize

I, Too and *The Negro Speaks of Rivers*

Langston Hughes

Before Reading

Building Background Have a volunteer read "Meet Langston Hughes" and the Building Background note in *Glencoe Literature*. Then tell students that the poem "I, Too," by Langston Hughes, was written in response to the poem "I Hear America Singing," by Walt Whitman. Review Whitman's poem with students (in Unit 3 of *Glencoe Literature*).

Making Predictions Have students look at the pen-and-ink drawing that accompanies "I, Too." Ask students to describe the emotions or attitudes conveyed by the image of this man. (*This drawing depicts a man who is dignified, inspired, aspiring, strong, graceful, proud.*) Ask students to predict, on the basis of this image, what the poem will be about. (*Possible response: The upward-reaching arm suggests that the poem may be about someone who wants to be counted too.*)

Building Vocabulary Write on the board the following words (without definitions) from "The Negro Speaks of Rivers": *ancient* (old, existing many years), *bathed* (washed), *lulled* (soothed), *pyramids* (ancient, massive stone structures built by the Egyptians), *bosom* (the chest, conceived of as the center of emotions and intimate feelings). Pair students to define the words, consulting dictionaries as they need to. Remind students to copy the words and their definitions into their vocabulary logs or journals.

Word Study: Contractions The poet Langston Hughes uses the contractions *I'll, nobody'll, they'll* and *I've* in the poems. Ask students what words form these contractions and why the poet may have chosen to use this form. (*I will, nobody will, they will, I have. Contractions are more informal, intimate, and conversational; they fit because the speaker tells of personal, deeply felt emotions.*)

Setting a Purpose for Reading Suggest that students read the poems to understand how each speaker views himself.

During Reading

Analyzing Diction Remind students that **diction** is a writer's choice of words. Diction helps establish the tone and mood of a poem. **Have a volunteer read aloud "I, Too."** Ask students to notice the kind of words Hughes uses and what those words describe. (*The words are simple and short and describe the most basic of human activities—eating. The tone created by the words is one of dignity.*) Ask students to analyze the diction in "The Negro Speaks of Rivers." Have them cite examples of the poet's diction and the mood created by the poet's choice of words. (*The example "rivers . . . older than the flow of blood in human veins" conveys a mood of timelessness.*)

Identifying the Speaker Have students silently read **"The Negro Speaks of Rivers."** Model the process of analyzing the text to understand who the speaker is.

> ***Modeling*** The title suggests that the "I" in this poem is probably an African American. In the second line, the speaker's saying that he has "known rivers ancient as the world" suggests one who has traveled widely and has a grasp of history. Lines 4 and 6 tell of bathing in the Euphrates and building the pyramids in ancient times, however, so I know that the speaker cannot be an ordinary person. No one lives for centuries. The speaker must be a voice for a group. The poet's use of the word "Negro" in the title supports this interpretation. The speaker recounts the scenes viewed by African and African American people through time. By using this technique, the poet offers a historical perspective of the past and the roots of African American people.

p. 84

Invite students to compare their analysis of the speaker with yours. Then call on a volunteer to model an analysis of the speaker in "I, Too." Have students complete Interacting with Text **Analyzing the Speaker,** student workbook page 84.

After Reading

You may also use the selection questions and activities in *Glencoe Literature*.

Summarizing After students have read "I, Too," have volunteers **summarize**—restate in other words—the main ideas expressed by the speaker. (*The speaker, a proud African American man, is forced to eat in the kitchen when company comes. Nevertheless, he maintains his sense of humor and vows that in the future he will "eat at the table"—participate on an equal basis with others—because he too is an American. People will see his beauty and feel ashamed of their past attitudes.*)

Synthesizing Remind students that, when they **synthesize** information, they view in new ways ideas that they have read about. Ask why Hughes may have decided to write "I, Too" in response to Whitman's "I Hear America Singing." (*In "I Hear America Singing," Whitman celebrates the roles Americans play and portrays a robust American life. African Americans, however, have not been allowed to act in these roles.*) Ask what may have motivated the speaker to use the word *too* in the title. (*The speaker points out the value of his own experiences as an American—one who has been forgotten and treated dishonorably.*)

Reviewing and Analyzing Ask the following questions to help students review and analyze the poems.

1. What words suggest that the speaker in "I, Too" feels anger toward his "family" of Americans? (*"Nobody'll dare / Say to me, / 'Eat in the kitchen.'"*)
2. What words suggest that the speaker in "I, Too" is proud of his race? (*"how beautiful I am"*)
3. In "The Negro Speaks of Rivers," why do you think the speaker mentions "the flow of human blood in human veins" when talking about ancient rivers? (*Possible response: The phrase suggests the bond of human beings with nature—blood flows like rivers. Some readers may identify the rivers with human history.*)

OBJECTIVES

- To use the reading strategies of questioning and clarifying in monitoring comprehension; to analyze connotations

FROM

Songs for Signare

Léopold Sédar Senghor

Translated by John Reed and Clive Wake

Before Reading

Activating Prior Knowledge Explain that the poem students will read, from *Songs for Signare*, describes African furnishings that the speaker has carefully chosen. Ask students to think about significant objects in their homes that remind them of who they are. Ask students to imagine their future homes and to identify the objects with which they want to surround themselves. Invite students to tell what they will include and why.

Building Vocabulary On the board, write the following words, without definitions: *steeped* (saturated, immersed), *somber* (dark), *serene* (calm), *hereditary* (ancestral), *leisure* (repose), *antiphonal* (sung responsively), *obsessive* (excessive). Then present each word in a sentence that is rich in context clues and have students suggest the word's meaning. As they read, students can check their definitions for sense against the poem's context.

During Reading

Questioning and Clarifying Remind students that **questioning** (asking themselves questions during reading) and **clarifying** (rereading, reading slowly, or reading on) can help them understand a poem. Place students in small groups and assign a leader to each group. **The leader is to read aloud each three lines in the poem,** stopping to ask the group questions about content and meaning. For example, read aloud the first two lines of the poem and ask: *Whom is the speaker talking to? What is the "presence of Africa"?* Point out that the speaker mentions furniture in the second line, so "presence of Africa" may refer to objects made in Africa or those that represent beliefs and customs of Africa.

After Reading

You may also use the selection questions and activities in *Glencoe Literature.*

Interactive Reading Workbook
p. 85

Inferring Meaning from Connotations Explain that poets choose words carefully, both for their meanings and their associations. The feelings that readers associate with a word affect how they react to what they have read. Point out that the word *steeped* in line 1 could be replaced by *soaked* and convey the same literal meaning. However, the word *steeped* suggests saturation, something that penetrates over a period of time. The connotations of the word *steeped* add to the reader's understanding and also enhance the reader's emotional response to the line. Then have students complete **Interacting with Text** **Analyzing Connotations,** student workbook page 85.

OBJECTIVES

- To analyze sensory language; to analyze speaker's viewpoint

Sonnet to a Negro in Harlem

Helene Johnson

Before Reading

Activating Prior Knowledge Tell students that the poem they will read, "Sonnet to a Negro in Harlem," describes someone who stands out in a crowd. Invite students to recall someone they have observed who attracted their admiration. What traits made the person magnetic? As they read, students can note the qualities of the person described and can consider whether they would respond to such a person in the same way as the poem's speaker does.

Building Vocabulary On the board, write the following words and definitions: *incompetent* (incapable), *imitate* (to copy), *despise* (to detest), *barbaric* (fierce, uncivilized), *arrogant* (egotistical). Ask students what feelings the words evoke. Then have volunteers use each word in a sentence that conveys its meaning. Have students write the words and definitions in their vocabulary logs or journals.

During Reading

Analyzing Sensory Language **Instruct students to read the poem silently.** Remind them that poets often use sensory details to evoke the sight, sound, smell, taste, and feel of a subject. **Then have students reread the poem,** picking out details that appeal to the senses. List these details on the board. Have students arrange the words in categories according to the sense they appeal to. (*sight: "perfect body," "pompous gait," "dark eyes flashing," "shoulders towering high above the throng"; sight and hearing: "head thrown back in rich, barbaric song"; hearing: "laughter arrogant and bold"*) Guide students in summarizing aspects of the physique and attitude of the person who is described by these words. (*The person is beautiful, tall, and slow moving, unlike the fast-moving crowd; he or she has a fearless, haughty, defiant attitude.*)

After Reading

You may also use the selection questions and activities in *Glencoe Literature.*

Analyzing Speaker's Viewpoint Have students review the poem to note paired adjectives. Tell students that these adjectives give clues to the speaker's viewpoint. Model the analysis of adjectives in the first line of the poem.

> ***Modeling*** I see that the speaker calls someone both "disdainful" and "magnificent." The first adjective describes a quality that has negative connotations, and the second one describes a quality that has positive connotations. The contrast is intriguing and suggests to me that the speaker has mixed feelings about the subject.

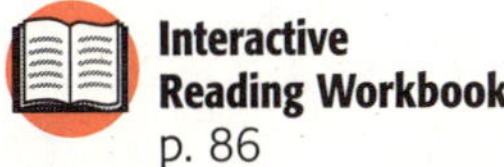

Then have students complete Interacting with Text **Analyzing Speaker's Viewpoint,** student workbook page 86. After they complete the page, have students explain what they think the poem means.

OBJECTIVES

- To paraphrase a poem; to identify the effects of caesura; to evaluate a poem

Storm Ending and *November Cotton Flower*

Jean Toomer

Before Reading

Building Background Review with students "Meet Jean Toomer" and the Building Background note in *Glencoe Literature*. Explain that in the 1920s many African Americans in the South were sharecroppers, people who worked the land in return for a small percentage of the crop. Ask students how the destruction of the cotton crop might affect the everyday lives of sharecroppers. (*The sharecroppers might not have money for necessities; they might not be able to buy seed for the next year's crops; they might be forced to find other jobs.*)

Activating Prior Knowledge Tell students that in "Storm Ending" the speaker vividly describes a storm. Build three word webs on the board, placing one of the following words in the center of each: *thunder, lightning, storm clouds*. Then use questions such as the following to prompt discussion about stormy skies: *To what would you compare storm clouds?* (Possible responses: billowing smoke, angry dark waves.) *Lightning?* (Possible responses: fireworks, neon lights.) *Thunder?* (Possible responses: cannon fire, sounds of a building demolition.) As students suggest words or phrases, place them in the correct web.

Building Vocabulary On the board, write the following words, without definitions: *clappers* (metal ringers in bells), *boll weevil* (an insect that feeds on cotton plants), *pinched* (cut back), *startled* (surprised), *assumed* (took on), *significance* (importance), *trace* (a tiny amount). Have volunteers define familiar words. Provide the definitions in parentheses and have students use the words in sentences to confirm that they have understood the meaning of each. Point out that *pinched*, *assumed*, and *trace* have multiple meanings; therefore, students should rely on context clues to infer which meaning is intended in each case.

Word Study: Synonyms The poems contain **synonyms,** or words that have similar meanings (*hollow/bell-like*, *bleeding/dripping*, *branch/stream*). Ask students how using more than one word to describe an idea helps the reader visualize images evoked by the details in a poem. (*Detailed, vivid descriptions can often create specific, defined images in the reader's mind.*)

Setting a Purpose for Reading Have students read the poems to help them appreciate the poet's use of language.

During Reading

Visualizing Tell students that **visualizing** is a helpful tool to use when reading or listening to a poem. **Have students close their eyes as you read "Storm Ending" aloud.** Tell students to let the words you read help them to create pictures in their minds. After you read, ask students these questions: *What does the speaker compare a storm to?* (flowers) *How are thunder and clouds like flowers?* (Possible responses: The thunder is a deep, full, and satisfying sound that could be compared to the depth of color and the roundness of flowers. The clouds might form shapes that resemble flowers. Each is unique and continuously changing) *What kind of flowers did you picture as you read? What words in the poem helped to form that picture?*

Paraphrasing Remind students that paraphrasing parts of a poem as they read can help them understand the writer's message more easily. **Call on a volunteer to read aloud the first eight lines of "November Cotton Flower."** Invite students to paraphrase this part of the poem. (*Boll weevils will soon arrive, and frost has damaged the cotton plants, making cotton scarce. The streams have dried up, the water level in wells is low, and birds have died because of the drought.*) **Ask another student to read the last six lines and then to paraphrase them.** (*A cotton plant blossoms in these hostile conditions, startling people but giving them hope. If nature can recover from this attack, so can they survive hostile conditions.*)

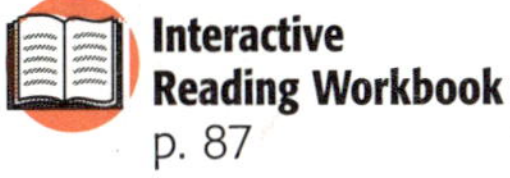
Interactive Reading Workbook
p. 87

Understanding Caesura Explain that **caesura** is a pause between lines or within a line of poetry. It can vary the rhythm in a poem and calls attention to the place where the pause occurs, often signaling a sudden change in thought. **Read aloud the first five lines of "November Cotton Flower"** and have students locate the caesura in line 4. Then have students comment on the effect of this pause. (*It breaks up the flow of the line and calls attention to the vanishing of the cotton.*) Then have students complete Interacting with Text **Analyzing Caesura,** student workbook page 87.

After Reading

You may also use the selection questions and activities in *Glencoe Literature.*

Evaluating Tell students that, when they judge an author's work, they are **evaluating** it. Ask students to select the Toomer poem they enjoyed more and to judge the poet's skill in recreating the scene. List the following criteria on the board and suggest that students consider each item as they evaluate the poem's effectiveness. Students might rank the poem as superior, good, or average, in each category.

- Uses original and striking imagery
- Involves the senses vividly
- Handles language skillfully and naturally
- Makes full use of the sound values of words
- Uses figurative language in ways that enrich meaning
- Focuses on themes that are meaningful to me

Have students find an example of each element in the poem of their choice.

OBJECTIVES

- To identify images and infer meaning; to analyze figurative language; to compare and contrast two poems

A black man talks of reaping

Arna Bontemps

Any Human to Another

Countee Cullen

Before Reading

Previewing the Selections Have students read the title of the poem by Arna Bontemps and the title of the poem by Countee Cullen in *Glencoe Literature*. Then ask students to look at the artwork and read the caption that accompanies each poem. Ask students to anticipate the subject matter of each poem. To encourage students to suggest likely topics for "A black man talks of reaping," ask questions such as the following: *What is a sharecropper?* (a farm worker who does not own the land he or she works) *What kind of labor are the people in the picture doing?* (hoeing)

Next, draw attention to "Any Human to Another." Ask: *What does the image show?* (different-colored hands grasping each other) *Why are the hands different colors?* (to represent different races) *What does the title "Any Human to Another" suggest in contrast to the title "A Black Man Talks of Reaping"?* ("Any Human to Another" suggests a common human experience; "A Black Man Talks of Reaping" suggests the viewpoint of one person.)

Building Vocabulary On the board, write the following terms and definitions: *reaping* (harvesting, gathering), *sown* (planted), *stark* (desolate, grim), *yields* (produces). Ask students what kind of life and land the terms refer to. (*farming life, poor land*) Then add the following terms and definitions: *marrow* (the center part of the bone, producing blood cells; essence), *intertwine* (weave or twist together), *mingle* (join), *diverse* (varied), *wreathed* (formed in a circle like a wreath). Ask students to copy the terms and definitions in their vocabulary logs or journals and to write a sentence using each word according to the meaning given. Have students share their sentences in class.

Word Study: Synonyms and Antonyms In "Any Human to Another," the poet uses a number of words that have similar meanings (*intertwine/fused/mingle; sorrow/grief; alone/single*) and words with opposite meanings (*sun/shadow; joy/sorrow; false/true*). Discuss why the poet may have made these word choices. (*to enable the reader to create specific mental images; to emphasize the contrasts within the poem*)

Setting a Purpose for Reading Point out to students that both titles imply communication between human beings. Invite students to find out the message of each speaker.

During Reading

Identifying Imagery Remind students that writers often create "word pictures" through descriptive language. **Call on a volunteer to read aloud "A Black Man Talks of Reaping."** Tell students to pay particular attention to the pictures the poet's words create. After each stanza, have students tell about the emotions or work that the poet describes. Invite students to point out images that stand out to them.

Analyzing Figurative Language Remind students that poets use figures of speech as tools to help them imply additional meaning. **Read aloud the first stanza of "Any Human to Another."** Then model the process of analyzing the simile in the stanza.

> ***Modeling*** In the first stanza, the speaker talks about "ills" that have pierced him "like an arrow." The word "like" indicates that this description is a simile. The phrase "Ills I sorrow at" possibly symbolizes the ills of society. In the simile, the hurt these ills cause the speaker is compared to the hurt caused by the piercing of an arrow. Considering the simile helps me picture how painful the ills of society are for the speaker.

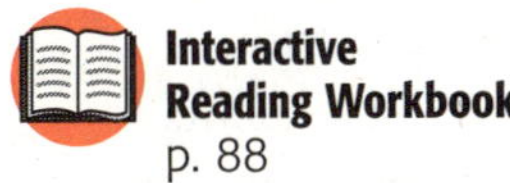
Interactive Reading Workbook p. 88

Have students read silently the rest of "Any Human to Another." Then have students complete Interacting with Text **Analyzing Figurative Language,** student workbook page 88.

After Reading

You may also use the selection questions and activities in *Glencoe Literature*.

See graphic organizers, Part 1, Venn Diagram p. T31

Comparing and Contrasting Remind students that **comparing** is telling how things are alike. **Contrasting** is telling how things are different. Point out that a Venn diagram is a good tool to use for comparing and contrasting. Create a transparency of a Venn diagram and display it on the overhead projector. Write "A Black Man Talks of Reaping" at the top of one circle of the diagram and "Any Human to Another" at the top of the other. Then show students how to complete the diagram. Write an example of a similarity in the intersection of the circles and an example of a difference in the appropriate circle. (*Similarities: both have rhyme, vivid images, figurative language, and a dignified tone. Differences: "A Black Man Talks of Reaping" has structured, traditional stanzas and meter and a consistent rhyme scheme; it addresses the experience of African Americans in the United States. "Any Human to Another" has varying stanza length and meter and more formal syntax; it speaks to all people in all times about their common experience.*)

Focusing on Theme Have students read the "Literary Purposes" note in Building Background of *Glencoe Literature*. Review with students that the writers of this literary movement and era often disagreed about topics for their works and purposes for their writing. Have groups of students review the poems by Bontemps and Cullen, comparing their differing views. (*Bontemps expresses bitterness about the unfair treatment of his people; Cullen records the common human experience that binds all people, regardless of race.*)

OBJECTIVES

- To make inferences; to identify sequence of events; to appreciate humor

The Second Tree from the Corner

E. B. White

Before Reading

Activating Prior Knowledge Explain to students that "The Second Tree from the Corner" is about a man who struggles to overcome depression and anxiety. Ask students to recall a time when their spirits were low or they felt fearful about something. How did their outlook affect their ability to enjoy the world around them?

Building Vocabulary On the board, write the following words, without their definitions, in one column: *corridor* (narrow passage), *conscientious* (painstaking, meticulous), *maneuvering* (scheming), *asylum* (care center for the mentally ill), *resignation* (acceptance), *neurotic* (irrational, disturbed). Write the definitions in random order in a second column. Ask students to use in sentences words that they know and then to match each word with its definition. Encourage students to consult a dictionary to look up the meanings of words that they do not know. Ask students to record the words and definitions in their vocabulary logs or journals.

Word Study: Base Word and Affixes Remind students that dividing a word into parts—prefix, base word, and suffix—can help them to discover its meaning. Identifying each of these parts and combining the separate meanings can help them to determine the meaning of the unknown word. Create a transparency of the Three-Column Chart graphic organizer and display it on the overhead projector. In the first column, list *inexpressible*, *uncertainly*, *unattainable*. Have students identify the base words and affixes and write each in the second column. Review the meanings of the prefixes *un-*/*in-* ("not") and the suffixes *-able*/*-ible* ("able," "capable of") and *-ly* ("in like manner or nature"). Explain the meanings of the base word and each affix to define the word *inexpressible*. Tell students that *in-* means "not" and *-ible* means "able" or "capable of." *Express* means "to put into words" or "to say or tell." When these meanings are combined, they define *inexpressible*, "not capable of being said." Write the meaning of the word in the third column of the chart. Have students determine the meanings of the other words listed.

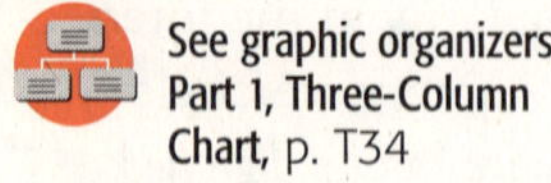

See graphic organizers, Part 1, Three-Column Chart, p. T34

Word	Prefix + Base Word + Suffix	Definition
inexpressible	in + express + ible	not able to be said
uncertainly	un + certain + ly	not in a certain manner
unattainable	un + attain + able	not able to have or achieve

Setting a Purpose for Reading Have students read the story to find out whether the main character overcomes his depression and feelings of anxiety—and if so, how.

During Reading

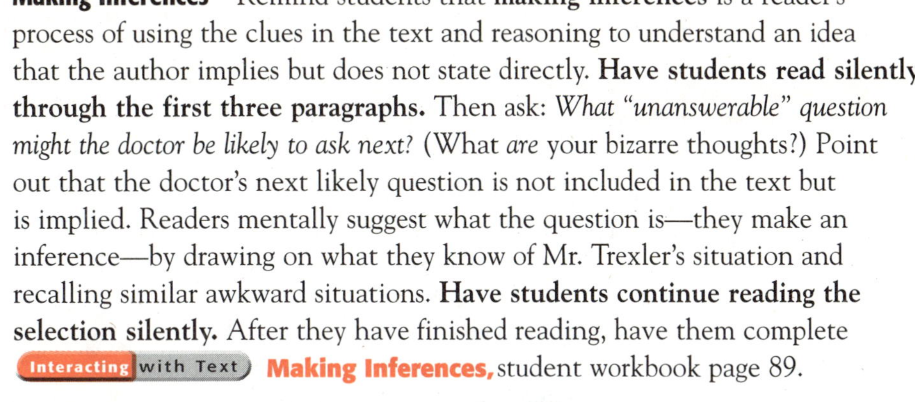

Making Inferences Remind students that **making inferences** is a reader's process of using the clues in the text and reasoning to understand an idea that the author implies but does not state directly. **Have students read silently through the first three paragraphs.** Then ask: *What "unanswerable" question might the doctor be likely to ask next?* (What *are* your bizarre thoughts?) Point out that the doctor's next likely question is not included in the text but is implied. Readers mentally suggest what the question is—they make an inference—by drawing on what they know of Mr. Trexler's situation and recalling similar awkward situations. **Have students continue reading the selection silently.** After they have finished reading, have them complete Interacting with Text **Making Inferences,** student workbook page 89.

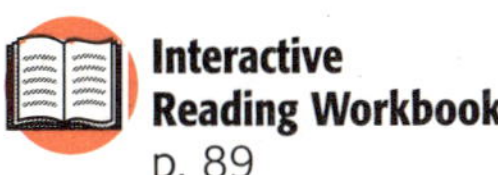

Interactive Reading Workbook
p. 89

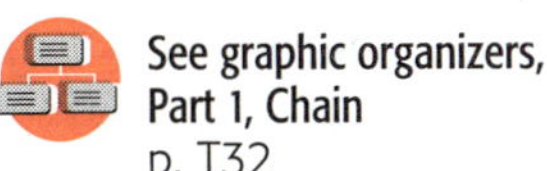

See graphic organizers, Part 1, Chain p. T32

Identifying Sequence of Events Explain that identifying the sequence of events helps readers to understand and remember a story. Create a transparency of the Chain graphic organizer and display it on the overhead projector. Distribute copies of the Chain graphic organizer. Work with students to complete the Chain graphic organizer as you model the process of listing the order of events.

> ***Modeling*** As I read the story, I noticed these important events: First, Mr. Trexler goes to a psychiatrist for help with his fears, anxieties, and troubling thoughts. I'll write *Mr. Trexler sees a psychiatrist* in the first box. Second, I see that, in subsequent weeks, he settles into a routine with the doctor. He even begins to change places mentally with the doctor and to see his own fears in the doctor. In the second box, I'll write *Settles into routine. Mentally changes places with doctor*. I read that, on the fifth visit, the doctor asks Trexler what Trexler wants. Trexler asks the doctor the same question. The doctor's answer does not satisfy Trexler. In the third box, I'll write *Trexler doesn't know what he wants; doctor does–doctor wants material things*. Then I read that Trexler, as he walks home, discovers that he knows what he wants, although he cannot put it into words. In the last box, I'll write *Trexler learns about himself.*

After Reading

You may also use the selection questions and activities in *Glencoe Literature*.

Appreciating Humor Explain that humorous details prevent this story from being overwhelming or sad. Ask students to read aloud parts of the story that they found amusing. (*Possible responses: Descriptions such as the ones that compare the doctor to a lizard and Trexler to a bug or Trexler's thought process to a darting hummingbird lighten the mood. Students may also point out the way Trexler knocks "the ashes out of his brain" as the doctor empties his pipe and Trexler's amusing turns of phrase: "can't stay on life's little bucky horse" and "Scared as a rabbit . . . Look at him scoot!"*)

OBJECTIVES

- To analyze imagery; to visualize; to interpret

Ode to My Socks

Pablo Neruda

Translated by Robert Bly

Before Reading

Activating Prior Knowledge Ask students to think of an everyday object that they own that has great personal meaning. Some students may wish to identify objects to which they attach personal value and to explain why the objects are meaningful. Then tell students that the speaker in "Ode to My Socks" finds something extraordinary about a pair of socks he receives as a gift. As students read, invite them to compare their feelings about special objects with the speaker's feelings about his socks.

Building Vocabulary On the board, write the following words, without definitions: *ode* (a lyric poem of praise), *immense* (huge), *decrepit* (wasted, weakened), *temptation* (something that entices one to do wrong), *learned* (educated, cultured), *sacred* (holy), *remorse* (regret for wrongdoing). Invite volunteers to define words that they already know. Explain meanings where necessary. Encourage students to record each word and its meaning in their vocabulary logs or journals.

During Reading

See graphic organizers, Part 1, Web p. T27

Interactive Reading Workbook p. 90

Analyzing Imagery **Have a volunteer read the poem aloud.** Remind students that **analyzing** is thinking critically about what they have read. Often breaking a concept into smaller parts helps the reader to understand the whole better. Create a web transparency and display it on the overhead projector. Write *socks* in the center circle. Have students suggest words from the poem that the poet uses to describe the socks and record these in the outer circles of the web. ("*soft as rabbits*," "*threads of twilight and sheepskin*," "*violent*," "*sharks*," "*immense blackbirds*," "*cannons*," "*heavenly*," "*handsome*") Now have students complete **Interacting with Text** **Analyzing**, student workbook page 90.

After Reading

You may also use the selection questions and activities in *Glencoe Literature*.

Visualizing and Interpreting Tell students that **visualizing** is using the details in a selection to help one mentally picture what is being described; **interpreting** is using one's own knowledge and experiences to attach meaning to what has been read. Point out that interpreting is a personal process. **Ask a volunteer to read aloud lines 17–26 of the poem.** Ask students to identify each image that applies to the socks and to describe what they picture. Then have them explain how they interpret the meaning of the imagery.

Reviewing **Ask students to reread the poem** and to decide why the speaker wears the socks instead of saving them. Guide students by asking them what happens to fireflies that are kept in a jar. (*The fireflies lose what makes them beautiful, and they eventually die.*)

OBJECTIVES

- To analyze descriptive details; to analyze characterization

Breakfast

John Steinbeck

Before Reading

Building Background Ask students what they know about John Steinbeck. Invite them to identify works by Steinbeck and to share their impressions of the works that they have read. Then have students read "Meet John Steinbeck" and the Building Background notes in *Glencoe Literature*. Point out that this selection was ultimately adapted and included as part of one of the author's most famous novels, *The Grapes of Wrath*, a story about a destitute family that migrates from Oklahoma to California to seek relief from misfortune during the Great Depression. Ask students to discuss anything they know about the Depression and about migrant workers.

Building Vocabulary On the board, write the following words, without definitions: *lavender* (pale purple), *draft* (air current), *interfere with* (prevent), *practiced* (skilled), *frantically* (in a frenzied or disordered way), *scalded* (burned with liquid). Ask students to use each word in a sentence that suggests its meaning. Call on volunteers to state the meanings of the words. Have students verify meanings in a dictionary. Encourage students to record the words, definitions, and sentences in their vocabulary logs or journals.

Word Study: Vivid Verbs Explain that "Breakfast" is filled with colorful, vivid verbs that help readers to visualize the action that is taking place. On the board, write the following sentence: "And it was cold . . . I *rubbed* my hands and *shoved* them deep into my pockets, and I *hunched* my shoulders up and *scuffled* my feet on the ground." Call on a volunteer to point out the verbs in the sentence and to act out the sentence. Explain that the vivid verbs help readers visualize the scene. Suggest that students list sentences with verbs that they find particularly effective as they read the selection.

Setting a Purpose for Reading Have students read the story to find out what the narrator does as he meets a migrant family.

During Reading

Analyzing Descriptive Details Invite students to define *descriptive writing*. If necessary, explain that **descriptive writing** includes details that appeal to the five senses—sight, hearing, smell, taste, and touch. Point out that John Steinbeck uses descriptive writing in "Breakfast" to present the setting and reveal information about the narrator. **Read aloud the first two paragraphs of the selection** and model the process of analyzing descriptive details.

> ***Modeling*** When the narrator says, "This thing fills me with pleasure," at first I don't understand what he is talking about. He calls it a "sunken memory." He replays it in his head. These details make me think that he is recalling an experience that means a lot to him. Next, I read the description of a setting just before dawn. "The eastern mountains were black-blue, . . .

the light stood up faintly colored . . . , growing colder, grayer and darker." The author uses color words that appeal to the sense of sight and words such as "growing colder" that appeal to the sense of touch. These details help me picture and almost experience the setting. Knowing that the narrator replays a memory is important information about him. I'll read on to find out why he does this.

Have students read the rest of the story silently. Afterward, have them reread the description in the paragraph beginning "And it was cold . . . " Ask volunteers to point out the images in the text that make the description vivid. Then have students complete  **Analyzing Description,** student workbook page 91.

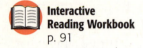

Interactive Reading Workbook p. 91

Analyzing Characterization Remind students that authors reveal a character through that character's thoughts, words, actions, and appearance and through how others react to the character. On the board, draw a five-column chart with the headings *Thoughts*, *Words*, *Appearance*, *Actions*, and *Reactions of Others*. Have students suggest details from the story that help characterize the narrator. In the appropriate columns in the chart, record the details that students suggest. (*Possible responses: thoughts—notices beauty of mountains, is hungry, notices the graceful woman, notices that men are not especially friendly; words—simple, friendly, polite; appearance—is cold, has hands shoved in pockets, has hunched shoulders; actions—stops in tent to see young woman, warms hands, squats to eat with others; reactions of others—receives invitations to eat with men, receives offer of work*) Engage students in a discussion of other characters. Ask what is suggested by the young mother's precise, practiced way of preparing the breakfast and nursing her baby. (*She knows how to take care of her family and does so with skill and grace.*) Have a volunteer generalize about the character of the migrant workers—the two men and the young woman. (*They are hard-working people who know the value of work and food. They are hospitable, caring people who offer to help others and share what little they have.*)

After Reading

You may also use the selection questions and activities in *Glencoe Literature.*

Reviewing and Analyzing Have students answer the following questions.

1. How is the migrant family's food cooked? (*The family cooks on top of an old iron cookstove.*)
2. Why do the migrant workers live in a tent? (*They move often to find agricultural work; they cannot afford a more permanent home.*)
3. Why are the men's new clothes important? (*Their pride in having new clothes suggests that the characters seldom have money to buy clothes; the clothes help convey the family's success.*)
4. The narrator says that there was "some element of great beauty" in his recalled experience. What "element of great beauty" does the narrator detect in the migrant family? (*Possible response: The family's graciousness and gratitude for what they have represent great beauty. The family's behavior is moving; the generosity of the characters contrasts sharply with the poverty and uncertainty of their situation.*)

OBJECTIVES

- To use the reading strategies of questioning, clarifying, summarizing, and predicting; to analyze time order

A Rose for Emily and *Address upon Receiving the Nobel Prize for Literature*

William Faulkner

Before Reading

Building Background Have students read "Meet William Faulkner" and the Building Background notes in *Glencoe Literature*. Point out that Faulkner creates a fictional county based on the region in Mississippi where he was brought up. In this setting, characters behave according to the Southern mores and values with which Faulkner is familiar. Ask students to discuss the role of women early in the twentieth century. Point out that, especially in the South, women were "put on a pedestal"; however, they were dependent on others—most often fathers and husbands—to provide for them.

Building Vocabulary On the board, write the following words, without definitions: *encroached* (invaded), *obliterated* (wiped out), *vanquished* (defeated), *teeming* (busy, active), *diffident* (timid), *idol* (symbol of an object of worship), *materialized* (taken shape), *earthiness* (commonness, lack of refinement), *remitted* (canceled, set aside), *contemporary* (person of the same age), *inextricable* (incapable of being disentangled). Use each word in a sentence and invite students to suggest its meaning. Have students check their definitions in the dictionary before adding the words and definitions to their vocabulary logs or journals.

Word Study: Suffixes On the board, write the word *deprecation*. Explain to students that a **suffix** is a word part that is added at the end of a base word or word root. Tell students the meaning of the suffix *–ion* or *–tion*. (*action or process of; state or condition of being; or result of*). On the board, have a volunteer erase the suffix and write the base word, restoring the final *e*. Tell students that *deprecate* means "to express disapproval of." Then ask them what *deprecation* means. (*the process of expressing disapproval*) Lead students to understand that, when they know the meaning of a base word, they can usually determine the meaning of the word after a suffix is added.

Setting a Purpose for Reading Have students read to discover Miss Emily's secrets.

During Reading

Using Reading Strategies Review with students the strategies of questioning, clarifying, summarizing, and predicting. Explain that using these strategies can help them to check their understanding of what they read. **Then read aloud the first paragraph of the story** and model the process of applying the reading strategies.

Modeling As I read, I **question** why Miss Emily's house is so neglected and shabby, an "eyesore." After all, she was important enough for the whole town to turn out at her funeral, and her name will have a place of honor in the cemetery. I also question why no one has seen the inside of her house in years. To **clarify**, I reread and note that the whole neighborhood has become industrial and that her home is the only remaining residence. Perhaps she couldn't afford to move, as other people had. This seems like a good time to **summarize** what I've read so far: Miss Emily, an institution from the town's upper-class society, has died, and the whole town attends her funeral. From the description so far, I **predict** that the story will be about misfortunes and setbacks that befall Miss Emily.

Tell students that **they will read and discuss the story in groups of five.** Designate a leader for each group. Review with students the role of the leader and that of the group. (See Part 1, page T3.) Explain to students that they should designate, within their groups, a stopping point for reading. **Students will read silently** to that point and then discuss the segment they have just read, following the procedure of questioning, clarifying, summarizing, and predicting. Circulate in the room as student discussions are taking place to guide the groups' efforts. Have students read the entire selection. **Then have students read "Address upon Receiving the Nobel Prize for Literature"** silently and follow the same process.

Understanding Time Order Tell students that understanding the order of events can help them to understand a story. Ask students to define **chronological order**. (*events in a story arranged according to the logical forward progression of time*) Ask whether Faulkner uses chronological order in "A Rose for Emily." (*No.*) To establish the time order of the story, have students reread section 1. Establish when the story begins. (*at Miss Emily's funeral*) Help students organize when other key events in section 1 occur. Have students designate these events as occurring in the present, recent past, or distant past. (*present—Miss Emily's funeral; distant past—Colonel Sartoris's remitting of taxes; recent past—visits of city delegation*) Explain that when the chronological order of events in a story is interrupted to show an event that took place earlier, the interruption is called a **flashback.** The interrupting event "flashes back" to a previous time.

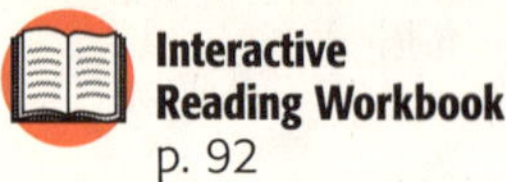

Encourage students to notice how time order changes in each section of the story. Have students complete Interacting with Text **Establishing Time Order,** student workbook page 92.

After Reading

You may also use the selection questions and activities in *Glencoe Literature.*

Analyzing Theme Ask students to consider the events of "A Rose for Emily." Have students summarize in a sentence or two the gist of the story. (*Emily is limited and restricted by the conventions of society; finally, she uses her own methods to hold onto the one she loves.*) Then have them suggest what overall idea or message the story communicates. Ask students to explain their choice of theme. (*Possible theme: People will struggle toward happiness and love, no matter the limitations or setbacks.*)

OBJECTIVE

- To make inferences based on details and images in a poem

Father's Bedroom

Robert Lowell

Before Reading

Building Background Review with students "Meet Robert Lowell" and the Building Background notes in *Glencoe Literature*. Point out that Robert Lowell came from an accomplished family. Ask how being in a family of high achievers might affect a family member. (*Having an accomplished family would probably create high expectations for all family members.*) As students read the poem, have them look for details that might suggest the father's personality and the son's feelings about his father.

Building Vocabulary On the board, write the following words, without definitions: *plush* (velvety), *broad-planked* (made from wide, thick, heavy boards), *warped* (twisted out of shape), *olive* (drab yellowish green). Read the following sentences aloud. Have students choose a word to complete each one. Verify definitions with a dictionary. Encourage students to record the words, definitions, and sentences in their vocabulary logs or journals.

- The box slanted oddly because it had been ________ by rain. *warped*
- Covered with a ________ material, the pillow felt irresistibly soft. *plush*
- Our footsteps echoed hollowly on the ________ wood floor. *broad-planked*
- The soldiers' camouflage fatigues were dirt brown and ________. *olive*

During Reading

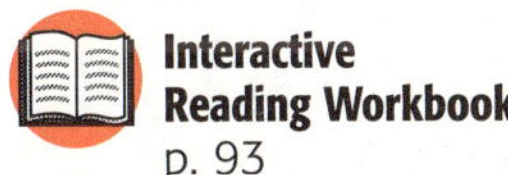

Interactive Reading Workbook p. 93

Making Inferences **Have students read the poem silently. Then ask a volunteer to read the poem aloud.** Encourage students to pay close attention to images and details in the poem to recognize what these convey about the father's character. Remind students that **making inferences** is making reasoned guesses about events or characters in a literary work. Point out the first three lines of the poem. Explain that the bedspread has blue lines of thread that are so thin they remind the speaker of a line of ink. Lines suggest straightness and regularity. Ask students what they can infer that the thin lines might suggest about the father. (*Thin lines may suggest rigidity and preciseness.*) Then have students complete Interacting with Text **Making Inferences,** student workbook page 93.

After Reading

You may also use the selection questions and activities in *Glencoe Literature*.

Analyzing Connotations Remind students that **connotations** are the emotions and values associated with words. Words have literal dictionary definitions, or **denotations.** Many words also have connotations. Ask students to define and then to identify the connotations of the following words: *thin, blue, warped, punished.* Then have them reread the poem and explain what the words add to the portrait of the father. (thin—*weakness, inadequacy*; blue—*coldness, sadness*; warped—*deformity, mental instability*; punished—*anger, hurt*)

OBJECTIVES

- To identify cause-and-effect relationships; to analyze dialogue

FROM

Black Boy

Richard Wright

Before Reading

Building Background Have students read "Meet Richard Wright" and the Building Background notes in *Glencoe Literature*. Point out that this selection is part of Richard Wright's autobiography. Ask students to define *autobiography*. (*An* ***autobiography*** *is the true story of a person's life, written by that person.*) Explain that this selection presents Wright, poor and hungry, at about six years of age. Ask students what point of view they expect to find in an autobiography. (*An autobiography is told from the first-person point of view.*) Have students share how they might react to hearing the true story, in the first person, of a child's hunger and poverty.

Building Vocabulary On the board, write the following words, without definitions: *jauntily* (in a dashing, cheerful manner), *acute* (intense), *spurned* (ignored), *gaunt* (thin), *intervals* (brief periods), *impressionable* (easily influenced), *eluded* (escaped), *elapse* (pass), *indestructible* (permanent, not possible to destroy), *destinies* (fates). Assign one or two of the words to pairs of students. Ask partners to locate the words in context and to suggest the meaning of each word. Add students' correct definitions to the board. Encourage students to write the words and definitions in their vocabulary logs or journals.

Word Study: Adverbs Explain that an **adverb** is a word that modifies a verb, an adjective, or another adverb. When modifying a verb, an adverb expresses when, where, or how the action of a sentence takes place. Write the following words on the board: *angrily, finally, continuously*. Ask students what these words have in common. (*They end in -*ly.) Tell students that most adverbs end in *-ly*. As students read, have them identify at least three adverbs that end in *-ly*. (Examples: *rapidly, correctly, sharply, completely*.)

Setting a Purpose for Reading Have students read to learn about Wright's experiences as a young boy.

During Reading

Analyzing Dialogue **Have students read the selection silently.** When students have finished reading, ask them to define *dialogue*. If necessary, explain that **dialogue** is the spoken words of characters. Tell students that authors use dialogue to help reveal the personality of characters in a story or an autobiographical selection. Have students reread from the paragraph that begins "'Step up close to the desk' . . . " up to the paragraph that begins "I began to cry. . . . " Ask them to describe the way Miss Simon communicates with Wright. (*She barks out commands and speaks more and more sharply to Wright as she becomes frustrated by his failure to obey.*) Guide students in assessing Miss Simon's words, discerning what they reveal about her personality.

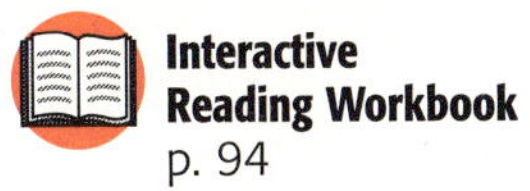

Interactive Reading Workbook p. 94

(*She is abrupt, unsympathetic, and authoritarian.*) Then have students complete Interacting with Text **Analyzing Dialogue,** student workbook page 94.

See graphic organizers, Part 1, Cause-and-Effect Chart, p. T29

Identifying Cause-and-Effect Relationships Tell students that many incidents in this selection are linked by cause-and-effect relationships. Explain that when one action or event causes another action or event to take place, the first action or event is the cause of the second action or event. The first action or event can be labeled *cause* and the second *effect*. Create a cause-and-effect chart transparency such as the one that follows and display it on the overhead projector. In the "cause" column, write the following: "Because Wright's mother could not provide for her children . . ." Then have a volunteer suggest the effect. (*The boys are put in an orphan home.*) List additional causes, such as the following, and have students identify their effects.

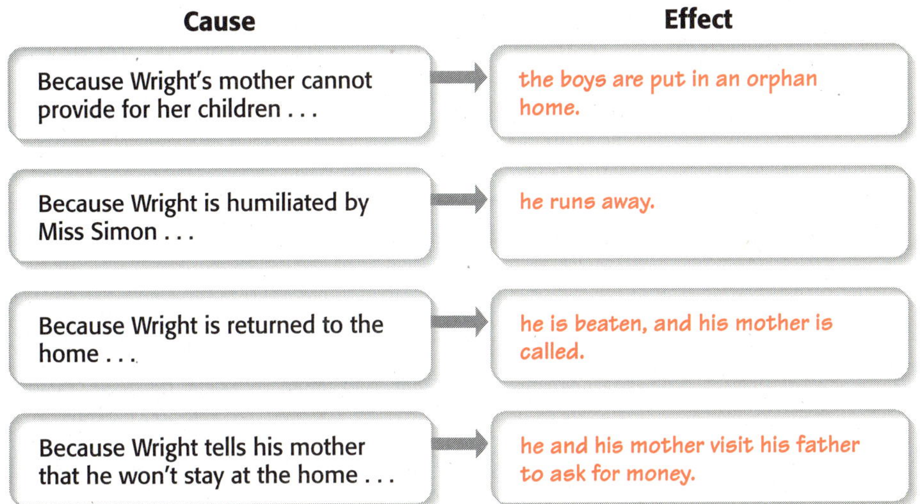

Cause
Effect
Because Wright's mother cannot provide for her children . . .
the boys are put in an orphan home.
Because Wright is humiliated by Miss Simon . . .
he runs away.
Because Wright is returned to the home . . .
he is beaten, and his mother is called.
Because Wright tells his mother that he won't stay at the home . . .
he and his mother visit his father to ask for money.

After Reading

You may also use the selection questions and activities in *Glencoe Literature*.

Responding Explain to students that their spontaneous thoughts and feelings during reading show their personal responses. Ask students to identify the passages of the selection that they found most moving. Have them record in their journals the passages that stirred them, explaining how they reacted and why.

Reviewing and Analyzing Help students review and analyze the selection by discussing together the following questions.

1. Why does the meeting with his father and the "strange woman" make Wright hate his father? (*Wright's father laughs at his mother's anguish and shows that he does not care about his children's hunger or regret abandoning them. The strange woman's superficial interest and indifference about the harm she has caused enrages the boy.*)
2. Seeing his father twenty-five years later, Wright is able to pity and forgive him. What phrases tell you that Wright sees his father as an incomplete person? (*Possible responses: "his soul was imprisoned," "how chained were his actions and emotions to the direct, animalistic impulses," "as a creature of the earth."*)

OBJECTIVES

- To visualize; to analyze figurative language; to analyze symbolism

A Worn Path

Eudora Welty

Before Reading

Building Background Have students read "Meet Eudora Welty" and the Building Background notes in *Glencoe Literature*. Point out that the Natchez Trace was a compelling road for Eudora Welty, although it was not used as a major thoroughfare in her lifetime. Explain that the Natchez Trace provides the setting and the atmosphere for much of Welty's fiction. Welty ascribes to it a timeless, mythic atmosphere that lends the characters walking along it a universal quality. Have students preview the photographs and illustrations that accompany the story. Invite students to speculate—on the basis of the title, the photographs, and the background information—about the kind of life the woman in the story has. Ask: *What do you think the setting looks like? How old do you think the woman in the story is? Why do you think so? Do you think her life is difficult or easy? Why do you think so?*

Building Vocabulary On the board, write the following words, without definitions: *pendulum* (free-swinging body suspended from a fixed point), *persistent* (continuing), *meditative* (thoughtful, contemplative), *solitary* (lone), *live-oaks* (durable evergreen oaks planted for shade and shelter), *lolling* (drooping), *springy* (bouncy), *bob-whites* (quail), *inclined* (bowed), *obstinate* (stubborn). Assign a word to each student. Have each student find its definition and then use the word in a sentence that gives clues to the meaning. After classmates guess the meaning, have the student supply the actual definition. Encourage students to write the words, definitions, and example sentences in their vocabulary logs or journals.

Word Study: *ph* for /f/ Tell students that the name of the main character is Phoenix Jackson. Write *Phoenix* on the board and point out that *ph* makes the sound of /f/. Have students suggest other words that contain *ph*. Record on the board the words students suggest and discuss the spelling of those words. Then have students take out a piece of paper. Dictate the following words and have students record them: *pharmacy*, *photography*, *phase*, *paragraph*, *phobia*, *philosophy*, *apostrophe*, *phantom*, *phony*, *physical*. Review together the correct spellings of the words.

Setting a Purpose for Reading Have students read to find out how the woman in the story manages the challenges of a journey.

During Reading

Visualizing As students read, remind them to **visualize,** or form mental pictures, as the author's descriptions prompt. Explain that imagining the sound, sight, smell, taste, and touch experiences presented in a scene will make the scene come alive and will also make it easier to comprehend and recall. **Call on a volunteer to read aloud the first two paragraphs of the story**. On the basis of the description in the paragraphs, have students visualize Jackson and imagine what she is doing. (*She is a tiny, old African American woman, plainly and poorly dressed, who walks with the aid of a home-made cane. She is walking in a rural, forested area.*) **Have students continue reading the story silently.** Encourage them to visualize as they read.

Analyzing Figurative Language Remind students that **figurative-language** expressions are not literally true but express some truth and are used for descriptive effect. Explain that **metaphors** and **similes** are **figures of speech,** specific literary devices or kinds of figurative (nonliteral) language. **Read aloud the first paragraph** and model the process of analyzing figurative language.

> ***Modeling*** The author uses a simile and compares the tapping of Phoenix Jackson's cane on the frozen ground to the chirping of a bird. I find myself picturing a tiny bird, making its lonely chirp, on a branch. Connecting the sound of the cane with the sound of a bird seems to link Phoenix Jackson with the natural scene surrounding her. The comparison also reminds me that Jackson is light, small, and frail—like a bird.

Interactive Reading Workbook
p. 95

Ask a volunteer to read aloud the second paragraph and to analyze the comparisons used in describing the pattern of wrinkles on Jackson's face. Then have students complete Interacting with Text **Analyzing Figurative Language,** student workbook page 95.

Analyzing Symbolism Remind students that a **symbol** is any object, person, place, or experience that exists on a literal level but that also represents something else, usually an abstract concept. Tell students that the path that Jackson walks can be seen as both a physical trail and something else. Invite students to speculate on what the path might symbolize. (*The path could be seen as symbolizing Jackson's journey through life.*) Guide students to list the snags and pitfalls on Jackson's journey and what each represents. Then have students record her response to each snag and what that response reveals about her character. On the board, create a chart such as the following and work with students to analyze the symbolism of Phoenix's "worn path."

Snag and Pitfall	What It Represents	Phoenix's Response	Character Traits Revealed
"a quivering in the thicket"	fears	"Out of my way . . . !"	courage, determination
"path ran up a hill"	a challenge	argues with herself but continues	awareness of the challenge; perseverance
"bush caught her dress," dress snags on thorns	series of delays and frustrations	tells thorns she understands their role; finally goes on	unruffled in the face of problems

After Reading

You may also use the selection questions and activities in *Glencoe Literature.*

Visualizing Follow-Up Ask students to share their visualizations of places along the path, the characters, or the dramatic action of the story. Have students read aloud the details in the text on which they based their visualizations. Invite classmates to comment on what each visualization reveals about the characters, setting, or plot of the story.

OBJECTIVES

▶ To analyze poetry; to identify tone

The Explorer

Gwendolyn Brooks

Before Reading

Activating Prior Knowledge Explain to students that "The Explorer" describes someone who is passing through a confused and confusing place. Have them recall a time when they felt overwhelmed by a situation. Ask: *What made it hard to think calmly and rationally?* Invite volunteers to describe the kinds of events that cause a reaction of distress and confusion.

Building Vocabulary On the board, write the following terms, without definitions: *frayed* (torn, ragged), *tatters* (shreds), *din* (racket, clamor), *vague* (uncertain, indefinite), *spiraling* (twisting, veering), *wee* (tiny). Invite volunteers to define the words they know. Provide definitions for any remaining words. Have students record the words and their definitions in their vocabulary logs or journals.

During Reading

Analyzing Remind students that thinking critically about what they have read will help them to understand complex ideas. **Then ask students to listen as you read the poem aloud.** Have students offer their impressions and reactions to the poem. Then guide them in analyzing the poem by having them answer the following questions. Have them support their answers.

1. Where is the explorer who is mentioned in the title of the poem? What does he seek? (*The explorer is in a place that is noisy and confusing. He seeks to find "a still spot in the noise."*)
2. Is the place in which the explorer finds himself a real place or a state of mind? (*The place may be a state of mind—the halls are "scrambled"; the door-knobs are "throbbing"; and the "high human voices" suggest shouting or nervous piercing noise.*)
3. What is the effect on the reader of the descriptive details? (*The details have a nightmarish quality. The reader may begin to feel anxious and frightened.*)
4. Who is the explorer? Why is he called an "explorer"? (*Possible response: The explorer may be a person who is confused or overwhelmed by a difficult time in his life. He may be called an "explorer" because he is exploring dark, frightening places within himself.*)

After Reading

Identifying Tone Tell students that the **tone** of a piece of writing is a reflection of the writer's or speaker's attitude toward a subject. Remind students that poets carefully choose words that will establish the appropriate tone in their writing. Have students complete Interacting with Text **Identifying Tone,** student workbook page 96. Encourage students to discuss their answers with the class.

You may also use the selection questions and activities in *Glencoe Literature.*

Interactive Reading Workbook
p. 96

OBJECTIVES

- To note sequence of events; to analyze symbols; to analyze theme

February

Ralph Ellison

Before Reading

Activating Prior Knowledge Tell students that the personal essay "February" describes an incident in which the author makes a discovery about himself. Have students think of an incident that taught them something important about their abilities or qualities. As students read, have them compare Ellison's discoveries about himself with what they have learned about themselves.

Building Vocabulary On the board, write the following words and meanings: *precise* (definite, exact), *immensity* (vastness), *snowscape* (snowy landscape), *drowsing* (slumbering, inactive), *wavery* (flickering, quivering), *phase* (stage). Invite students to compose oral sentences that convey the meaning of the vocabulary words. Have them write the words, definitions, and an example sentence for each word in their vocabulary logs or journals.

During Reading

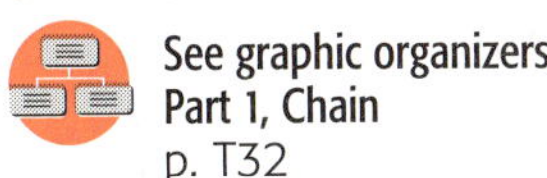
See graphic organizers, Part 1, Chain p. T32

Noting Sequence of Events Explain to students that they will read a personal essay that includes the thoughts and insights of its writer, Ralph Ellison. Tell students that listing the events in such a piece of writing can sometimes help them recall later not only what happened but what thoughts each event evoked. Distribute copies of the Chain graphic organizer. **Have a volunteer read aloud the first paragraph of the essay.** Ask students to discuss where Ellison is, why he has gone there, and what he does. (*He is in a woods near Dayton, where he has gone to forget his grief and worries. He observes quail tracks, drinks from a brook, looks at the distant city, and finds an old sleigh in a shed.*) Have students record this information in brief notes in the first box of their graphic organizers. **Have another volunteer read aloud the rest of the selection.** Pause with students to record each event that occurs and the writer's associated thoughts.

Interactive Reading Workbook p. 97

Understanding Symbols Ask students what a symbol is. (*A **symbol** is any object, color, person, place, or experience that exists on a literal level but that also represents something else, usually an abstract idea.*) **Call on a volunteer to reread the first paragraph.** Ask: *What does the month of February symbolize to the author?* (Students may suggest that it symbolizes a time of solitude, self-discovery, and finally hope.) Then have students complete Interacting with Text **Analyzing Symbols,** student workbook page 97.

After Reading

You may also use the selection questions and activities in *Glencoe Literature.*

Analyzing Theme Have students summarize what Ellison learned from his experience. Have students write a sentence stating the **theme,** or the message, of the essay that is based on their summaries. (*By surviving a cold, comfortless time in his life and seeing how the world permits him to nourish himself, body and soul, Ellison gains confidence in his vitality and ability to survive. The theme of the essay may be that peace and hope ultimately emerge even in the bleakest of times.*)

OBJECTIVES

- To map a story; to analyze theme; to make inferences from dialogue; to evaluate realism

The Portrait

Tomás Rivera

Before Reading

Activating Prior Knowledge Have students read "Meet Tomás Rivera" and the Building Background notes in *Glencoe Literature*. Point out that the story takes place in the 1950s when the United States was involved in the Korean War. Tell students "The Portrait" is about a treasured family photograph. Ask them to think of an irreplaceable object that they treasure. Have students describe their feelings about it.

Building Vocabulary On the board, write the following words, without definitions: *inlays* (decorative patterns set into the surface of another material), *installments* (partial payments), *demanding* (difficult, making many demands), *responsible* (reliable, trustworthy), *sacrifices* (things given up or lost), *overlays* (coverings over existing layers), *enlargements* (photographic prints larger than their original negatives, or "blown up" prints), *swindled* (cheated). Ask students to provide definitions for words they know and to find definitions for the remainder in a dictionary. Encourage students to record the words and their definitions in their vocabulary logs or journals.

Word Study: Silent *gh* On the board, write the word *right*. Explain to students that the letters *gh* are often silent when they appear together in a word. Have volunteers write on the board the following words from the selection and ask them to underline the silent letters: *frightened*, *thought*, *brought*. As students read, encourage them to notice words that contain silent *gh*.

Setting a Purpose for Reading Have students read to find out who is pictured in the portrait named in the title and why the portrait is valued.

During Reading

See graphic organizers, Part 1, Story Map p. T28

Mapping the Story Distribute copies of the Story Map graphic organizer (see Part 1, page T28). Create a transparency of the Story Map and display it on the overhead projector. Write "The Portrait" on the title line. With students, review the meaning of the terms **setting** (the time and the place of events), **conflict** (the struggle between opposing forces in the plot), **resolution** (the outcome of the conflict), and **theme** (the main message of the story). Ask students to recall the setting from the Building Background notes. (*Texas, 1950s*) **Read aloud the first two paragraphs.** Have students name the characters that have been introduced up to this point in the story. (*Don Mateo and a salesman*) Add these names to the story map. Ask students what clues they noticed that hint at a conflict or problem that may arise. (*Possible response: The insistence on cash suggests that the salesman will try to cheat Don Mateo.*) **Have students read the story silently.** Ask them to complete the story map after reading.

Analyzing Theme To complete the story map, students will need to analyze the theme. Model the process of determining the theme of the story.

> ***Modeling*** To understand the theme, I'll first summarize what happened: The parents of a young man who was killed in Korea pay an excessive amount of money for a portrait enlargement of their beloved son. They give their only photograph to the salesman, a stranger. Surrendering the photograph is an act of faith. The salesman has no intention of creating the portrait the parents pay for. When Don Mateo discovers the scam, he seeks out the salesman and forces the salesman to honor the sale. The portrait that is completed is not of Don Mateo's son but of himself; however, Don Mateo does not recognize that this is so. Instead, he is pleased that his son looks so much like him.
>
> I think Don Mateo's reaction shows his love of his child. He accepts that his son looks like him, and this acceptance gives Don Mateo a sense of peace. The theme of the story may be that people who are good and honorable radiate those qualities and find peace in the world.

Discuss other possible themes that students suggest. Then fill in the theme box of the story map.

Making Inferences Point out that most of this story is told through **dialogue,** or the characters' spoken words. Tell students that readers can, by analyzing dialogue, make inferences about the characters, including such things as a character's intentions or personality traits. (Remind students that **making inferences** is the skill of using clues in the text and readers' own knowledge to help them understand what the author implies but does not state directly.) **Call on two volunteers to read aloud the dialogue from the paragraph that begins "Good afternoon"** through the paragraph that begins "Boy, that's expensive!" Ask students what concerns Don Mateo and why. (*Don Mateo is concerned about the cost of the portrait because he is poor.*) Then have students analyze the salesman's words to discern what they show about the salesman. (*The salesman stresses quality and downplays cost. He does not want his customer to think about price, because he knows the family is poor and cannot afford the portrait.*) Guide students to recognize what these clues reveal about the salesman. (*The salesman does not have his customers' interests at heart. Rather, he is interested only in taking their money.*) Have students complete Interacting with Text **Making Inferences from Dialogue,** student workbook page 98.

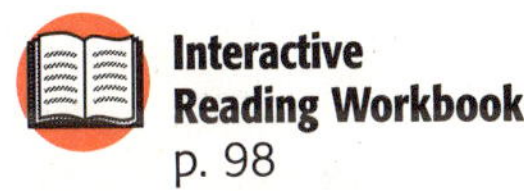
Interactive Reading Workbook
p. 98

After Reading

You may also use the selection questions and activities in *Glencoe Literature.*

Evaluating Realism Explain to students that **realism** is a literary style that portrays situations in a true-to-life way. Invite students to recall the characters' actions and reactions in this story and evaluate their level of realism. Have students discuss whether Don Mateo's acceptance of the portrait is realistic. (*Possible responses: Don Mateo's acceptance of the portrait is realistic because he has already begun to forget details of his son's features; he takes pleasure in thinking that his son looked like him; and, unable to get back the photograph, he wants to hold on to some image of his lost son.*)

OBJECTIVES

- To interpret figurative language; to analyze an explanation

The Death of the Ball Turret Gunner

Randall Jarrell

Before Reading

Previewing the Selection Have students look at the photograph and read the title of the selection and "Note from the Author" in *Glencoe Literature.* Invite students to predict what the poem will be about. (*Possible response: The poem may describe how a World War II gunner dies.*) Have students discuss what they know about World War II bombers.

Building Vocabulary On the board, write the following words and definitions: *plexiglass* (acrylic plastic sheet), *revolved* (moved in a curved path around an axis), *fetus* (developing unborn baby), *fighters* (airplanes, with a crew of one or two, designed for use against enemy planes or ground crews), *turret* (transparent plastic bubblelike structure on military aircraft, used to house antiaircraft guns and their gunners). Have volunteers use each word in a sentence that conveys the meaning of the word.

During Reading

Understanding Figurative Language **Have a volunteer read the poem aloud.** After students have listened to the poem, remind them that most poems include **figurative language,** language used for descriptive effect in order to convey ideas or emotions—expressions that are not literally true. Such language helps the poet express truths beyond the literal meaning of the words. **Call on a volunteer to reread the poem aloud.** Ask students, as they listen to the poem, to identify parts that contain figurative language. Ask students to consider the following phrases in the context of the gunner's situation and to suggest meanings for each: "*my mother's sleep*" (his private or civilian life); "*fell into the State*" (became a soldier, part of the government's fighting force); "*my wet fur*" (his uniform, also suggests his animal vulnerability); "*its* [earth's] *dream of life*" (living things' desire to live).

Interactive Reading Workbook p. 99

Analyzing Metaphor Guide students to understand that the images compare the gunner in the turret to a fetus inside its mother. Have students complete Interacting with Text **Analyzing Metaphor,** student workbook page 99.

After Reading

You may also use the selection questions and activities in *Glencoe Literature.*

Using Explanation Point out the unusual "Note from the Author" that follows the poem. Ask a volunteer to reread it aloud. Ask students what key points they learn from this note. (*Students may learn what a ball turret is; the characteristics of the gunner; the type of gun included in the ball turret; how the ball turret moves; how the gunner appears in the turret—like a fetus; the type of fire that enemy fighters use; the type of hose that cleans the ball turret after the gunner's death.*) Invite students to share their views on whether the information in the note is crucial to understanding the meaning of the poem.

OBJECTIVES

- To analyze parts of speech; to paraphrase a poem

The Beautiful Changes

Richard Wilbur

Before Reading

Activating Prior Knowledge Ask students to think about what makes something beautiful and have them suggest a definition of *beauty*. As students read the poem, have them compare their ideas about beauty with the speaker's.

Word Study: Parts of Speech Remind students that a word can have more than one meaning; a word can also be used as more than one part of speech. For example, the word *shade* can be a noun, meaning "a spot sheltered from light," or a verb, meaning "to shelter from glare." Ask students to read the title of the poem and to suggest the parts of speech for the words *beautiful* and *changes*. (Beautiful *can be an adjective describing* changes, *a noun;* or beautiful *can be a noun and* changes *a verb.*) Write the following sentences on the board and ask volunteers to explain the difference in meaning.

The changes are beautiful.		*The beautiful changes.*	
noun	adjective	noun	verb

(*Possible explanation: The first sentence describes changes that are attractive; the second statement means that what is considered beautiful inevitably changes.*) Write *valleys* and *finding* on the board and have students predict what part of speech each word will be in the poem. (*Possible answers:* Valleys *is a noun, and* finding *is a verb form.*) Encourage students to notice how meaning changes according to the part of speech that is associated with a word. Then have students complete **Interacting with Text** **Parts of Speech,** student workbook page 100.

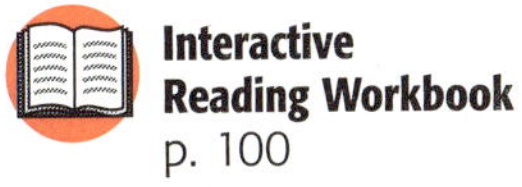
Interactive Reading Workbook
p. 100

During Reading

Paraphrasing Remind students that **paraphrasing** a poem, or restating it in their own words, will help clear up questions and clarify the poem's meaning. **Read aloud the first stanza.** Guide students in paraphrasing. (*The speaker is walking in a meadow in fall. Tall grass acts like water, rippling outward from his steps. The ripples cause the flowers to sway away from him gracefully. This pleasing sight reminds him of the effect on him of someone he loves.*) **Read the rest of the poem aloud,** continuing to guide students in paraphrasing it.

After Reading

You may also use the selection questions and activities in *Glencoe Literature.*

Interpreting Remind students that **interpreting** is attaching meaning to what they have read. Help students interpret the poem with these questions. Ask: *What does it mean to "sunder things and things' selves"?* (A thing, or how we perceive it, and the essential reality of it are different.) *What is the "second finding," and why does it result in wonder?* (The vision of a thing perceived in a new way evokes awe; the world has so many levels and intricacies.)

Prior Knowledge Follow-Up Ask students to review their definition of beauty and to discuss how they would change the definition or expand it. Has their view of what is beautiful changed? If so, how?

OBJECTIVES

- To visualize setting and action; to summarize; to compare and contrast characters

The Rockpile

James Baldwin

Before Reading

Activating Prior Knowledge Have students read "Meet James Baldwin" and the Building Background notes in *Glencoe Literature*. Then tell students that "The Rockpile" presents a family in which fears and tensions overshadow love. Point out that there are some similarities between James Baldwin's own strict stepfather and the father described in the story. Then have a volunteer read aloud the title and ask students what a *rockpile* is. (*In this story, the rockpile is an outcropping of natural rock in a city lot.*) Invite students to suggest why a story about strained family relations might be titled "The Rockpile."

Building Vocabulary On the board, write the following words, without definitions: *challenged* (called into question), *indifference* (lack of concern), *latent* (potential, hidden), *superficial* (shallow), *apprehension* (dread, worry), *exasperated* (beyond endurance), *relapsing* (slipping back). Invite volunteers to give the meanings of the words they know. Provide definitions as necessary. Encourage students to record the words and their definitions in their vocabulary logs or journals.

Word Study: Latin Roots Tell students that Latin roots appear in many English words. Learning the roots' meanings helps to unlock the meanings of many words. Write the words *decent* and *decorate* on the board and ask students what group of letters they share. (*dec*) Explain that the Latin root *decere* means "to be fitting." Invite students to tell how this meaning applies to these two words. (Decent *behavior is fitting or appropriate;* to decorate *a place is to make it fit the circumstances or occasion.*) Then write the following sentence on the board and have students infer the meaning of decorum: *The family behaved with decorum while the minister visited.*

Setting a Purpose for Reading Have students read to find out whether two brothers obey their parents' order to stay away from the rockpile.

During Reading

Visualizing Remind students that the story is set in Harlem in the 1930s—a poor, crowded, busy, urban setting. **Call on a volunteer to read aloud the first two paragraphs of the story.** Have students describe the scene as they **visualize,** or picture, it. (*Students should describe the rockpile and the children playing on it. The rockpile is located in a city lot. Rough and uneven, it rises sharply out of the ground. Possible visualization: Boys play on the rockpile as if they were playing "King of the Mountain," sometimes slipping down the side of the "mountain," screaming and raising dust.*)

Summarizing **Have students read silently up to the paragraph beginning "In the summertime . . ."** Ask students what questions a summary answers. (*who*, *what*, *why*, *when*, and *where* questions) Then model the process of summarizing.

> ***Modeling*** To summarize the story so far, I see that most neighborhood children fight on the rockpile. John and Roy are forbidden by their parents to go anywhere outside the apartment other than the fire escape. Roy seems adventurous, but John fears the danger of the rockpile. Both boys long to escape the apartment. They fear their father. He considers anything of the outside world wicked and sinful.

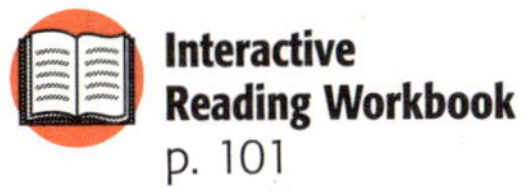
Interactive Reading Workbook
p. 101

Comparing and Contrasting Point out that an author may create strong similarities and differences in characters in order to emphasize their personalities or make a point. **Have students read the rest of the story silently.** As they read, ask them to observe what each character is like and to jot down notes about the characters' personalities. Then have students list the story's main characters. (*Roy*, *John*, *Elizabeth*, *Gabriel*) Ask students to suggest adjectives that describe each character. (*Possible response: Roy—impatient, bold, and spoiled; John—bookish, worried, and terrified of his father; Elizabeth—protective, nurturing; Gabriel—stern, forbidding, violent.*) Write the appropriate adjectives beside each character's name. Have students complete Interacting with Text **Comparing and Contrasting Characters,** student workbook page 101.

After Reading

You may also use the selection questions and activities in *Glencoe Literature*.

Understanding Symbols Call on a volunteer to define a symbol. (*A* ***symbol*** *is any object, color, person, place, or experience that exists on a literal level but also represents something else, usually an abstract concept or value.*) Have students tell what they think the rockpile represents. Ask a volunteer to explain in brief its importance to the family. (*The rockpile seems to represent all the dangers and wickedness of the outside world. To Roy it represents a fearsome but desirable place. After Roy's injury, the rockpile's continued attraction fuels the ongoing conflict between Elizabeth and her husband and John and his stepfather. Ironically, the rockpile proves less hurtful to Roy than Gabriel's words are to John.*)

Interpreting Use the following questions to help students interpret parts of the story.

1. Why did Baldwin include the incident about the drowning of the boy Richard? (*The incident illustrates the real dangers of the outside world and the anguish a mother feels at the loss of a child. This incident emphasizes the warning to the boys.*)
2. What does the description of John's position beneath Gabriel's "heavy shoe" emphasize? (*The description emphasizes John's helplessness before his father and suggests the violence that John has probably experienced at his father's hands.*)

OBJECTIVES

- To make predictions; to identify internal conflict in a character

The Magic Barrel

Bernard Malamud

Before Reading

Activating Prior Knowledge Have students read the Building Background notes in *Glencoe Literature*. Tell students that "The Magic Barrel" is about a man who is trying to choose a wife. As he tries to identify the qualities he looks for, he learns a great deal about himself. Encourage students to talk about choices that lead to self-discovery.

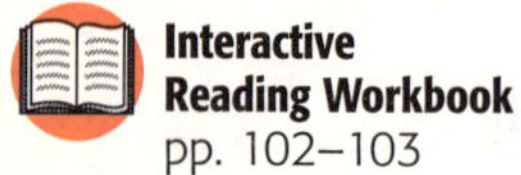
Interactive Reading Workbook
pp. 102–103

Building Vocabulary Have students turn to Interactive Reading **Reading Guide** on student workbook page 102. Read aloud and discuss with students the Key Vocabulary and Terms. Tell students that, as they read, they should note the way the words are used in the context of the story.

Word Study: Suffixes *-ation, -tion* Remind students that a **suffix** is a group of letters added to the end of a base word (or word root) to create a new word with a new meaning. Explain that identifying base words and suffixes can help them learn the meanings of unfamiliar words. Tell students the meanings of the suffixes *–ion*, *-tion* and *-ation*: "state or condition of being"; "action or process of." On the board, write the word *anticipation*, and below it write the base word and the suffix used to form *anticipation*. (*anticipate + -tion*) Point out the difference in spelling of the base word when the suffix is added. Then guide students to give a meaning for *anticipation*. (*"the act of anticipating;" "feeling of excited expectation"*) Add the following story words to the list on the board: *revelation, consolation, redemption*. Have students identify the base word and suffix in, and define, each word. (*reveal + -ation, "disclosure"; console + -ation, "that which comforts"; redeem + -tion, "salvation"*) Have a volunteer suggest a general rule that explains what happens to the part of speech of a base word when *-tion* or *-ation* is added. (*A verb becomes a noun.*)

Setting a Purpose for Reading Suggest that students read to find out whether a young man is successful in finding a wife.

During Reading

Making Predictions Remind students that reviewing what they know so far and predicting what will happen next in a story can help them read with more enjoyment and understanding. **Read aloud the first three paragraphs of the story**. Model how to make inferences in order to predict what will happen.

> ***Modeling*** I know that Leo Finkle is poor and has been studying for six years but believes that he needs to marry quickly. He has no experience in dating. Matchmaker Pinye Salzman is also poor but seems eager to please. Because Salzman is not prosperous, it is likely that he will not have many desirable women among his clients. I predict that Finkle will be disillusioned by the process of matchmaking.

Pair students and have them read the story silently in two sections: the first section from the beginning of the selection up to the paragraph that begins "He was infuriated with the marriage broker" and the second section from the paragraph beginning "He was infuriated . . . " to the end of the story. As students read, encourage them to predict what will happen to Finkle. Remind students to base their predictions on clues in the text and on their own awareness about how various situations usually work out.

Using the Reading Guide Ask students to return to the reading guide on student workbook pages 102–103. Explain that they will use the reading guide to help them keep track of story events. Partners may complete this section together.

Identifying Internal Conflict Explain to students that **internal conflict** in a story is a struggle between two opposing thoughts or desires within the mind of a character. After students read the first section of the story, ask them to identify Finkle's internal conflict. Guide students to see that Finkle's questions and responses provide a clue to what is bothering him. (*Although he knows that matchmaking is an accepted practical arrangement in traditional Jewish culture, he is ashamed of its loveless nature and the focus on marketing. Finkle sees focusing on appearance and money as degrading.*) Ask students to identify changes in Leo Finkle's conflict through the story. (*1. Finkle struggles with the knowledge that he is interested in women and in God for shallow reasons. 2. He struggles with the knowledge that he is unloved and loveless and hates the idea of a loveless marriage. 3. His intimidation by Stella's broader experience conflicts with the appeal of the knowledge that her suffering has brought her and with the longing to make her "his redemption."*)

After Reading

You may also use the selection questions and activities in *Glencoe Literature*.

Analyzing Changes in a Character Ask students to read aloud passages that describe the matchmaker Salzman and to note how he changes physically through the story. (*He goes from looking thin and poor to becoming weak and emaciated. At the end, he is "transparent to the point of vanishing."*) Encourage students to speculate about reasons that Salzman's appearance changes and what the changes may mean. (*The changes could indicate that his death is nearing, which might motivate him to lure Finkle into marrying his daughter.*)

Evaluating Theme Ask students to scan the story again to locate passages that tell about truths that Finkle learns about himself. (*Finkle learns the following truths: (1) that he is shallow in what he wants in a wife, (2) that he has not learned to love God because he has not interacted with and loved people, (3) that he wants to love the woman he marries, (4) that giving love may save him.*) Invite students to discuss what these discoveries might mean to Finkle's life. (*Understanding his shortcomings and needs makes him more human and lovable and could help him serve his congregation with more understanding, but his belief in Stella's ability to "help him seek whatever he was seeking" is naïve and may cause him further disappointment.*) Ask students to suggest the theme of the story. (*Possible themes: Love is often found where one least expects it; love that is not encouraged is sweeter than love that is approved of; our struggles often lead to self-discovery.*)

OBJECTIVES

- To identify main idea and supporting details; to evaluate author's opinions

FROM

Stride Toward Freedom

Martin Luther King Jr.

Before Reading

Activating Prior Knowledge Tell students that the selection from *Stride Toward Freedom* that is in *Glencoe Literature* is by Martin Luther King Jr., the principal leader of the American Civil Rights movement of the 1950s and 1960s. Ask students to tell what they know about the Civil Rights movement and the philosophy of Martin Luther King Jr. Then have students read "Meet Martin Luther King Jr." and the Building Background notes in *Glencoe Literature*.

Building Vocabulary On the board, write the following words, without definitions: *emancipation* (freedom from oppression or control by another), *resignation* (acceptance), *segregation* (separation; isolation of a group by discriminatory means), *annihilate* (destroy completely), *monologue* (speech performed by one actor), *reconcile* (unite; bring together), *perpetrators* (those who carry something out or bring it about, as a crime), *unrelentingly* (constantly; without yielding), *militant* (aggressively active). Ask volunteers to identify and define the words they know and then to consult a dictionary to find the meanings of unfamiliar words. Encourage students to record the words and definitions in their vocabulary logs or journals.

Word Study: Antonyms Remind students that **antonyms** are words with opposite meanings. Write the word *respect* on the board and invite students to think of antonyms for it. (*disrespect*, *scorn*, *contempt*) Point out that sometimes antonyms are formed by adding a prefix that means "not," such as *un-*, *in-*, *non-*, or *dis-*, to the base word or word root. Write the words *violence* and *justice* on the board and have students suggest prefixes to make the words antonyms. (*nonviolence*, *injustice*) Explain that antonyms are more likely to be unlike words, however, such as *slavery* and *freedom*. Explain that, in an essay about oppressed peoples and their oppressors, antonyms help to define and establish opposing or conflicting ideas. Tell students to list antonyms that they notice in the essay as they read.

Setting a Purpose for Reading Have students read to find out about the ways that people can combat oppression.

During Reading

Identifying Main Idea and Supporting Details Remind students that a paragraph presents a main idea and details that support it. Explain that the first or last sentence often expresses the main idea in a paragraph but that the reader may at times have to infer the main idea from information in the text. **Read aloud the first paragraph of the selection** and model the process of identifying the main idea and supporting details.

Modeling The first sentence in the paragraph states that there are three ways oppressed people deal with their oppression. King names the first method: "acquiescence"—the process of adjusting and resigning oneself to an injustice until one becomes conditioned to it. Next, he gives an example: He points out how the children of Israel preferred slavery, which they knew, over suffering unknown horrors in the struggle for freedom. I know that definitions and examples are forms of support used to prove and expand on an idea. I can express the main idea of this paragraph as follows: King believes that one of the three ways oppressed people cope with oppression is by acquiescing to injustice.

Call on volunteers to continue reading the selection aloud. Encourage students to identify the main idea and supporting details of each paragraph.

Evaluating Validity of Opinions Remind students that **facts** can be proved or verified; **opinions** are expressions of attitudes, feelings, or personal beliefs, and they cannot be proved or disproved. Explain that opinions can be powerfully persuasive if they are supported by convincing facts. On the board, write *Violence as a way of achieving racial justice is both impractical and immoral.* Ask students to identify this as a fact or an opinion and explain how they know. (*It is an opinion; it expresses King's belief and cannot be proved or disproved absolutely.*) **Have students reread the fifth paragraph.** Model the process of evaluating the soundness of the facts that King uses to decide whether the opinion is valid.

Modeling King calls violence impractical. He explains his belief by pointing out that it is destructive and intensifies rather than solves problems. He mentions "an eye for an eye," a biblical phrase used to justify striking back. However, King points out that this kind of logic will lead to everybody's being blinded. With each incidence of violence, hatred will increase, and nothing will be resolved. King's reasoning is logical and compelling.

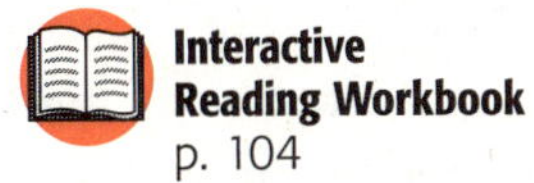

Invite a volunteer to model the process of evaluating the validity of King's description of violence as immoral. Then have students complete Interacting with Text **Evaluating the Validity of Opinions,** student workbook page 104.

After Reading

You may also use the selection questions and activities in *Glencoe Literature.*

Word Study Follow-Up After students have read the selection, ask them to share their lists of antonyms. (*Possible responses:* cooperation/noncooperation, moral/immoral, resistance/nonresistance, oppressed/oppressor, temporary and momentary/permanent, oppression/emancipation, integration/segregation, perpetrators/recipients, immoral/sublime *and* moral, anarchy/community.)

Purpose for Reading Follow-Up Ask students to state the three parts of King's argument in their own words. (*1. Do not accept oppression because acquiescing to it fails to show the oppressor that he or she is doing evil. 2. Do not resort to violence because violence causes an increasing level of harm and hatred. 3. Engage in nonviolent resistance because it is moral and avoids the evils of violence and passivity while it fights against oppression and refuses to harm others.*)

OBJECTIVES

- To visualize scenes and actions; to analyze causes and effects; to identify author's purpose

Choice: A Tribute to Dr. Martin Luther King Jr.

Alice Walker

Before Reading

Building Background Have students read "Meet Alice Walker" and the Building Background notes in *Glencoe Literature*. Point out to students that demonstrations such as sit-ins and protest marches were strategies of the Civil Rights movement. They proved effective, in part, because television cameras captured the violent responses of white segregationists contrasting with the nonviolent resistance of protesters. Slowly the public conscience was stirred, and public opinion came to favor civil rights.

Building Vocabulary On the board, write the following words, without definitions: *dispossession* (deprival of property), *acknowledge* (to admit), *sensibility* (understanding, perceptiveness), *abandonment* (surrender, desertion), *disinherit* (to cut off, disown), *municipal* (related to local laws), *revolutionary* (bringing about fundamental change), *assuredly* (confidently), *heritage* (ancestry; birthright). Encourage students to study the words and to identify the word parts that they know. Guide students by underlining the base words (or word roots) within words, such as *possess* in *dispossession* and *sens* in *sensibility*, and asking them to define the base words. Invite volunteers to suggest the meanings of the longer words on the basis of what they already know. Then have them check meanings in a dictionary before adding the words and their definitions to their vocabulary logs or journals.

Word Study: Past-Tense Verbs On the board, write the following words: *inherit, expect, learn, force, watch, appear, handcuff,* and *shove*. Remind students that the ending of most verbs changes as the tense of the verb changes. On the board, write the following sentence from the selection: "We loved the land and worked the land." Have students identify the actions in this sentence as taking place in the present, past, or future. (*past*) Point out the *-ed* ending on *loved* and *worked*. Have students change the words on the board to past tense.

Setting a Purpose for Reading Have students read the selection to learn Alice Walker's personal reasons for honoring Martin Luther King Jr.

During Reading

Visualizing Remind students that **visualizing,** creating mental pictures based on the details in the text, can help them to understand their reading better. **Read aloud the first two paragraphs of the selection** and then invite students to describe the scenes they visualized. (*Possible responses: the great-great-great-grandmother first as a young mother carrying two babies and then as a 125-year-old woman; a simple country church and cemetery.*) Point out that Walker's personal reminiscences allow the reader to see what living in the Southern United States was like for African Americans. These images serve as a backdrop for the changes Martin Luther King Jr. would launch. As students read, remind them to read actively by visualizing the people and the scenes that Walker describes.

See graphic organizers, Part 1, Cause-and-Effect Chart, p. T29

Analyzing Cause and Effect Remind students that a **cause** is an action or an occurrence that makes something happen; an **effect** is the result of that action or occurrence. Point out that Walker explains why various events occurred and what happened as a result of other events. **Call on a volunteer to read aloud the third and fourth paragraphs.** Create a cause-and-effect chart transparency and display it on the overhead projector. Then model the process of identifying causes and effects in these paragraphs. As you model, write causes in boxes on the left-hand side of the transparency and effects in boxes on the right-hand side.

> ***Modeling*** According to Walker, although African American Southerners worked the land and lived on it, they were not allowed to own it. What happened as a result of this unjust situation? First, not allowing people to own the land they worked created poverty and a sense of hopelessness. These conditions in turn caused bitterness and the loss of love for the land. Walker tells how she left her birthplace when she became a young adult so that she would not come to hate it for the brutal conditions there in which her people were forced to live. The act of denying African Americans land rights caused two social ills—one outward and easily seen and the other inward and invisible but just as painful.

Have students fill in the causes and effects on their papers. **Ask students to read the rest of the speech silently,** noting other causes and effects.

After Reading

You may also use the selection questions and activities in *Glencoe Literature*.

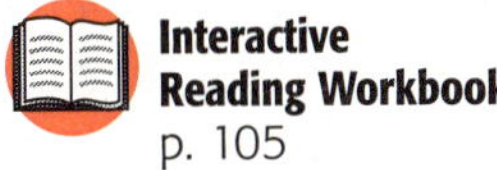
Interactive Reading Workbook p. 105

Cause-and-Effect Follow-Up Have students complete Interacting with Text **Cause-and-Effect Relationships,** student workbook page 105. Explain that students' responses to the questions can help them understand the profound effect of Martin Luther King Jr. on the African American community. Use the following questions to guide students' analysis of other causes and effects.

1. What causes Walker's mother to pray for King every night? (*Walker's mother understands that King is the leader for whom they have waited and fears that he may be killed.*)
2. What causes public facilities such as the restaurant to open to African Americans? (*federal law enforcement, which results from King's activism and leadership*)

Identifying Author's Purpose Ask students: *What is an author's purpose in writing?* (An **author's purpose** is the accomplishment of one or more of the following goals: to persuade, to inform, to explain, to entertain, or to describe.) Have students discuss Alice Walker's purposes for writing and presenting her speech "Choice: A Tribute to Dr. Martin Luther King Jr." Guide students to understand that one purpose is to inform her audience of what living in the southern United States was like for African Americans before civil rights legislation and how King's courage, eloquence, philosophy, and accomplishments were inspirational to the Civil Rights movement and to Alice Walker.

OBJECTIVES

- To recognize dialect; to read dialogue with expression; to summarize; to make predictions; to analyze plot

The Crucible

Arthur Miller

Before Reading

Building Background Explain to students that *The Crucible*, a play by Pulitzer Prize-winning playwright Arthur Miller, is about the Salem witch trials. Have students read the Building Background notes in *Glencoe Literature*. Invite them to share what they know about the witch trials that took place in Salem, Massachusetts, in the late 1600s. Make students aware of the overriding fear and suspicion that pervaded the Puritan settlement, leading the authorities to place teenage girls and women on trial as witches. Ask students to imagine being unfairly accused of a crime. Ask: *How would you feel? How would you react? What might you do to vindicate yourself? What would you do if no one believed you?*

Characteristics of Genre: Drama Invite students to discuss differences between how a play and a story are presented. Remind students that drama, on the printed page, looks different from other literature. A drama appears as a **script**—a set of words and instructions to be followed by actors. Longer scripts are divided into sections called **acts,** and each act may be divided into smaller sections called **scenes.** Have students read the Literature Focus introduction "Drama" which precedes the selection in *Glencoe Literature*. Review with students the elements of drama: characters, setting, plot, dialogue, and acts and scenes. As students read the play, encourage them to notice the way characters are introduced and how playwright Miller reveals their character traits.

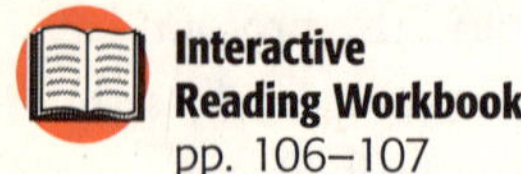
Interactive Reading Workbook pp. 106–107

Building Vocabulary Have students turn to Interactive Reading **Introductory Reading Guide,** pages 106–107. Tell students that two reading guides are provided for *The Crucible*: Introductory Reading Guide, for act 1 and act 2 of the play; and Reading Guide for Act 3 and Act 4. Then explain that the play takes place in the late 1600s and that some of the vocabulary and terms may sound old-fashioned. Together with students, read over the Key Vocabulary and Terms listed for act 1. Invite students to share what they know about each word. After reading act 1, return to the list of words and discuss the words as they are used in the context of the play. Repeat the process as students read each subsequent act of the play.

Word Study: Dialect Remind students that **dialect** is a variation of a language spoken by a particular group, often within a particular region and time. Dialect may differ from the standard language in grammar, pronunciation, or vocabulary. Write on the board the words *goin'* and *doin'*. Ask students to give the Standard English form of these words. (*going, doing*) Explain that speakers of the English language, in various regions of the United States, drop the /g/ sound when pronouncing words that end in *-ing*. Ask students for other examples of dialect that they are accustomed to hearing or using themselves.

Then remind students that a play is made up of **dialogue,** or the words that the characters say. A playwright often uses dialect to make a character's words and manner of speaking seem realistic. Ask what using dialect adds to the meaning of a play. (*It gives the reader a clear impression of the characters and the time and place in which the characters live.*) Explain to students that they will find other examples of dialect as they read. They will also encounter the use of archaic words and phrases, words and expressions that were commonly used at the time and place in which the play is set but that are not necessarily familiar today. Encourage students to read the footnotes for help in interpreting dialect and archaic language.

Setting a Purpose for Reading Suggest that students read the play to find out what events took place in the Massachusetts Bay Colony that affected the lives of so many in the community.

During Reading

Using the Reading Guides Have students turn to the reading guides (student workbook pages 106–110). Remind students that two reading guides are provided: Introductory Reading Guide, for act 1 and act 2 (pages 106–108) and Reading Guide for Act 3 and Act 4 (pages 109–110). Tell students that, before they read each act, they should refer to the corresponding reading guide. Point out that the first page of the Introductory Reading Guide lists the characters in the play, in the order in which they appear, and provides a brief description of each one. Review the Key Vocabulary and Terms for act 1 with students. Review the exercises with students so that they know what information to be looking for as they read. As students read through each act, have them complete the sentences or answer the questions in the reading guide.

Reading with Expression Tell students that a play is intended to be performed before an audience. **Assign character roles to students, with one person reading all of the stage directions, and tell them that they will read aloud act 1.** Remind students that dialogue read aloud includes not only a character's words but also the feelings of the character. Readers should try to read their character's words with the emotion they think the character might be feeling. **Call on volunteers to read aloud through Tituba's second bit of dialogue.** Then model the reading of dialogue with expression.

> ***Modeling*** I have to think about how the character is feeling, and what he is doing, as I read the words aloud. At the beginning of act 1, I know that the Reverend Samuel Parris is distressed about the illness of his young daughter Betty. ***(Read with feeling Parris's speech from "Out of my . . . " through "Betty, little one . . . ")*** Now let me show you how those words might sound if I read them without any expression. ***(Reread the same part without expression.)*** You can hear how the expression in my voice makes Parris's feelings clear.

Have students with assigned roles continue reading act 1 aloud, using tone of voice and expression to show each character's feelings.

Summarizing Remind students that to **summarize** means to restate briefly, in one's own words, the main ideas and the most important details in a passage or a selection. Tell students that summarizing is a reading strategy that can enhance their understanding of what they read by helping them to identify and organize the main ideas. Model the process of summarizing act 1 of the play.

> ***Modeling*** At the beginning of act 1, we learn that Parris has seen a group of girls dancing and acting strangely in the woods at night. He fears that witchcraft may be involved. When his own daughter Betty seems to be in a trance of some kind, he becomes terrified. His niece Abigail denies involvement in witchcraft, or "conjuring spirits," but her conversation with Mercy and Mary shows that she is lying. She also seeks revenge against Elizabeth Proctor for firing Abigail after the girl apparently had a romantic involvement with John Proctor. The words and actions of several towns-people show the central idea—the people of Salem are desperately afraid of witchcraft and suspicious of one another.

Have students read the rest of the play independently in small groups. After students read each act of the play, ask them to work together to write a summary of the act. Remind students to complete the exercises for each act in the reading guide. Suggest that they refer to the completed reading guide exercise to help them with their summaries.

Making Predictions Point out to students that **making predictions,** the process of thinking ahead about what may happen, is a reading strategy that can help readers focus on the important ideas in a selection. After students read and discuss act 1, write the following chart on the board. Work with students to supply predictions for the class chart that are based on the events that occur and the character traits that are revealed in act 1. (A sample prediction is developed in the chart.) Then distribute copies of the Two-Column Chart graphic organizer. As students read subsequent acts of the play, encourage them to record their own predictions and then to revise those predictions as necessary in light of additional information.

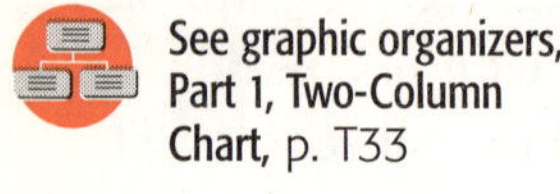
See graphic organizers, Part 1, Two-Column Chart, p. T33

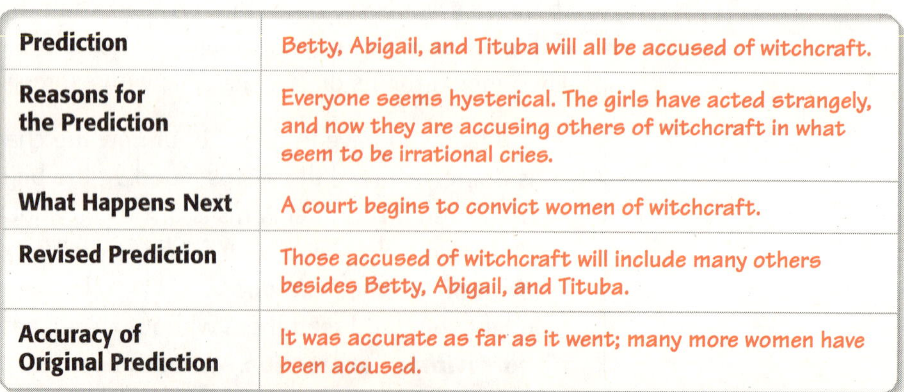

Prediction	Betty, Abigail, and Tituba will all be accused of witchcraft.
Reasons for the Prediction	Everyone seems hysterical. The girls have acted strangely, and now they are accusing others of witchcraft in what seem to be irrational cries.
What Happens Next	A court begins to convict women of witchcraft.
Revised Prediction	Those accused of witchcraft will include many others besides Betty, Abigail, and Tituba.
Accuracy of Original Prediction	It was accurate as far as it went; many more women have been accused.

Analyzing Plot Remind students that the **plot** is the sequence of events in a drama or narrative work of fiction. Usually, the main character faces a problem, or **conflict.** The plot includes all action that takes place while the main character faces and solves the problem. On the board, create a chart such as the following. Have students use it as an outline to aid them as they read the play. Review with students each of the plot elements listed in the first column. Work with students to fill in the second column of the chart with examples from *The Crucible*.

Elements of Plot	Examples in *The Crucible*
Exposition Introduction of the setting, the characters, and the problem	The list of characters and the stage direction at the beginning of act 1 introduce the characters and establish the setting. The problem develops in act 1, when people are faced with the possibility that members of their group are practicing witchcraft.
Rising Action Events that show the basic conflict and complications that occur	More people are accused of witchcraft. The perceived threat of witchcraft becomes clear. Elizabeth Proctor is arrested for witchcraft. Her husband vows to bring out the truth. Then he also is accused of witchcraft.
Climax The high point of the action; the point of highest interest, excitement, and importance	Several respected citizens, including Proctor, are to be hanged. After talking to his pregnant wife, Proctor decides to sign a confession in order to gain his freedom. Then he destroys his false confession, knowing that he will be hanged with the others.
Falling Action Events that follow the climax; logical result of the climax; winding down of the plot	Proctor and the others proceed to the gallows. Others beg Elizabeth to persuade her husband to change his mind to save himself, but she refuses.
Resolution or Dénouement The solution to the problem; the final outcome	Elizabeth knows that her husband demonstrates his true goodness as the hanging proceeds.

Clarifying Invite students to suggest several reading strategies and techniques that they find helpful. Point out how useful it is to jot down notes or questions as they read, identifying any part of the play that they do not understand. Later they can reread that section silently to **clarify** its meaning. Model the process of clarifying.

> ***Modeling*** I'm not sure I understood the discussion, between Parris and Abigail at the beginning of act 1, about witchcraft. As I read, I wrote down the page number and my question: *What does Parris see in the woods that makes him suspect that the girls practice witchcraft?* Now that I have I finished reading act 1, I'll reread that section. ***(Read aloud Parris's dialogue in the second column of the second text page of the play, beginning "Now then in the midst of such disruption . . . " through his dialogue that begins "I saw it!")*** After reading, I have a better idea of the situation. Parris saw Abigail, Betty, and other girls dancing in the woods the night before. He also saw a dress lying on the ground, suggesting that one of the girls was naked. These strange sights Parris assumes are evil. He believes that witches and the Devil are behind all evil. (*On the third text page of the play,* ***read aloud Parris's part, from "Abigail, I have fought here three long years . . . " through the end of the paragraph.***)

From the piece of dialogue, I understand that because of Parris's position in the church, he is especially worried about accusations that anyone in his family is involved with witchcraft. He knows that he will lose his job. Now I understand better why he is so anxious and why he is looking for someone else to blame.

Invite students to take turns modeling the reading strategy of clarifying. Encourage them to explain how clarifying helps them to check their understanding of important plot events or situations.

After Reading

You may also use the selection questions and activities in *Glencoe Literature*.

Summarizing Have volunteers share the summaries they wrote for acts 2 through 4. Sample summaries follow.

Act 2 Abigail, along with Mary Warren and others, accuses many women of being witches. Elizabeth Proctor wants her husband to expose Abigail's true character to the town. John and Elizabeth's marriage is strained. Elizabeth is arrested as a witch. John vows to bring out the truth.

Act 3 To defend his wife, Proctor has Mary Warren tell the court that the accusations of witchcraft are false. Abigail responds by accusing Mary. Enraged, Proctor reveals his affair with Abigail. Weakened by ridicule and scorn, and fearful of the legal consequences of having lied, Mary accuses Proctor of being the "Devil's man." He is arrested for witchcraft.

Act 4 Many of those accused of witchcraft, including John Proctor, are convicted and sentenced to hang. Elizabeth Proctor, who is pregnant, is allowed to speak with her husband. Elizabeth maintains her belief in Proctor. He reluctantly signs a false confession, which may enable him to be saved. When Proctor realizes that the confession will be posted on the church door, he destroys the confession. He goes to his death with the others, proving his goodness by refusing to make a false confession. His action also reinforces the stance of many of his friends and neighbors who have remained honest and have not confessed.

Identifying Secondary Conflict Remind students that the **conflict** is the central problem that moves a story along. A character may struggle against another person, nature, society, or self. Ask students to identify the conflict in *The Crucible*. (*The religious leaders, wanting to eradicate witchcraft from the community, arrest and prosecute many citizens, including the main character and his wife.*) Have students characterize the conflict. (*The main character struggles against society.*) Tell students that many stories, including this drama, have a secondary conflict running concurrently with the first. Ask students what other conflict simmers beneath the surface; have them describe how it affects the characters and the action. (*Proctor and his wife are in conflict because he has had a personal relationship with their house servant, Abigail. Elizabeth cannot forgive John, and he lashes out at her while also blaming himself. This relationship affects the plot because Elizabeth's firing of Abigail causes Abigail to strike back later by accusing Elizabeth of witchcraft.*) Ask how the final scene resolves not only the primary conflict but also the secondary one. (*The conflict of Proctor against society is resolved as Proctor is hanged. However, by choosing death over giving a* *false confession, he does not compromise his own beliefs or put in jeopardy his friends and neighbors who have not confessed. The conflict of Proctor against Elizabeth is resolved through his receiving her genuine forgiveness and love. By accepting death and not compromising his honor with lies, he demonstrates his own goodness to himself, his wife, and the community.)*

Reviewing and Evaluating Help students review and evaluate the play by asking them the following questions.

1. In act 1, how do the Putnams differ from Proctor on the issue of witchcraft? (*The Putnams want to prove that witchcraft exists. Proctor seeks a natural explanation for the children's behavior.*)
2. What is your opinion of Proctor's character? Do you think he brings about his own downfall? Why or why not? (*Possible response: Proctor ultimately shows himself honorable, but his pride in refusing to publicly admit his mistake with Abigail until it is too late is his downfall.*)
3. Who do you think is the most sympathetic character in the play? Who do you think is the most unsympathetic character? Explain. (*Students should provide reasons for their choices.*)

Analyzing Character Ask students to discuss how a playwright reveals the characters in a drama. (*The audience learns about the characters through their actions and through the dialogue.*) Point out to students that a playwright often provides short descriptions of major characters upon their first entrance onstage. Explain to students that the character John Proctor is the principal protagonist in "The Crucible." A **protagonist** is the character around whom the action revolves. Tell students: *Think about Proctor's actions and dialogue. What makes John Proctor a complex character?* (Possible responses: Proctor is a reasonable man as shown by the way he respects and defers to the reasonable opinions of Rebecca Nurse rather than listen to the flawed arguments of Parris or Putnam. Proctor knows that he is guilty of unfaithfulness, yet he acts morally superior to others. His decision to sign a confession but to refuse to have it publicly posted or to accuse others shows his determination to defend his principles and at the same time retain his dignity.) Encourage students to choose a character from the play that they find particularly interesting and to analyze that character on the basis of his or her actions and the dialogue.

Connecting to the Theme Point out to students that the title of this theme is Acting on an Idea. Ask: *What do you think "acting on an idea" means?* (being prompted by an idea or a conviction to take action) *How is this theme reflected in* The Crucible? *What idea prompts various characters to take actions, and what actions do they take?* (Some characters act upon their fear of witchcraft and persecute those who are accused of evil. Others risk their lives to oppose what they believe are unjust accusations of witchcraft.) *Do you think that acting on an idea can be dangerous? Why or why not? Can it be a positive thing to do? Under what circumstances?*

OBJECTIVES

- To identify similes and metaphors; to distinguish fantasy from reality

Nineteen Thirty-Seven

Edwidge Danticat

Before Reading

Activating Prior Knowledge Briefly review the Salem witch trials as depicted in *The Crucible*. Point out that, although the people's fears and suspicions about witchcraft were real, no actual evidence of witchcraft or other supernatural powers existed. Then tell students that the story "Nineteen Thirty-Seven" is also about someone who is accused of practicing witchcraft. Encourage students to use what they already know, from their reading and from personal knowledge and experiences, about possible outcomes when people make false accusations based on superstitions and fear.

Building Background To provide background into the historic setting, have students read the Building Background notes and "Meet Edwidge Danticat" in *Glencoe Literature*. In addition, prepare students for the brutal events described in this selection by explaining, and expanding upon, the information contained in footnote 3 concerning General Rafael Trujillo.

Building Vocabulary On the board, write the following vocabulary words, without definitions: *escorted* (accompanied), *nauseated* (revolted, disgusted), *mute* (not speaking), *ration* (fixed portion), *pilgrimage* (long journey for a noble purpose), *indistinguishable* (unable to be identified distinctly), *implied* (suggested without being directly expressed), *disciplines* (systems of rules for conduct). Ask students to tell what they know about these words. Have students use each word in a sentence that conveys its meaning. Encourage them to consult a dictionary to verify their definitions and then to write the words and definitions in their vocabulary logs or journals. Ask students to notice, as they read the selection, the context in which the words are used.

Word Study: Irregular Verb Forms On the board, write the words *talk* and *talked*. Ask a student to use each verb in a sentence and to use the sentences to review present-tense and past-tense verbs. Remind students that **regular verbs** form their past tense through the addition of *ed*. Write the following verbs on the board: *build, seek, go, keep*. Lead students to understand that these are **irregular verbs** because their past tense is *not* formed through the addition of *ed*. Then write, on the board, the past-tense forms *built, sought, went*, and *kept*. Have students use both the present-tense and past-tense forms of the irregular verbs in sentences. Challenge students to note at least three other irregular past-tense verb forms as they read.

Setting a Purpose for Reading Suggest that students read the selection to learn the outcome of suspicions of witchcraft.

During Reading

Identifying Similes and Metaphors Point out that many writers use figurative language to create vivid descriptions and imaginative comparisons. Write the following sentences on the board: *The lamb's wool was as white as snow.*

Your smile is like sunshine. Our friendship is a treasure. Point out that a **simile** is one type of figurative language in which the word *like* or *as* is used in a comparison of two things that are basically quite different. Point to the first two sentences on the board as examples, circling the words *as* and *like*. Invite students to suggest other examples. Write them on the board, circling *as* or *like*. Then point out that a metaphor is another type of figurative language. A **metaphor** is a comparison in which something or someone is stated or implied actually to be another. Point to the third sentence on the board as an example of a metaphor. Invite students to suggest other examples. Write them on the board. Briefly discuss the pairs of items that the similes and metaphors compare. Point out that one major goal of figurative language is to create vivid pictures in the reader's mind. **Have students read the selection silently.** After students have finished reading, have them complete Interacting with Text **Identifying Similes and Metaphors,** student workbook page 111.

Interactive Reading Workbook p. 111

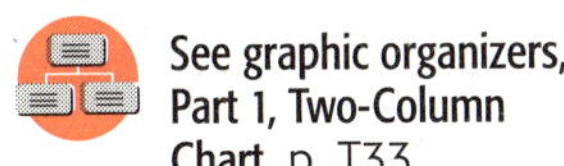
See graphic organizers, Part 1, Two-Column Chart, p. T33

Distinguishing Fantasy from Reality Discuss with students the differences between reality and fantasy in a story. Create a two-column chart graphic organizer transparency and display it on an overhead projector. Label one column *reality* and the other *fantasy*. Invite students to define *reality* in a literary work. (***Reality*** *is a state represented by events, characters, and settings that could be found in real life.*) Provide the example of a rainstorm. Explain that a rainstorm is real because it exists in real life. Lead students to understand that ***fantasy*** can be defined as "a state in which events that could not really occur, or in which certain characters or places that could not really exist, are present." For example, a rainstorm in which coins fell instead of water could not occur. **Read aloud the paragraph that begins "The yellow prison building . . . "** and model the process of distinguishing fantasy from reality.

> ***Modeling*** As I read, I pause and think about what seems real and what does not seem real. The description of the prison is realistic. The simile in the first sentence ("like a fort") helps me picture a strong, yellow building, perhaps made of stone. Details that follow include facts about the building—it was built by American Marines during the occupation. All of this seems believable. However, something in the last sentence doesn't seem real. The speaker says that Manman has been imprisoned because she has been accused of having wings of flame. I know that people can't really have burning wings. Therefore, I know that this statement is fantasy.

Work with students to fill in the two-column chart, noting elements of reality and fantasy in the appropriate sections.

After Reading

You may also use the selection questions and activities in *Glencoe Literature*.

See graphic organizers, Part 1, Venn Diagram p. T31

Comparing and Contrasting Remind students that **comparing** is finding similarities and **contrasting** is finding differences between ideas, persons, or events. Distribute copies of the Venn Diagram graphic organizer. Have students work in small groups to compare and contrast the events in "Nineteen Thirty-Seven" with those that occurred in *The Crucible*. Encourage students to discuss how the two literary works are alike and how they are different and to record their findings in a Venn diagram.

OBJECTIVE

- To identify details that support the main idea

Snow

Julia Alvarez

Before Reading

Building Background Read and discuss with students the Building Background note in *Glencoe Literature*. Draw attention to the accompanying photograph of children participating in an air-raid drill. Discuss with students how such children may have felt about the information they were given and the drills they participated in.

Word Study: Compound Words On the board, write the selection words *cornflakes, wide-eyed, air-raid, radioactive, fallout, blackboard, chalkmarks, daydreaming, sidewalk.* Remind students that a **compound word** is a word formed from two or more words. When combined, the original words work together to form a new meaning. Use each word on the board as an example, calling on volunteers to identify the words that have been combined, the meaning of each of these words, and the new meaning that is derived from combining them into a compound word. Be sure to use the words *wide-eyed* and *air-raid* to demonstrate that some compound words contain hyphens. Explain that one effective strategy for unlocking the meaning of an unfamiliar word is to determine whether it is a compound word and to use the meanings of the word parts to figure out its meaning.

During Reading

Identifying Main Idea and Supporting Details **Read the first paragraph aloud,** as students follow along in the textbook. Ask students to notice the details. Then ask what main idea these details suggest. (*The nuns at the narrator's school are a powerful and kindly influence on her, and they give her special attention.*) **Have students read the rest of the selection silently,** noting details of each paragraph and discerning what main idea they support. Ask them to jot down the main idea of each paragraph in their own words. Then have students complete Interacting with Text **Identifying Main Idea and Supporting Details,** student workbook page 112.

Interactive Reading Workbook p. 112

After Reading

Identifying Main Idea Follow-Up Invite students to read their main-idea statements of selection paragraphs. As a class, create a main-idea statement for the selection. (*Possible response: A kindly teacher helps the narrator through a frightening experience and helps the narrator to learn to value herself and others as loving, unique human beings.*)

You may also use the selection questions and activities in *Glencoe Literature*.

OBJECTIVES

- To make inferences about characters; to compare and contrast characters

FROM

The Woman Warrior

Maxine Hong Kingston

Before Reading

Building Background Read and discuss with students the Building Background notes in *Glencoe Literature*. Ask students to describe some of the emotions that immigrants to the United States might feel. Point out that many Asian immigrants of the mid-twentieth century experienced conflicts because their American-born children understood little of their parents' experience and felt more American than Asian.

Activating Prior Knowledge Tell students that, in this selection from *The Woman Warrior*, an old woman waits to greet a sister whom she has not seen in thirty years. Have students imagine how they would feel as they waited at the airport to see someone they loved, from whom they had been separated for a long time. Ask volunteers to share their ideas.

Building Vocabulary On the board, list the following words, omitting the definitions: *hysterically* (in a frenzied way), *beaming* (sending out rays, like light or radio beams), *encampment* (camping site), *conveyor belts* (continuously moving belts for moving bulky objects), *lure* (to draw or tempt away), *alien* (foreign), *grooves* (ruts or creases). Have students work with partners. Assign each pair a word to define, using a dictionary. Then have each pair write a sentence that uses the word in a way that suggests its meaning. As the pairs read their sentences aloud, have students guess the meanings of the words. Have students write all of the words and meanings in their vocabulary logs or journals.

Word Study: Suffixes On the board, write the selection words *useless*, *gladly*, *Chinese*, *confusedly*, *momentarily*, *politeness*, *gravity*, and *silliness*. Remind students that a **suffix** is a word part that is added to the end of a word. A suffix changes the meaning of the word to which it is added. Draw attention to the word *silliness*. Identify the base word as *silly*—reviewing, if necessary, that in words ending in a consonant plus *y*, the *y* is changed to *i* before a suffix is added. Ask a volunteer to define *silly*. (*funny, inane, not serious*) Then underline the suffix *-ness*. Define it as meaning "the state of," leading students to understand that *silliness* means "the state of being silly" or "the state of being not serious." Have a volunteer use the word in a sentence that shows its meaning. Repeat the activity with the remaining words, having students identify the base word and providing them with the definition of each suffix. Close the activity by stressing that recognizing suffixes and understanding their meanings will help students to unlock the meanings of many unfamiliar words.

Setting a Purpose for Reading Have students read the selection to see how an elderly Chinese American woman views her relatives and her adopted country.

During Reading

Making Inferences Remind students that authors do not always state main ideas directly. Writers often provide clues through details. Readers can then use these clues, plus their own knowledge and experience, to help them **make inferences,** or logical guesses, about the writer's main ideas. **Read the introductory paragraph of the selection aloud** and then model the process of making an inference about Brave Orchid's state of mind.

> ***Modeling*** This paragraph tells me that Brave Orchid is at the airport waiting to meet her sister, whom she last saw thirty years ago. My own knowledge and experience tells me that thirty years is a long time to be separated from a close relative. The last sentence in the paragraph indicates that Brave Orchid got up early, even before her sister's flight took off from Hong Kong. Clearly, Brave Orchid is excited. I make the inference that Brave Orchid has missed her sister and is eager to see her again.

Make sure that students understand how you drew on your own knowledge and experience as well as specific clues and suggestions from the writer in this passage. **Ask a volunteer to read the second paragraph aloud** and to use clues in the passage, as well as his or her own knowledge and experience, to make inferences about what the writer suggests about Brave Orchid. (*Brave Orchid is a strong-willed woman who feels responsible for her sister and believes that she can control her sister's safety.*) **As students read the rest of the story silently,** have them continue to rely on details from the text and their own knowledge and experience to make inferences about the characters and the plot events.

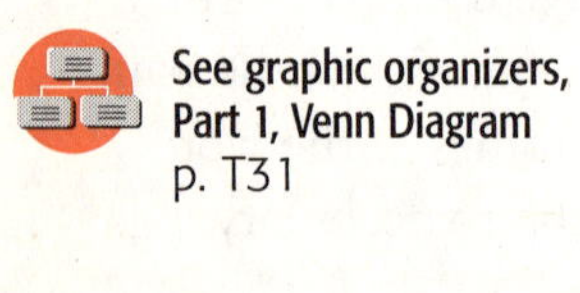

See graphic organizers, Part 1, Venn Diagram p. T31

Comparing and Contrasting Remind students that **comparing** is finding ways in which items or ideas are alike and **contrasting** is finding ways in which they are different. Then create a Venn diagram graphic organizer on a transparency and display it on an overhead projector. Work with students to use the diagram to jot down specific details that compare and contrast Brave Orchid and her children. (*Everyone is eager to see Moon Orchid; the children are impatient, distracted, and embarrassed by their mother's stubborn standing, while Brave Orchid is focused and determined to carry out her duty. Her suspicions contrast with her children's enthusiasm for America.*) Have students complete Interacting with Text **Comparing and Contrasting,** student workbook page 113. **Then have students reread the selection** to observe how the author contrasts Brave Orchid with other characters.

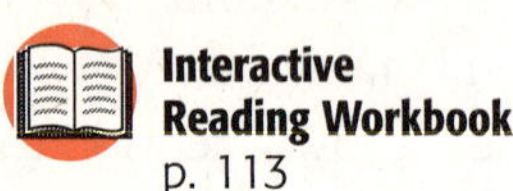

Interactive Reading Workbook p. 113

After Reading

You may also use the selection questions and activities in *Glencoe Literature.*

Comparing and Contrasting Follow-Up Ask students to identify places in the selection that show contrasts between Brave Orchid and one or more other characters. (*She and her niece eat Chinese food that she has prepared, while her own "bad boy and bad girl" waste their money on hamburgers. Unlike her niece, Brave Orchid has an unrealistic perception of what her sister should look like. Brave Orchid is argumentative, whereas her niece is soothing. Brave Orchid is "fat" and unhappy, but Moon Orchid is thin and smiling.*) Guide students to understand that these contrasts help readers grasp how Brave Orchid is isolated from her "Americanized" children and from her sister.

OBJECTIVES

- To note story structure and the sequence of story events; to identify theme

Son

John Updike

Before Reading

Activating Prior Knowledge Tell students that "Son" is an exploration of several generations of father-son relationships in a family. Ask students to suggest ways in which fathers and sons might be alike and different and what activities they might enjoy sharing.

Previewing the Selection Have students scan the selection for the red capital letters that denote section breaks and to find the dates that show a shift in time and setting in each section. Ask students to predict how this structure will affect the story. Lead them to understand that the story will move back and forth in time showing key moments for fathers and sons in the narrator's family.

Building Vocabulary On the board, write the following story words, omitting the definitions: *infantile* (babyish, immature), *leonine* (lionlike), *irksome* (annoying), *docile* (tame, gentle), *seminary* (a school that educates future members of the clergy), *camaraderie* (comradeship, friendship), *demolition* (destruction), *obscenities* (offensive or foul language). Ask students to define the words they know and to use them in sentences. Provide context sentences for all unfamiliar words and have students guess their meanings. On the board, write appropriate definitions for each word and encourage students to add the words and definitions to their vocabulary logs or journals.

Setting a Purpose for Reading Have students read the selection to discover the narrator's thoughts and observations regarding different father-son relationships in his family.

During Reading

Noting Story Structure and Sequence **Have small groups read the first section of the story silently.** Remind students that the **sequence of events**—the order in which the action occurs—is chronological in most stories. Then point out that this story, by contrast, is divided into seven distinct sections and that each section is set in a different period of time. Point out that this structure enables the narrator to focus on important moments in each of four generations in a family's history. However, because this structure is unconventional, readers must read carefully, pause to ask questions, and perhaps reread to discover the time period of each section and the identity of each son. On the board create a three-column chart similar to the following one. Write the section numbers in the first column as shown but do not add the notations shown in the second and third columns. Distribute copies of the Three-Column Chart graphic organizer to students.

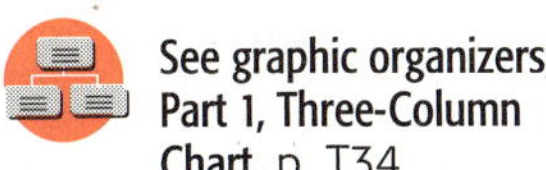
See graphic organizers, Part 1, Three-Column Chart, p. T34

Section of Story	Time Period	Son
1	1973	narrator's son
2	1949	narrator
3	1913	narrator's father
4	1887–1889	narrator's grandfather
5	1973	narrator's son
6	probably 1950s–1960s	narrator
7	1973	narrator's son

Refer students to the first section of the story and model the process of completing the second and third columns of the chart.

> ***Modeling*** **The last sentence in this section tells me that the actions take place in 1973. (*Write* 1973 *in the second column of the chart.*) The narrator is a father talking about his son, who is almost sixteen. He describes the son in detail and seems to want to show how thoroughly he understands what the boy is thinking and feeling. The narrator's son is the central focus of this section. (*Write* narrator's son *in the third column.*)**

Have students read the remaining sections of the story in small groups. As they complete each section, have group members work together to determine the time period and the identity of the son. Call on a different group each time to report its findings.

After Reading

You may also use the selection questions and activities in *Glencoe Literature.*

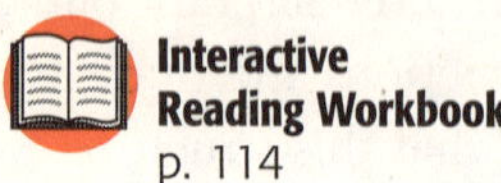
Interactive Reading Workbook p. 114

Inferring Theme Remind students that the **theme** of a piece of literature is a dominant or central idea, often a message about life. Sometimes the writer states the theme directly, but most often the writer uses story events and details to suggest the theme. Readers can then use these hints, together with their own knowledge and experiences, to **make inferences,** or reasoned guesses, about the theme. Have volunteers explain the important ideas about fathers and sons that they think the story presents. Have them tell what events or details have led them to each inference. Then have students complete Interacting with Text **Inferring Theme,** student workbook page 114. Use the displayed three-column chart to help students recall what happens in each section. Encourage students to find additional passages that point to the nature of father-son relationships. After students have completed the page, call on volunteers to share and discuss their responses. Then sum up the activity by asking: *In the events that the narrator shares, what message does he seem to communicate about what happens to a son's view of his father as he moves from childhood to adulthood?* (As youths, sons are impatient, feel superior to their fathers and families, and long for escape. As men and fathers, sons understand what their fathers endured and can, if they choose, use that understanding to empathize with the feelings of their own sons.) *How would you condense this message into a theme?* (Sons can learn from conflicts with their fathers to become understanding fathers themselves.)

OBJECTIVES

- To monitor comprehension; to understand tone; to analyze imagery

FROM

The Way to Rainy Mountain

N. Scott Momaday

Before Reading

Building Background Tell students that this selection from *The Way to Rainy Mountain* is set in Oklahoma. Explain that during the nineteenth century the United States government relocated many Native American people to reservations in Oklahoma. The government usually moved native people to less desirable land, making their old lands available for white settlers.

Building Vocabulary On the board, write the following words, omitting the definitions: *tornadic* (like a tornado, a violent whirling wind), *disposition* (nature, character), *ill-provisioned* (poorly supplied with food), *brooding* (sober, grim), *caldron* (kettle), *compensation* (payment, reward), *servitude* (slavery). Invite volunteers to select words from the list to define and use in sentences. Provide definitions and sentences that suggest the meanings of any remaining words. Then have students write the words, definitions, and example sentences in their vocabulary logs or journals.

Word Study: Using Context Clues Remind students to use clues in the **context,** the words and sentences near an unfamiliar word, to help them determine the word's meaning. **Read the first two sentences of the selection aloud as students follow along silently.** Then model the process of using context clues.

> ***Modeling*** The selection begins "A single knoll rises out of the plain in Oklahoma." I'm not sure what *knoll* means, but I know that a plain is flat. The next sentence says that the knoll is a landmark for the Kiowas; I know that a landmark is a feature of the landscape that stands out. A raised area of land would stand out on the plains. The Kiowas called the knoll "Rainy Mountain." These clues all suggest that a knoll is a steep-sided hill or mound. I'll consult a dictionary to confirm this definition.

List the following words on the board: *brittle, alliance, affliction, nomadic, divinity, confinement, reverence.* As students read, have them use context clues to help them determine the meaning of each word.

Setting a Purpose for Reading Have students read the selection to learn how legends and ancestral experiences helped to shape the narrator's beliefs.

During Reading

Monitoring Comprehension On the board, write *Summarizing, Questioning, Clarifying,* and *Predicting.* Explain that these are four key strategies that help readers to improve their understanding and enjoyment of what they read. **Summarizing** is briefly retelling the main ideas in a passage. **Questioning** is asking questions about information that is unclear. **Clarifying** is finding answers to questions about the text. **Predicting** is using information that has been presented and plot events that have already occurred to make reasoned guesses about what might happen.

Read the introductory paragraph of the selection aloud and model the process of using each of the strategies.

> **Modeling** I can *summarize* this paragraph by briefly restating the main ideas: The narrator's people live on the plains that surround a hill called Rainy Mountain. The weather and landscape are harsh. Broad spaces isolate people and things. I can ask *questions* such as What does the author mean that to look on this landscape "is to lose the sense of proportion"? To *clarify,* I reread. The paragraph makes me picture flat spaces, great distances, and only a few people or large objects. I think the writer is referring to his feeling small while standing in these giant spaces. The writer mentions "imagination" and "Creation." I *predict* that in the paragraphs that follow, he will provide some history of his people, such as how they came to live in Oklahoma.

Divide the selection into sections: the first four paragraphs, the middle seven paragraphs, and the final five paragraphs. **Create groups of three students and have them read the selection aloud by sections, taking turns.** Have members take turns leading the group in using the four strategies. The leader should initiate and provide examples of each strategy; the other group members should contribute additional questions and insights.

After Reading

You may also use the selection questions and activities in *Glencoe Literature*.

Understanding Tone Remind students that tone is a reflection of a writer's attitude toward his or her subject matter. **Have a volunteer read aloud the paragraph beginning "A dark mist lay over the Black Hills. . . . "** Ask students whether this language sounds formal or informal. (*The language is formal.*) Have students point out words and phrases that convey the impression of formality. (*The phrases "as if in the birth of time" and "engender an awful quiet in the heart of man" are examples.*) Point out that this formality helps create a serious, dignified tone. Have volunteers explain why this tone is appropriate for Momaday's subject. (*His memoir reveals truths and events that represent the core of his identity. He wants to ascribe to his grandmother the dignity and honor that she deserves.*)

Analyzing Imagery Point out that Momaday uses vivid imagery throughout this selection to enable the reader to "see" features of the Kiowas' historic landscape. Point out examples in the first paragraph, such as "At a distance in July or August the steaming foliage seems almost to writhe in fire." Explain that such language not only helps the reader visualize the scene; it also helps create a sense of living and thriving under harsh conditions. Have students find other examples of imagery in the selection. Ask students to explain the effect each image has on their view of the narrator, the grandmother, the physical setting, and the Kiowas' challenges. Then have students complete Interacting with Text **Analyzing Imagery,** student workbook page 115.

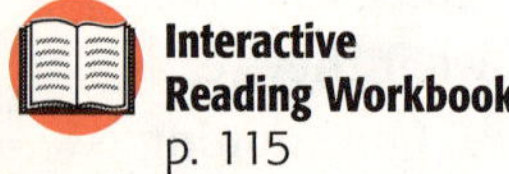
Interactive Reading Workbook
p. 115

OBJECTIVES

- To make inferences; to visualize

Ambush

Tim O'Brien

Before Reading

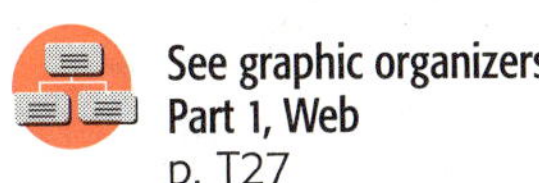
See graphic organizers, Part 1, Web p. T27

Activating Prior Knowledge Explain that "Ambush" tells of an incident that occurred during the Vietnam War. Have students read the Building Background note in *Glencoe Literature*. Then create a web graphic organizer on a transparency and display it on an overhead projector. Write *Vietnam War* in the center circle. Invite volunteers to tell what they know about this conflict. Jot responses in outer circles. Lead students to understand, and to note on the web, such terms as *guerrilla warfare*; and to identify the opposing forces (the South Vietnamese government and the United States against the North Vietnamese and the "Vietcong").

Building Vocabulary On the board, write the following words, omitting the definitions: *absolutely* (completely), *ambush* (a trap or surprise attack), *gradually* (a little at a time), *slivers* (small, thin shafts of light), *repellent* (a substance that keeps away insects), *morality* (virtue, a code of honorable behavior), *evaporate* (vanish), *peril* (danger). Ask students to identify and define any familiar words and to use each one in a sentence that shows its meaning. Have students consult a dictionary for definitions of any unfamiliar words. Then encourage students to record words, definitions, and example sentences in their vocabulary logs or journals.

Word Study: Contractions Write the following contractions on the board: *must've*, *he'll*, *I'd*, *she's*. Remind students that a **contraction** is a word that is formed by combining two words. An apostrophe takes the place of letters that are removed when the contraction is formed. Point to the contractions on the board and guide students to tell what two words have been combined to form each one and what letters were removed and replaced by an apostrophe. Point out that *he'll* can have two meanings, *he will* and *he shall*; that *I'd* can mean *I would* or *I had*; and that *she's* can mean *she is* or *she has*.

Setting a Purpose for Reading Have students read the selection to see how one soldier is affected by a disturbing war experience in Vietnam.

During Reading

Making Inferences Remind students that authors do not always make their points directly. Instead, they may provide clues and suggestions through facts and details. These clues and suggestions help readers to **make inferences,** or reasoned conclusions, concerning the author's full meaning and intent. **Call on a volunteer to read aloud most of the first paragraph of the selection, ending with " . . . she was absolutely right."** Then ask students what they can infer about the narrator from the details in the paragraph. (*The narrator did kill someone in the war.*) As students read the story, encourage them to use clues that the author provides to help them make inferences.

Visualizing Point out that a good strategy for making sure that students understand what they are reading is for them to **visualize,** or mentally picture, each scene or action that is described. Explain that visualizing helps readers not only to "see" the story but also to understand the motivations and feelings of the characters. **Reread aloud the first paragraph.** Then model the process of visualizing events.

> ***Modeling*** In this paragraph, the narrator's nine-year-old daughter asks her father whether he killed someone during the war. The narrator says that this was a difficult moment for him, so I picture him looking at her seriously and hesitating. Then he says that he "did what seemed right." These words tell me that he weighed the effect that his words would have and decided that the whole truth would be too hard for a child to understand. I picture him holding his daughter on his lap. She can't see his face, so he lets his sadness show.

Have a volunteer read aloud the second paragraph in the story and model the process of visualizing the event that takes place. **Divide the class into partners and direct them to take turns reading the rest of the story aloud to each other.** Encourage partners to pause at the end of each student's turn to discuss their visualizations of the setting, events, and character's emotions.

After Reading

You may also use the selection questions and activities in *Glencoe Literature.*

Making Inferences Follow-Up **Have students reread the paragraph beginning "Shortly after midnight . . . "** through the sentence ending " . . . seeing the young man come out of the fog." Ask what inferences they can make about the narrator's mood and physical state, from the details. (*Details: He is sleepy, hot, plagued by mosquitoes, and unable to see much. His troop is waiting to ambush enemy soldiers, a dangerous situation. Inferences: The narrator must be miserable both physically and mentally. He is nervous and uncertain what to expect. The fog and darkness make the situation seem like a dream to him.*) Discuss the details that led students to make specific inferences. For additional practice, have students complete Interacting with Text **Making Inferences,** student workbook page 116.

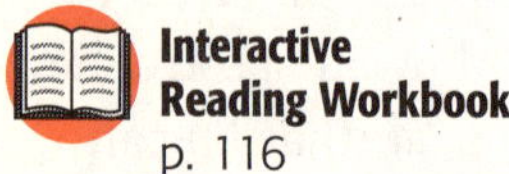
Interactive Reading Workbook
p. 116

Identifying Theme Remind students that the **theme** of a piece of literature is its central message or underlying meaning. Have students suggest the theme of "Ambush." To stimulate their thinking, ask such questions as *What did the narrator learn through the act of killing the enemy soldier?* (He regrets having killed the man, who would probably just have passed by quietly. He is haunted by his act and wishes that he could undo it.) Invite a volunteer to form a sentence that explains the theme. (*Possible response: One of the most horrifying things about war is learning that you are capable of killing someone and understanding that the "enemy" is often a person much like yourself.*)

OBJECTIVES

- To draw conclusions; to analyze figurative language

Rain Music

Longhang Nguyen

Before Reading

Activating Prior Knowledge Tell students that in "Rain Music" a young woman named Linh must choose between two men who love her. Ask students to recall situations they have read about or have seen in movies or television programs that involved such divided feelings. Ask: *What conflicts can result when someone must choose one person over another? What factors might influence a person's decision? What feelings might arise out of this choice?*

Building Vocabulary On the board, write the following words, omitting the definitions: *rivalry* (competition, struggle to surpass), *assaulting* (attacking), *intimate* (close, very personal), *breathtaking* (awe-inspiring), *harmonizing* (sounding agreeable or pleasing to the senses), *residency* (a period of advanced training in a medical specialty), *hamper* (a covered basket), *linear* (forming a straight line). Have students offer definitions and sentences for any familiar words. Provide definitions and sentences for any unfamiliar words. Have students add the words and definitions to their vocabulary logs or journals.

Word Study: Multiple-Meaning Words Copy the following chart onto the board.

Word	Meaning #1	Meaning #2
penned	restrained in a cage or corral	wrote
set	a unified group, as in a *set* of dishes	a portion of a tennis match
bright	smart or intelligent	shining with light
patient	a client of a doctor or hospital	kind, calm, and understanding

Remind students that **multiple-meaning words** are words that have more than one meaning. Draw attention to the words listed in the first column of the chart. Explain that the chart shows two possible meanings for each word. Point out that some of the words, such as *set*, have more than two meanings. Explain that when readers come to words that have more than one meaning, they must use context clues to be sure that they understand which meaning the author intended. Review the meanings of each word in the chart with students.

Setting a Purpose for Reading Have students read to learn about Linh's conflicting feelings for the two young men.

During Reading

Drawing Conclusions Remind students that **drawing conclusions** means making general statements that are based on details, reasons, and facts in a selection. **Call on a volunteer to read aloud the first three paragraphs of the story.** Ask students what conclusions they can draw about the narrator's feelings regarding her sister Linh, according to facts and details in this passage. (*The narrator considers Linh's beauty breathtaking; she believes that her parents are prouder of Linh than they are of her; although the narrator expresses some jealousy, she honestly admires her sister.*) As they **read the rest of the story silently,** encourage students to draw conclusions about David and Thanh and about why Linh has conflicting feelings about them.

Analyzing Figurative Language: Metaphors and Similes Remind students that **metaphors** and **similes** are two forms of figurative language. Explain that a **metaphor** is a direct comparison of two things, and a **simile** is a comparison in which the word *like* or *as* is used. **Have students reread the second paragraph of the story** to find a metaphor. (*"She is the red rose of the family and I am the green thorn."*) Model the process of analyzing this metaphor.

> ***Modeling*** In this metaphor, Linh is compared to a red rose and the narrator to a green thorn. I know the figure of speech is a metaphor rather than a simile, because it is a comparison that does not contain the word *like* or *as.* To analyze this metaphor, I'll use what I know about roses and thorns. A rose has a sweet scent and is lovely; it has shades of color and rounded, velvety petals. A thorn is unvarying in color; it is sharp and can cause pain. The comparison suggests that Linh is accommodating and is pleasing, like a rose; her sister is not so flexible and is "sharper," perhaps cutting in her remarks, like a thorn. The fact that roses and thorns exist together on a single branch suggests the closeness of the two sisters.

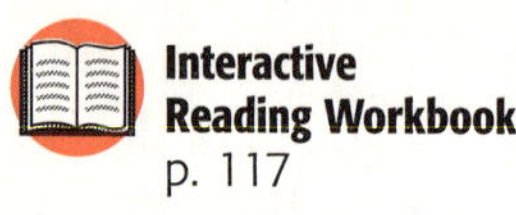
Interactive Reading Workbook
p. 117

Invite a volunteer to find a simile in the paragraph. (*"She has wide, almond-shaped eyes like black, pearl-black reflecting pools."*) Ask the volunteer to explain how he or she recognized the simile. (*The word* like *indicates that the comparison is a simile.*) Then work with students to analyze the meaning of the simile. (*Her eyes are a deep black, and they seem to flash with reflected light.*) After students have finished reading, have them complete **Interacting with Text** **Analyzing Figurative Language: Metaphors and Similes,** student workbook page 117.

After Reading

You may also use the selection questions and activities in *Glencoe Literature.*

Drawing Conclusions Follow-Up Ask students to share the conclusions they drew about Linh's feelings about David and Thanh and point out details in the selection that support their conclusions. (*Possible conclusions: Linh appears to love David deeply but is concerned about their cultural differences and his ability to support a family; she feels fondness and admiration for Thanh but not passion, and she feels obligated, perhaps because of her parents' expectations, to marry him.*) Stress that students must use many conclusions, rather than direct statements by the narrator, to help them explore Linh's feelings.

OBJECTIVES

- To determine author's viewpoint; to analyze sensory images

Kitchens

Aurora Levins Morales

Before Reading

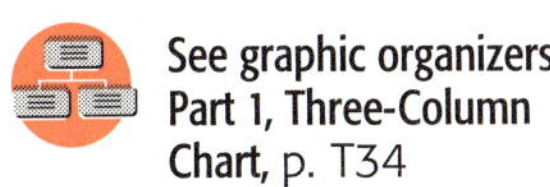

See graphic organizers, Part 1, Three-Column Chart, p. T34

Activating Prior Knowledge Tell students that the essay "Kitchens" explores a Puerto Rican woman's memories of her ancestors' cooking. Read and discuss with students the Building Background note in *Glencoe Literature*. Create a three-column K-W-L chart on a transparency and display it on an overhead projector. Have students offer information they already know about Puerto Rican cooking. Write these items in the *K* (for *know*) column. Then have students name things they would like to learn about this topic. Write these questions in the *W* (for *want to learn*) column. Explain that, after reading, they will use the *L* column for facts that they *learned* from reading.

Building Vocabulary On the board, write the following words in a vertical list; in a second column, write their definitions in random order: *defects* (imperfections or flaws), *scum* (filmy covering floating on the top of a liquid), *basin* (large bowl-like container for holding water), *cilantro* (leaves of the herb coriander, used as a seasoning), *oregano* (a type of mint plant used as a seasoning), *gnarled* (knotted, disfigured), *apprentice* (a person learning a skill by training with an experienced worker), *novice* (beginner). Provide a sentence using one of the words in context. Challenge students to use the context clues to help them match the word with the appropriate definition on the board. Repeat the process with the remaining words. Ask students to write the words and definitions in their vocabulary logs or journals.

Word Study: Words with Foreign Origins Explain to students that, as a result of populations' immigrating to the United States, words from foreign languages are introduced into common language usage and eventually become part of English. For example, many names of common foods in the United States have foreign origins. On the board, write the following words, omitting the countries or continents of origin: *zucchini* (Italy), *pretzel* (Germany), *yogurt* (Turkey), *spaghetti* (Italy), *cocoa* (Spain), *tofu* (Japan), *yam* (Africa), *meringue* (France), *gumbo* (Africa), *chow mein* (China), *chowder* (France). Call on a volunteer to define the first word on the board. Then have the volunteer consult a dictionary to find the word's country or continent of origin. Write the name of the place on the board. Repeat this process with the remaining words.

Setting a Purpose for Reading Have students read the essay to learn how cooking traditional foods from her native culture affects a woman who was born in Puerto Rico and who now lives in the United States.

During Reading

Determining Author's Viewpoint Point out to students that, when they read nonfiction, they should determine the **author's viewpoint**—the author's attitude, opinions, or beliefs about his or her subject. Explain that the author's feelings naturally flavor the content of a piece, because the author carefully chooses words, phrases, and sensory images that will best express his or her ideas or feelings. Identifying the author's viewpoint helps readers become aware of how the information in the selection may be slanted and how the selection may subtly influence themselves as readers. Recognizing the author's viewpoint requires readers to separate facts from opinions and to decide whether they agree with the author's views and attitudes. **Read the first paragraph of the selection aloud.** Then model the process of analyzing content to determine the author's viewpoint.

> ***Modeling*** **In the first part of this paragraph, the author states that she is standing in her kitchen in California, making a vegetable dish that is traditional in her Puerto Rican culture. The sights and smells of the cooking make her think of older women in her family, whom she remembers cooking similar dishes during her childhood. She uses words and phrases —such as *so deftly, so swiftly*—that show her affection and respect for the skills of these women. These context clues, plus what I already know about family relationships, can help me determine that the author has a positive attitude about, and a sense of pride in, these women and the skills that they have passed down to her.**

Have students continue to read the essay silently. As they read, encourage them to watch for more details that indicate the author's viewpoint.

Analyzing Sensory Images Remind students that **sensory images** are words and phrases that appeal to one or more of the reader's senses (sight, hearing, smell, taste, and touch). Point out that Aurora Levins Morales makes strong appeals to the senses in the introductory paragraph. **Ask students to reread the paragraph silently** and to identify phrases that appeal to the senses of sight and touch. (*Possible responses: sight—"shiny black beans floating"; touch—"smooth . . . beans sliding through their fingers."*) Have students discuss how such details affect their understanding of this scene. (*Sensory images help readers to visualize the scene and feel as though they are experiencing it with the author.*) Have students complete Interacting with Text **Analyzing Sensory Images,** student workbook page 118.

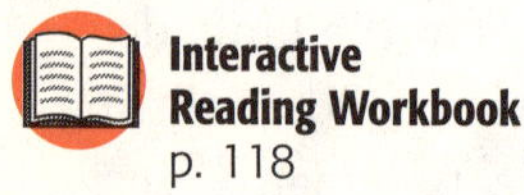
Interactive Reading Workbook
p. 118

After Reading

You may also use the selection questions and activities in *Glencoe Literature.*

Author's Viewpoint Follow-Up Ask students to summarize the author's viewpoint toward her subject. (*She feels both affection for and pride in her ancestors' kitchens and cooking; she feels satisfaction in her own kitchen as a place where she can renew her connection with her past and her culture.*)

Connecting Have students discuss feelings about their own family traditions, relationships with grandparents, and favorite foods and pastimes. What feelings might they share with Morales? What questions might they like to ask Morales? With what family member might they share and discuss Morales's essay?

OBJECTIVES

- To use the strategy of questioning; to identify tone; to analyze symbols

Bread

Margaret Atwood

Before Reading

Activating Prior Knowledge Ask students to think about their favorite foods. Ask: *If you could have for lunch today any foods you choose, what would you have? Would anyone choose to eat just bread?* Lead students to understand that many people, particularly in abundant situations, think of bread as a basic and ordinary food. Ask students to think of the significance of bread to those who are starving. What is the value of bread in those circumstances? Encourage students to keep these ideas in mind as they read the selection.

Building Vocabulary On the board, write the following words, omitting the definitions: *breadboard* (smooth board on which bread is sliced), *famine* (a period of severe food shortage), *infested* (overrun, contaminated), *corpses* (dead bodies), *traditional* (historic, customary), *yeast* (a tiny fungus used to make bread dough rise). Invite students to provide definitions for words they know. Then have students consult dictionaries to find meanings for the remaining words. Assess students' grasp of the words' meanings by having them make up sentences using the words in context. Ask students to add the words and definitions to their vocabulary logs or journals.

Word Study: Homophones Tell students that **homophones** are words that sound alike but have different meanings and usually different spellings. Write the words *weak* and *week* on the board as examples. Call on a volunteer to pronounce and define each word and to use each in a context sentence. Then write the following sentence from "Bread" on the board: "Should you share the bread or give the whole piece to your sister?" Ask students to identify the five words in this sentence that have homophones. (*bread/bred; whole/hole; piece/peace; to/two/too; your/you're/yore*) Invite students to watch, as they read, for other homophones. (Other selection words that have homophones include *know, do, die, pears, pain, right, here, tale, whether.*)

Setting a Purpose for Reading Have students read the selection to observe how the meaning and value of bread changes, depending on the situation.

During Reading

Monitoring Comprehension Remind students that pausing, as they read, to ask themselves questions helps them to make sure that they understand the author's ideas and the information that has been presented. **Call on a volunteer to read aloud the opening paragraph of "Bread."** Encourage students to frame questions silently about the subject as they listen. Then model the process of asking questions to clarify text.

> ***Modeling*** I wonder why the author wants me to "imagine a piece of bread." The description I've read makes me feel as though I am touching, cutting, and eating the bread. Why does she describe different types of

bread? Perhaps these details are meant to give me a sense of plenty and of choice. These details help me imagine the bread's look, feel, texture, and taste. They suggest how good bread is and how basic it is to life.

Point out to students that the essay is divided into sections; each section begins with a colored capital letter. **Direct partners to take turns reading sections aloud.** After reading each section, have partners ask each other questions to monitor comprehension. When reading is complete, call on volunteers to share questions that they asked and answered to help them understand the author's ideas.

Identifying Tone Explain that the **tone** of a piece of writing is a reflection of the writer's overall attitude toward the subject matter. For example, the tone may be sympathetic, objective, humorous, or angry. Point out that authors reveal the tone through word choice, sentence structure, sensory images, and figures of speech. Ask students to review the opening paragraph of the story and to identify its tone. (*homey, friendly*) Invite volunteers to point out elements that support this tone. (*The words are simple. The images are positive, warm, and homey—the bread knife was "picked up at an auction"; "the word BREAD carved into the wooden handle." The sentences are simple and direct.*) Explain that the tone shifts in the remaining sections of the essay. Encourage students to be aware of word choice, sentence structure, sensory images, and figures of speech that contribute to the tone of a piece of writing. Have students complete Interacting with Text **Identifying Tone,** student workbook page 119.

Interactive Reading Workbook
p. 119

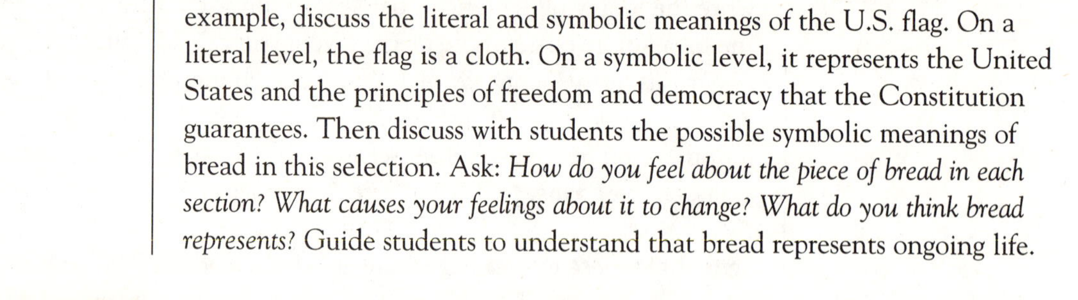

Analyzing Symbols Review with students the following explanation: A **symbol** is an object, person, place, or experience that exists on the literal level but also represents something beyond itself, usually something abstract. As an example, discuss the literal and symbolic meanings of the U.S. flag. On a literal level, the flag is a cloth. On a symbolic level, it represents the United States and the principles of freedom and democracy that the Constitution guarantees. Then discuss with students the possible symbolic meanings of bread in this selection. Ask: *How do you feel about the piece of bread in each section? What causes your feelings about it to change? What do you think bread represents?* Guide students to understand that bread represents ongoing life.

After Reading

You may also use the selection questions and activities in *Glencoe Literature.*

Evaluating Remind students that to **evaluate** a literary work is to judge it. Readers might evaluate an author's techniques, or they might evaluate a character's course of action. Ask students to think about each vignette in the selection. Which decision about bread—the one during the famine or the one made in prison—do they think would be most difficult to make? (*Possible response: Both are equally difficult in a moral sense in that both assign to the decision maker the power of life and death over another.*) Then have students judge how effectively Margaret Atwood makes her point.

OBJECTIVE

- To identify and analyze imagery

Picture Bride

Cathy Song

Before Reading

Building Background Review and discuss with students "Meet Cathy Song" and the Building Background note in *Glencoe Literature*. Ask how students would expect Song's Asian American heritage to influence her poems. (*Possible response: She might explore her ancestors' culture or the difficulties they may have experienced moving to a new land.*)

Word Study: Regular and Irregular Verbs Write the words *wait* and *waited* on the board, identifying them as the present- and past-tense forms of the verb *wait*. Circle the *-ed* ending and remind students that most verbs are changed to the past tense through the addition of *ed* and that these verbs are known as **regular verbs.** Then write the following words on the board: *leave, light, grow, blow*. Identify these as **irregular verbs,** explaining to students that their past tense is not formed through the addition of *ed*. Challenge a volunteer to skim "Picture Bride" to find the past-tense form of *leave*. (*left; line 3*) Discuss why this verb is considered "irregular." Repeat the process with the remaining verbs. (*light/lit, line 18; grow/grew, line 20; blow/blew, line 33*)

During Reading

Analyzing Imagery Remind students that **imagery** is the "word picture" that readers create in their minds as they read descriptive writing. To create imagery, writers use **sensory details,** or descriptions that appeal to one or more of the five senses—sight, hearing, smell, taste, and touch. **Have a volunteer read aloud lines 1–12 of the poem.** Discuss with students the "word picture" that these lines create in their minds. (*A young Korean woman leaves home and walks through her town to a pier where a ship waits to take her away.*) Ask students what emotions they feel and how they think the young woman feels. Guide them to recognize that the poet chose this imagery to encourage a response of sympathy in readers. **Have students finish reading the poem silently.** Then, to provide students with further practice in identifying and analyzing imagery, have them work independently to complete Interacting with Text **Analyzing Imagery,** student workbook page 120.

Interactive Reading Workbook p. 120

After Reading

Connecting Discuss with students how they might feel if they were in the situation of the young Korean woman: having to journey to a faraway land and marry a stranger who was thirteen years older than they? What questions would they ask the "picture bride" if she were their grandmother?

You may also use the selection questions and activities in *Glencoe Literature*.

OBJECTIVES

- To identify understatement; to distinguish between fact and opinion

Prime Time

Henry Louis Gates Jr.

Before Reading

Building Background Read and discuss with students "Meet Henry Louis Gates Jr." and the Building Background note in *Glencoe Literature*. Explain that "Prime Time" is an autobiographical essay about what living in Piedmont, West Virginia, was like for an African American during the late 1950s and 1960s.

Building Vocabulary On the board, list the following words, omitting the definitions: *chafed* (felt irritated or impatient), *light-complected* (light-skinned—*a regionalism*), *contested* (challenged, controversial), *even-steven* (having an equal score), *primal confrontation* (conflict or showdown of a basic, prevailing nature), *foibles* (minor failings, frailties), *awry* (amiss, wrong). On the board, write a sentence for each word that suggests the word's meaning. Have students suggest a meaning for each word; then have them check their definitions against those in the dictionary. Ask students to add the words and definitions to their vocabulary logs or journals.

Word Study: Idioms Explain to students that **idioms** are words or phrases that take on special meaning, often different from the words' usual meanings. Idioms are often used in everyday conversation and may come into wide use and then fade, like fashions. On the board, write such examples as *in the meantime*, *living on Easy Street*, *puppy love*, and *tried and true*. Identify each one as an idiom, and explain its meaning. Invite students to suggest other, currently popular idioms. Then write the following idioms from the selection on the board: "fashion plate," "shut it down," "down-and-out," "rednecks," "spectator sport." Define each one, pointing out that such idioms were widely used in the 1950s and 1960s, when the author was a child.

Setting a Purpose for Reading Have students read the essay to understand the situations that many African Americans endured prior to the Civil Rights movement.

During Reading

Identifying Understatement Explain that **understatement** is language that makes something seem less important than it really is. **Read the first paragraph aloud.** Then model the process of identifying and analyzing an understatement.

> ***Modeling*** I can identify the statement "It's no disgrace to be colored, but it is awfully inconvenient" as an understatement. The information that follows this statement makes clear that African Americans were treated unjustly: In the 1950s and 1960s, African Americans were denied such simple privileges as eating in certain restaurants, sleeping in hotels, using public bathrooms, and trying on clothes in a store. The turmoil and pain that they faced was far greater than mere "inconvenience."

Lead students to understand that the author uses this understatement to show irony and to make a strong emotional statement. **Have students read the story silently.** Encourage them to note examples of understatement as they read.

Distinguishing Between Fact and Opinion Remind students that a **fact** is a statement that can be proven true—by observation ("The sky is blue"), by consulting a reference source ("Thomas Jefferson was the third president of the United States"), or through personal experience ("My father works for the telephone company"). By contrast, an **opinion** is a statement of belief that cannot be proven or disproven. Sometimes, but not always, opinions contain such expressions as *I believe* or *I think*. Writers and speakers usually support their opinions with evidence—facts, details, and reasons. Stress that readers must be alert to distinguish between fact and opinion.

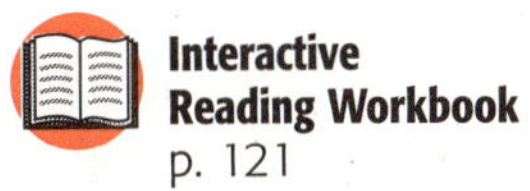
Interactive Reading Workbook
p. 121

Have students reread the opening paragraph of the selection and locate one or more facts. (*Possible response: "For most of my childhood, we couldn't eat in restaurants or sleep in hotels. . . ."*) Ask a volunteer to explain why this is a fact. (*The author's everyday experience proved it to be true.*) Have students continue reading silently until they locate an opinion. (*Possible response: "But I believe it was in part because Daddy was so light-complected. . . ."*) Ask them to explain what makes this statement an opinion. (*It is a belief and cannot be proven.*) For independent practice, have students complete Interacting with Text **Distinguishing Between Fact and Opinion,** student workbook page 121.

After Reading

You may also use the selection questions and activities in *Glencoe Literature*.

Connecting to Theme Remind students that this selection appears in the theme "Generations." Ask students how this selection fits in with the theme. If necessary, point out that the essay deals with situations that the author and other African Americans endured in the "generation" that lived at the beginning of the Civil Rights movement. Point out that the author states that he is now a parent; discuss how the situations that his children face today may be different from the situations he faced as a child. Then turn the discussion to the views of the author and his father regarding Martin Luther King Jr. and the beginnings of the Civil Rights movement. Ask: *Why do you think the author's father was so cynical about Martin Luther King Jr., whereas the author was so hopeful?* (Possible response: The father probably was afraid to hope that changes were possible because he did not want to be disappointed.)

OBJECTIVES

- To analyze problems and solutions; to identify and analyze similes

Se me enchina el cuerpo al oír tu cuento . . .

Norma Elia Cantú

Before Reading

Previewing the Selection Have students read the Building Background note in *Glencoe Literature.* Then have them read the translation of the title provided in the footnote on the first page of the selection. If necessary, define *goosebumps.* Ask students to study the painting above the title. Then ask students to relate the facts in Building Background to the title and the painting and to suggest what the selection might be about. (*Possible response: The face is haunted by anger or pain, and the title is suggestive of a suspenseful or grim tale.*)

Building Vocabulary Provide the following words orally, omitting the definitions: *board* (to cover with boards), *wrath* (anger, rage), *smothered* (suffocated). Ask students to suggest definitions for any familiar words. Define and provide context sentences for any unfamiliar words. Have students add the words and definitions to their vocabulary logs or journals.

During Reading

Analyzing Problems and Solutions Remind students that the plots of most stories involve central conflicts, or **problems,** that the character or characters must solve. The characters' actions in finding **solutions** to the problem make up the plot events and help reveal the personalities of the characters. As they read the selection, ask students to notice the problems that the family of migrant workers face. **Have students read the selection silently. Then call on a volunteer to read the first five paragraphs aloud.** Point out that the first problem encountered is the place the family is given to live in. It is not even "good enough for the chickens." Explain that the solution is to clean and furnish the chicken coop as best the family can.

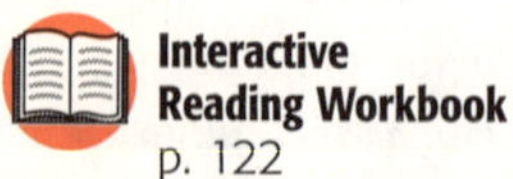

Interactive Reading Workbook p. 122

Have students complete Interacting with Text **Analyzing Problems and Solutions,** student workbook page 122.

After Reading

You may also use the selection questions and activities in *Glencoe Literature.*

Interpreting Figurative Language: Simile Remind students that a **simile** is a type of figurative language—it is a comparison in which the word *like* or *as* is used. Have students identify two similes in the last three paragraphs of the selection. (*"You hold your words like caged birds"; the memory is "like an old war wound or surgical scar."*) Ask students to tell what makes these comparisons appropriate to the situation. Discuss what is compared in each example and why the author compares such seemingly unlike things as words to caged birds and memories to scars. (*The man refuses to talk about the experience; the memory is the mark of a healed wound that recalls an extremely painful time.*)

OBJECTIVES

- To monitor comprehension; to analyze cause-and-effect relationships

FROM

Kubota

Garrett Hongo

Before Reading

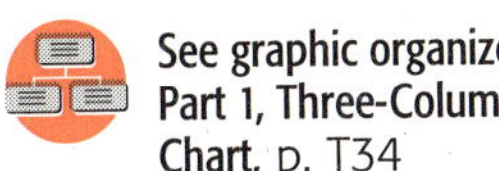

See graphic organizers, Part 1, Three-Column Chart, p. T34

Activating Prior Knowledge Tell students that the selection from a book titled *Kubota* describes how events during World War II affected many Japanese Americans. Read and discuss with students the Building Background note in *Glencoe Literature*. Then create a three-column K-W-L chart on a transparency and display it on an overhead projector. Ask students to share any prior knowledge they have regarding what happened to Japanese Americans who lived in the United States during World War II. Write these details in the K (for *know*) column. Then ask students to pose questions they would like to learn the answers to about this topic. Write these questions in the W (for *want to learn*) column. As they read, students can note answers to their questions and other new information in the L (for *learned*) column.

Building Vocabulary On the board, write the following words, omitting the definitions: *designated* (determined, chosen), *dutiful* (obedient, responsible), *judo* (a form of martial arts used for self-defense), *treachery* (treason, disloyalty), *scion* (descendant, heir), *exemplary* (ideal, flawless), *injunction* (order, command). Define and provide for each word a sentence that clearly conveys its meaning. Then have students add the words, definitions, and example sentences to their vocabulary logs or journals.

Word Study: Compound Words Remind students that a **compound word** contains two or more small words. When combined, these smaller words blend their meanings to form a word with a new meaning. On the board, write the following compound words from the selection: *roundup*, *offshore*, *wholesale*, *firearms*, *undertone*, *mainland*, *cupboard*. Call on volunteers to identify the two words that make up each compound word. Then work with the students to help them define each compound word and use it in a sentence that clearly conveys its meaning. As students read the selection, encourage them to find other examples of compound words.

Setting a Purpose for Reading Have students read the selection to find what happened to a boy's grandfather and to other Japanese Americans during World War II.

During Reading

Monitoring Comprehension Point out to students that they should pause periodically during reading to ask themselves questions about anything that seems unclear. Questioning is a helpful strategy to use when reading longer or more complex selections. Emphasize that good readers reread, adjust their reading rate, and read on to find clarification, or answers to their questions. **Call on a volunteer to read the opening paragraph aloud.** Then demonstrate how to monitor comprehension.

Modeling In the first paragraph, I read that after the Japanese attack on Pearl Harbor the narrator's grandfather was questioned by FBI agents. He was arrested at night, and no one in his family knew what had happened to him or what to expect. Why was he arrested? Reading on, I learn that the grandfather seems to have been Japanese American. Did that, and the Japanese attack on Pearl Harbor, have something to do with his arrest? The answer may be in the last statement, which explains that suspected enemy sympathizers were arrested. Did the grandfather sympathize with the enemy? What happened to him? As I read further, I'll try to find answers to these questions.

Have students read the rest of the selection silently.

Analyzing Cause-and-Effect Relationships Point out to students that in literature, as in real life, many events are linked by cause-and-effect relationships. A **cause** is an action or occurence that makes something else happen. An **effect** is the result or outcome. Give a simple example, such as *I drop a glass of water on the floor. What happens because I dropped the glass?* Identify the dropping of the glass as a cause; broken glass and a puddle of water are effects—they are the results of the glass's being dropped. Point out that readers look for causes and effects as they read to understand what happens and why.

See graphic organizers, Part 1, Cause-and-Effect Chart p. T29

Interactive Reading Workbook p. 123

Have students reread the second paragraph in the selection, which begins "My grandfather was suspected of espionage." Have students explain what caused U.S. government agents to suspect Kubota of espionage. (*Kubota was often seen at the fishing grounds where Japanese fighters had attacked. He had hosted people from Japan in his home. He had a radio and access to firearms.*) Create a cause-and-effect chart on a transparency and display it on an overhead projector. (See graphic organizers, Part 1.) Record the effect—Kubota's arrest—in the second box in the first row. Write the causes of the arrest in the first three boxes. Have students review the remainder of the selection, looking for additional causes and effects that will help them understand why certain events take place. Have students complete Interacting with Text **Recognizing Cause-and-Effect Relationships,** student workbook page 123.

After Reading

You may also use the selection questions and activities in *Glencoe Literature.*

Reviewing Call students' attention to the K-W-L chart they began prior to reading. Add to the *L* column new facts and answers to the *W* questions. Use questions such as the following to help students recall outcomes: *What happened to most of the Japanese Americans who were rounded up?* (They spent years in relocation centers, which were much like concentration camps.) *After the war, how did many Japanese Americans respond to their internment?* (They became silent and tried to "blend in" to the culture.)

OBJECTIVES

- To analyze repetition and extended metaphor; to analyze imagery

Speaking

Simon J. Ortiz

apprenticeship 1978

Evangelina Vigil-Piñon

Before Reading

Building Background Read and discuss with students the Building Background note in *Glencoe Literature*. Ask volunteers to describe stories that are part of the oral tradition of their families or cultural heritage. Point out that people have always used stories to connect to other people and to express their joys and sorrows.

Building Vocabulary On the board, write the following words, omitting the definitions: *cricket* (a type of insect), *murmurs* (speaks in a low and gentle voice), *tremble* (to shake, as in fear or excitement), *brilliant* (glowing, brightly colored), *masterpieces* (exceptional and rare paintings or other pieces of art), *galleries* (places where art is displayed and admired). Call on volunteers to define the words as used in the poems and to use them in sentences that suggest their meaning. Then have students add the words and definitions to their vocabulary logs or journals.

Setting a Purpose for Reading Have students read the poems to explore the connections between father and son and granddaughter and grandmother.

During Reading

Word Study: Connotations Explain to students that every word has a **denotation,** its dictionary definition. Additionally, words may have **connotations,** emotional or underlying impressions that add to a word's meaning. Connotations may be negative or positive. Use as examples the words *fragrance* and *odor*. Point out that each of these words has the same general denotation—"smell." However, *fragrance* has a positive connotation; it conveys the meaning of "a pleasant smell." *Odor*, on the other hand, has a negative connotation. It suggests "an unpleasant smell." Write the following selection words on the board: *murmurs*, *bubbles*. Next to *murmurs*, write *mutters*. Model the process of identifying and comparing the connotations of words that have similar denotations.

> ***Modeling*** Both *murmurs* and *mutters* have the same denotation: They mean "to talk in a low voice." *Murmurs* means "to talk in a low, soothing, gentle voice." A mother might murmur a lullaby to her baby. *Murmurs* has a happy, relaxing, positive connotation. Someone who *mutters* also speaks in a low voice but in an angry or complaining way. A student might mutter about a long homework assignment. *Mutters* has a negative connotation.

Call on a volunteer to read aloud "Speaking." Discuss with students how the positive connotation of *murmurs* contributes to the image of the little son and the happy experience. Then discuss the connotation of *bubbles*. (*positive connotation*)

Analyzing Repetition **Have students reread the poem "Speaking" silently,** identifying repeated words. (*crickets, cicadas, ants; listen; my son; this boy; speaking*) Remind students that repetition emphasizes ideas. Ask students why they think the speaker puts this emphasis on insects, his son, and the acts of listening and speaking. (*The speaker is showing the connection between his son and the natural world. He is emphasizing the idea that his son is part of nature.*) **Call on a volunteer to reread "Speaking" aloud** as the class listens to the effect of the repetition. Then ask: *If in the first stanza, the father introduces his son to the natural world, and in the second stanza, the natural world seems to be listening to the son, why does nature respond to the child?* Lead students to understand that the child, because of his youth and innocence, is more a part of the natural world than is his father.

Analyzing Extended Metaphor Review with students that a **metaphor** is a type of figurative language in which a comparison is made by stating that one object *is* another object. Give the following example of a metaphor: *Your friendship is a great treasure to me.* Point out that friendship is compared to a treasure. Then explain that an **extended metaphor** extends the comparison of the two objects or ideas over a paragraph, a stanza, or a poem. An example of a line that extends the friendship metaphor is *The jewel of your understanding sparkles between us.* Have students **listen as you read "apprenticeship 1978" aloud.** Lead them to observe that the speaker compares her grandmother's stories of her life with works of art. Then ask students to tell how these things are alike. (*Possible responses: Both may inspire. Both may be kept, and treasured, and used to stir memories.*) Ask students how this metaphor helps them understand the importance of the grandmother's stories and memories.

Rereading "apprenticeship 1978" If possible, call on a Spanish-speaking student to read "apprenticeship 1978" aloud. As they listen to the poem a second time, encourage students to think about how the Spanish language adds to the mood and meaning of the poem. (*The blended Spanish and English connect the girl to her grandmother and to her Spanish-speaking heritage.*)

After Reading

You may also use the selection questions and activities in *Glencoe Literature.*

Interactive Reading Workbook
p. 124

Analyzing Imagery Remind students that poets use **imagery,** or descriptive language that creates "pictures" in a reader's mind, to enable the reader to visualize the scene or understand an idea. Ask students to practice their skill in analyzing images by rereading "apprenticeship 1978" to observe what pictures the words of the poem create in their minds. Then have students complete **Interacting with Text** **Analyzing Imagery,** student workbook page 124.

OBJECTIVE

▶ To analyze simile and personification

Prayer to the Pacific

Leslie Marmon Silko

Before Reading

Activating Prior Knowledge Tell students that "Prayer to the Pacific" is a poem written by Leslie Marmon Silko, a Native American woman from the Laguna Pueblo in New Mexico. Invite students to discuss what they know about Native American beliefs or views about the relationship between human beings and nature. Then have students preview the poem. After they have read the title and looked at the painting, encourage students to suggest what they think the tone of the poem might be (**tone** is a reflection of the poet's attitude toward the subject) and have them provide reasons for their ideas.

Building Vocabulary On the board, write the following words from the poem, without the definitions: *myth of origin* (a traditional tale of creation), *turquoise* (a blue-green mineral that may be polished into a gemstone, commonly found in the American Southwest), *coral* (a stony substance composed of the skeletons of tiny sea animals; often used in jewelry). Ask students to define or describe these items. Lead students to suggest the definitions shown in parentheses.

During Reading

Analyzing Simile and Personification Review with students some of the kinds of figures of speech poets use in their work. Invite students to define *simile* (*a* ***simile*** *is a comparison of two seemingly unlike things in which the word* like *or* as *is used*) and *personification* (***personification*** *is a figure of speech in which human qualities are ascribed to an animal, an object, or an idea*). Ask volunteers to give examples of personification and simile. (Examples: personification—*the wind sighed*; simile—*as gentle as a lamb.*) **Have a volunteer read the poem aloud** while students follow along in the textbook. Have students look for examples of personification and simile in the poem. Then have students complete Interacting with Text **Analyzing Simile and Personification,** student workbook page 125.

After Reading

You may also use the selection questions and activities in *Glencoe Literature.*

Prior Knowledge Follow-Up Ask students to characterize the tone of the poem. (*Possible response: The tone is respectful, dignified.*) Have them point out some of the poem's elements that suggest the tone. (*Possible response: The word "prayer" in the title suggests respect for the ocean; the main idea of the poem is about the ocean's importance to the survival of the Native American peoples; students may suggest that the shape of the poem mirrors the waves of the ocean.*) Encourage students to tell whether the tone of the poem is what they expected.

Connecting Invite students who have seen an ocean to share their reactions to it. What sights, sounds, and smells of the ocean do they recall? Ask: *In what ways does Silko help re-create your own impressions of the ocean?*

OBJECTIVE

▸ To interpret poetry

Riding the Elevator into the Sky

Anne Sexton

Before Reading

Activating Prior Knowledge Invite students to brainstorm for images, or mental pictures, that the title "Riding the Elevator into the Sky" brings to mind. Use students' ideas in developing a concept web for *elevators* on the board. Encourage students to review the concept web after they have read the poem so as to compare their ideas with ideas from the poem.

Word Study: Latin Root Explain to students that the word *elevator* is derived from the Latin word *ēlevāre* (to raise, lift up). Write the Latin word and its definition on the board. Then ask students the meaning of the word *elevator*. (*a movable cage that is used for carrying people and things from one level to another*)

Analyzing Figurative Language Tell students that the poet of "Riding the Elevator into the Sky" uses an extended metaphor to express her thoughts, comparing the speaker's inner life to an elevator ride. Have a volunteer define *metaphor* and *extended metaphor*. (*A* ***metaphor*** *is a figure of speech in which two seemingly unlike things are compared or equated. In an* ***extended metaphor,*** *the comparison is elaborated on throughout a paragraph, a stanza, or an entire piece of writing.*) As students read the poem, ask them to notice what they think the speaker is rising above on her elevator ride.

During Reading

Interpreting **Ask a volunteer to read aloud "Riding the Elevator into the Sky."** Then tell students that *surreal* means "having the strange qualities of exaggerated reality that a dream might have." Discuss the surreal elements in the poem. Remind students that readers **interpret** by making sense of a work in light of their life experiences, their general knowledge, and the comparisons and contrasts they make to other works. Explain that interpreting is especially important when a poet or an author uses symbolism to convey an idea. For instance, in "Riding the Elevator into the Sky," going past each floor might symbolize how the speaker gets further away from the familiar. Have students complete **Interacting with Text** **Interpreting Poetry,** student workbook page 126.

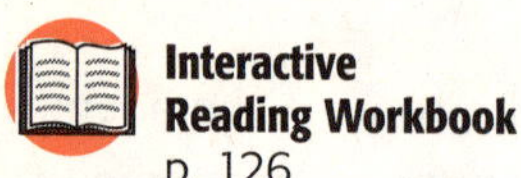
Interactive Reading Workbook p. 126

After Reading

You may also use the selection questions and activities in *Glencoe Literature*.

Analyzing Explain to students that, like the speaker in "Riding the Elevator into the Sky," people take risks and ignore warnings. Ask students to point out some images from the poem that they consider the most vivid. Ask: *Do you think Sexton's images spring primarily from the logical part or from the creative part of her mind? Why might she have chosen the elevator as a central image? Does the poet seem afraid of riding elevators? Explain.*

OBJECTIVES

- To identify noun-forming suffixes; to use the reading strategy of clarifying

Game

Donald Barthelme

Before Reading

Building Background Have students read "Meet Donald Barthelme" and the Building Background note in *Glencoe Literature*. Point out that Barthelme experimented with new forms and ideas and is noted for his use of **irony,** a form of expression in which the meaning of a passage is the opposite of that which the words convey. Then tell students that the title of the selection, "Game," can be interpreted several ways. Ask students to preview the story by looking at the painting on the first page of the story and reading the inset quotation in the center of the following page. Ask: *On the basis of the title, the picture, the quotation, and what you know about the author, what do you expect the story to be about? Why?*

Building Vocabulary On the board, write the following words in one column and their definitions in random order in a second column: *attaché case* (a briefcase), *flawed* (damaged; incomplete), *maneuver* (a procedure), *relief* (substitute), *oversight* (a failure to notice or think of something), *precedence* (priority), *concession* (the granting of a right or privilege). Have volunteers match the words to their definitions. Direct students to write the words and definitions in their vocabulary logs or journals.

Word Study: Noun-Forming Suffixes On the board, write the word *enjoy*. Ask students what part of speech the word is. (*verb*) Review with students how adding a **suffix** to the end of a word can change the meaning as well as the part of speech of the word. Ask: *How would you change the verb* enjoy *to make it into a noun?* (add *-ment* to form *enjoyment*) Write *enjoyment* on the board and identify *-ment* as a suffix. Explain to students that suffixes added to words to make them into nouns are called **noun-forming suffixes.** Tell students that several examples of words having noun-forming suffixes appear in the selection. Have students complete Interacting with Text **Noun-Forming Suffixes,** student workbook page 127.

Interactive Reading Workbook p. 127

Setting a Purpose for Reading Suggest that students read the story to find out what is ironic about the title "Game."

During Reading

Clarifying Remind students that they can increase their understanding of what they read by developing the habit of **monitoring their own comprehension**—checking to make sure that they understand what they are reading. Have students identify strategies that they can use to help them understand what they read. Then explain that clarifying is one strategy that they might find useful as they read the story "Game." **Clarifying** a passage may involve **rereading** to check information or **reading on** to see whether the meaning of a confusing passage becomes clear in a subsequent passage. **Read aloud the first paragraph of the story.** Model the process of clarifying.

> ***Modeling*** As I read this paragraph, I'm not sure I really understand what's going on. Who is Shotwell, and why is he playing jacks? Are he and the narrator of the story supposed to be children? I think so, because jacks is a game that children play, yet Shotwell keeps them in an attaché case, and it would be odd for a child to have a briefcase. These points may become clear later in the story, so I decide to read on. (*Read through the third paragraph.*) The references to carrying guns, living underground, and to a "twisted childhood" make clear that the characters are adults.

Divide students into small groups and have students read the story aloud. Remind students to monitor their own comprehension as they read. Groups should pause between readers to give everyone an opportunity to check his or her comprehension and clarify confusing passages.

Analyzing Repetition Discuss with students the author's frequent use of repetition. Have volunteers **point out and read aloud passages that contain examples of repetition.** (Example: "my hand resting idly atop my attaché case, my hand resting idly atop my attaché case, my hand. My hand resting idly atop my attaché case.") Ask: *Why do you think the author uses repetition?* (Possible response: To emphasize the boredom that comes from confinement and to emphasize the narrator's mental state.) *What effect does the author's use of repetition have on the reader?* (The repetition helps convey the on-edge, confused state of mind of the narrator and is effective in communicating the boredom the men experience.)

Making Inferences Remind students that they must make inferences frequently as they read. When **making inferences,** readers use common sense and their own knowledge to help them reason out things that the author does not state directly. Discuss with students what "the bird" in the story might be. Ask: *What inference can you make about what the bird is? Explain on what the inference is based.* (The bird is a missile. Students might make this inference from the setting and the description of what the men need to do to make the bird fly.)

After Reading

You may also use the selection questions and activities in *Glencoe Literature.*

Purpose for Reading Follow-Up Tell students that **irony** is a contrast or discrepancy between appearance and reality. Remind students that their purpose for reading was to find the irony in the title "Game." Ask the following questions.

1. What simple games do the men play in the story? (*The men play jacks.*)
2. What is the larger game? (*launching a missile that could kill thousands of people*)
3. Why is the title ironic? (*The title is ironic because the story is about life and death. It is not about something as trivial as a child's game.*)

OBJECTIVES

- To use context clues; to identify dialogue

Waiting for the Barbarians

C. P. Cavafy

Translated by Edmund Keeley and Philip Sherrard

Before Reading

See graphic organizers, Part 1, Web p. T27

Building Background Tell students that "Waiting for the Barbarians" is about the Romans' waiting for their enemy, the barbarians. Create a transparency of the Web graphic organizer and display it on the overhead projector. Write *barbarian* in the center circle. Ask students to suggest meanings and associations for the word. Write the suggestions in the circles that extend from the center of the web. (Examples: *savage, uncivilized person.*) Explain that in ancient times the Romans thought that foreigners (especially those who did not share their culture, language, or beliefs) were uncivilized, or barbaric.

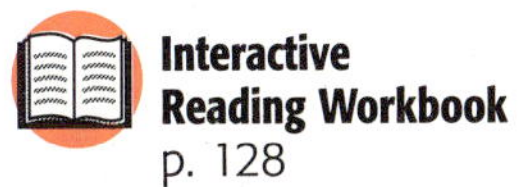

Interactive Reading Workbook p. 128

Building Vocabulary On the board, write the following words, without their definitions: *legislating* (making laws), *enthroned* (placed on a throne), *worked* (shaped or decorated by skill), *orators* (speech makers), *bewilderment* (confusion). Invite students to discuss ways to determine the meaning of an unfamiliar word from **context,** the words and sentences that surround the unknown word. Have students complete Interacting with Text **Using Context Clues,** student workbook page 128.

During Reading

Identifying Dialogue Help students recall that **dialogue** is the conversation between characters in a work of literature. Explain that the poem "Waiting for the Barbarians" takes the form of an extended dialogue—although quotation marks, the familiar indicators of dialogue, do not appear. The words of the two speakers are indicated by the way the lines are set on the page. Point out that the first speaker asks a question and the second speaker answers it. Ask: *Do you know what this question-and-answer pattern is called?* (It is referred to as "call and response.") Encourage students to share any experience with call and response. (*Students may mention prayers and church liturgy or musical forms such as gospel music and jazz.*) **Ask two volunteers to take the two parts and read aloud the poem.**

After Reading

You may also use the selection questions and activities in *Glencoe Literature*.

Reviewing and Interpreting Ask the following questions to help students review and interpret the poem.

1. Who do you think the two speakers are? (*Both are citizens of the city.*)
2. How do you interpret the last line of the poem? (*The barbarians are seen as a solution instead of a problem. Ironically, it is a threat from the outside that keeps the Romans united.*)

OBJECTIVE

▸ To analyze a poem

Mirror

Sylvia Plath

Before Reading

See graphic organizers, Part 1, Concept-Definition Map p. T25

Building Background Tell students that the poem "Mirror" is by Sylvia Plath. Distribute copies of the Concept-Definition Map graphic organizer to students and have them explore associations with the word *mirror*. After they read the poem, urge students to refer to their concept-definition maps to remind them of the associations and connections they made with the word *mirror*.

Building Vocabulary Explain to students that poets carefully select the words in their poems—not only for their meaning but also for their connotation, sound, and rhythm. Tell students that poet Sylvia Plath uses several precise-sounding, multisyllabic words, such as *preconceptions* and *agitation*. The meanings of the words, their connotations, and their formal sound all reinforce the theme of the poem. Review the meaning of *preconceptions* (ideas or opinions formed before acquiring actual knowledge or experience) and that of *agitation* (excited movement). Ask students to listen for other formal-sounding words in the poem.

During Reading

Interpreting Explain that personal knowledge and experience help readers to understand a literary work. Tell students that poetry in particular, with its condensed use of language, relies on readers to make connections and to **interpret** (to attach meaning to) what they read. **Read aloud the first stanza of the poem.** After students have listened to the first stanza, ask them what they know about the speaker. (*The speaker is a mirror.*) **Have a volunteer read aloud the second stanza.** Ask: *On the basis of the second stanza, who or what do you conclude the speaker is?* (The speaker is a lake.) *What qualities do a mirror and a lake share?* (Both reflect images.) *In what ways do the mirror and the lake featured in the poem reflect images differently?* (Possible response: The mirror is flat and cold and offers "truth"; the lake has depth—"reaches"; the lake offers depth that can hold—and reflect—all of life's experiences.)

After Reading

You may also use the selection questions and activities in *Glencoe Literature*.

Interactive Reading Workbook p. 129

Analyzing Tell students that **analyzing** a poem is looking carefully at its elements in order to understand it as a whole. Identifying the topic, main idea, sound devices, figurative language, and theme may all be involved when analyzing a poem. Have students complete Interacting with Text **Analyzing a Poem,** student workbook page 129.

Evaluating Tell students that Sylvia Plath's poetry often dealt with psychic anguish—a painful exploring of the self. Her husband, poet Ted Hughes, once said that Plath shared with a few other prominent poets of her day "the central experience of a shattering of the self, and the labor of fitting it together again or finding a new one." Ask students how "Mirror" helps illustrate Hughes's comment.

OBJECTIVES

- To summarize a poem; to connect with a poem

Traveling Through the Dark

William Stafford

Before Reading

Activating Prior Knowledge Tell students that the poem "Traveling Through the Dark" describes an experience that might seem an unlikely inspiration for poetry. Invite students to recall any experience they have had while traveling at night. Ask them to describe the situation and how it made them feel. Ask: *Where were you? What did you find disturbing or enjoyable about the situation?* To make sure that students are aware of poet William Stafford's interest in reflecting the Midwest and West, have them read the Building Background note in *Glencoe Literature*.

Word Study: Homophones Remind students that **homophones** are words that sound alike but have different meanings and usually different spellings. Write the word *deer* on the board and ask a volunteer to suggest a homophone for *deer* and to define both words briefly. (*deer, "animal"—dear, "beloved"*) As they read the poem, ask students to list at least three words that have homophones and then to write a homophone for each. (Examples: *road/rode, roll/role, tail/tale, doe/dough, born/borne, red/read, hear/here.*)

During Reading

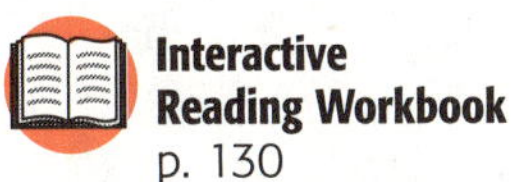
Interactive Reading Workbook
p. 130

Summarizing **Ask a volunteer to read the poem aloud** and to pause only where punctuation dictates. Have other students follow along in the textbook as they listen to the poem. Remind students that **summarizing** is retelling the main ideas and important details in their own words. Ask a volunteer to summarize the first stanza of the poem. (*Possible response: At night, I saw a dead deer on the road and moved it out of the way so that no one would get hurt.*) Have students complete Interacting with Text **Summarizing,** student workbook page 130.

After Reading

You may also use the selection questions and activities in *Glencoe Literature*.

Connecting Review with students that **connecting,** or relating their own life experiences to something that is read, often makes the selection more meaningful and memorable. Invite discussion of the ways that students connect with the situation and the feelings expressed in the poem. Ask the following questions.

1. How have you responded when you saw a dead animal by the side of the highway? Why?
2. To whom is the speaker referring when he says, "I thought hard for us all"? (*The speaker may be referring to human beings and animals or to the doe, the unborn fawn, and himself.*)
3. How do you think the speaker will feel about his decision when he thinks about it later? Why? How would you feel in a similar situation?

OBJECTIVES

- To recognize author's purpose; to analyze and interpret a poem

Frederick Douglass

Robert Hayden

Before Reading

Building Background Tell students that the poem "Frederick Douglass," by Robert Hayden, is about the famous abolitionist. Have students read and review "Meet Frederick Douglass," the Building Background notes, and the selection from *My Bondage and My Freedom* in Theme 4 of *Glencoe Literature*. Ask: *Why is Frederick Douglass a hero to all Americans?* (He championed the rights of African Americans and women and worked tirelessly for freedom.)

Building Vocabulary On the board, write the following vocabulary words, without their definitions: *gaudy* (showy in a tasteless way), *mumbo jumbo* (language that is impossible to understand), *rhetoric* (pompous writing). Ask students to offer definitions and to use the words in sentences. Provide definitions as necessary and ask students to record the words, definitions, and sentences in their vocabulary logs or journals.

During Reading

Recognizing Author's Purpose **Ask a volunteer to read the poem aloud.** Remind students that an author's purpose for writing a piece of literature is to accomplish one or more of the following purposes: to persuade, to inform, to explain, to entertain, or to describe. Have students read "Meet Robert Hayden" in *Glencoe Literature*. Then ask students to speculate about why Hayden wrote a poem about Frederick Douglass.

Interactive Reading Workbook p. 131

Analyzing and Interpreting Remind students that **interpreting** is applying personal knowledge and experience to help them discern meaning in what they read. **Analyzing** is breaking something into parts, studying the parts, and seeing what the parts contribute to the meaning of the whole. Point out that the poem "Frederick Douglass" consists of just two sentences. **Invite a volunteer to read aloud the first sentence of the poem.** Because the sentence is long and complex, students may benefit from an informal analysis. To help them do this, ask students to complete Interacting with Text **Analyzing and Interpreting,** student workbook page 131.

After Reading

You may also use the selection questions and activities in *Glencoe Literature*.

Rereading After students have completed the workbook page, suggest that they **reread the poem silently.** Encourage students to consider what they have gained from their own analysis and interpretation that changes their understanding of the poem. Students may enjoy presenting a choral reading of the poem.

OBJECTIVES

- To recognize rhythm in free verse; to respond to poetry; to identify personification

#2 Memory and Poem

Victor Hernández Cruz

Before Reading

Activating Prior Knowledge Tell students that the two short poems by Victor Hernández Cruz in *Glencoe Literature* give advice. Ask: *Do you like getting advice? What makes advice easy or hard to accept?* Have students recall and discuss times when they received valuable advice.

Word Study: Irregular Verbs On the board, write the verbs *think* and *dance*. Ask students what the past tense of *think* is. (*thought*) Then ask what the past tense of *dance* is. (*danced*) Remind students that the past tense of **regular verbs** is formed through the addition of *ed* to the end of the word. However, the past tense of **irregular verbs** is formed through respelling. As students read "#2 Memory," encourage them to note the irregular verbs. Have students write the present and past tenses of each irregular verb that they note. (*says/said, have/had, know/knew, buy/bought*)

During Reading

Reading Poetry Ask a volunteer to read aloud the Building Background note in *Glencoe Literature*. Point out that free verse does not lack rhythm. Remind students that **rhythm** is the pattern of beats created by the arrangement of stressed and unstressed syllables. **Have partners read aloud "#2 Memory" and "Poem,"** concentrating on the rhythm of the poem. Suggest that students pause slightly for breath after they read lines 3 and 8 of "#2 Memory." Ask what other breaks make sense to them. (*Readers should pause fully only after line 1, which has punctuation.*)

Responding Invite students to respond to the poems by offering their personal reactions and sharing how they might apply the advice to their own lives. Ask students: *What is your opinion of the advice in these two poems? Is it similar to any advice you have received?* Then have students complete Interacting with Text **Responding**, student workbook page 132.

Interactive Reading Workbook
p. 132

After Reading

Identifying Personification Tell students that **personification** is a figure of speech in which an animal, an object, an idea, or a force of nature is assigned human qualities. Ask what is personified in "#2 Memory" and which human characteristics are assigned. (*The words people say are personified. The human traits assigned to the words are the ability to travel and the ability to wear clothes.*)

You may also use the selection questions and activities in *Glencoe Literature*.

OBJECTIVES

- To analyze sensory imagery; to identify the theme of a poem

Weaver

Sandra María Esteves

Before Reading

Activating Prior Knowledge On the board, write the word *weaver* and tell students that "Weaver" is the title of a poem by Sandra María Esteves. Engage students in a discussion of what a weaver does and list, on the board, words suggested by students that describe the tasks of a weaver. Then have a volunteer explain what a *symbol* is. (*A* ***symbol*** *is an object, a person, a color, an idea, a place, or an experience that has a literal meaning but also represents something else.*) Read aloud to students the Building Background notes in *Glencoe Literature.* Ask students to suggest what the weaver in the poem might symbolize.

Word Study: Coined Words On the board, write the words *wildgrowth* and *sweatseeds.* Remind students that poets often use language in fresh and surprising ways to create powerful images. Explain that one way poets use language is to coin, or make up, new words. Invite speculation about the possible definitions of the words *wildgrowth* and *sweatseeds.* Ask: *How can you figure out the meaning of the words?* (Use context clues to help figure out the meaning of the words.) As students read, encourage them to look for and to figure out the meaning of the coined words.

During Reading

Analyzing Sensory Imagery Remind students that **imagery** is the word pictures that writers create to evoke an emotional response. Help students recall that **sensory imagery** appeals to one or more of the senses of smell, taste, hearing, sight, and touch. Such imagery gives poems a feeling of immediacy and sense of reality. **Read aloud the following lines from the poem: *"Weave us a red of fire and blood / that tastes of sweet plum."*** Have students identify the senses to which the imagery appeals. (*The images appeal to the senses of sight—"red of fire and blood"—and taste—"tastes of sweet plum."*) Suggest that students look for sensory imagery as they read to increase their enjoyment of the poem. **Have volunteers take turns reading aloud the stanzas of the poem** as the rest of the students follow along in the textbook. Then ask volunteers to identify and reread some of their favorite sensory images in the poem. Have students complete **Interacting with Text** **Analyzing Sensory Imagery,** student workbook page 133.

Interactive Reading Workbook
p. 133

After Reading

You may also use the selection questions and activities in *Glencoe Literature.*

Identifying Theme Remind students that the **theme** of a work of literature is its central meaning. Ask students to identify and discuss possible themes of the poem "Weaver." Ask: *What one overarching idea do you think Esteves wants readers to remember from the poem?* (Possible response: Unity among people brings peace.)

OBJECTIVES

- To identify main idea; to identify theme; to visualize

For Georgia O'Keeffe

Pat Mora

Most Satisfied by Snow

Diana Chang

Before Reading

Building Background Tell students that the poems "For Georgia O'Keeffe," by Pat Mora, and "Most Satisfied by Snow," by Diana Chang, are both about the effects of the natural environment on each poem's speaker. Have students read the Building Background note about Georgia O'Keeffe in *Glencoe Literature*. Call students' attention to the painting by O'Keeffe that accompanies the poem. Encourage a brief discussion of O'Keeffe, showing students other examples of her paintings, if possible. Invite students to respond to O'Keeffe's art and to discuss anything they know about her life and work.

Building Vocabulary On the board, write the following words, without their definitions: *bouquet* (a bunch of attractive objects together, such as flowers), *pelvis* (bones that form a cavity with the hipbones and the end of the backbone), *glaring* (shining so brightly that it hurts the eyes), *blooms* (flowers), *pervade* (to spread through every part of), and *occupied* (taken up, filled). Have students supply the meanings of any words they can define. Then have them look up the remaining words in a dictionary. Write the definitions on the board. Ask students to write the words, meanings, and a sentence using each word in their vocabulary logs or journals.

Word Study: Spelling Explain to students that many words include silent letters, which can make the words difficult to spell. On the board, write the following words from the poems: *straight* and *windows*. Ask students to underline the letters in each word that are silent. (igh *in* straight *and the second* w *in* windows) Invite students to add to the list other words that include silent letters. (*Common examples:* thought, science, island, climb.) Then ask students to look through the poems to find other examples of words that have silent letters. (*Examples:* walk, bone, know, snow.)

Setting a Purpose for Reading Suggest that students read "For Georgia O'Keeffe" to find out what inspired Pat Mora to write a poem dedicated to the famous painter. Suggest that students read "Most Satisfied by Snow" to learn about the poet's connection with nature.

During Reading

Analyzing Main Idea Ask a volunteer to read "For Georgia O'Keeffe" aloud. Model the process of finding the main idea of the poem.

Modeling I know that the *main idea* of a poem is the most important idea in it, or what the poem is all about. The title and the text confirm that the main idea has to do with Georgia O'Keeffe. I reread the poem. Then I determine that all of the details support the idea that the speaker wants to be able to experience the landscape through O'Keeffe's eyes, to feel a living connection to the environment.

Identifying Theme Remind students that the **theme** of a piece of literature is a dominant idea, often a universal message about life, that the writer communicates to the reader. Authors rarely state a theme outright. Instead, they use an **implied theme** in which the meaning of the selection is revealed through events, dialogue, or descriptions. **Have partners read "Most Satisfied by Snow" aloud.** Invite students to identify the theme. (*People are part of nature.*) Ask students to compare the two poems and to consider similarities in their themes. Guide students toward understanding that both poems are about the natural world and that people sense the world in different ways. Extend the discussion to include the Theme 12 title, Variety Is Richness. Ask: *How do these two poems fit into that theme? What variety do they offer? What richness?* (Students should describe the ways in which the settings of the poems differ and should note the difference in the poets' approaches to the general theme of the relationship between people and nature.)

After Reading

You may also use the selection questions and activities in *Glencoe Literature*.

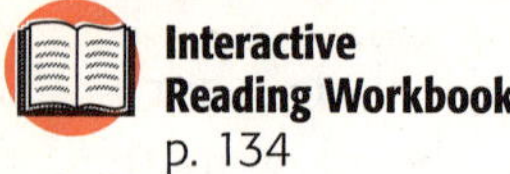

Interactive Reading Workbook p. 134

Visualizing Discuss with students the process of visualizing. Help them recall that **visualizing** is creating mental images based on the words in the text in combination with their own knowledge and experiences. **Ask students to reread each poem.** Encourage them, as they read, to visualize the images described in the text. Then have students complete Interacting with Text **Visualizing,** student workbook page 134. After students have completed the workbook page, invite them to discuss the painting accompanying the poem "For Georgia O'Keeffe" in *Glencoe Literature*. Ask them what stands out to them about the painting, *Red Hills and Bones* by Georgia O'Keeffe. Ask whether the painting represents the way they visualized the setting and action described in the poem. Then have students share the imagery the poet uses in "Most Satisfied by Snow" that best helps them visualize the scene. (*Possible responses: heavy fog outside windows; snow covering a landscape.*)

Connecting Ask students to recall a time when they felt especially connected to the natural world. Ask: *Where were you? What was happening? Is that feeling of connection to nature a common one for you, or does it happen only under unusual circumstances? Which aspect of nature, desert or snow, described in the poems appeals to you more?* Then ask students: *If you were to dedicate a poem to an artist, which artist would you choose? Why? What is there about the artist's work that is especially meaningful to you?*

OBJECTIVES

- To analyze figurative language; to identify theme

Geometry

Rita Dove

Before Reading

Activating Prior Knowledge Tell students that they will read a poem "Geometry" by Rita Dove. Invite students to define *geometry*. (*Geometry is a branch of mathematics that deals with the properties, measurements, and relations of points, lines, angles, surfaces, and solids.*) Have students express their feelings about studying geometry. Then ask: *How do you feel after solving a problem in geometry, such as proving a theorem?* Encourage students to recall problems they have solved in other subjects and to discuss the feelings they experience when they solve a problem. Suggest that students, as they read the poem, compare their feelings about solving problems in geometry or other disciplines with the speaker's feelings.

Building Vocabulary Ask students to explain what a *theorem* is. (*A theorem is a statement that can be proved on the basis of certain assumptions and definitions.*) Have students read the Building Background notes in *Glencoe Literature* to find out about the history of theorems. As they read "Geometry," encourage students to note why the word *theorem* is important to the poem.

Word Study: Word Origins Explain that the word *theorem* comes from a Greek word *theōrēma*,which means "to observe, look at." The word *theorem* is related to other English words derived from the same root, such as *theory* (an idea that explains a group of facts). Encourage discussion about the relationship of the words' meanings to the root.

During Reading

Analyzing Figurative Language Remind students that **figurative language** refers to expressions that are not literally true but express some truth beyond the literal level. Ask students what a metaphor is. (*A* ***metaphor*** *is a figure of speech in which two seemingly unlike things are compared or equated.*) Have students define *personification*. (***Personification*** *is a figure of speech in which an animal, an object, a force of nature, or an idea is assigned human characteristics.*) **Ask a volunteer to read the poem aloud** while students follow along in the textbook. Then have students complete Interacting with Text **Analyzing Figurative Language,** student workbook page 135.

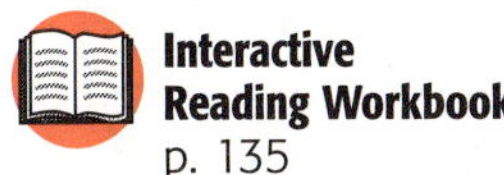
Interactive Reading Workbook p. 135

After Reading

You may also use the selection questions and activities in *Glencoe Literature.*

Identifying Theme Remind students that the **theme** is the central message of a work of literature. Encourage them to explain the theme of the poem. (*Possible responses: Knowledge sets us free; there will always be truths that need to be proved; there is value to inspiration, but it is limited.*) Ask: *What action of the speaker prompted her to write the poem?* (Proving a theorem inspired the speaker.) *How does performing that action make the speaker feel?* (She feels ecstatic and free.) *Why do you think she feels this way?* (Students may suggest the satisfaction that comes from completing a difficult task.)

OBJECTIVE

- To compare and contrast

The Welder

Cherríe Moraga

Before Reading

Activating Prior Knowledge Tell students that they will read the poem "The Welder" by Cherríe Moraga. Have volunteers explain what a welder does. (*A welder permanently connects pieces of metal by heating them until they soften and then holding them together until they fuse, or melt together.*) Have students read about welders in the Building Background note in *Glencoe Literature.*

Building Vocabulary Write the words *fusion* and *adhesion* on the board. Ask students to explain the difference in meaning between the two words. Explain to students that *adhesion* means "the sticking of one thing to another." For instance, an adhesive bandage sticks to the skin. Point out that adhesion is usually temporary. Then discuss the word *fusion.* Make sure students understand that fusion is a much stronger process than adhesion and that it is considered permanent. *Fusion* is "the act or process of melting together." Explain that in fusion two substances are bonded together, usually permanently. As they read, encourage students to observe why understanding the meanings of *fusion* and *adhesion* is critical to understanding the theme of "The Welder."

During Reading

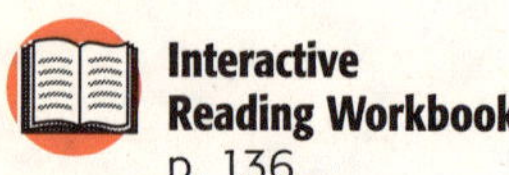
Interactive Reading Workbook p. 136

Comparing and Contrasting Remind students that **comparing** is looking for the similarities, and **contrasting** is looking for the differences. **Have volunteers take turns reading the stanzas of the poem aloud.** Ask: *According to the speaker, how are a poet and a welder alike? How are they different? Why does the speaker describe herself as a welder rather than as an alchemist?* Have students continue comparing and contrasting by completing Interacting with Text **Comparing and Contrasting,** student workbook page 136.

After Reading

You may also use the selection questions and activities in *Glencoe Literature.*

Understanding Extended Metaphor Remind students that an **extended metaphor** is a metaphor that compares two essentially unlike things throughout a passage or a work of literature. Ask: *What is the extended metaphor that is carried throughout the poem?* (The speaker, a writer, is compared to a welder.) Discuss the effect of this extended metaphor. Ask: *How powerful do you find this metaphor? In what ways does it help you understand the speaker's motivations and feelings?*

Vocabulary Follow-Up Review with students the difference between *adhesion* and *fusion.* Then invite them to discuss how the words are used in the poem. Ask a volunteer to reread aloud the fourth verse, in which the words are used. Ask: *What is the speaker talking about fusing together?* (people) *What is the main point that is made about adhesion in the comparison?* (Adhesion is temporary, a "patching up.")

OBJECTIVES

- To analyze English and Spanish versions of a poem

The House/ La Casa

María Herrera-Sobek

"The House" Translated by Tey Diana Rebolledo

Before Reading

Activating Prior Knowledge Explain to students that the poems "The House" and "La Casa" are the same poem written in different languages—English and Spanish. "La Casa" is the original poem, which was translated into English as "The House." Explain that the strong visual images described in the poem were inspired by the poet's view through her window. Have students recall thoughts and daydreams that they have had as they gazed out a window. Ask: *Where were you? What did you see? What images did you find particularly interesting?* Suggest that students read the poem to compare their own thoughts on gazing out a window to the speaker's.

Building Vocabulary On the board, write the following words, without their definitions: *desolate* (deserted and dreary) and *hermit* (a person who lives alone without interaction with others). Have students brainstorm about possible meanings of the words. If necessary, use the words in sentences that contain context clues that convey the words' meanings.

During Reading

Interactive Reading Workbook p. 137

Comparing and Contrasting Invite students who speak more than one language to discuss the difficulties of translation. Remind students that most English words have multiple meanings and point out that the same is true of other languages. Explain that the similarities in origin of some languages can be helpful to translators. For example, Spanish is a Romance language, which means that it evolved from Latin, the language of Rome. English has many words based on Latin roots. Therefore, many words in Spanish are similar enough to their English counterparts to be understood by non-Spanish speakers. Ask students to **compare and contrast** the two versions of the poem. Have students follow along in the textbook for a reading of each version of the poem. **Then have a volunteer read aloud the English version of "The House." Have a Spanish-speaking student read aloud the Spanish version, "La Casa."** Encourage students to note similarities and differences between the two versions of the poem by looking closely at similar words. Have students complete Interacting with Text **Using Language Clues,** student workbook page 137.

After Reading

You may also use the selection questions and activities in *Glencoe Literature.*

Paraphrasing Remind students that **paraphrasing** is retelling what they have read, using their own words. Ask volunteers to paraphrase the poem. Ask: *What words would you use to express what the poet communicates in "The House" or "La Casa"?*

OBJECTIVE

- To analyze characterization

Salvador Late or Early

Sandra Cisneros

Before Reading

Activating Prior Knowledge Have students discuss distinctions between poetry and prose. (***Prose*** *is written language that is not versified. Novels, short stories, and essays are written in prose.* ***Poetry*** *is language that emphasizes the line, rather than the sentence.*) Explain that other characteristics of poetry are compact and imaginative uses of language; figures of speech; and sound devices such as rhyme, alliteration, and rhythm. Then tell students that the selection "Salvador Late or Early" by Sandra Cisneros, is a short short story distinguished by poetic language, imagery, and poetic devices such as alliteration. On the board, write the title "Salvador Late or Early." Ask students to prepare to read Cisneros's poetic style by writing freely for five minutes, jotting down the ideas, associations, and speculations that the title brings to mind.

Word Study: Alliteration On the board, write the following sentence, without the underlining: "*Helps his mama, who is busy with the business of the baby.*" Remind students that **alliteration** is the repetition of consonant sounds at the beginnings of words in close proximity. Then ask a volunteer to point out the alliteration in the sentence on the board. Encourage students to observe the way the author uses alliteration throughout the story.

During Reading

Analyzing Characterization **Ask a volunteer to read aloud the first paragraph of the story** as other students follow along in their textbooks. Note that the author not only describes what Salvador looks like and how he behaves; she briefly sketches a picture of his harsh life. **Ask two other volunteers to read aloud the remaining two paragraphs of the story.** Discuss Salvador with students. Ask: *What kind of a person is Salvador? How do you feel about him?* Tell students that Cisneros uses **direct characterization** in this story, as she makes explicit statements about Salvador, and **indirect characterization,** in which she reveals the character through his actions. Have students complete Interacting with Text **Analyzing Characterization,** student workbook page 138.

After Reading

You may also use the selection questions and activities in *Glencoe Literature.*

Word Study Follow-Up Ask students to identify sentences or groups of sentences that contain alliteration. Have volunteers read aloud passages from the story that seem most rhythmic to them. Students in small groups might plan and perform choral readings of the story. (Examples of alliteration: "color of caterpillar," "history of hurt.")

OBJECTIVES

- To visualize; to analyze sensory imagery; to connect

Embroidering:

A Response to "Somnad" by Carl Larsson

Rita Magdaleno

El Olvido

(Según las Madres)

Judith Oritz Cofer

Before Reading

Activating Prior Knowledge Tell students that the poems they will read—"Embroidering: A Response to 'Somnad' by Carl Larsson" by Rita Magdaleno and "El Olvido (Según las Madres)" by Judith Ortiz Cofer—both have subtitles. Direct students to check the footnotes in *Glencoe Literature* for the translation of the title of the second poem. [*"The Forgotten (According to Mothers)."]* Explain that each of the poems concerns a memory of the relationship between the speaker and her mother. Encourage students to discuss some of the things that trigger memories. (*Examples: a photograph, a scent, a place, a dream, an object, a phrase.*)

Building Vocabulary On the board, write the following words, without definitions: *strand* (one of the threads of a piece of cloth), *fervor* (intense enthusiasm), *exposure* (the state of being unprotected). After they offer their ideas about what these words mean, let students verify meanings in a dictionary. Ask students to use each word in a sentence that conveys its meaning. Have students record the words, definitions, and sentences in their vocabulary logs or journals.

Word Study: Greek Roots On the board, write the word *choreography*. Ask students to identify a familiar Greek word root in *choreography*. Help them realize that the Greek root *graph*, meaning "to write," is part of the word. Explain that the beginning of the word also comes from a Greek root, *khorōs*, meaning "dance, chorus." Invite students to brainstorm and to compile a list of other English words that include the Greek root *graph*. (*Possible words: geography, autograph, photograph, telegraph.*) Volunteers might also point out other English words from the Greek root *khorōs*, such as *chorus* and *chorale*. Interested students may want to consult a dictionary for the etymologies, or word histories, of other words that may have these Greek roots.

Setting a Purpose for Reading Suggest that students read for details in the poems that may bring memories to mind.

During Reading

Visualizing Remind students that often they can **visualize,** or form mental pictures, from descriptions that a poet provides. **Read aloud the first sentence of "Embroidering."** Model the process of visualizing.

> ***Modeling*** I remember seeing hydrangeas—big, puffy, dramatic flowers, some on bushes. Many people pick hydrangeas for bouquets. The poet says that the room is "blue and clear, everything solid and in its place." I picture a neat, tidy room painted blue. The vase of hydrangeas sits, carefully centered, on a table. The large white flowers contrast with the room's blue walls.

Encourage students to visualize the scene as they read, using both the details in the poem and their own knowledge and experiences.

Interactive Reading Workbook
p. 139

Analyzing Sensory Imagery Recall with students that poets use **sensory imagery**—words, phrases, and descriptions that appeal to the five senses: smell, taste, hearing, sight, and touch. **Read aloud the second sentence of "Embroidering," from line 3 ("Here, two women . . . ") through line 6 (" . . . beautiful threads").** Ask: *What sense is the poet appealing to most in this passage?* (touch) Suggest that students listen for other sensory images as you **read the poem aloud** while students follow along in the textbook. Then have students complete Interacting with Text **Analyzing Sensory Imagery,** student workbook page 139.

Connecting Invite students to share their personal responses to the poem, including ways in which they **connect** its message and feelings to people, events, or situations in their own lives. **Have students read "El Olvido" independently.** Then ask: *In what ways do these poems remind you of feelings you have experienced in your own life? In what ways are the two poems similar?* Have students respond in their journals.

After Reading

You may also use the selection questions and activities in *Glencoe Literature*.

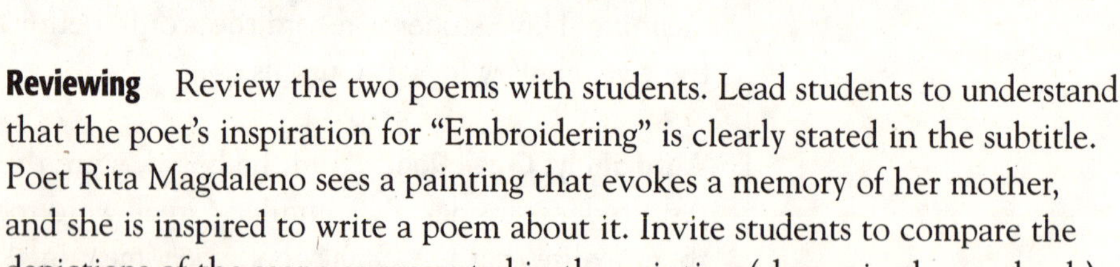

Reviewing Review the two poems with students. Lead students to understand that the poet's inspiration for "Embroidering" is clearly stated in the subtitle. Poet Rita Magdaleno sees a painting that evokes a memory of her mother, and she is inspired to write a poem about it. Invite students to compare the depictions of the scene as presented in the painting (shown in the textbook) and the poem.

Analyzing Ask students to suggest important ideas in "Embroidering" and have them find the text that illustrates each of their ideas. Have students explore the idea of connections—between people and between generations. Ask them to find imagery in the poem that addresses this idea. ("*two women / sit together, their knees / touching*"; "*threads*"; "*filaments*"; "*string*"; "*this rhythm of breathing and needles / sliding slowly through the cloth*"; "*for guests*"; "*passed through / generations, needle of the mother, / needle of the daughter crossing*"; "*a choreography / of hands and needles*")

OBJECTIVES

- To use summarizing, questioning, clarifying, and predicting

The Names of Women

Louise Erdrich

Before Reading

Building Background Have students read "Meet Louise Erdrich" and the Building Background note in *Glencoe Literature*. Point out that Erdrich's Native American heritage inspires much of her writing.

Characteristics of Genre: Personal Essay Remind students that an **essay** is a short work of nonfiction on a single topic. The purpose of an essay is to communicate an idea or an opinion. Explain that in a **personal essay,** such as "The Names of Women," an author may reflect upon personal experiences or present personal views on an issue. Specific details of the writer's life and experiences encourage readers to connect their own experiences to those of the writer. Such connections make readers more likely to accept the author's views.

Building Vocabulary On the board, write the following words, without definitions: *mystique* (an attitude of mystery), *icon* (a formal representation of a sacred personage, someone greatly revered), *clan* (an extended family), *materialize* (to appear), *adhering* (following devotedly), *configurations* (arrangements), *homely* (plain and ordinary). Ask students to define the words, using a dictionary as necessary. Have students write the words and their meanings in their vocabulary logs or journals.

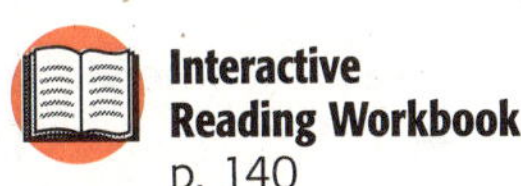
Interactive Reading Workbook p. 140

Word Study: Homographs and Homophones Remind students that **homographs** are words that are spelled alike but have different meanings and may have different pronunciations. (Example: the words *well*, meaning "a place to get water from the ground," and *well*, meaning "not sick.") **Homophones** are words that sound similar but have different spellings and different meanings. (Example: the words *to*, *too*, and *two*.) Have students complete Interacting with Text **Homographs and Homophones,** student workbook page 140.

Setting a Purpose for Reading Have students read to learn about names and the author's ancestors.

During Reading

Using Reading Strategies On the board, write the names of the following reading strategies: summarizing, questioning, clarifying, and predicting. Tell students that **summarizing** is thinking back over what you have read and briefly retelling its most important ideas; **questioning** is asking yourself questions about what is being read; **clarifying** is answering your own questions and making sure you understand what you are reading; and **predicting** is using what you have read in combination with personal knowledge to make a logical guess about what will happen next. **Read aloud the first paragraph of "The Names of Women."** Model the process of using the strategies.

Modeling I summarize to check my understanding of the information that has been presented: The history of the Anishinabe tribe, like the histories of other Native American groups, is of a culture that was altered and destroyed. Next, I question: Why does the author say that "only the names survive"? I will reread the paragraph to clarify my understanding. (***Reread the paragraph aloud.***) I read that the Anishinabe intermarried with the French. Then I read that the culture and way of life of the woodland Anishinabe were altered by disease, wars with other tribes, and loss of land to European settlers. The Anishinabe seem to have been destroyed. What's left of this heritage, which is the author's Native American heritage, is only the Anishinabe names. I predict, on the basis of the first paragraph and the title of the selection, that the rest of the essay will concern the meaning and cultural significance of various Anishinabe names.

Monitoring Comprehension Divide the class into groups of four. **Have the groups read the selection silently.** Provide students with a copy of the following chart. Divide the selection into four parts: part 1, from the beginning up to "It is no small thing . . . " Each subsequent part begins with a large print letter *I* in color. Explain that groups, after reading each part, will use the reading strategies on the chart. Review the strategies with students. Have each group name a group leader. Monitor the groups and guide their efforts as they discuss each part of the selection.

Strategy	How Student Leader Helps	The Group's Response
Summarize	The leader briefly restates the main points of the text that may answer the questions *who? what? where? why?* and *when?*	The group offers ideas for additions and corrections to the leader's summary.
Question	The leader identifies questions about what was just read.	Group members try to answer the questions. They propose additional questions.
Clarify	The leader guides the group to answer the questions and rereads confusing passages aloud.	Group members seek answers and ask for additional clarification when information is unclear.
Predict	The leader predicts what may happen in the next reading segment and explains why he or she thinks so.	Group members offer their own predictions about what may happen.

After Reading

You may also use the selection questions and activities in *Glencoe Literature*.

Reviewing Comprehension Strategies Bring the small groups together for a whole-class discussion of the strategies students used to help them understand the selection. Ask volunteers to model how using particular strategies helped them understand specific passages in "The Names of Women."

OBJECTIVES

- To paraphrase a passage; to summarize, to make predictions

Naming Myself
Poniendome un Nombre

Barbara Kingsolver

Before Reading

Activating Prior Knowledge Tell students that the poem titled "Naming Myself" is by Barbara Kingsolver, who is part Cherokee. Ask: *If you could name yourself, what name would you choose?* Then ask: *Under what circumstances do people change their names?* Students may mention that a woman in the United States may change her surname to her husband's when she marries, or she may hyphenate her own and her husband's last names. Explain that some women who marry choose to keep their maiden names. Encourage students who are familiar with the naming conventions of other cultures to describe those conventions, such as that of a surname's preceding a given name.

Building Vocabulary On the board, write the following words, without their definitions: *ancestor* (one from whom a person is descended), *legend* (a story handed down by tradition and popularly regarded as historical). Ask students to suggest the meaning of the words and to use the words in sentences that convey their meaning. Elicit from students definitions similar to those in parentheses. Encourage students to record the words and definitions in their vocabulary logs or journals.

Word Study: Variant Spellings Write the word *moustache* on the board and tell students that they will encounter this word in "Naming Myself." Explain that occasionally the spelling and pronunciation of a word, such as *moustache*, change over the years. Then, on the board, write the word *mustache*. Point out that this spelling is now more common, although both spellings are acceptable. Remind students that some words are spelled differently in British English, such as the British *colour* for *color* and *practise* for the verb *practice*. Point out that some spellings are simply replaced with more modern spellings, such as *archaeology* / *archeology* and *encylopaedia* / *encyclopedia*. Tell students that a dictionary is the most reliable source of preferred and variant spellings. In the dictionary, the preferred or most usual spelling appears first.

Setting a Purpose for Reading Suggest that students read the poem to determine how the speaker feels about her name and to decide whether they feel the same way about their own names.

During Reading

Paraphrasing **Have a volunteer read aloud the first two stanzas of "Naming Myself"** as students follow along in the textbook. Then invite students to discuss paraphrasing. If necessary, remind students that **paraphrasing** means restating what is read in one's own words. Ask: *What makes paraphrasing an effective comprehension strategy?* Explain that if they are unable to paraphrase a passage, they probably do not understand it and need to clarify it before reading on. Encourage volunteers to paraphrase the grandfather's story in "Naming Myself."

Summarizing Tell students that **summarizing** is the process of stating the most important ideas in what they have read, in a logical order. Explain that summarizing requires readers to evaluate which ideas are most significant. Students then synthesize that information and create a statement that incorporates the text's key ideas in the student's own words. To provide students with practice in summarizing, have them complete Interacting with Text **Summarizing,** student workbook page 141.

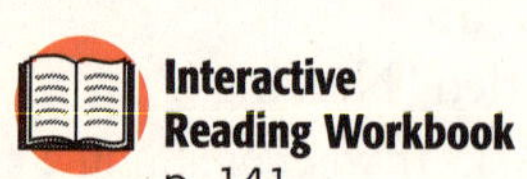
Interactive Reading Workbook
p. 141

Making Predictions Have a volunteer explain the reading strategy of making predictions. (***Making predictions*** *calls for making reasoned-out guesses, based on clues in the text, about what may happen next in a selection.*) Ask: *Now that you have heard the first two stanzas of "Naming Myself," would you predict in the final two stanzas of the poem that the speaker is likely to consider changing her name?* Model the process of making predictions.

> ***Modeling*** **In the poem are several clues that lead me to predict that the speaker is unlikely to consider changing her name. In the very first line of the poem, she says, "I have guarded my name. . . . " She says that her grandfather lost his name and invented the one she now has. That must have made the name special to her. These clues lead me to predict that the speaker will not consider giving up her name.**

Have students finish reading the poem independently. Ask them to verify the accuracy of your prediction. Explain to students that the author provides a Spanish version of the poem, titled "Poniendome un Nombre." **Invite Spanish-speaking students to present an oral reading of the poem as classmates follow along in their textbooks.**

After Reading

You may also use the selection questions and activities in *Glencoe Literature.*

Connecting Discuss with students their reactions to the speaker's determination to keep her own name. Have students discuss how they would feel if they changed their names.

Paraphrasing Follow-Up Have students reread the second stanza of "Naming Myself." Remind students that paraphrasing is a good way for them to check their understanding of a passage. Call on volunteers to paraphrase the last three lines of the second stanza. (*Possible response: The speaker sees a photograph of her Cherokee grandmother, who wears braids and old-fashioned clothes, but the speaker does not know her grandmother's name.*)

Reviewing Tell students that the speaker in this poem considers whether to give up her name. Ask: *According to the speaker, where (in a figurative sense) would her name go?* (Her name would go to the "Limbo for discontinued maiden names.") *What else does the speaker believe that she would lose along with her name?* (Possible response: The speaker believes she would lose part of her past and her history.)

OBJECTIVES

- To identify main idea; to compare and contrast

A Poet's Job

Alma Luz Villanueva

Emily Dickinson

Lucha Corpi

Translated by Catherine Rodríguez-Nieto

Before Reading

Building Background Tell students that "A Poet's Job" and "Emily Dickinson" are about poetry and the reasons that poets write. Initiate a discussion of the poet's vocation. Ask: *Why do you think people write poems? What special skills and qualifications should a poet have? What inspires one to write a poem? Is it a feeling, an experience, a memory, or even an opinion? What does poetry offer a reader that prose does not?* Let students discuss the reasons they like and dislike certain poems or types of poetry. For additional information about Emily Dickinson, have students read the Building Background note "Emily Dickinson" in *Glencoe Literature*.

Building Vocabulary On the board, write the following words, without their definitions: *contours* (shape, outline), *migrant* (traveling), *persistent* (stubbornly continuing), *progression* (the activity of moving forward, advancement), and *unsown* (unplanted). Ask volunteers to define the words, consulting a dictionary as necessary, and to use each word in a sentence that conveys its meaning. Encourage students to record the words, definitions, and sentences in their vocabulary logs or journals.

Word Study: Punctuation Ask students to discuss briefly the purpose of punctuation marks such as periods, commas, and dashes. Review that the marks signify to readers such things as where a thought ends, how thoughts are connected, and whether a sentence is a question, a statement, or an exclamation. Explain that punctuation provides guidance on how readers should read the words on a page. When reading aloud, punctuation can indicate whether readers pause, hesitate, or stop, as well as when to use inflection by dropping or raising the voice. Point out that typographic cues, such as paragraph indention and spacing, contribute to the organization of ideas and the unity of written thoughts. Encourage students to pay careful attention to punctuation and typographic conventions so as to discern meaning as they read the poems aloud or silently.

Setting a Purpose for Reading Suggest that students read the poems to discover the poets' opinions of the job of the poet.

During Reading

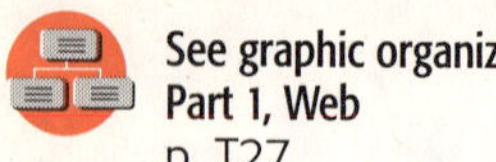

See graphic organizers, Part 1, Web p. T27

Identifying Main Idea **Ask a volunteer, paying particular attention to the punctuation marks, to read aloud "A Poet's Job"** while other students follow along in the textbook. Create a web graphic organizer on a transparency and display it on an overhead projector. Provide each student with a copy of the Web graphic organizer from Part 1. Have students fill in their own webs as you begin filling in the web on the transparency. Discuss with students the topic of the poem. (*The topic is "a poet's job."*) Write in the center of the web *What a Poet Does*. Tell students that this phrase expresses the **main idea**—the most important or central idea of the poem. Then brainstorm with students, filling in the extended circles of the web with details that tell more about the phrase at the center. As students reread the poem, have them write in the circles paraphrases of the aspects of the poet's job. (Examples: "to see the contours of the world" could be restated as "to see realistically"; "make a myth to share" could be restated as "to create a myth.")

See graphic organizers, Part 1, Venn Diagram p. T31

Comparing and Contrasting **Ask a volunteer to read "Emily Dickinson" aloud** as classmates follow along in the textbook. Recall with students how Alma Luz Villanueva describes the job of a poet in "A Poet's Job." Remind students that **comparing** is looking for the ways things are alike and that **contrasting** is looking for the ways things are different. Initiate a discussion of the two poems in which the ideas about poets and poetry are compared and contrasted. Create a Venn diagram graphic organizer transparency and display it on an overhead projector. Tell students that a Venn diagram can help them organize information as they make comparisons. Write the titles of the poems on the outside circles. Model the process of comparing and contrasting.

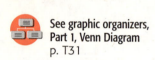

> ***Modeling*** **Both poems describe what poets do, so I write "Describe Poet's Job" in the overlapping circles of the Venn diagram. One idea that Villaneuva expresses in "A Poet's Job" is that poets make up myths for others to share. Corpi doesn't mention that idea in "Emily Dickinson," so I record that point under Villanueva on her circle. I continue this way to list shared and unshared ideas in the poems.**

Interactive Reading Workbook p. 142

Ask students to complete Interacting with Text **Analyzing and Interpreting,** student workbook page 142.

After Reading

You may also use the selection questions and activities in *Glencoe Literature.*

Evaluating Invite students to evaluate the two poems by discussing questions such as the following: *Do you have to know Emily Dickinson's poetry to understand the poem "Emily Dickinson"? Is the comparison made between the speaker and Emily Dickinson meaningful and effective? Why or why not? Which of the two poems do you think gives a clearer picture of what a poet does or should do? How? Which poem holds the most personal meaning for you? Explain.*

PART 3

Interactive Reading Workbook, Teacher Annotated Edition

INTERACTIVE Reading Workbook

American Literature

New York, New York Columbus, Ohio Chicago, Illinois Peoria, Illinois Woodland Hills, California

Acknowledgments

"The Fish" from *The Complete Poems 1927–1979* by Elizabeth Bishop. Copyright © 1979, 1983 by Alice Helen Methfessel. Reprinted by permission of Farrar, Straus, & Giroux, Inc.

"To His Excellency, George Washington" from *The Poems of Phillis Wheatley,* edited by Julian D. Mason Copyright © 1989 by the University of North Carolina Press. Used by permission of the publisher.

"Follow the Drinking Gourd," adapted by John L. Haag, from *All American Folk, Vol. #1.* Copyright © 1982 and 1986 Creative Concepts Publishing Corp. Used by permission.

"The Gift in Wartime" by Tran Mong Tu. Reprinted by permission of the author.

"The Useless" by Thomas Merton from *The Way of Chuang Tzu*. Copyright © 1965 by The Abbey of Gethsemane. Reprinted by permission of New Directions Publishing Corp.

Poem #1732 reprinted by permission of the publishers and the Trustees of Amherst College from *The Poems of Emily Dickinson*, Thomas H. Johnson, ed., Cambridge, Mass: The Belknap Press of Harvard University Press, copyright © 1951, 1955, 1979, 1983 by the President and Fellows of Harvard College.

"A Pact" by Ezra Pound, from *Personae*. Copyright © 1926 by Ezra Pound. Reprinted by permission of New Directions Publishing Corp.

"This Is Just to Say" by William Carols Williams, from *Collected Poems: 1909–1939, Volume I.* Copyright © 1938 by New Directions Publishing Corp. Reprinted by permission of New Directions Publishing Corp.

"Anecdote of the Jar" from *Collected Poems* by Wallace Stevens. Copyright © 1923 and renewed 1951 by Wallace Stevens. Reprinted by permission of Alfred A. Knopf, Inc., a division of Random House, Inc.

"Richness" by Gabriela Mistral, translated by Doris Dana. Reprinted by arrangement with Doris Dana, c/o Joan Daves Agency as agent for the proprietor. Copyright © 1971 by Doris Dana.

"Ars Poetica" from *Collected Poems 1917–1982* by Archibald MacLeish. Copyright © 1985 by The Estate of Archibald MacLeish. Reprinted by permission of Houghton Mifflin Company. All rights reserved.

"Dirge Without Music" by Edna St. Vincent Millay. From *Collected Poems,* HarperCollins. Copyright © 1928, 1955 by Edna St. Vincent Millay and Norma Millay Ellis. All rights reserved. Used by permission of Elizabeth Barnett, literary executor.

"anyone lived in a pretty how town," copyright 1940, © renewed 1968, 1991 by the Trustees for the E. E. Cummings Trust, from *Complete Poems: 1904–1962* by E. E. Cummings. Edited by George J. Firmage. Reprinted by permission of Liveright Publishing Corporation.

"Poetry," reprinted with the permission of Simon & Schuster from *Collected Poems* by Marianne Moore. Copyright © 1935 by Marianne Moore; copyright renewed © 1963 by Marianne Moore and T. S. Eliot.

Excerpts from *Songs of Gold Mountain: Rhymes from San Francisco Chinatown* by Marion K. Hom. Copyright © 1987 The Regents of the University of California. Reprinted by permission of the University of California Press.

"The Death of the Hired Man" from *The Poetry of Robert Frost,* edited by Edward Connery Lathem. Copyright 1944, 1951, © 1956, 1958 by Robert Frost, © 1967 by Lesley Frost Ballantine, copyright 1916, 1923, 1928, 1930, 1939 © 1969 by Henry Holt & Co., Inc. Reprinted by permission of Henry Holt & Co., Inc.

"My City," copyright 1935 by James Weldon Johnson, © renewed 1963 by Grace Nail Johnson, from *Saint Peter Relates an Incident* by James Weldon Johnson. Reprinted by permission of Viking Penguin, a division of Penguin Putnam Inc.

"I, Too" from *Collected Poems* by Langston Hughes. Copyright © 1996 by the Estate of Langston Hughes. Reprinted by permission of Alfred A. Knopf, Inc., a division of Random House, Inc.

"An We Shall Be Steeped" from *Nocturnes* by L. S. Senghor. Copyright © Editions du Seuil, 1964. Reprinted by permission of Editions du Seuil.

"November Cotton Flower" from *Cane* by Jean Toomer. Copyright 1923 by Boni & Liveright, renewed 1951 by Jean Toomer. Reprinted by permission of Liveright Publishing Corporation.

"Any Human to Another" from *On These I Stand* by Countee Cullen. Copyrights held by the Amistad Research Center, administered by Thompson and Thompson, New York, NY.

"Ode to My Socks" from *Neruda and Vallejo: Selected Poems,* translated by Robert Bly and James Wright, Boston, Beacon Press 1976. © 1972 by Robert Bly. Reprinted with the translator's permission.

"Father's Bedroom" from *Selected Poems* by Robert Lowell. Copyright © 1976 by the Estate of Robert Lowell. Reprinted by permission of Farrar, Straus & Giroux, Inc.

"The Explorer" by Gwendolyn Brooks, from *Blacks,* published by Third World Press, Chicago © 1991. Reprinted by permission of the author.

"The Death of the Ball Turret Gunner" from *The Complete Poems* by Randall Jarrell. Copyright © 1969 by Mrs. Randall Jarrell. Reprinted by permission of Farrar, Straus & Giroux, Inc.

"The Beautiful Changes" from *The Beautiful Changes and Other Poems,* copyright © 1947 and renewed 1975 by Richard Wilbur, reprinted by permission of Harcourt Brace & Company.

"Picture Bride" from *Picture Bride* by Cathy Song. Copyright © 1983 by Cathy Song. Reprinted by permission of Yale University Press.

"apprenticeship 1978" reprinted by permission of the author, Evangelina Vigil-Piñon.

"Prayer to the Pacific," copyright © 1981 by Leslie Marmon Silko. Reprinted from *Storyteller* by Leslie Marmon Silko, published by Seaver Books, New York, New York.

"Riding the Elevator Into the Sky" from *The Awful Rowing Toward God* by Anne Sexton. First published in the *New Yorker*. Copyright © by Loring Conant Jr., executor of the Estate of Anne Sexton. Reprinted by permission of Houghton Mifflin Company. All rights reserved.

"Waiting for the Barbarians" from Keeley, Edmund, and Sherrard, Philip (translators); *C. P. Cavafy: Selected Poems*. Copyright © 1972 by Edmund Keeley and Philip Sherrard. Reprinted by permission of Princeton University Press.

"Mirror" from *Crossing the Water* by Sylvia Plath. Copyright © 1963 by Ted Hughes. Originally appeared in the *New Yorker*. Reprinted by permission of HarperCollins Publishers, Inc.

"Traveling Through the Dark," copyright © 1962, 1998 by the Estate of William Stafford. Reprinted from *The Way It Is: New & Selected Poems* by William Stafford with the permission of Graywolf Press, Saint Paul, Minnesota.

"Frederick Douglass," copyright © 1966 by Robert Hayden, from *Collected Poems of Robert Hayden* by Frederick Glaysher, editor. Reprinted by permission of Liveright Publishing Corporation.

"#2 Memory" and "Poem" from *Mainland* by Victor Hernandez Cruz. Copyright © 1973 by Victor Hernandez Cruz. Reprinted by permission of Random House, Inc.

"Weaver" copyright © 1974 by Sandra María Esteves reprinted with permission from the author.

"For Georgia O'Keeffe," by Pat Mora, is reprinted with permission from the publisher of *Chants* (Houston: Arte Publico Press–University of Houston, 1985).

"Most Satisfied By Snow" first appeared in *The Virginia Quarterly Review*, Autumn, 1973. Copyrighted by Diana Chang and reprinted by permission of the author.

"Geometry" from *Rita Dove, Selected Poems,* © 1980, 1993 by Rita Dove. Used by permission of the author.

"The Welder" from *This Bridge Called My Back: Writings by Radical Women of Color.* Copyright © 1983 by Cherrie Moraga and Gloria Anzaldua. NY: Kitchen Table Press, 1983.

"The House" and "La Casa" by María Herrera-Sobek, from *Chasqui*, published in *Infinite Divisions,* by Tey Diana Rebolledo (University of Arizona Press, 1993).

"Embroidering: A Response to 'Somnad' by Carl Larsson" by Rita Magdaleno, from *New Chicano/Chicana Writing 2*, University of Arizona Press, 1992. Reprinted by permission of the author.

"Naming Myself" by Barbara Kingsolver. Copyright © 1994 by Barbara Kingsolver. Reprinted from *Another America*, by Barbara Kingsolver, and published by Seal Press.

"A Poet's Job" by Alma Villanueva, from *Bloodroot*, Place of Herons Press, 1982. Reprinted by permission of the author.

Glencoe/McGraw-Hill

A Division of The ***McGraw-Hill*** *Companies*

Send all inquiries to:
Glencoe/McGraw-Hill
8787 Orion Place
Columbus, OH 43240-4027

ISBN 0-07-825179-6

Printed in the United States of America

1 2 3 4 5 6 7 8 9 10 066 08 07 06 05 04 03 02

Table of Contents

UNIT 2 A NEW NATION

THEME 2 Breaking Free

THEME 3 Gaining Insight

THEME 4 The Union Is Tested

THEME 5 Two New American Voices

THEME 6 The Energy of the Everyday

THEME 7 New Directions

THEME 8 The Harlem Renaissance

THEME 9 Personal Discoveries

THEME 10 Acting on an Idea

UNIT 7 INTO THE TWENTY-FIRST CENTURY

THEME 11 Generations

Name .... Class .... Date ....

The Life You Save May Be Your Own

Interactive Reading Reading Guide

EXERCISE A. Read the Key Characters and the Key Vocabulary and Terms sections. Then read "The Life You Save May Be Your Own" in *Glencoe Literature*. As you read the story, use the information obtained to help you answer the questions in Sorting It Out.

KEY CHARACTERS

Mrs. Crater–an old woman who lives on a rundown farm with her daughter

Lucynell Crater–Mrs. Crater's mentally disabled, unmarried daughter

Tom Shiftlet–a young homeless man

KEY VOCABULARY AND TERMS

afflicted–distressed by persistent suffering or anguish

moral–relating to principles of right and wrong behavior

crabbed–marked by a forbidding moroseness

guffawing–loudly or boisterously laughing

SORTING IT OUT

EXERCISE B. Answer the questions that follow. Write on the lines provided.

1. What is the setting as the story begins? The setting is Mrs. Crater's deserted, dilapidated farm, in the South, during the Depression in the 1930s.

2. Who walks up to Mrs. Crater's house one evening? Tom Shiftlet, a drifter, walks up to the Crater house.

3. Why is the drifter's coat sleeve folded up? He has only half an arm.

4. What is Mrs. Crater's first response to the drifter? She thinks that he is a tramp, but she is not afraid of him; she expresses casual interest in him.

5. What information does Tom Shiftlet give about himself? He says that he is twenty-eight years old and has done a variety of things, such as being a gospel singer, a railroad foreman, a mortuary assistant, and a soldier. He says that he is single.

6. What agreement do Mrs. Crater and Tom Shiftlet make? He will stay at the farm and do odd jobs in exchange for food, and he will sleep in Mrs. Crater's old car.

7. Does Tom Shiftlet prove to be a good helper at the Crater farm? Explain. Yes; he repairs a fence and the front and back steps of the house and builds a new hog pen.

8. How would you characterize Mrs. Crater's daughter, Lucynell? She has a mental disability that makes her childlike; she cannot hear or talk.

9. In what condition is Mrs. Crater's old car? Although it is well built, it does not run.

10. How does Tom Shiftlet get Mrs. Crater's car running? He figures out what is wrong with it, obtains the necessary parts, and repairs it.

11. After Shiftlet repairs Mrs. Crater's car, what request does Mrs. Crater make of Shiftlet? She asks Shiftlet to marry Lucynell and remain on the farm.

12. How does Mrs. Crater describe Shiftlet as she speaks to him? She calls him a "poor disabled friendless drifting man."

13. What deal do Mrs. Crater and Shiftlet make? In exchange for Shiftlet's marrying Lucynell, Mrs. Crater agrees to let him use the car and some of her savings for a trip after the wedding.

14. What event takes place in town? Lucynell and Shiftlet get married.

15. How does Shiftlet feel when he looks over at Lucynell in the car seat? He feels ill-tempered and depressed.

16. What is Lucynell doing when Shiftlet looks over at her in the car? She is picking the cherries off her hat and throwing them out the car window.

17. What happens to Lucynell in the diner called The Hot Spot? She falls asleep in the diner, and Shiftlet abandons her.

18. Whom does Shiftlet pick up on the road? What does Shiftlet tell the person? Why? Shiftlet picks up a young boy who is hitchhiking. He tells him why a boy's mother is important. Possibly Shiftlet is trying to discourage the boy from running away.

19. How does Shiftlet feel after the boy jumps out of the car? He feels "the rottenness of the world" is about to overwhelm him.

20. What does Shiftlet do as the rainstorm starts? He steps on the gas and continues driving by himself into Mobile.

Name .... Class .... Date ....

The Fish

Interacting with Text Identifying Figurative Language

Sensory details are words or phrases that appeal to one or more of the five senses. A **metaphor** is a comparison of two seemingly unlike things in which one is said to be another. A **simile** is a comparison of two seemingly unlike things in which the word *like* or *as* is used.

EXERCISE A. Read the following passage and notice the sensory details.

[The fish] was speckled with barnacles,
fine rosettes of lime,
and infested
with tiny white sea-lice,
and underneath two or three
rags of green weed hung down.
. . . .
I thought of the coarse white flesh
packed in like feathers,
the big bones and the little bones,
the dramatic reds and blacks
of his shiny entrails,
and the pink swim-bladder
like a big peony.

EXERCISE B. Read the items below. Follow the directions for marking the passage. Write explanations and answers to the questions on the lines provided.

1. Underline three of the sensory details in the passage that help the reader picture the fish's exterior. Briefly describe the fish's exterior. Any three of these answers: (1) "speckled with barnacles," (2) "fine rosettes of lime," (3)"infested with tiny white sea-lice," (4) "green weed" hanging from it.

2. Double-underline three of the sensory details in the passage that help the reader picture the fish's interior. Briefly describe the fish's interior. Any three of these answers: (1) "coarse white flesh," (2) "big bones," (3) "little bones," (4) "reds and blacks of his shiny entrails," (5) a "pink swim-bladder like a big peony."

3. Does the fish literally have rags hanging from it? Identify the figure of speech the poet is using and the two things being compared. The rags are part of a metaphor: The poet compares the appearance of hanging "weed" to that of hanging rags.

4. Circle two similes in the passage. Write down each simile that you circled. "coarse white flesh packed in like feathers," "pink swim-bladder like a big peony"

Name .... Class .... Date ....

Thoughts on the African-American Novel

Interacting with Text Questioning

Questioning is the strategy of asking oneself questions during or after reading to help make sure that the important ideas of the selection are understood.

EXERCISE A. Read the following passage from "Thoughts on the African-American Novel."

In the books that I have written, the chorus has changed but there has always been a choral note, whether it is the "I" narrator of *Bluest Eye*, or the town functioning as a character in *Sula*, or the neighborhood and the community that responds in the two parts of town in *Solomon*. Or, as extreme as I've gotten, all of nature thinking and feeling and watching and responding to the action going on in *Tar Baby*, so that they are in the story: the trees hurt, fish are afraid, clouds report, and the bees are alarmed. Those are the ways in which I try to incorporate, into that traditional genre the novel, unorthodox novelistic characteristics–so that it is, in my view, Black, because it uses the characteristics of Black art. I am not suggesting that some of these devices have not been used before and elsewhere—only the reason why I do.

EXERCISE B. Read the following items. Follow the directions for marking the passage. Complete answer-choice questions as directed.

1. Underline the sections of the passage in which Toni Morrison explains how the chorus functions in her novels.
2. Underline the word *unorthodox* in the passage. What does *unorthodox* mean? Circle the letter before the correct answer choice.
   - a. nontraditional
   - b. inflexible
   - c. tolerant
3. Underline the context clue that helped you to figure out the meaning of *unorthodox*.
4. What is the main idea of the passage? Circle the letter before the correct answer choice.
   - a. Morrison uses a chorus in her novels because she considers it a characteristic of African American art.
   - b. Morrison uses a chorus in her novels as a personal trademark.
   - c. Morrison uses a chorus in her novels because she likes to use unorthodox literary devices.

Name .... Class .... Date ....

The Sky Tree

Interacting with Text Recognizing Cause-and-Effect Relationships

Sometimes a story or an article explains why something happens. It may even tell of a series of events that cause other events. One event that sets another event in motion is called a **cause**. The outcome of the event is called the **effect**. Origin myths explain how Earth was created or why certain features of Earth are the way they are.

EXERCISE A. Read the following passage from "The Sky Tree."

It came to be that the old chief became sick and nothing could cure him. He grew weaker and weaker until it seemed he would die. Then a dream came to him and he called Aataentsic to him.

"I have dreamed," he said, "and in my dream I saw how I can be healed. I must be given the fruit which grows at the very top of Sky Tree. You must cut it down and bring that fruit to me."

Aataentsic took her husband's stone ax and went to the great tree. As soon as she struck it, it split in half and toppled over. As it fell a hole opened in Sky Land and the tree fell through the hole.

EXERCISE B. Now read the following questions. Find the text in the passage that will help you answer each question. Underline the text. Then use the text you have marked to help you answer the questions on the lines provided.

1. What causes the chief to think the fruit of the Sky Tree will help him? The chief has a dream that conveys that the fruit of the Sky Tree can heal him.

2. Why does Aataentsic cut down the Sky Tree? Aataentsic cuts down the tree because her husband instructs her to do so. She needs to get the fruit from the tree in order to help her husband.

3. What is the effect of Aataentsic's first blow to the Sky Tree? Because of Aataentsic's first blow, the Sky Tree splits in half and topples over.

4. Why does the Sky Tree fall out of Sky Land? The Sky Tree falls out of Sky Land because a hole opens in Sky Land and the tree falls through the hole.

Name .... Class .... Date ....

from *The Iroquois Constitution*

Interacting with Text Summarizing

To **summarize** a text is to state briefly the main ideas and important details. Summarizing can help readers understand and remember passages that are complicated.

EXERCISE A. Read the following passages from *The Iroquois Constitution*. Follow the directions for marking text and then answer the questions that follow.

The Lords of the Confederacy of the Five Nations shall be mentors of the people for all time. The thickness of their skin shall be seven spans—which is to say that they shall be proof against anger, offensive actions, and criticism. Their hearts shall be full of peace and good will and their minds filled with a yearning for the welfare of the people of the Confederacy. With endless patience they shall carry out their duty, and their firmness shall be tempered with a tenderness for their people. Neither anger nor fury shall find lodgment in their minds, and all their words and actions shall be marked by calm deliberation.

1. Whom is this passage about? Underline the title of leaders whom this passage describes. Write the title on the lines provided. The title of the leaders is "Lords of the Confederacy of the Five Nations."

2. With what should the hearts of the Lords of the Confederacy be filled? Double-underline the text that describes the hearts of the Lords. Then restate what you have underlined in your own words. The hearts of the leaders should be filled with peace and good will.

EXERCISE B. Answer the following questions. Find the text in the passage that will help you answer each question. Circle the letter in front of the correct answer.

1. Which detail would **not** be necessary in a summary of this passage?
   - (a.) The Confederacy leaders will have skin that is seven spans thick.
   - b. The Confederacy leaders must work for the welfare of their people.
   - c. The Confederacy leaders should not have quick tempers.

2. Which of the following statements is the best summary of the passage?
   - a. The people of the Confederacy should have big hearts and thick skins.
   - (b.) The Lords of the Confederacy of the Five Nations should with good will work for the welfare of the people.
   - c. The laws of Five Nations should be built on calm deliberation and thick skins.

Name .... Class .... Date ....

from *La Relación*

Interacting with Text **Analyzing Mood**

The **mood** of a literary work is its atmosphere or emotional quality. An author can create a particular mood through word choice, subject matter, setting, and tone.

EXERCISE A. Read the following passage from *La Relación*. Notice the mood that the author creates.

Since the surf was very rough, the sea wrapped all the men in its waves, except the three that had been pulled under by the boat, and cast them on the shore of the same island. Those of us who survived were as naked as the day we were born and had lost everything we had. Although the few things we had were of little value, they meant a lot to us.

It was November then and the weather was very cold. We were in such a state that our bones could easily be counted and we looked like the picture of death.

EXERCISE B. Read the following items. Follow the directions for marking the text. Then use the text you have marked to help you answer the questions or list terms on the lines provided.

1. Circle words and phrases in the passage that indicate where and when the action takes place. What is the setting of the passage? The setting is the ocean and a wilderness island in November.

2. Underline words and phrases in the passage that help set a particular mood. List these on the lines provided. "rough," "pulled under by the boat," "survived," "naked," "the picture of death"

3. According to the passage, what is the condition of the men? The men are naked and so thin that their ribs can be counted. They look "like the picture of death."

EXERCISE C. Read the following questions. Circle the letter before the correct answer.

1. What mood does the author create with the setting?
   a. cautious
   b. lazy but happy
   c. cold and lonely

2. What is a good description of the topic of the narrative?
   a. adventures in the New World.
   b. hardships endured while exploring a new land.
   c. how to negotiate with people from another culture.

Name .... Class .... Date ....

from *Of Plymouth Plantation*

Interacting with Text Analyzing Style

An author's style is his or her own unique way of communicating. **Style** is indicated by such elements as word choice, sentence length, sentence structure, and use of figurative language.

EXERCISE A. Read the following passages from *Of Plymouth Plantation*. Notice the style of the writing.

Passage 1

Being thus arrived in a good harbor, and brought safe to land, they fell upon their knees and blessed the God of Heaven who had brought them over the vast and furious ocean, and delivered them from all the perils and miseries thereof, again to set their feet on the firm and stable earth, their proper element.

Passage 2

Being thus passed the vast ocean, and a sea of troubles before in their preparation (as may be remembered by that which went before), they had now no friends to welcome them nor inns to entertain or refresh their weather-beaten bodies; no houses or much less towns to repair to, to seek for succor.

EXERCISE B. Now read the following items. Mark the passage as directed. Then circle your answer choice for each item below.

1. Underline the longest sentence in the first passage. Circle the letter before the answer choice that best describes the sentence.
   - a. The sentence is filled with details.
   - b. The sentence gets right to the point.
   - c. The sentence tells only facts.
2. What is the best description of the author's sentence structure?
   - a. simple
   - b. complex
   - c. parallel
3. Underline a use of figurative language in the second passage.
4. Which words best describe the author's style? The author's style can be described as
   - a. direct and matter-of-fact.
   - b. formal and descriptive.
   - c. light and colorful.

Name .... Class .... Date ....

To My Dear and Loving Husband

Interacting with Text Paraphrasing

To **paraphrase** is to state the meaning of a passage in one's own words. In paraphrasing a poem, it is helpful to change lines to logical word order (subject/verb/direct object) and to change unusual or unfamiliar words to common words.

EXERCISE A. Read the following lines from "To My Dear and Loving Husband." Then follow the directions for the items that follow. Find and mark the text in the passage that will help you answer each question.

> Thy love is such I can no way repay,
> The heavens reward thee manifold, I pray.
> Then while we live, in love let's so persevere
> That when we live no more, we may live ever.

1. An **archaic word** is a word that is no longer in common use. Underline the archaic word in the passage that means the same thing as *your*.
2. Double-underline the archaic word in the passage that means the same as *you*.
3. Circle the word in the second line that can be changed to a simpler, more modern phrase.

EXERCISE B. Answer the following questions. Draw a circle around the letter in front of the correct answer choice.

1. What pronoun is a synonym for *thy*?
   a. you b. your c. her
2. What pronoun is a synonym for *thee*?
   a. you b. your c. her
3. What is the definition of the word *manifold*?
   a. "something given in compensation"
   b. "in many ways"
   c. "without assistance"
4. Which is the best paraphrase of the last two lines of the passage above?
   a. Staying in love requires perseverance.
   b. We love each other so much that we will live forever.
   c. Let us persist in loving so that our love lives even when we are dead.

Name .... Class .... Date ....

from *A Narrative of the Captivity and Restoration of Mrs. Mary Rowlandson*

Interacting with Text Recognizing Theme

The **theme** of a literary work is a general truth that can be gleaned from it.

EXERCISE A. Read the following passages from *A Narrative of the Captivity and Restoration of Mrs. Mary Rowlandson*.

Passage 1

I had often before this said, that if the Indians should come, I should choose rather to be killed by them than taken alive; but when it came to the trial my mind changed; their glittering weapons so daunted my spirit, that I chose rather to go . . .

Passage 2

But I was fain to go and look after something to satisfy my hunger; and going among the wigwams, I went into one, and there found a squaw who showed herself very kind to me, and gave me a piece of bear. . . . I have seen bear baked very handsomely amongst the English, and some liked it, but the thoughts that it was bear made me tremble: but now that was savory to me that one would think was enough to turn the stomach of a brute creature.

EXERCISE B. Write a sentence stating a general truth based on the first passage. Underline parts of the passage that helped lead you to this generalization.

Generalization People do not know how they will react in a crisis until they actually experience it.

EXERCISE C. Read the following items. Find and underline the text in the second passage that will help you follow the directions for each item–on the lines provided or by circling the letter before the best answer choice.

1. How has the author felt in the past about eating bear? It disgusted her.
2. Write a sentence stating a general truth shown by the second passage.
   Generalization To a person in a desperate situation dislikes are insignificant.
3. According to these two passages, the theme of this selection is the following.
   a. People are likely to do what they have to do in order to survive.
   b. It is important to blend in with others in times of hardship.
   c. In the face of danger, people should take a stand for their principles.

Name .... Class .... Date ....

from *Stay Alive, My Son*

Interacting with Text — Analyzing Dialogue

Dialogue is the exact words people speak in a fiction or nonfiction narrative. Dialogue helps to characterize people and to move along the action of a narrative.

Speaker tags, such as "he said," usually precede or follow a character's words. They indicate who is speaking. Speaker tags also can indicate how the speaker feels.

EXERCISE A. Read the following passage from *Stay Alive, My Son*. The dialogue is between the narrator and his wife.

> Better that I should get away, and give myself a chance to live, or at least die on my own terms. . . .
>
> "You can live on here with Nawath," I went on. "It's the only answer. I'll take my chances in the forest. If I succeed, we'll meet again. But I have to go soon. In one week, it'll be too late."
>
> "You'll leave?" she said. "Leave me here with Nawath?" And suddenly she began to sob as if she were being torn apart.
>
> "Yes, my dearest. It's the only way," I said, desperately. . . .
>
> . . . With hesitations and bitter sobs, she went on, "It's impossible, my dearest Thay . . . I don't want to be separated from you. . . . I prefer to die with you rather than to stay here . . . "

EXERCISE B. Read the following questions. Follow the directions for each question.

1. What conflict is the narrator experiencing? Underline the sentence in the passage that states his conflict. Then write it in your own words on the lines provided.
   His conflict is whether to stay with his family and die or to save his life by leaving them.

2. How does the narrator feel about his conflict? Circle the word included in a speaker tag that tells how the narrator feels. On the lines provided, explain his feelings.
   The narrator feels desperate and guilty.

3. How do the narrator and his wife feel about one another? Underline the words in their dialogue that indicate their feelings. Then explain how their dialogue communicates how they feel about each other.
   They love each other very much. They call each other "my dearest." The narrator's wife says that she would rather die with him than be left alone without him.

Name .... Class .... Date ....

from *Sinners in the Hands of an Angry God*

Interacting with Text Understanding Figurative Language

In some **figures of speech**, two unlike things are compared in a nonliteral way. In a **simile**, the figure of speech is signaled by the word *like* or *as*. In a **metaphor**, a comparison is made without the use of *like* or *as*.

EXERCISE A. Read the following passages from *Sinners in the Hands of an Angry God*.

Passage 1

The God that holds you over the pit of hell, much as one holds a spider, or some loathsome insect, over the fire . . .

Passage 2

The bow of God's wrath is bent, and the arrow made ready on the string, and justice bends the arrow at your heart, and strains the bow, and it is nothing but the mere pleasure of God, and that of an angry God, without any promise or obligation at all, that keeps the arrow one moment from being made drunk with your blood.

EXERCISE B. Read the following questions for the first passage. Find the text that will help you answer each question. Underline the text. Then answer the questions on the lines provided.

1. What two things are being compared in a figure of speech? God's holding a person over hell and someone's holding a spider over a fire are being compared.
2. What word indicates whether the figure of speech is a simile or a metaphor? The word as indicates that the passage contains a simile.

EXERCISE C. Read the following questions for the second passage. Find the text that will help you answer each question. Underline the text. Then answer the questions on the lines provided.

1. What two main things are being compared? God's sending his wrath to people and an arrow's being shot by a bow.
2. According to the author, in what way are these two things alike? God is as ready to express his wrath as a bow is ready to shoot an arrow.
3. What specific figure of speech is the author using? Explain how you know. The figure of speech is a metaphor: it is an implied comparison. The comparison is not signaled with the word *like* or *as*.

Name .... Class .... Date ....

Offer of Help

Interacting with Text — Main Idea and Supporting Details

The **main idea** of a passage is the most important idea in the passage. **Supporting details** are the sentences that add information about the main idea.

EXERCISE A. Read the following passage from "Offer of Help."

> Several of our young people were formerly brought up in the colleges of the northern provinces; they were instructed in all your sciences; but, when they came back to us, they were bad runners, ignorant of every means of living in the woods, unable to bear either cold or hunger, knew neither how to build a cabin, take a deer, or kill an enemy, spoke our language imperfectly, were therefore neither fit for hunters, warriors, nor counsellors, they were totally good for nothing.

EXERCISE B. Read the following questions. Follow the directions for each item below.

1. What were the Native American young people taught in the colleges of the northern provinces? Circle the part of the text that identifies the subject matter in which they were instructed. Write what you have underlined on the lines provided.

   The young people "were instructed in all your sciences."

2. According to the author, in what ways were the Native American college-educated young people unfit for life in the tribe? Underline the part of the text that tells of their shortcomings. Then record what you have underlined on the lines provided.

   "They were bad runners, ignorant of every means of living in the woods, unable to bear either cold or hunger, knew neither how to built a cabin, take a deer, or kill an enemy, spoke our language imperfectly, were therefore neither fit for hunters, warriors, nor counsellors, they were totally good for nothing."

3. What statement best expresses the main idea of the passage? Circle the letter in front of the correct answer choice.

   a. What is useful for one culture is not necessarily useful and valuable for another.

   b. To prepare for everyday life, all young people should study the sciences.

   c. The colleges of the northern provinces should include classes in hunting.

Name .... Class .... Date ....

from *The Autobiography of Benjamin Franklin*

Interacting with Text ## Analyzing Setting

The **setting** of a literary work is the time and place in which the events in the literary work occur.

EXERCISE A. Read the following passage from *The Autobiography of Benjamin Franklin*.

However, walking in the evening by the side of the river, a boat came by, which I found was going toward Philadelphia with several people in her. They took me in, and as there was no wind we rowed all the way; and about midnight, not having yet seen the city, some of the company were confident we must have passed it and would row no further; the others knew not where we were, so we put toward the shore, got into a creek, landed near an old fence, with the rails of which we made a fire, the night being cold, in October, and there we remained till daylight.

EXERCISE B. Read and answer the following questions. For each question, find the text in the passage that will help you answer it. Follow the directions with each question for marking the text.

1. What is the specific time in which the events in this passage take place? Underline the text that gives information about the specific time. Identify the time in which these events occur, according to the text you have underlined.

   The time is a night—from evening to daylight—in October.

2. What is the specific place described in the passage? Double-underline the text that describes the specific place. Then identify the place, using the lines provided.

   The place described in the passage is a river and the shore of a river near Philadelphia.

3. What details in the setting appeal to the sense of touch? Circle the text that describes details that appeal to the sense of touch and answer on the line provided.

   "we made a fire, the night being cold"

4. In this passage, what is the mood or atmosphere created by the setting? Circle the letter that identifies the correct answer.

   a. windy, cold, and hopeless

   b. frightening, destructive, and desperate

   c. dark, chilly, yet friendly

Name .... Class .... Date ....

Dichos

Interacting with Text Understanding Figurative Language

Figurative language creates an effect by making a nonliteral comparison between two unlike things. A **simile** is a comparison in which the word *like* or *as* is used. A **metaphor** is an implied comparison. A **symbol** is a person, place, or thing that represents an abstract idea.

EXERCISE A. Read each *dicho*. Think about whether each one has only a literal meaning or makes a point through figurative language.

a. Where can the ox go that he will not have to plow?

b. We see their faces, but we do not know their hearts.

c. If you're born to be a *tamal*, heaven will send you the cornshucks.

d. I'm as gentle as a lamb, as long as I'm doing what I want to do.

EXERCISE B. Read the following questions. For each question, find the text in the passage that will help you answer it. Underline the text. Then use the text you have marked to help you answer the questions.

1. In *dicho* b, find and underline *hearts*. What do *hearts* represent? Answer on the lines provided. Hearts represent the emotions and intentions of people.

2. In which *dicho* is an animal used as a metaphor for a person? Find and underline the name of the animal. Write it on the lines provided.
   dicho a–ox

3. Which *dicho* uses a simile to make a point? Find and underline the simile. Then write it on the lines provided.
   dicho d–"as gentle as a lamb"

4. Explain how symbolism is used in *dicho* c. Write on the lines provided.
   Tamal stands for a person destined to do a certain thing; cornshucks stand for what the person needs in order to achieve that destiny.

Name .... Class .... Date ....

Speech to the Second Virginia Convention

Interacting with Text **Identifying Persuasive Techniques**

Speakers and writers use **persuasive techniques** to convince their listeners or readers of their views. These techniques include **loaded language** (words that have strong positive or negative connotations), **rhetorical questions** (questions asked for effect with no expectation of an answer), and **figures of speech** (nonliteral comparisons).

EXERCISE A. Read the following passage from "Speech to the Second Virginia Convention." Notice the persuasive techniques Patrick Henry uses.

Are fleets and armies necessary to a work of love and reconciliation? . . . Let us not deceive ourselves, sir. These are the implements of war and subjugation; the last arguments to which kings resort. I ask gentlemen, sir, what means this martial array, if its purpose be not to force us to submission? . . . Has Great Britain any enemy, in this quarter of the world, to call for all this accumulation of navies and armies? No, sir, she has none. . . . They are sent over to bind and rivet upon us those chains which the British ministry have been so long forging.

EXERCISE B. Read the following directions. For each item, find the text in the passage that will help you. Underline the text. Then use the text you have marked to help you supply the information on the lines provided.

1. List the rhetorical questions in the passage.

1) "Are fleets and armies necessary to a work of love and reconciliation?"

2) "I ask gentlemen, sir, what means this martial array, if its purpose be not to force us into submission?"

3) "Has Great Britain any enemy, in this quarter of the world, to call for all this accumulation of navies and armies?"

2. Find and record two examples of loaded language in the passage.

Possible answer: "These are the implements of war and subjugation"; "what means this martial array, if its purpose be not to force us into submission?"

3. Find and underline an example of figurative language in the last sentence. Record the two things being compared? Identify the comparison as literal or figurative.

Great Britain's limiting political freedom for American colonists is compared to creating chains and putting them on Americans. The language is figurative.

Name .... Class .... Date ....

from *The Crisis, No. 1*

Interacting with Text — Recognizing Author's Purpose

Author's purpose refers to an author's reason for writing. Authors write to entertain, inform, explain, persuade, or describe, or for a combination of purposes.

EXERCISE A. Read the following passage about Americans' role in the struggle against the British in the selection from *The Crisis, No. 1*. Think about how the author's purpose affected his choice of style, diction, and content.

> Let it be told to the future world that in the depth of winter, when nothing but hope and virtue could survive, that the city and the country, alarmed at one common danger, came forth to meet and to repulse it. Say not that thousands are gone—turn out your tens of thousands; throw not the burden of the day upon Providence, but "*show your faith by your works*," that God may bless you. It matters not where you live, or what rank of life you hold, the evil or the blessing will reach you all. The far and the near, the home counties and the back, the rich and poor, will suffer or rejoice alike. The heart that feels not now is dead; the blood of his children will curse his cowardice who shrinks back at a time when a little might have saved the whole, and made *them* happy.

EXERCISE B. Read the following questions. For each question, find the text in the passage that will help you answer it. Underline the text. Then use the text you have marked to help you answer the questions on the lines provided.

1. Does Thomas Paine's language appeal to the audience's intellect, emotions, or sense of humor? Paine's language appeals to the audience's emotions.
2. What two words in the first sentence have positive connotations? The words with positive connotations are hope and virtue.
3. What phrase in the first sentence creates a negative mood? The phrase "depth of winter" creates a negative mood.
4. According to Paine, what role should God and religion play in people's behavior in this situation? People shouldn't expect God to make things right but should show their faith by working for the cause.
5. What is Thomas Paine's overall purpose in the passage? Paine's purpose is to persuade everyone to get involved in the struggle for freedom.

Name .... Class .... Date ....

from *The Histories*

Interacting with Text **Analyzing Dialogue**

In **dialogue** an author provides the exact words of a character.

EXERCISE A. Read the following passage from *The Histories*. Think about how the dialogue brings out the plot, theme, and characterization of the selection.

[Xerxes] sent for Demaratus, . . . who had come with the army, and questioned him . . . in the hope of finding out what the unaccountable behavior of the Spartans might mean. "Once before," Demaratus said, "when we began our march against Greece, you heard me speak of these men. I told you then how I saw this enterprise would turn out, and you laughed at me. I strive for nothing, my lord, more earnestly than to observe the truth in your presence; so hear me once more. These men have come to fight us for possession of the pass, and for that struggle they are preparing. It is the common practice of the Spartans to pay careful attention to their hair when they are about to risk their lives. But I assure you that if you can defeat these men and the rest of the Spartans who are still at home, there is no other people in the world who will dare to stand firm or lift a hand against you."

EXERCISE B. Read the following items. Follow the directions for marking the text. Then use the text you have marked to help you respond.

1. Read and underline the segment of the text that characterizes the way Demaratus speaks. On the basis of this segment, characterize the manner in which Demaratus speaks. Circle the letter of the correct answer choice.
   a. Demaratus is reasonable and polite.
   b. Demaratus is angry.
   c. Demaratus is filled with joy.
2. Describe the character of Demaratus, from what he says, on the lines provided.
   Possible answer: Demaratus seems respectful, insightful, and earnest.
3. Describe the character of Xerxes, from what Demaratus says to him, on the lines provided. *Possible answer: He is arrogant and not respectful of the advice and opinions of others.*
4. Cite the custom of the Spartans that Demaratus mentions, on the lines provided.
   The Spartans attend to their hair when they are about to risk their lives.

Name .... Class .... Date ....

Declaration of Independence

Interacting with Text Summarizing

When you **summarize** a passage, you briefly state its main ideas.

EXERCISE A. Read the following passages from the Declaration of Independence.

Passage 1

In every stage of these oppressions we have petitioned for redress in the most humble terms; our repeated petitions have been answered only by repeated injury. A prince whose character is thus marked by every act which may define a tyrant is unfit to be ruler of a free people.

Passage 2

We, therefore, the representatives of the United States of America, in General Congress assembled, appealing to the Supreme Judge of the world for the rectitude of our intentions, do, in the name and by the authority of the good people of these colonies, solemnly publish and declare that these United Colonies are, and of right ought to be, free and independent states; that they are absolved from all allegiance to the British crown, and that all political connection between them and the state of Great Britain is, and ought to be, totally dissolved.

EXERCISE B. Read the following items. Follow the directions for each item.

1. Circle the letter of the best summary of the first passage.
   a. A prince should rule free people by using repeated petitions.
   b. A leader who ignores his subjects' requests for justice is not fit to rule.
   c. We have been humble because the king has ignored our petitions.

2. Circle the main (most important) idea in the second passage.

3. Underline the details that elaborate, or explain more about, the main idea in the second passage. List the details you have underlined on the lines provided.
   "... that they are absolved from all allegiance to the British crown, and that all political connection between them and the state of Great Britain is ... dissolved."

4. Write a summary of the second passage on the lines provided.
   As representatives of the United Colonies, we declare the colonies free and independent, with no further loyalty or political connection to Great Britain.

Name .... Class .... Date ....

To His Excellency, General Washington

Interacting with Text Analyzing Personification

Personification is a figure of speech in which human characteristics are attributed to something that is not human—an animal, an object, a force of nature, or an idea.

EXERCISE A. Read the following passage from "To His Excellency, General Washington" and the footnote that follows it. Notice all instances of the poet's use of personification.

33 Fix'd are the eyes of nations on the scales,
For in their hopes Columbia's arm prevails.
Anon Britannia° droops the pensive head,
While round increase the rising hills of dead.
Ah! cruel blindness to Columbia's state!
38 Lament thy thirst of boundless power too late.

°Britannia is Great Britain, personified as a goddess.

EXERCISE B. Read the following questions. For each question, find the text in the passage that will help you answer it. Then follow the directions for each item.

1. What is the figure of speech in line 33? Underline the text that presents personification. What object or idea is assigned a human characteristic? What is the human characteristic? Nations are not human, but they are assigned the human characteristic of sight.

2. Read line 35 and the footnote. Who is Britannia? What country does she represent? Britannia is a goddess. She represents Great Britain.

3. What characteristic is attributed to Britannia in line 35? Underline the example of personification in the passage. Britannia "droops the pensive head."

4. What does Britannia's action mean? Britannia's drooping head suggests that the spirit of the government and the people of England is beginning to break.

5. Underline the parts of the text that show personification in lines 36 through 38. Explain each figure of speech. "Cruel blindness" is an instance of personification. It refers to Britannia's ignoring the condition of America. "Thirst of boundless power" is personification; it shows England's desire to rule America.

Name .... Class .... Date ....

Letter to Her Daughter from the New and Unfinished White House

Interacting with Text Making Generalizations

Making generalizations is stating broad conclusions on the basis of several particular facts or examples. A generalization is a broad statement that applies to more than one or to a group of items or instances. Generalizations can be made from the following passage. However, to make sure such a generalization was valid, you would need to find other supporting information in several sources.

EXERCISE A. Read the following passage from "Letter to Her Daughter from the New and Unfinished White House." Notice the use of specific details.

The house is upon a grand and superb scale, requiring about thirty servants to attend and keep the apartments in proper order. . . . To assist us in this great castle, and render less attendance necessary, bells are wholly wanting, not one single one being hung through the whole house, and promises are all you can obtain. This is so great an inconvenience, that I know not what to do, or how to do. . . . —If they will put me up some bells, and let me have wood enough to keep fires, I design to be pleased. I could content myself almost anywhere three months; but, surrounded with forests, can you believe that wood is not to be had, because people cannot be found to cut and cart it!

EXERCISE B. Read the following questions. For each question, find the text in the passage that will help you answer it. Underline the text. Then use the text you have marked to help you answer the questions. Circle the letter of the correct answer choice.

1. Which of the following generalizations seems correct, according to the details in the text?
   a. Bells were very expensive in 1800.
   b. Bells were used to get servants' attention in 1800.
   c. Bells were used to provide music in 1800.

2. Which generalization about Abigail Adams is valid according to this text?
   a. Abigail Adams was a difficult and demanding woman.
   b. Abigail Adams was mainly concerned with her personal comfort.
   c. Abigail Adams did her best to deal with difficult situations.

Name .... Class .... Date ....

from *The Life of Olaudah Equiano*

Interacting with Text Analyzing Characterization

Characterization is the methods a writer uses to reveal the personality of a character. Authors use a variety of methods to characterize the people they write about. In **direct characterization,** the writer makes explicit statements about a character. In **indirect characterization,** the writer reveals a character through the character's words and actions and through what other characters think and say about the character.

EXERCISE A. Read the following passage from *The Life of Olaudah Equiano*. Notice how Equiano characterizes the white men.

I asked them if we were not to be eaten by those white men with horrible looks, red faces, and long hair. . . .

. . . They gave me to understand, we were to be carried to these white people's country to work for them. I then was a little revived. . . . but still I feared I should be put to death, the white people looked and acted. . . . in so savage a manner; for I had never seen among any people such instances of brutal cruelty; and this not only shown towards us blacks, but also to some of the whites themselves. One white man in particular I saw . . . flogged so unmercifully with a large rope near the foremast, that he died in consequence of it; and they tossed him over the side as they would have done a brute.

EXERCISE B. Read the following questions. For each question, find the text in the passage that will help you answer it. Underline the text. Then use the text you have marked to help you answer the question.

1. In what phrase does the author characterize the men by their looks? Write the phrase on the lines provided. What traits does the description bring to mind?

"white men with horrible looks, red faces, and long hair"—This phrase suggests that the white men are mean, angry, and unkempt.

2. What word and phrase give a direct description of the men's characters? Write the word and phrase on the line provided.

"savage," "brutal cruelty"

3. What action helps characterize the men? Write the answer on the lines provided.

The author describes the men's flogging another white man to death and tossing him overboard.

Name .... Class .... Date ....

The Devil and Tom Walker

Interactive Reading **Reading Guide**

EXERCISE A. Read the Key Characters and Key Vocabulary and Terms sections. Then read the selection. Look back at the lists as needed during reading.

Part 1: The Devil

KEY CHARACTERS

Tom–a miserly man living near Boston in 1727

Tom's wife–a woman with a bad temper, who is as miserly as her husband

A stranger–a man (the devil) whom Tom meets in the swamp

KEY VOCABULARY AND TERMS

stagnant–not flowing in a current or stream

treacherous–marked by hidden dangers, hazards, or perils

eminent–prominent; important

consecrated–dedicated

persecutions–acts of harassing; causing to suffer because of belief

avarice–excessive desire for wealth; greed

resolute–marked by firm determination

sullen–gloomily or resentfully silent

propitiatory–intended to appease or pacify

SORTING IT OUT

EXERCISE B. As you read "The Devil and Tom Walker," use the reading guide to help you keep track of key events. Read the first seven pages of the story from the beginning through the paragraph that begins "Tom consoled himself for the loss of his property. . . ." Answer the following questions on the lines provided.

1. Near what city is "The Devil and Tom Walker" set? The setting for the story is a few miles from Boston, Massachusetts.

2. Where does Tom Walker's shortcut lead him? For what is the area known? Instead of leading him home, the shortcut leads Tom Walker through a treacherous swamp. Pirates hid treasure there, and Indians built a fort.

3. Describe the stranger that Walker meets. Who is he? He has a dark, dirty face, wild black hair, and large red eyes. He is dressed in crude clothes and carries an ax on his shoulder. He has a harsh voice. He is the devil.

4. What offer does the stranger make Walker? The stranger says that he will tell Tom Walker where to find the buried pirate treasure if Tom meets certain conditions.

5. What does Walker's wife do when she finds out about Tom's meeting? She urges Tom to meet the devil's terms. When he says that he will not do it, she goes to see the devil herself.

6. What happens to Walker's wife? She disappears. She does not return home.

Part 2: Tom Walker's Bargain

KEY VOCABULARY AND TERMS

haggle–bargain

obstinate–stubborn

squeamish–easily offended or disgusted

consideration–recompense; payment

security–something given or pledged to make certain the fulfillment of an obligation

censurer–someone who finds fault with and criticizes as blameworthy

zeal–eagerness in pursuit of something

superfluous–extra; not needed

parish–a local church community

piety–devoutness in religion

foreclose–to take legal steps to bar a mortgager's right to redeem a mortgaged property

SORTING IT OUT

EXERCISE C. Read the Key Vocabulary and Terms section. Then read from "At length, it is said, when delay had whetted Tom's eagerness . . . " to the end of the story. Answer the following questions on the lines provided.

7. What deal does Tom Walker make with the devil? What is the result of the deal? The devil will let Tom Walker find the pirate's treasure, but he insists that it must be used to do the devil's work. Tom Walker becomes a usurer and cheats many people out of their money. He becomes very wealthy.

8. What does Walker tell the land jobber who begs him to extend his loan for a few months because Tom already has so much money? Tom says that he himself did not make any money and that, if he is lying, the devil should take him.

9. What finally happens to Walker? The devil takes him away on a horse, and Walker is never seen again.

10. What happens to Walker's riches? All of his riches disappear.

11. What is the saying or proverb that became popular in New England as a result of the story? The proverb is of "the devil and Tom Walker."

Name .... Class .... Date ....

Thanatopsis

Interacting with Text Analyzing Imagery

Imagery is the "word pictures" that writers create to evoke an emotional response. These vivid descriptions generally appeal to one or more of the senses: sight, hearing, touch, taste, and smell.

EXERCISE A. Read the following passage from "Thanatopsis." Notice the imagery and the senses to which the images appeal.

. . . The hills
Rock-ribbed and ancient as the sun,—
the vales
Stretching in pensive quietness between;
The venerable woods—rivers that move
In majesty, and the complaining brooks
That make the meadows green; and, poured
round all,
Old Ocean's gray and melancholy waste,—

EXERCISE B. Read the following items. Follow the directions for marking the passage. Write your answers to the questions on the lines provided.

1. Underline the details that include colors. Then write on the lines the phrases that include colors. To which sense does each image appeal? The phrases that include the names of colors are "meadows green" and "Ocean's gray . . . waste." Both images appeal to the sense of sight.

2. What sensory detail does the poet include in the line that begins "In majesty" and ends with "brooks"? Underline the sensory detail. To which sense does the detail appeal? The detail "the complaining brooks" appeals to the sense of hearing.

3. What images do the lines "The hills / Rock-ribbed and ancient as the sun" bring to mind? What do you picture as you read? Possible answer: I picture rolling hills with giant rocks jutting out of them. The hills look as though they have been there since the beginning of time.

4. What mood do the images in the passage create? Double-underline four words in the passage that you think help convey that mood. Explain your choices.
Possible answer: The mood is quiet, dignified, and awe inspiring. The words "ancient," "pensive," "venerable," and "majesty" contribute to the mood.

Name .... Class .... Date ....

The Chambered Nautilus

Interacting with Text: Identifying Metaphor and Personification

Metaphor and personification are both figures of speech. A **metaphor** is a comparison between two seemingly unlike things. In **personification** an animal, an object, a force of nature, or an idea is assigned human characteristics.

EXERCISE A. Read the following passage from "The Chambered Nautilus." In the passage, the poet first describes the chambered nautilus.

Thanks for the heavenly message brought by thee,
    Child of the wandering sea,
    Cast from her lap, forlorn!
From thy dead lips a clearer note is born
Than ever Triton blew from wreathèd horn!
    While on mine ear it rings,
Through the deep caves of thought I hear a voice that sings:—

EXERCISE B. Follow the directions for marking the passage shown above.

1. Underline the parts of the text that show personification in line 23.
2. Underline the parts of the text that show personification in line 24.
3. Underline the words in the text that name human body parts in line 25.

EXERCISE C. Read the following questions. Use the text you have already marked to help you answer each question. Answer the questions on the lines provided.

1. In line 23, what human traits are assigned to the chambered nautilus and to the sea? The chambered nautilus is called "child," and the sea is the parent; the sea also has the human trait of "wandering."
2. In line 24, what human attribute is assigned to the sea? What human emotion is assigned to the chambered nautilus? The sea has a "lap." The chambered nautilus is "forlorn."
3. In line 25, who or what is personified as having "dead lips"? What is the meaning of the personification? The chambered nautilus has "dead lips." This personification reminds the reader that the chambered nautilus is dead but that it is communicating with the speaker nonetheless.

Name .... Class .... Date ....

The First Snow-Fall

Interacting with Text Characterizing a Speaker

The **speaker** of a poem is the person who is narrating it. To understand and appreciate a poem, identify and characterize the speaker.

EXERCISE A. Read the following passages from "The First Snow-Fall."

Passage 1

I thought of a mound in sweet Auburn
Where a little headstone stood;
How the flakes were folding it gently,
As did robins the babes in the wood.

Up spoke our own little Mabel,
Saying, "Father, who makes it snow?"
And I told of the good All-father
Who cares for us here below.

Passage 2

Then, with eyes that saw not, I
kissed her;
And she, kissing back, could
not know
That *my* kiss was given to her sister,
Folded close under deepening snow.

EXERCISE B. Follow the directions to mark the passages shown.

1. In the first passage, underline the parts of the text that convey important information about the speaker.
2. Underline the parts of the text that show whether the speaker is a religious man.
3. In the second passage, underline the parts of the text that reveal what kind of a father the speaker is.

EXERCISE C. Read the following questions. For each question, review the text you have marked. Use it to help you answer the question. Circle the letter of the correct answer choice.

1. What important fact about the speaker do you learn in the first stanza of passage 1?
   a. He has buried a baby robin.
   b. He has had a child who died.
   c. He enjoys snow.
2. What phrase from the poem shows that the speaker is a religious man?
   a. "And I told of the good All-father"
   b. "the babes in the wood"
   c. "sweet Auburn"

Name .... Class .... Date ....

The Tide Rises, the Tide Falls

Interacting with Text — Analyzing Sound Devices

Sound devices such as rhyme make poetry memorable and interesting. Other sound devices are **repetition,** the recurring of words, phrases, lines, or stanzas; and **alliteration,** the repetition of a series of initial consonant sounds. Another sound device is **onomatopoeia,** the use of a word, such as *croak*, that imitates or suggests the sound it describes.

EXERCISE A. Read the following passage from "The Tide Rises, the Tide Falls." Notice the sound devices and the effects they create.

The morning breaks; the steeds in their stalls
Stamp and neigh, as the hostler calls;
The day returns, but nevermore
Returns the traveler to the shore,
And the tide rises, the tide falls.

EXERCISE B. Now read the following items. Mark the text as directed. Write on the lines provided.

1. Does the stanza have rhyme? Underline the words that rhyme. Write the rhyming words on the lines provided. The rhyming words are "stalls," "calls," "falls"; "nevermore" and "shore."

2. Find two examples of repetition in the stanza. Double-underline the words that are repeated. Write the repeated words on the lines provided. The words "returns" and "tide" are repeated.

3. Circle the words that contain alliteration. What words in lines one and two contain alliteration? What sound is repeated? Write your answers on the lines provided. The words "steeds," "stalls," and "stamp" contain alliteration. The st sound is repeated.

4. In line 2, the word *neigh* is an example of what sound device? The sound device is called onomatopoeia.

Name .... Class .... Date ....

from *Self-Reliance*

Interacting with Text **Summarizing**

Summarizing a passage is briefly stating its main ideas in different words.

EXERCISE A. Read the following passage from "Self-Reliance." The passage describes Ralph Waldo Emerson's ideas about moral standards.

What I must do, is all that concerns me, not what the people think. This rule, equally arduous in actual and in intellectual life, may serve for the whole distinction between greatness and meanness. It is the harder, because you will always find those who think they know what is your duty better than you know it. It is easy in the world to live after the world's opinion; it is easy in solitude to live after our own; but the great man is he who in the midst of the crowd keeps with perfect sweetness the independence of solitude.

EXERCISE B. Now find and mark the text in the passage as directed.

1. Find and underline the author's statement of his concern.
2. Find and double-underline the detail in the passage that states what the author is not concerned about.
3. Find and underline the details in the passage that explain what makes it hard to follow one's own conscience or moral standards.
4. Find and underline the phrase that defines a "great man."

EXERCISE C. Read and answer the following questions about the passage. Circle the letter of the correct answer choice.

1. Who are the most admirable people, according to Ralph Waldo Emerson?
   a. The most admirable people are those who do what they think is right, not what others think they should do.
   b. The most admirable people advance the world by conforming with others.
   c. The most admirable people form opinions based on others' opinions.
2. What is the best summary sentence for the passage?
   a. Solitude prepares a person for forming strong, secure opinions. These opinions should be used to influence others.
   b. A great man is one who has a gentle nature and a trusting reliance on others but who values orthodoxy.
   c. It is easy to hold firm opinions when alone and to go along with the crowd when with others. What is important is to maintain your own ethical standards in all circumstances.

Name .... Class .... Date ....

from *Civil Disobedience*

Interacting with Text **Paraphrasing**

When you retell something in your own words, you are **paraphrasing.**

EXERCISE A. Read the following passage from "Civil Disobedience." Henry David Thoreau is describing his ideas about American government in the passage.

> . . . Yet this government never of itself furthered any enterprise, but by the alacrity with which it got out of its way. *It* does not keep the country free. *It* does not settle the West. *It* does not educate. The character inherent in the American people has done all that has been accomplished; and it would have done somewhat more, if the government had not sometimes got in its way. For government is an expedient by which men would fain succeed in letting one another alone; and, as has been said, when it is most expedient, the governed are most let alone by it. Trade and commerce, if they were not made of india-rubber, would never manage to bounce over the obstacles which legislators are continually putting in their way.

EXERCISE B. Follow the directions for each of the following items. If you are unsure of the meaning of a word, you may consult your textbook or a dictionary.

1. Paraphrase the first sentence of the passage. The only way the government has helped an enterprise is by the speed with which it left the enterprise alone.

2. Underline three details in the passage that Thoreau uses to support the idea of the first sentence. To whom does "*It*" refer in the passage? Explain.
"It" refers to the government, specifically the American government.

3. Find and underline the words *inherent*, *expedient*, and *fain* in the passage. Write the meaning of each word as it is used in the context of the sentence.
Inherent means "belonging to by nature."
Expedient means "means to an end; appropriate or advisable."
Fain means "gladly."

4. Paraphrase the last sentence of the passage. Trade and commerce are flexible, and that is why they have succeeded even though government has often gotten in the way.

Name .... Class .... Date ....

The Minister's Black Veil

Interactive Reading **Reading Guide**

Section 1: The Minister's Veil

KEY CHARACTERS

Mr. Hooper–minister of the Milford church

Elizabeth–Mr. Hooper's fiancée

Members of the Milford church congregation

KEY VOCABULARY AND TERMS

obscurity–the state of being hidden from view

countenance–a face

oratory–the art of speaking eloquently in public

indecorous–conflicting with accepted standards of good conduct or taste

ostentatious–in a way that attracts notice

bewildered–confounded; completely confused

SORTING IT OUT

EXERCISE A. Read the Key Characters and the Key Vocabulary and Terms sections. Then read the story from the beginning to the paragraph that begins "The next day the whole village of Milford talked of little else than Parson Hooper's black veil." Answer the questions on the lines provided.

1. Where and when does the story take place? The story is set in a New England town in the seventeenth century.

2. What is unusual about Mr. Hooper's appearance at the beginning of the story? He is wearing a black veil over his face.

3. What effect does Mr. Hooper's appearance have on his congregation? Members are startled, amazed, nervous, frightened, and curious.

4. What is the subject of Mr. Hooper's sermon? The subject is secret sin—the sin we conceal from everyone, even ourselves sometimes.

5. In the afternoon, Mr. Hooper prays at a funeral service for a young woman. What strange thing do some people say that they think they see during the funeral procession? They think they see the minister and the dead maiden's spirit walk hand in hand.

6. Why is the wedding that Mr. Hooper performs that night not a happy occasion? The guests become depressed because of Mr. Hooper's veil, and the bride quivers and becomes pale.

Section 2: A Black Veil on Every Face

KEY VOCABULARY AND TERMS

emblem–a symbol

impertinent–rudely bold

remonstrance–protest, complaint

deputies–persons appointed with power to act

unappalled–not shocked or dismayed

obstinacy–stubbornness

eccentric–strange

plausibility–the state of seeming worthy of belief

ambiguity–the possibility of two or more meanings

consorted–associated

aghast–shocked

SORTING IT OUT

EXERCISE B. Read the Key Vocabulary and Terms section. Then read from the paragraph that begins "The next day the whole village of Milford . . . " to the end of the story. Answer the questions on the lines provided.

7. What happens when a group of parishioners tries to ask Mr. Hooper about his veil? They are too intimidated to ask about it, so they tell the congregation that a synod would be required to handle the problem.

8. How does Mr. Hooper respond when Elizabeth asks him to remove the veil and tell her why he put it on? He refuses to do so.

9. What happens to the relationship between Mr. Hooper and Elizabeth? Elizabeth says farewell because he will not confide in her about the veil.

10. What is the rest of Mr. Hooper's life as a minister like? People come from far away to hear him preach. He lives a long, good life but has no close friends or relationships.

11. Who takes care of Mr. Hooper at the end of his life? Elizabeth takes care of Mr. Hooper until he dies.

12. Mr. Hooper is often called upon by people in "mortal anguish." What title does Mr. Hooper acquire? Mr. Hooper acquires the title of "Father": Father Hooper.

13. What does the Reverend Mr. Clark ask of Mr. Hooper as Mr. Hooper lies dying? He asks Mr. Hooper for permission to remove the veil.

14. How does Mr. Hooper respond to the request for permission to remove the veil? Mr. Hooper refuses. He holds the veil down with both hands. As he dies, he says that he sees a black veil on every face around him.

Name .... Class .... Date ....

The Three-Piece Suit

Interacting with Text Questioning

Asking questions during reading helps readers understand a passage and contributes to their understanding of the whole selection.

EXERCISE A. Read the following passage from "The Three-Piece Suit."

I bought several items and held them in my arms against my chest. The salesgirl greeted me and unhooked a suitable basket. I had no other alternative but to deposit my purchases inside, and since the proper sort of people, my sort, buy without consideration for the price, I did not even bother to look at the cash register total. When I had returned home, my blood pressure was at its peak, my head was literally boiling, my tongue twisted and my chest heaving. I no longer saw where I walked or where I threw my jacket, vest, and trousers. I clenched my teeth and gritted them as I cursed the traps of this century and the folly of fools. I finally went back to being my old self and since that day no one has troubled me anymore.

EXERCISE B. Now read the following items. Follow the directions for marking the passage. Write on the lines provided.

1. What does the narrator buy? Underline the phrase that tells what he bought. Write on the line the phrase that indicates what he purchased. The narrator bought "several items."

2. Why does the narrator avoid looking at the cash register total? Underline the part of the text that shows the reason he does not look at the total. Restate what you have underlined on the lines. The sort of people with whom the narrator wants to be associated buy without concern for the price.

3. Underline the parts of the text that describe the narrator's physical reactions when he returns home.

4. Is the narrator's head "literally boiling"? If not, why does he use these words? No, he is exaggerating to express how upset he is.

5. What does the narrator curse? Explain. He is lamenting the materialistic obsession of the times and thinks it is foolish.

Name .... Class .... Date ....

The Pit and the Pendulum

Interactive Reading **Reading Guide**

Part 1: The Pit

KEY CHARACTERS

Narrator–a man who has been imprisoned in a small chamber by Spanish Inquisitors

KEY VOCABULARY AND TERMS

indeterminate–not definitely clear

delirious–affected by a mental disturbance marked by confusion and hallucinations

imperceptible–extremely slight, gradual, or subtle; impossible to recognize

fancy–imagination, especially of a delusive sort

subterranean–being under the surface of the earth

prostrate–lying flat

masonry–something constructed of stone or brick

hearkened–listened

SORTING IT OUT

EXERCISE A. Read the Key Character and the Key Vocabulary and Terms sections. Then read the first section of the story. Stop reading at the paragraph that begins, "Looking upward I surveyed . . . " Answer the following questions on the lines provided.

1. What is the narrator's physical and mental condition at the beginning of the story?
He is in a dreamlike state, barely conscious; he is weak and anxious.

2. Where is the narrator imprisoned? Describe the prison. He is in a small, dark room with cold stone walls.

3. What does the narrator do to find out how large his cell is? He paces around it; he rips a piece of cloth off his gown and puts it into the wall as a marker.

4. In trying to measure his cell, the narrator trips. Where does he find himself when he does so? He finds himself at the brink of a circular pit.

5. When the narrator wakes up from a nap, how has his position been changed?
He has been tied to a low wooden frame with a long strap so that he can move his arm only to feed himself.

Name .... Class .... Date ....

Part 2: The Pendulum

KEY VOCABULARY AND TERMS

ravenous–extremely hungry or greedy for food

confounded–baffled

acrid–sharp and harsh in odor

cessation–a temporary or final ceasing

voracity–having hunger that seems impossible to satisfy

abstraction–the state of being lost in thought

conjecture–a conclusion reached by guessing

fissure–a narrow opening or crack of considerable length and depth

discordant–quarrelsome

SORTING IT OUT

EXERCISE B. Read the Key Vocabulary and Terms section. Then read the second section, which begins "Looking upward I surveyed . . . ," through the end of the story. Answer the following questions on the lines provided.

6. What animals share the cell with the narrator? He is surrounded by rats.

7. What unusual features does the narrator notice about the pendulum when he looks at it more carefully? Its sweep is increasing, and it is descending; its bottom is formed into a razor-sharp crescent.

8. What does the narrator realize will happen to him? The pendulum will eventually reach him and cut his chest open.

9. What hope for survival does the narrator have? His hope is that the blade will cut the rope binding him so that he can escape.

10. Why will this hope for survival not succeed? The narrator realizes that the ropes that bind him are arranged so as not to fall beneath the blade of the pendulum.

11. How does the narrator use the rats to help him? He wipes oil from his food dish on onto the rope; the rats gnaw through rope, and he frees himself.

12. After the narrator overcomes the threat of the pendulum, what new threat does he face? The iron walls of his cell are heating and contracting, threatening to burn him to death or force him into the pit.

13. What finally happens to the narrator? He is saved by the general of the French army, which has entered Toledo and halted the Inquisition.

Name .... Class .... Date ....

from *My Bondage and My Freedom*

Interacting with Text Drawing Conclusions

To **draw conclusions** is to use one's own reasoning to make broad statements that are based on information in the text.

EXERCISE A. Read the following passage from *My Bondage and My Freedom.* In the passage, Frederick Douglass describes attitudes about slavery.

Although slavery was a delicate subject, and very cautiously talked about among grown up people in Maryland, I frequently talked about it—and that very freely—with the white boys. I would, sometimes, say to them, while seated on a curb stone or a cellar door, "I wish I could be free, as you will be when you get to be men." "You will be free, you know, as soon as you are twenty-one, and can go where you like, but I am a slave for life. Have I not as good a right to be free as you have?" Words like these, I observed, always troubled them; and I had no small satisfaction in wringing from the boys, occasionally, that fresh and bitter condemnation of slavery, that springs from nature, unseared and unperverted.

EXERCISE B. Read the following questions. Follow the directions for marking the text. Write your answers to questions 5 and 6 on the lines provided.

1. What subject do the adults approach with caution? Circle the subject that the grown-ups think is delicate.
2. How often do the children talk about the subject? Double-underline the text that indicates how often the subject is discussed among the children.
3. What is Douglass's wish? What is his argument? Underline the parts of the text that show what Douglass says to the other children.
4. What does Douglass observe about the other children's reactions to his argument? Circle the parts of the text that tell how the children react.
5. What can you conclude about socializing between enslaved African or African American children and white children from the details in the passage? The children played together freely.
6. What conclusion might you draw about why Frederick Douglass has "no small satisfaction" from provoking condemnations of slavery from the white children? He is pleased that his logical argument proves his point that slavery is unnatural.

Name .... Class .... Date ....

Follow the Drinking Gourd

Interacting with Text Analyzing Imagery

Imagery evokes an emotional response in readers. **Images** are mind pictures that make poems, songs, and stories seem real by appealing to the reader's senses: sight, touch, hearing, smell, and taste.

EXERCISE A. Read the following passages from "Follow the Drinking Gourd."

Passage 1

When the sun comes back and the first
quail calls, 1
Follow the drinking gourd,*
For the old man is a-waiting for to carry
you to freedom
If you follow the drinking gourd.

*the Big Dipper constellation

Passage 2

The river bank will make a very good
road, 9
The dead trees show you the way,
Left foot, peg foot traveling on
Follow the drinking gourd.

EXERCISE B. Read the following items. Follow the directions for marking the passages. Then answer the questions on the lines provided.

1. In passage 1, underline the parts of the text that tell what the speaker sees and hears. To which senses do the images appeal? The image "the sun comes back" appeals to sight and possibly touch—the warmth of the sun; "the first quail calls" appeals to hearing.

2. In passage 2, underline the parts of the text that create a picture of the road north to freedom. On the basis of these words, how can you describe the road to freedom? Possible answer: Dead trees along the river bank mark the road to freedom.

3. To what sense does the image of "The dead trees show you the way" appeal? The image "The dead trees show you the way" appeals to sight.

4. Circle the first instance of the line in passage 1 that is later repeated. According to the footnote, to what senses does "the drinking gourd" appeal? Explain. The repeated reference to "the drinking gourd," as both a gourd and a star constellation, appeals to the sense of sight. It also suggests the process of drinking, which appeals to the senses of touch and taste.

Name .... Class .... Date ....

And Ain't I a Woman?

Interacting with Text **Analyzing Style**

The term **style** refers to the elements that make an author's writing unique. Style includes the author's diction and sentence structure, as well as the use of imagery and figurative language.

EXERCISE A. Read the following passage from "And Ain't I a Woman?"

Look at me! Look at my arm. I have ploughed and planted, and gathered into barns, and no man could head me! And ain't I a woman? I could work as much and eat as much as a man—when I could get it—and bear the lash as well! And ain't I a woman? I have borne thirteen children, and seen them most all sold off to slavery, and when I cried out with my mother's grief, none but Jesus heard me! And ain't I a woman?

Then they talk about this thing in the head; what's this they call it? [Intellect, someone whispers.] That's it, honey.

EXERCISE B. Read the following questions and follow the directions for marking the text. Write your answers on the lines provided.

1. Underline each occurrence of a refrain in the passage. Copy the refrain. What does the refrain add to the speech's style? "And ain't I a woman?" is the refrain. The refrain is emphatic, emotional, and attention getting.

2. Underline the punctuation marks, other than periods or commas, in the passage. What do these punctuation marks suggest about the techniques that Sojourner Truth uses in her speech? Question marks here draw attention to rhetorical questions, questions asked for effect with no answer expected. Exclamation points convey Truth's strong feelings. Dashes suggest asides, or comments

3. What do words and phrases such as "ain't" and "honey" reveal about Truth's style? The words give the speech an informal tone.

4. What painful facts does Truth reveal about her life? Circle the facts that tell the audience what Truth has endured. What response might she expect as she reveals these facts? How does using these facts contribute to her style? Truth has been whipped and has lost her children to slavery. The audience is likely to react with sympathy to her hardships. These facts make her speech raw, honest, and effective.

Name .... Class .... Date ....

from *His Promised Land*

Interacting with Text Analyzing Characters

Analyzing characters means thinking critically to determine the traits and personalities of the people or characters in narratives. To analyze a character, consider the character's words, thoughts, and actions as well as how others react to the character.

EXERCISE A. Read the following passage from *His Promised Land.*

These unnerving things set [Eliza] more determinedly on her way, until again she broke through the ice, and again she threw the baby from her, while she held on to the rail. Now cold, wet, and weary, she struggled out to find her baby and wearily continued her journey. A third time she broke through and a third time she had to go through the same efforts to secure her baby. This time she was so weak and exhausted, her clothes frozen to her body, she did not have the strength to even pull the rail along with her, so simply left to trust that the ice would hold. . . .

. . . As she stepped off the shore ice onto the land, weary and disheartened, a caring hand came from some unknown source out of the dark and grabbed her. . . . She sank down on the ground and began to cry, feeling she was lost.

EXERCISE B. Read the following items. Follow the directions for marking the passage. Then write your responses on the lines provided.

1. The first sentence of the passage describes obstacles that Eliza must overcome. Underline the phrase used to describe Eliza's attitude. Write the phrase that shows Eliza's attitude. The phrase "more determinedly" describes Eliza.

2. The second sentence describes Eliza's physical state. Underline the parts of the text that give information about how she feels. Write one sentence to describe how Eliza feels. Eliza is cold, wet, and weary.

3. How is Eliza described? Underline the words in the remainder of the passage that describe Eliza. Tell what the words reveal about Eliza. Possible answer: The words "weak," "exhausted," "weary," "disheartened," and "lost" reveal how Eliza feels about the difficulties she faces on her almost impossible journey.

4. Tell what personality traits Eliza's actions reveal. Eliza's actions show her courage, determination, and love for her child.

Name .... Class .... Date ....

from *Mary Chesnut's Civil War*

Interacting with Text Summarizing and Questioning

To summarize a passage, first determine its main ideas and then express them briefly in your own words. To be sure of understanding text, ask yourself questions as you read.

EXERCISE A. Read the following passage from "Mary Chesnut's Civil War."

April 12, 1861. Anderson will not capitulate.

Yesterday was the merriest, maddest dinner we have had yet. Men were more audaciously wise and witty. We had an unspoken foreboding it was to be our last pleasant meeting. Mr. Miles dined with us today. Mrs. Henry King rushed in: "The news, I come for the latest news—all of the men of the King family are on the island"—of which fact she seemed proud.

While [Mrs. Henry King] was here, our peace negotiator—or envoy—came in. That is, Mr. Chesnut returned—his interview with Colonel Anderson had been deeply interesting—but was not inclined to be communicative, wanted his dinner. Felt for Anderson. Had telegraphed to President Davis for instructions.

EXERCISE B. Read the following questions. Follow the directions for marking the text. Then write your answers to the questions on the lines provided.

1. Underline the word in the first paragraph that suggests that the dinner party may not be simply a joyous gathering. What word suggests a feeling of approaching misfortune? The word "foreboding" suggests that difficult times may lie ahead.

2. What is an *envoy*? Explain how Colonel Chesnut is acting as an envoy. An envoy is someone sent as a messenger or a representative of another. Chesnut is acting as a "peace negotiator" for President Davis.

3. Underline the text that tells what Colonel Chesnut has found "deeply interesting." Why does Chesnut not want to discuss what is "deeply interesting"? Chesnut has been involved in a private, extremely important talk with Colonel Anderson.

4. Read over the passage and your responses to the questions. Then write a summary of the passage. Possible summary: At a dinner party, guests are merry yet filled with foreboding. Colonel Chesnut is noncommunicative about his discussion with Colonel Anderson. Chesnut wires President Davis to ask how to proceed.

Name .... Class .... Date ....

Letters to His Family

Interacting with Text Analyzing Tone

The **tone** of a literary work is a reflection of the writer's attitude toward a subject. Tone may be conveyed through elements such as word choice and sentence structure.

EXERCISE A. Read the following passage from "Letters to His Family."

Secession is nothing but revolution. The framers of our Constitution never exhausted so much labor, wisdom, and forbearance in its formation, and surrounded it with so many guards and securities, if it was intended to be broken by every member of the Confederacy at will. It was intended for "perpetual union," so expressed in the preamble, and for the establishment of a government, not a compact, which can only be dissolved by revolution or the consent of all the people in convention assembled. . . . Anarchy would have been established, and not a government, by Washington, Hamilton, Jefferson, Madison, and the other patriots of the Revolution.

EXERCISE B. Read the following items. Mark the text as directed. Then follow the directions for each item.

1. What attitude toward secession does author Robert E. Lee convey in the first sentence? Circle the letter of the correct answer choice.
   - a. Lee is pleased because he believes that secession is unlikely.
   - (b.) Lee believes that the threat of secession is frightening.
   - c. Lee finds the threat of secession exciting.
2. Underline the second sentence in the passage. What does the statement suggest about Lee's thoughts and attitudes? Circle the letter of the correct answer choice.
   - a. Lee thinks that the Constitution is mainly a symbolic document.
   - b. Lee is trying to impress his reader with grandiose ideas.
   - (c.) Lee has given deep thought to the meaning of the Constitution.
3. What tone do the words "exhausted" and "forbearance" convey in the passage? Circle the letter of the best answer choice.
   - a. The words convey an argumentative tone.
   - b. The words convey a casual tone.
   - (c.) The words convey an earnest tone.
4. Write a sentence to describe the overall tone in the passage on the line provided.

   Possible answer: The overall tone of the passage is serious, formal, and concerned.

Name .... Class .... Date ....

An Occurrence at Owl Creek Bridge

Interacting with Text Analyzing Plot

The **plot** is the series of events in a story. The center of a plot is the conflict that the main character experiences. A **flashback** is an interruption in the chronological order of a narrative. It presents an event that took place earlier.

EXERCISE A. Read the following passages from "An Occurrence at Owl Creek Bridge." The events in passage 1 occur as Farquhar stands on the bridge with a noose around his neck.

Passage 1

[Farquhar] unclosed his eyes and saw again the water below him. "If I could free my hands," he thought, "I might throw off the noose and spring into the stream. By diving I could evade the bullets and, swimming vigorously, reach the bank, take to the woods and get away home. . . ."

As these thoughts . . . were flashed into the doomed man's brain, . . . the captain nodded to the sergeant. The sergeant stepped aside.

Passage 2

Peyton Farquhar was a well-to-do planter, of an old and highly respected Alabama family. . . .

One evening while Farquhar and his wife were sitting on a rustic bench near the entrance to his grounds, a gray-clad soldier rode up to the gate and asked for a drink of water. . . . While [Mrs. Farquhar] was fetching the water her husband approached the dusty horseman and inquired eagerly for news from the front.

EXERCISE B. Read the following questions and answer them on the lines provided. Follow the directions for marking the text.

1. In passage 1, underline the part of the text that identifies the conflict. What conflict is presented? *Farquhar is about to be hanged and wonders whether he might somehow escape.*

2. How does the author create suspense in passage 1? *Farquhar's thoughts are so detailed that the reader begins to think it possible that Farquhar can escape. Suspense builds as the reader wonders whether Farquhar will escape or be executed.*

3. The passages are presented in the order in which they appear in the story. Which passage is a flashback? Underline the part of the text that begins the flashback.

Name .... Class .... Date ....

Shiloh

Interacting with Text — Recognizing Irony

Irony is a contrast or discrepency between appearance and reality. Recognizing irony helps the reader understand the author's theme.

EXERCISE A. Read the following passage from "Shiloh."

Through the pause of night
That followed the Sunday fight
Around the church of Shiloh—
The church so lone, the log-built one,
That echoed to many a parting groan
And natural prayer
Of dying foemen mingled there—
Foemen at morn, but friends at eve—
Fame or country least their care:
(What like a bullet can undeceive!)
But now they lie low,
While over them the swallows skim,
And all is hushed at Shiloh.

EXERCISE B. Read the following items and write your responses on the lines provided. Follow the directions for marking the text.

1. Underline the part of the text that indicates the setting of the poem. Describe the setting. The events take place in the area around a log church in Shiloh. It is Monday.

2. Circle the part of the text that indicates what event took place there. What has happened recently? What is the result of this event? A battle took place at Shiloh, and men on both sides died.

3. What irony does the poet present in the lines "Foeman at morn, but friends at eve / Fame or country least their care"? In life the men were enemies; in death, the causes that they died for are of no significance. They are brothers in death.

4. Explain the irony presented through the setting and the imagery. What is the difference between what the reader might expect at the place described and what actually happened there? What is the difference between the scene as it is now and as it was before? One might expect joyful, peaceful events to take place at the church. Instead, a brutal battle with many deaths has occurred there. The images of nature—beautiful, graceful swallows skimming over the hushed field—at the end of the poem are ironic because such imagery contrasts with that of men dying.

Name .... Class .... Date ....

The Gettysburg Address

Interacting with Text Paraphrasing

To **paraphrase** is to restate a passage in one's own words. In the process, one changes unfamiliar words to simple ones and rewrites sentences that have complex structures so as to simplify them.

EXERCISE A. Read the following passage from The Gettysburg Address.

But, in a larger sense, we can not dedicate—we can not consecrate—we can not hallow—this ground. . . . It is for us the living, rather, to be dedicated here to the unfinished work which they who fought here have thus far so nobly advanced. It is rather for us to be here dedicated to the great task remaining before us—that from these honored dead we take increased devotion to that cause for which they gave the last full measure of devotion—that we here highly resolve that these dead shall not have died in vain—that this nation, under God, shall have a new birth of freedom—and that government of the people, by the people, for the people, shall not perish from the earth.

EXERCISE B. Follow the directions for marking the text.

1. Read the following paraphrase: *In reality, we cannot make this ground holy.* Underline the sentence in the passage that is paraphrased.
2. Read the following paraphrase: *that we increase our commitment to the cause that the soldiers gave their lives for.* Double-underline the part of the passage that is paraphrased.

EXERCISE C. Read question 1 and circle the letter of the best answer choice. Then read item 2 and write your paraphrase on the lines provided.

1. Which statement is the best paraphrase of the sentence that begins "It is for us the living . . . "?
   a. We should finish the work started by the soldiers who fought here.
   b. Our advanced dedication is noble and supports those living today.
   c. The soldiers started their work in a noble, dedicated way.
2. Paraphrase the third sentence, which begins "It is rather for us to be here dedicated to the great task remaining before us . . . " We should devote ourselves to the cause for which these soldiers died, to show the dedication that the soldiers showed, and to resolve that their deaths were for a great purpose: a rebirth of freedom in our nation and the preservation of our government.

Name .... Class .... Date ....

The Gift in Wartime

Interacting with Text Recognizing Symbolism

A **symbol** is an object or an act that has a literal meaning but that also represents something more, such as an idea or a belief.

EXERCISE A. Read the following passages from "The Gift in Wartime." As you read, notice the symbolism.

Passage 1

I offer you roses
Buried in your new grave
I offer you my wedding gown
To cover your tomb still green with grass

You give me medals
Together with silver stars
And the yellow pips on your badge
Unused and still shining

Passage 2

I offer you clouds
That linger on my eyes on summer days
I offer you cold winters
Amid my springtime of life

EXERCISE B. Follow the directions in each item for marking the passages. Read the questions and answer them by writing on the lines provided or by circling the letter of the best answer choice.

1. Underline the objects that are symbols of love in the first stanza of passage 1. What items did you underline? roses, wedding gown

2. Underline all the objects in the second stanza of passage 1. What do these objects symbolize?
   a. The objects symbolize the strength of various types of metals.
   b. The objects symbolize military service.
   c. The objects symbolize the power of love.

3. Underline the symbols that have something in common in passage 2. What idea do these symbols represent?
   a. winter
   b. spring and summer
   c. the passing of the time

Name .... Class .... Date ....

Beat! Beat! Drums!

Interacting with Text Identifying Sound Devices

Poets use sound devices to help create the tone of a poem. Sound devices include **rhyme** and **repetition.** Other sound devices are **alliteration,** the repetition of initial consonant sounds in words in close proximity, and **onomatopoeia,** words that imitate the sound they describe.

EXERCISE A. Read the following passage from "Beat! Beat! Drums!" Notice the sound devices the poet uses.

Beat! beat! drums!—blow! bugles! blow!
Through the windows—through doors—burst like a ruthless force,
Into the solemn church, and scatter the congregation,
Into the school where the scholar is studying;
Leave not the bridegroom quiet—no happiness must he have now with his bride,
Nor the peaceful farmer any peace, ploughing his field or gathering his grain,
So fierce you whirr and pound you drums—so shrill you bugles blow.

EXERCISE B. Read the following items and follow the directions for marking the text. Then write your answers for the questions on the lines provided.

1. In the first four lines of the poem, which words are repeated? Underline the repeated words. Then explain how the repetition affects the sound and meaning of the poem. The words "beat," "blow," "through," and "into" are repeated; the repetition of these words lends a sharp, drumlike rhythm to the poem. The repeated words also increase the sense of unity in the poem.

2. Double-underline the words in lines 3 and 4 that show alliteration. What words show alliteration, and what consonant sounds are repeated? The words "solemn," "scatter," "school," "scholar," and "studying" show alliteration, and the s sound is repeated.

3. What five words from the stanza are examples of onomatopoeia? The words "beat," "blow," "whirr," "pound," and "shrill" are examples of onomatopoeia.

4. **Tone** is a reflection of the writer's attitude toward a subject. What is the poet's tone? How do sound devices emphasize the poet's tone? The tone is angry. The repetition and onomatopoeia produce an abrupt, angry sound.

Name .... Class .... Date ....

from Song of Myself

Interacting with Text Analyzing Imagery

Imagery is the vivid word pictures that writers create through descriptive writing. Imagery appeals to the reader's senses of sight, hearing, touch, taste, and smell.

EXERCISE A. Read the following passage from *Song of Myself.* Notice the imagery in the passage.

> The spotted hawk swoops by and accuses me, he complains of my gab and
>   my loitering.
> I too am not a bit tamed, I too am untranslatable,
> I sound my barbaric yawp over the roofs of the world.
> The last scud [cloudiness or rain] of day holds back for me,
> It flings my likeness after the rest and true as any on the shadow'd wilds,
> It coaxes me to the vapor and the dusk.
> I depart as air, I shake my white locks at the runaway sun . . .

EXERCISE B. Read the following items and follow the directions for marking the text. Write your answers to the questions on the lines provided.

1. What is described in line 104? a hawk Underline the words in the passage that help you picture this image.

2. To what two senses does the imagery of line 104 appeal? Explain. The imagery appeals to the sense of sight ("spotted hawk swoops") and sense of hearing ("accuses" and "complains").

3. What traits does the poet assign to the hawk in line 104? How does attributing these traits to the hawk make the image more powerful? The poet assigns to the hawk the human traits of accusing and complaining. The personification makes the image vivid and specific.

4. What two words are used to create sound imagery in line 106? Underline the words in the passage. How does each word function differently to describe the sound? The word "barbaric" describes the kind of sound it is; "yawp" imitates the sound.

5. What time of day is the poet describing? Underline three phrases that describe the time of day. Explain. The poet describes twilight: "the last scud of day," "the vapor and the dusk," "the runaway sun."

Name .... Class .... Date ....

The Useless

Interacting with Text Analyzing Analogy

An author may present an **analogy** to help clarify ideas. In an analogy, something unfamiliar is often compared to something familiar.

EXERCISE A. Read the following passage.

"If you have no appreciation for what
has no use
You cannot begin to talk about what
can be used.
The earth, for example, is broad and vast
But of all this expanse a man uses only
a few inches
Upon which he happens to be standing.
Now suppose you suddenly take away
All that he is not actually using
So that, all around his feet a gulf
Yawns, and he stands in the Void,
With nowhere solid except right under
each foot:
How long will he be able to use what
he is using?"

Hui Tzu said: "It would cease to serve any purpose."

EXERCISE B. Read the following items and follow the directions for marking the text. Write your answers to the questions and your explanation on the lines provided.

1. Underline the analogy in the passage.
2. To what does Chuang Tzu compare "what has no use"? Chuang Tzu compares what has no use to the broad Earth.
3. To what does Chuang Tzu compare "what can be used"? Chuang Tzu compares useful knowledge to the space on the earth taken up by a man standing.
4. In your own words, explain what the analogy means. Possible answer: If a person understands only a small part of the world, the information is useful. But without a broader knowledge of the world and its values and ideologies, the information is not connected to anything meaningful. A larger body of knowledge, containing values, ideals, and philosophies, greatly extends the meaning of "useful knowledge."

Name .... Class .... Date ....

I heard a Fly buzz when I died

Interacting with Text **Interpreting**

To **interpret** a text is to use details from the text and personal knowledge and experience to attach meaning to what is read.

EXERCISE A. Read the following poem by Emily Dickinson.

I heard a Fly buzz when I died

I heard a Fly buzz—when I died—
The Stillness in the Room
Was like the Stillness in the Air—
Between the Heaves of Storm—

The Eyes around—had wrung them dry—
And Breaths were gathering firm
For that last Onset—when the King
Be witnessed—in the Room—

I willed my Keepsakes—Signed away
What portion of me be
Assignable—and then it was
There interposed a Fly—

With Blue—uncertain stumbling Buzz—
Between the light—and me—
And then the Windows failed—and then
I could not see to see—

EXERCISE B. Read the following items and follow the directions for marking the text. Write your answers to the questions on the lines provided.

1. What is the speaker in the process of doing? The speaker is in the process of dying.

2. Underline the words in the poem that have unusual capitalization. Read over the words you have underlined. What do these words suggest about key ideas in the poem? Possible answer: The words emphasize death ("Stillness," "Room," "Windows"), the reactions of others to death ("Eyes," "Breaths"), the speaker's surrender to death ("Onset," "Keepsakes," "Signed," and "Assignable"), Christ ("King"), and the imposition of a minor, inconsequential thing ("Fly," "Blue," and "Buzz") into the process of something monumental, death.

3. Why is the fly's role significant? The fly interrupts the process of dying and distracts the dying person, assuming importance only because it is the last thing the speaker sees.

Name .... Class .... Date ....

The Celebrated Jumping Frog of Calaveras County

Interacting with Text Monitoring Comprehension

Monitoring comprehension means making sure that you understand what you are reading. This involves checking your understanding as you read.

EXERCISE A. Read the following passages from "The Celebrated Jumping Frog of Calaveras County." The passages describe Jim Smiley and include several examples of dialect–language from a particular region or language spoken among a particular group of people.

Passage 1

But still he was lucky, uncommon lucky; he most always come out winner. He was always ready and laying for a chance; there couldn't be no solitry thing mentioned but that feller'd offer to bet on it, and take any side you please, as I was just telling you.

Passage 2

He ketched a frog one day, and took him home, and said he cal'klated to edercate him; and so he never done nothing for three months but set in his back yard and learn that frog to jump.

EXERCISE B. Read the following questions. For each question, find and underline the text in the passage that will help you answer it. Write the answers for each question on the lines provided.

1. Reread the first sentence in passage 1. What do you think "he most always come out winner" means? Underline a part of the sentence that gives you a clue. Write one sentence defining the phrase. It means that Jim Smiley was so lucky that he almost always won his bets.

2. Reread the second sentence in passage 1. Underline the words *solit'ry* and *feller'd* in the passage. Write the correct form of each word to make its meaning clearer.

   solit'ry solitary

   feller'd fellow would

3. Reread passage 2. Find the following words and underline them: *ketched*, *cal'klated*, *edercate*, *learn*. Write the correct form of each word to make it easier to understand the passage.

   ketched caught

   cal'klated calculated

   edercate educate

   learn teach

Name .... Class .... Date ....

The Outcasts of Poker Flat

Interacting with Text **Recognizing Foreshadowing**

Foreshadowing is the author's use of clues to prepare readers for events that will take place later in a story. The clues may be words, phrases, or whole sentences.

EXERCISE A. Read the following passage from "The Outcasts of Poker Flat." Look for hints that signal what will happen later in the story.

The spot was singularly wild and impressive. A wooded amphitheatre, surrounded on three sides by precipitous cliffs of naked granite, sloped gently toward the crest of another precipice that overlooked the valley. It was, undoubtedly, the most suitable spot for a camp, had camping been advisable. But Mr. Oakhurst knew that scarcely half the journey to Sandy Bar was accomplished, and the party were not equipped or provisioned for delay. This fact he pointed out to his companions curtly, with a philosophic commentary on the folly of "throwing up their hand before the game was played out." But they were furnished with liquor, which in this emergency stood them in place of food, fuel, rest, and prescience.

EXERCISE B. Read the questions below. Answer on the lines provided.

1. What makes you think that the place at which the group stops may be dangerous for them? Underline the clues in the text that tell of danger. Explain. The group is surrounded by steep cliffs in a wild place. They are less than halfway to their destination and have no provisions with them.

2. From the information in the paragraph, what do you conclude is most likely to happen next? Underline parts of the text that provide clues to what might happen. Explain your prediction. For some reason, the group will stay in this spot. They will not have food or any way to camp safely. The author says that the spot is very wild with steep cliffs, which hints that it is dangerous. It is clear to Mr. Oakhurst that the group should not camp there. The members are not even halfway to their destination, and he knows that, because they have no supplies for camping, to camp now would be foolish. This is an emergency, but the others, nevertheless, drink liquor and do not think about the situation they are in.

Name .... Class .... Date ....

Chief Sekoto Holds Court

Interacting with Text Determining Fact and Opinion

A **fact** is a statement that can be proven. An **opinion** is a statement expressing a belief that cannot be proven.

EXERCISE A. Read the following passage from "Chief Sekoto Holds Court."

Every weekday morning, Chief Sekoto listened to cases brought before his court, while the afternoons were spent at leisure unless there were people who had made appointments to interview him. This particular Monday morning a lively and rowdy case was in session when, out of the corner of his eye, Chief Sekoto saw his brother Matenge drive up and park his car opposite the open clearing where court was held. Nothing upset Chief Sekoto more than a visit from his brother, whom he had long classified as belonging to the insane part of mankind.

EXERCISE B. Now read the following questions. For each question, find and underline the part of the passage that will help you answer it. Then write the answers on the lines provided.

1. List two facts about court cases from the passage and briefly explain why you think each one is a fact. Facts given may vary.

   Fact "Every weekday morning, Chief Sekoto listened to cases brought before his court."

   Verification This could be proven by asking people to verify that this was the usual routine.

   Fact "This particular Monday morning a . . . case was in session."

   Verification This could be proven by checking the court calendar or by asking people who were there.

2. What did Chief Sekoto think about his brother? Is what the chief thought about his brother a fact or an opinion? The chief thought his brother belonged to "the insane part of mankind." There would be no way to prove what the insane part of mankind was or whether the brother really belonged to it. Nothing in the statement can be proven; this is an opinion.

Name .... Class .... Date ....

To Build a Fire

Interactive Reading **Reading Guide**

Part 1: The Man

KEY VOCABULARY AND TERMS

significance–the meaning of things

meditate–think deeply

frailty–weakness

spat–ejected saliva from the mouth

spittle–saliva

warm-whiskered–heavily bearded

obtained–prevailed; gained

yearned–longed, desired greatly

SORTING IT OUT

EXERCISE A. Read the Key Vocabulary and Terms section. Then read the first section of the story. (Stop reading at the end of the paragraph that begins "When the man had finished . . .") Complete the following items on the lines provided.

1. It is the man's first winter in the Yukon. He is hiking in order to get to the camp where his friends are.
2. The dog is clearly not eager to go with the man because the dog's instinct seems to tell him that it is just too cold to make the journey.
3. The instant the man stops rubbing his cheeks, they become numb because it is so cold that his cheeks, which are not covered, freeze immediately.
4. The man is frightened when he stops to eat his lunch because his fingers freeze as he gets his biscuit and the ice around his mouth prevents him from taking a bite.

Part 2: The Fire

KEY VOCABULARY AND TERMS

foundation–a base or support

entanglement–a knot or a problem

sensation–a feeling

smote–attacked; hit

tip of the planet–the "top" or most northern part of the world

freighted–loaded

excruciating–terribly painful

the wires–the communication between brain and body

cherished–tended with love

disrupted the nucleus–broke into the center

SORTING IT OUT

EXERCISE B. Read the Key Vocabulary and Terms section. Then read the second section of the story (from "The man took a chew of tobacco . . . " through ". . . shifting its weight back and forth on them with wistful eagerness"). Answer the following questions on the lines provided.

5. What serious mishap occurs that makes the man even more miserable? He breaks through into the water of a spring, getting wet up to the knees.

6. Why is the mishap serious? Now he will have to stop, build a fire, and dry out his feet and clothing. His feet will freeze quickly in the terrible cold.

7. Why does the man have so much difficulty building a fire? He has some bad luck when a tree drops snow on his fire and puts it out, but his main problem is that his hands are so badly frozen that he cannot use them properly.

Part 3: The End

KEY VOCABULARY AND TERMS

carcass–a dead body

apprehension–fear

posture–the position of the body

unrelated to the earth–disconnected from the ground beneath

allegiance–loyalty

throttle–to choke

oppressive–heavy, bearing down on

ploughed–plowed, moved through

endurance–the ability to keep going

headlong–head first

simile–a comparison

SORTING IT OUT

EXERCISE C. Read the Key Vocabulary and Terms section. Then read the end of the story. (Start reading from the paragraph that begins "The sight of the dog . . . ") Complete the items below.

8. The man desperately needs to be able to build a fire in order to save himself, but his hands are so frozen that he is unable to do it. How does he think he can use the dog to save himself? He plans to kill the dog and bury his hands inside the dead dog's warm body in order to warm his hands.

9. Why doesn't this plan work? The man has forgotten that he cannot use his hands because they are frozen. He grabs the dog by putting his arms around it, but without hands that work, he cannot do anything else.

10. Why does the man begin to run? He thinks that the activity will keep his blood moving and will save him from freezing to death.

11. In the end, exposure to the extreme cold kills the man. What else causes his death? His lack of imagination keeps him from realizing the consequences of traveling in the extreme cold.

Name .... Class .... Date ....

I Will Fight No More Forever

Interacting with Text Drawing Conclusions

When you **draw a conclusion**, you make a judgment or form an opinion that is based on the information provided in a selection as well as your own knowledge and experience.

EXERCISE A. Read the following selection from "I Will Fight No More Forever."

Tell General Howard I know his heart. What he told me before, I have in my heart. I am tired of fighting. Our chiefs are killed. Looking Glass is dead. Too Hul Hul Suit is dead. The old men are all dead. It is the young men who say yes and no. He who led on the young men is dead. It is cold and we have no blankets. The little children are freezing to death. My people, some of them, have run away to the hills and have no blankets, no food; no one knows where they are—perhaps freezing to death. I want to have time to look for my children and see how many I can find. Maybe I shall find them among the dead.

EXERCISE B. Follow the directions for each item to find and mark the text in the passage.

1. Underline two details in the text that express Chief Joseph's concern for the children of his people.
2. Double-underline five sentences that convey that many of Chief Joseph's people have died.

EXERCISE C. Now read and answer the following questions. Write on the lines provided.

1. What conclusion can you draw about how Chief Joseph feels about the children of the tribe? Chief Joseph cares deeply for the children of the tribe and for his own children.
2. What clues from the passage could lead to the conclusion that Chief Joseph knows the people of his tribe and keeps track of them? Chief Joseph knows that the chiefs are all dead, including Looking Glass and Too Hul Hul Suit, as well as the one "who led on the young men." He knows that the old men are dead. He knows that many children are freezing to death and that some of his people are in the hills without blankets or food.

Name .... Class .... Date ....

Let Us Examine the Facts

Interacting with Text **Identifying Main Ideas**

The **main idea** of a paragraph or a selection is its main topic, or what it is about. A main idea may be stated directly anywhere in the paragraph. However, the main idea is not always stated. The details in the paragraph may simply imply the main idea.

EXERCISE A. Read the following passage from "Let Us Examine the Facts."

The great God of Nature has placed us in different situations. It is true that he has endowed you with many superior advantages; but he has not created us to be your slaves. *We are a separate people!* He has given each their lands, under distinct considerations and circumstances; he has stocked yours with cows, ours with buffalo; yours with hog, ours with bear; yours with sheep, ours with deer.

EXERCISE B. Follow the directions for each item to find and mark the text in the passage. Write on the lines provided.

1. In the passage, underline the details that identify the animals that "the great God of Nature" has provided on the Cherokees' land. List animals valued by the Cherokee.

   buffalo, bear, deer

2. In the passage, double-underline the details that identify the animals that were given white people. List animals valued by the white people.

   cows, hogs, sheep

EXERCISE C. Read and answer the following questions. Circle the letter in front of the best answer choice.

1. What is the main idea of the passage?
   - a. "It is true that he has endowed you with many superior advantages; but he has not created us to be your slaves."
   - (b.) "*We are a separate people!*"
   - c. Neither of the above.

2. What type of main idea is found in the passage?
   - (a.) The main idea of the passage is stated directly.
   - b. The main idea of the passage is not stated directly.
   - c. There is no main idea in the passage.

Name .... Class .... Date ....

The Story of an Hour

Interacting with Text Understanding Characterization

The personality of a character in a story is revealed through that character's words, thoughts, and actions. It is also revealed through what other characters think and say about that character. Understanding what a character is like helps you to understand the story.

EXERCISE A. Read the following passage from "The Story of an Hour."

"Go away. I am not making myself ill." No; she was drinking in a very elixir of life through that open window.

Her fancy was running riot along those days ahead of her. Spring days, and summer days, and all sorts of days that would be her own. She breathed a quick prayer that life might be long. It was only yesterday she had thought with a shudder that life might be long.

EXERCISE B. Read the following questions. Find the text in the passage that will help you to answer each question.

1. What does Mrs. Mallard say? Underline the text of Mrs. Mallard's spoken words.
2. What does Mrs. Mallard think? Circle the text that suggests what Mrs. Mallard thinks.
3. What does Mrs. Mallard do? Double-underline the text that describes Mrs. Mallard's actions.

EXERCISE C. Read the following questions. Find the text in the passage that will help you to answer each question. Circle the letter of the best answer choice.

1. Which of the following best describes Mrs. Mallard?
   a. She is a delicate person whose grief overwhelms her.
   b. She is excited to realize how liberating her husband's death will be for her.
   c. She is a strong person who takes charge of everything and everyone around her.
2. Which of the following best describes how Mrs. Mallard felt before finding out that her husband is dead?
   a. She felt depressed because she thought she might have a long life.
   b. She felt happy because she and her husband had plans to travel.
   c. She felt angry because she had too much work to do.

Name .... Class .... Date ....

A Wagner Matinée

Interacting with Text **Analyzing Cause-and-Effect Relationships**

A **cause** is an event or situation that makes something happen. An **effect** is the result, or what happens. Understanding the relationship between a cause and an effect can help you understand and predict events in the plot.

EXERCISE A. Read the following passage from "A Wagner Matinée."

One summer, while visiting in the little village among the Green Mountains where her ancestors had dwelt for generations, she had kindled the callow fancy of my uncle, Howard Carpenter, then an idle, shiftless boy of twenty-one. When she returned to her duties in Boston, Howard followed her, and the upshot of this infatuation was that she eloped with him, eluding the reproaches of her family and the criticism of her friends by going with him to the Nebraska frontier.

EXERCISE B. Now read the following questions. For each question, find the text in the passage that will help you answer it. Follow the directions for each item.

1. What was the cause of Howard Carpenter's following Georgiana? Underline the cause in the passage. Explain the cause on the lines provided. Georgiana "had kindled the callow fancy of [the narrator's] uncle." Howard Carpenter was infatuated with her.

2. What was the effect of Howard's infatuation with Georgiana? Circle the effect in the passage. Explain the effect on the lines provided. Georgiana eloped with Howard. She ran away with him to get married.

3. Reread the last sentence in the passage. What did Georgiana avoid as a result of running away to Nebraska with Howard? Double-underline the text in the passage that describes the effect.

4. Underline in the passage the phrase that describes how Georgiana eluded the reproaches of her family. On the lines provided, explain why Georgiana's action had this effect. By going with Howard to the Nebraska frontier, Georgiana avoided criticism because she was far away from friends and family.

Name .... Class .... Date ....

Douglass

Interacting with Text Paraphrasing

Paraphrasing is putting something you have read into your own words. When you paraphrase a poem, begin by paraphrasing one line or sentence at a time.

EXERCISE A. Read the first stanza of the poem "Douglass," which follows. Find the parts of the text that will help you to answer the questions. Then answer the questions, marking the text as indicated.

Ah, Douglass, we have fall'n on evil days,
  Such days as thou, not even thou didst know,
  When thee, the eyes of that harsh long ago
Saw, salient, at the cross of devious ways,
And all the country heard thee with amaze.
  Not ended then, the passionate ebb and flow,
  The awful tide that battled to and fro;
We ride amid a tempest of dispraise.

1. What word in the first line has been changed to fit the rhythm of the poem? Underline the word that has been shortened. On the line provided, write the customary spelling of the word. fallen

2. What word in the second line means *did*? Underline the word that means *did*.

3. What words in the stanza above mean "fall and rise"? Underline the words that mean "fall and rise."

EXERCISE B. Now read the following questions. Follow the directions for each item.

1. Reread lines 1–5 of the stanza above. Answer the following questions on the lines provided.
   a. Does the speaker think that Frederick Douglass had experiences similar to those the people are having now? How do you know? No. The speaker says "such days as even you did not know."
   b. When Douglass witnessed harsh days during his own time, what did he see? He saw bad days, in which devious or dishonest actions were evident.
   c. How did the whole country react to Douglass's speeches? Everyone in the country listened with respect.

2. How would you paraphrase lines 6–8? Use the lines provided. The passionate rise and fall of opinions continues. We must endure other people's disapproval of our conduct.

Name .... Class .... Date ....

Lucinda Matlock

Interacting with Text Making Inferences

To make an **inference**, you use one or more details that you have read to make a logical assumption about something that is not directly stated.

EXERCISE A. Read the following lines from the poem "Lucinda Matlock."

Passage 1

I went to the dances at Chandlerville,
And played snap-out at Winchester.

Passage 2

And then I found Davis.
We were married and lived together for seventy years,
Enjoying, working, raising the twelve children,
Eight of whom we lost
Ere I had reached the age of sixty.
I spun, I wove, I kept the house, I nursed the sick,
I made the garden, and for holiday
Rambled over the fields where sang the larks,
And by Spoon River gathering many a shell,
And many a flower and medicinal weed—
Shouting to the wooded hills, singing to the green valleys.

EXERCISE B. Read and answer the following questions. Find the parts of the text in the lines above that will help you answer each question.

1. Read passage 1. What logical inference can you make about Lucinda, from these lines? Circle the letter of the best answer choice.
   a. Lucinda was young.
   b. Lucinda was an expert dancer.
   c. Everyone feared playing Lucinda in games.

2. Circle the words in passage 2 that imply that Lucinda made home remedies for illnesses. Write the words on the lines provided. Lucinda gathered "medicinal weed." This implies that she used some weeds for medicines.

3. Underline the phrases in passage 2 that help you make the inference that Lucinda liked the area where she lived. Write the words and phrases on the lines provided. Lucinda showed that she liked the area where she lived by the way that she described the land and her actions when she was walking. She "rambled over the fields where sang the larks"; she was "shouting to the wooded hills"; she was "singing to the green valleys."

Name .... Class .... Date ....

Miniver Cheevy

Interacting with Text Visualizing

When you **visualize**, you picture something you are reading about. You use the details the author provides and your own experiences and imagination to help you picture mentally the action, setting, or characters as you read.

EXERCISE A. Read the following three stanzas from the poem "Miniver Cheevy."

Passage 1

Miniver loved the days of old
When swords were bright and steeds were
prancing;
The vision of a warrior bold
Would set him dancing.

Passage 2

Miniver cursed the commonplace
And eyed a khaki suit with loathing;
He missed the mediæval grace
Of iron clothing.

Passage 3

Miniver Cheevy, born too late,
Scratched his head and kept on thinking;
Miniver coughed, and called it fate,
And kept on drinking.

EXERCISE B. Now read and answer the following questions. Follow the directions for each item. Write the answers on the lines provided.

1. Miniver Cheevy himself likes to visualize. Reread passage 1 shown above. Underline words that tell what Miniver Cheevy is visualizing. How would you describe what he pictures? Students should describe warriors of the middle ages, with swords, riding prancing horses.

2. Tell how you visualize Miniver Cheevy dressed as he would like to be. Underline clues in the second passage that indicate how he would have liked to dress.
Students should describe Miniver Cheevy dressed in a suit of medieval armor.

3. Underline the words in passage 3 that provide clues to Miniver Cheevey's appearance and character. Then describe how you picture Miniver Cheevy.
Students should describe him as a pensive man scratching his head, dreaming, and drinking.

Name .... Class .... Date ....

The Open Boat

Interactive Reading **Reading Guide**

Parts I, II, and III

KEY CHARACTERS

cook

oiler–named Billie

correspondent–probably based on author Stephen Crane, who as a journalist had a similar experience to the one described in the story

captain–the only man in the boat who is injured in the shipwreck

KEY VOCABULARY AND TERMS

barbarously–in a cruel or brutal way

surmounting–overcoming

capsized–overturned

stern–the rear part of a boat or ship

mast–the vertical pole of a ship

ominous–threatening

dinghy–a small rowboat

sidled–moved sideways in a careful manner

cynical–not believing in the goodness of people

direful–dreadful, terrible

scatheless–untouched

SORTING IT OUT

EXERCISE A. Read the Key Characters and the Key Vocabulary and Terms sections. Then read parts I, II, and III of the story. Complete the following items on the lines provided.

1. The four men are in the small boat because their ship has sunk.

2. The author says that the boat is not much bigger than a bathtub.

3. Riding in the boat is compared to riding a bucking bronco.

4. The men who are rowing must from time to time engage in the dangerous and delicate activity of changing places in order to take turns rowing—dangerous because moving around on the boat could cause it to capsize.

5. The men take time to smoke the cigars that the correspondent finds in his pocket because they are getting close to land and can see a lighthouse, so they believe that they are about to be rescued.

Parts IV and V

KEY VOCABULARY AND TERMS

epithet–a descriptive word or phrase used in place of a person's name

rollers–huge waves

perchance–old fashioned term for *possibly*

conjure–think up, invent

formidable–difficult, threatening

discern–to determine; figure out

flounder–to struggle clumsily

haggard–appearing to be exhausted

grotesque–strange and distorted

phosphorescence–glowing light

SORTING IT OUT

EXERCISE B. Read the Key Vocabulary and Terms section. Then read parts IV and V of "The Open Boat." Answer the following questions on the lines provided.

6. The men in the boat see land that seems close. Why are they upset? No one on land seems to see them.

7. Why do the men suddenly decide to exchange addresses? They want to know whom to inform in case one of them does not make it safely to shore.

Parts VI and VII

KEY VOCABULARY AND TERMS

abominable–horrid; terrible

main–damage

supplicant–asking humbly and earnestly

myriad–a great or countless number

formulae–Latin or formal plural of *formula*, a prescribed method of doing something

respite–rest from a task

bequeathed–given as in a will

grapple–to content or attempt to deal with

SORTING IT OUT

EXERCISE C. Read the Key Vocabulary and Terms section. Then read parts VI and VII of "The Open Boat." Answer the questions on the lines provided.

8. The correspondent suddenly remembers a verse he once knew. What is the verse about? Why do you think the correspondent's mind returns to this verse at this time? The verse is about a dying soldier. His mind returns to the verse because he is afraid that he is dying away from home, just as the soldier was.

9. Why do the men take the boat farther out to sea even though they have seen shore? They know that getting to shore is dangerous because the sea is rough there, and they don't want to try it in the dark.

10. Which one of the four men does not make it to shore alive? The oiler does not make it to shore alive.

Name .... Class .... Date ....

A Pact

Interacting with Text — Analyzing Author's Viewpoint

A reader can discover an **author's viewpoint** about a subject by noticing word choices and the overall tone of the writing.

EXERCISE A. Read the following poem, "A Pact." Underline the words that reveal dislike or rejection of Walt Whitman. Circle the words that indicate affection or acceptance.

I make a pact with you, Walt Whitman–
I have detested you long enough.
I come to you as a grown child
Who has had a pig-headed father;
I am old enough now to make friends.
It was you that broke the new wood,
Now is a time for carving.
We have one sap and one root–
Let there be commerce between us.

EXERCISE B. Now read the following questions. Use the passage to help you answer each question. Write on the lines provided.

1. What did the poet Ezra Pound think about Whitman when he was younger? Pound did not like Whitman's poetry.

2. How does Pound feel about Whitman at the time he writes this poem? Pound is ready to "make friends" with Whitman because he now understands and appreciates Whitman's poetry.

3. What do the words *child* and *father* show about Pound's viewpoint? Pound feels closely related to Whitman, as though Whitman has given him the guidance that a father would.

4. What words show that Pound understands that both he and Whitman share a bond? Why are these words appropriate? Possible answer: "We have one sap and one root." The tree metaphor suggests a shared creative source connecting the poetry of these men.

5. What is the tone of the poem? Possible answer: It is harmonious and accepting.

Name .... Class .... Date ....

The Love Song of J. Alfred Prufrock

Interacting with Text Analyzing Figurative Language

Metaphors and similes are two kinds of figurative language in which two things that appear not to be alike are compared. In a **simile,** words such as *like* or *as* are used in the comparison. In a **metaphor,** the comparison is implied instead of being stated directly.

EXERCISE A. Read the following passages from "The Love Song of J. Alfred Prufrock." In each passage, underline the text in which a comparison is implied.

Passage 1

The yellow fog that rubs its back upon the
window-panes,
The yellow smoke that rubs its muzzle on the
window-panes,
Licked its tongue into the corners of the
evening,

Passage 2

The eyes that fix you in a formulated phrase,
And when I am formulated, sprawling on a
pin,
When I am pinned and wriggling on the wall,
Then how should I begin . . .

EXERCISE B. Read the following questions. For each question, find the text in the passage that will help you answer it. Then write the answer on the lines provided.

1. To what are the fog and the smoke of the city compared? List three comparisons that are included in the text above. 1. They are compared to a cat. 2. The fog "rubs its back on window-panes." 3. The smoke "rubs its muzzle on window-panes" and licks "its tongue into corners of the evening."

2. What characteristics does the poet attribute to the fog and smoke by using this metaphor? A cat suggests a smoothly moving, graceful creature. The comparisons to a cat's movements make the fog and smoke seem to creep quietly and slowly.

3. To what does Prufrock compare himself in the second passage? He compares himself to an insect that has been pinned by a collector.

4. What part of the comparison reveals his discomfort? He describes himself as sprawling and wriggling as a pinned insect would be. These words suggest Prufrock's pain and awkwardness.

Name .... Class .... Date ....

This Is Just to Say

Interacting with Text **Analyzing Sensory Language**

Sensory language describes how things look, sound, smell, feel, or taste. Poets use sensory details to help readers imagine seeing, hearing, smelling, tasting, or touching what they are reading about. Words that appeal to the senses help readers experience a scene or subject in the way the poet experiences them.

EXERCISE A. Read the following passages from "This Is Just to Say." Underline the words in these lines that suggest the use of one of the five senses.

Passage 1

I have eaten
the plums
that were in
the icebox . . .

Passage 2

. . . Forgive me
they were delicious
so sweet
and so cold

EXERCISE B. Now read the following questions. Use the underlined words to help you answer each question. Then write the answer on the lines provided.

1. What words appeal to the sense of taste? "eaten the plums," "delicious," "sweet," "cold"

2. What words appeal to the sense of touch? "eaten," "cold," "in the icebox"

3. What made this experience pleasurable to the speaker? The sweet, cold plums were irresistible to the speaker and tasted very good to him.

4. Why might the speaker have wanted the "you" he addresses to know how wonderful the plums were? Possible answer: "You" is someone he seems to care about and someone he regrets disappointing. Maybe he hoped that this person would understand his actions.

Name .... Class .... Date ....

Anecdote of the Jar

Interacting with Text Comparing and Contrasting

When you **compare** two things, you examine the ways in which they are alike. When you **contrast** them, you focus on their differences.

EXERCISE A. Reread the poem "Anecdote of the Jar." Circle the words that describe the wilderness. Underline the words that describe the jar.

I placed a jar in Tennessee,
And round it was, upon a hill.
It made the slovenly wilderness
Surround that hill.

The wilderness rose up to it,
And sprawled around, no longer wild.
The jar was round upon the ground
And tall and of a port in air.

It took dominion everywhere.
The jar was gray and bare.
It did not give of bird or bush,
Like nothing else in Tennessee.

EXERCISE B. Use the text in the passage to help you answer the questions on the lines provided.

1. What words describe the wilderness? What do these words tell you about the poet's impression of the wilderness? "slovenly," "sprawled," "wide"; Stevens paints a picture of nature as lacking a sense of order; it is untidy.

2. What words describe the jar? What is the speaker's thought about the jar? Some descriptive words are "round," "tall," "port in air," "took dominion," "gray," "bare": The speaker presents the jar as imposing a perception of order on the "slovenly wilderness."

3. Does Stevens compare or contrast the wilderness and the jar? Explain your answer. He contrasts the two because he is focusing on their differences.

4. How does this technique help you understand the message of the poem? Stevens uses the differences between familiar objects as a concrete means of describing the limits of civilization and artificially made inventions.

Name .... Class .... Date ....

The Jilting of Granny Weatherall

Interacting with Text Stream of Consciousness

Stream-of-consciousness writing seems to jump randomly from idea to idea instead of following a chronological order of events. If a passage becomes difficult to understand, readers can look for clues in the text that enable them to follow the flow of thoughts inside a character's head.

EXERCISE A. Read the following passage from "The Jilting of Granny Weatherall." Place a slash (/) in the text wherever her thoughts turn from one subject or time to another.

Yes, she had changed her mind after sixty years and she would like to see George. I want you to find George. Find him and be sure to tell him I forgot him. . . . Tell him I was given back everything he took away, and more./Oh, no, O God, no, there was something else besides the house and the man and the children. Oh, surely they were not all? What was it? Something not given back . . . /Her breath crowded down under her ribs and grew into a monstrous frightening shape with cutting edges; it bored up into her head, and the agony was unbelievable./Yes, John, get the doctor now, no more talk, my time has come.

EXERCISE B. Now use the passage to help you answer the following questions. Use the lines provided.

1. George is the man who "jilted" Ellen Weatherall. In the first sentences of the paragraph, what are her thoughts about him? Ellen Weatherall wants him to know that she did well in spite of him.

2. Where in the passage is the first example of a shift in Weatherall's thoughts? What new direction do her thoughts take? After "and more." She becomes aware that she has lost something that a home and family could not make up for.

3. There is a clue in lines 2–5 of column two that signals a change in thought. What happens to Weatherall to draw her attention away from her current train of thought? Why does it distract her? She experiences a sudden pain. Because it is so intense it temporarily pushes all other thoughts from her mind.

4. Where has her mind wandered in the last three lines of the passage? Why? Her thoughts have returned to the birth of one of her children; her pain reminds her of childbirth.

Name .... Class .... Date ....

Richness

Interacting with Text **Interpreting**

To **interpret** the language in a poem, consider different levels of meaning that the language may contain: figurative and literal. *Literal language* is simple and straightforward and is based on dictionary definitions of words. *Figurative language* contains expressions and imagery that convey ideas or emotions.

EXERCISE A. Read the following passage from "Richness." Underline the words that describe the "faithful joy." Circle the words that describe the "joy that is lost." Underline and circle the words that describe both.

I have a faithful joy
and a joy that is lost.
I am as rich with purple
as with sorrow.

Ay! How loved is the rose,
How loving the thorn!
Paired as twin fruit,
I have a faithful joy
and a joy that is lost.

EXERCISE B. Read the following questions. For each question, find the words in the passage that will help you answer it. Then write the answer on the lines provided.

1. Do you think the speaker is using *purple* figuratively or literally when she says she is "rich with purple?" What do you think the speaker means? Figuratively, purple may represent royalty or riches. Her joy is a type of wealth.

2. What emotion is associated with a "lost joy?" Why? Sorrow; something that is lost often brings sadness and pain.

3. What do you think the speaker is referring to when she says that she has a "faithful joy?" What type of language is she using in that description? The speaker may be referring to a constant joy in her life. She is using figurative language.

4. What do you think the speaker means when she refers to "a joy that is lost?" Why? The expression could refer to a sad event in the speaker's life, but this lost joy has also added to the richness of experiences in her life.

5. How are both joys like "twin fruit"? They are both necessary to life. As fruit grows from the same branch, both joys grow from a single full life.

Name .... Class .... Date ....

Ars Poetica

Interacting with Text **Analyzing Line Structure**

Remind students that poems are structured in groups of lines called **stanzas**. Studying the organization of stanzas and rhyming patterns can add to a reader's understanding and enjoyment of a poem.

EXERCISE A. Read the following stanzas from "Ars Poetica." On the blank before each line, write the number of syllables in the line. Underline the rhyming words.

8 A poem should be equal to:
2 Not true

8 For all the history of grief
10 An empty doorway and a maple leaf

2 For love
12 The leaning grasses and two lights above the sea—

EXERCISE B. Now read the following questions. Use the stanzas quoted to help you answer the questions. Use the lines provided.

1. How many lines are in each stanza? two lines

2. How do the lengths of the lines in each stanza differ? How are they alike?
In two of the stanzas, one line is long, and one is short; the final words rhyme in two of the stanzas.

3. What effect is gained by varying the length of lines in each stanza? The contrast is startling and draws attention. Emphasis is placed on the shorter line.

4. What is the effect of the pattern of rhyme in the first two stanzas? The sound is musical and holds the lines together.

Name .... Class .... Date ....

Dirge Without Music

Interacting with Text **Inverted Word Order**

Syntax is the arrangement of words in sentences. Usually, in a sentence, the subject comes first. Adjectives usually come before the noun they modify. When normal syntax is **inverted,** or reversed, special emphasis is placed on the reordered words. A change in word order may also call attention to a formal attitude or occasion.

EXERCISE A. Read the following passage from "Dirge Without Music." Underline the words that are not placed where they usually would be in everyday speaking.

The answers quick and keen, the honest look,
the laughter, the love,–
They are gone. They are gone to feed the
roses. Elegant and curled
Is the blossom. Fragrant is the blossom. I
know. But I do not approve.
More precious was the light in your eyes than
all the roses in the world.

EXERCISE B. Read the following questions. Use the underlined words to help you answer each question on the lines provided.

1. In line 1 of the passage, what adjectives come after the noun they modify? "Quick" and "keen" follow the noun "answers."

2. Find the subjects of sentences that come after the verbs. "The blossom" and "the light in your eyes" follow verbs.

3. How would these sentences be worded in more usual syntax? The blossom is elegant and curled. The blossom is fragrant. The light in your eyes was more precious.

4. What kind of words are emphasized by being placed first? Adjectives that communicate the beauty and value of what is lost to death are emphasized.

5. What effect do these reversals of standard sentence order have on the tone of the poem? These reversals of normal sentence order may cause the reader to pay closer attention to the descriptions. They contribute to a formal and thoughtful tone.

Name .... Class .... Date ....

anyone lived in a pretty how town

Interacting with Text Analyzing Repetition

Repetition adds to the musical effect of a poem. It also emphasizes the ideas contained in the repeated words.

EXERCISE A. Read the following passages from "anyone lived in a pretty how town." They show repeated words. Underline the repetitions.

spring summer autumn winter
he sang his didn't he danced his did.

. . . .

autumn winter spring summer)
that noone loved him more by more

. . . .

Women and men (both dong and ding)
summer autumn winter spring
reaped their sowing and went their came

EXERCISE B. Read the following questions. Use the text in the passages you have underlined to help you answer the questions. Write on the lines provided.

1. What words are repeated? "summer," "autumn," "winter," "spring"

2. What changes in each repetition? The order in which the seasons are listed changes.

3. What do you think the seasons represent in the poem? What idea do they emphasize? They represent the passing of time and mark the "seasons" of anyone's and noone's lives. They emphasize the measured way in which life goes on.

4. Why do you think the order in which the seasons are listed changes? This changing order may mark the "season" of anyone's or noone's life that the stanza describes. For example, spring is mentioned first in the first stanza, where anyone's early life is described.

Name .... Class .... Date ....

Poetry

Interacting with Text Summarizing

The main idea and most important details in a poem can be condensed into a short summary.

EXERCISE A. Read the following passage from "Poetry." Underline the words that suggest the poet's problem with some poetry. Place brackets ([ ]) around words that point to the solution of this problem.

. . . all these phenomena are important. One must make a distinction
however: when dragged into prominence by half poets, the result is not poetry,
nor till the poets among us can [be
'literalists of
the imagination']—above
insolence and triviality and can [present

for inspection, 'imaginary gardens with real toads in them',] shall we
have it.

EXERCISE B. Read the following questions. Use your markings in the passage to help you answer each question. Write on the lines provided.

1. What words suggest the speaker's difficulty in relating poetry to her own experience? Restate the problem in your own words. Some such words are "half poets," "insolence," "triviality." Bad poetry is written by those who are not genuine or who write of unimportant things in an arrogant way.

2. What phrases suggest how poets can avoid this type of poetry? The phrases "be 'literalists of the imagination,'" "present for inspection," and "'imaginary gardens with real toads in them'" make such suggestions.

3. Briefly summarize the speaker's ideas about poetry. What does she dislike? What does she think makes a good poem? The speaker dislikes poetry that describes trivial things in a needlessly complicated way. She appreciates poems that are written clearly about subjects of importance.

Name .... Class .... Date ....

The Bridal Party

Interactive Reading **Reading Guide**

Part I

KEY CHARACTERS

Michael Curly–young man of modest means

Caroline Dandy–the young woman whom Michael loves

Hamilton Rutherford–her fiancé, a wealthy stockbroker

KEY VOCABULARY AND TERMS

pathetic–pitiable

authoritative–commanding, masterful

humiliation–shame

intolerable–unbearable

concierge–hotel staff person who handles mail, special tours, luggage, etc.

brusque–curt and abrupt in manner

SORTING IT OUT

EXERCISE A. Read the Key Characters and the Key Vocabulary and Terms sections. Then read the first section of the story. Complete the following items on the lines provided.

1. Michael's mental and emotional state in Paris up to this point has been that of one who has been nursing a broken heart and wishing that Caroline could be his again.

2. He is astonished and anguished when he meets Caroline and her fiancé in the street.

3. Michael could not ask Caroline to marry him because he had no money or any prospects for getting any.

4. The reaction that causes Michael to believe Caroline may still have feelings for him is that she sees his hurt and is touched and confused by it.

5. Michael's situation changes suddenly when he finds out that he has inherited a quarter of a million dollars from his grandfather's estate.

Part II

KEY VOCABULARY AND TERMS

proximity–closeness

hysterical–excitable

potentialities–possibilities

stimulated–excited

sense–reason, cleverness

combative–aggressive, confrontational

assured–self-confident

turned out–dressed

Name .... Class .... Date ....

SORTING IT OUT

EXERCISE B. Read the Key Vocabulary and Terms section. Then read the second section of the story. Complete the following items on the lines provided.

1. When Michael attends the party at Chez Victor, he asks Caroline to dance.

2. Michael meets with Hamilton Rutherford in order to ask Hamilton to let Carolyn decide with her heart whom she wants to marry now that Michael has money.

3. Hamilton says that what Michael and Carolyn's attraction was based on was not love but sorrow.

4. The night of the bachelor party, Carolyn learns that Hamilton has lost all of his money and that Michael has become wealthy.

5. Carolyn chooses to marry Hamilton.

Part III

KEY VOCABULARY AND TERMS

dispense with–to forgo

gossamer–flimsy, delicate material

by and by–soon

charade–an act

modulated–softened

forcibly–by force; with compulsion

abducted–carried off

defiantly–with bold resistance

recede–to move back, withdraw

initiation–an introduction, induction

SORTING IT OUT

EXERCISE C. Read the Key Vocabulary and Terms section. Then read the third section of the story. Complete the following items on the lines provided.

1. Michael stands at the back of the church for the wedding because he feels improperly dressed, as though he doesn't belong.

2. When they meet in the reception line after the wedding, Carolyn kisses Michael, but he feels no contact or emotion.

3. Michael finds out that for two years Carolyn had been pursuing Hamilton even while she professed to love Michael.

4. That morning, Michael learns, Hamilton has been offered a job with a salary of $50,000.

5. Michael is surprised to realize that he has not thought of Carolyn for hours. He is "cured"; he no longer loves her.

Name .... Class .... Date ....

Chicago

Interacting with Text Identifying Apostrophe

Apostrophe is a device in which a poet addresses an object, an idea, or a person not present. By using this technique, a writer can add to the impact of a poem.

EXERCISE A. Read the following passage from "Chicago." It describes hard qualities of the city. Underline the words that tell you the speaker is directly addressing the city.

Hog Butcher for the World,
Tool Maker, Stacker of Wheat,
Player with Railroads and the Nation's
Freight Handler;
Stormy, husky, brawling,
City of the Big Shoulders:
They tell me you are wicked and I believe
them, for I have seen your painted
women under the gas lamps luring the
farm boys.
And they tell me you are crooked and I
answer: Yes, it is true I have seen the
gunman kill and go free to kill again.

EXERCISE B. Read the following items. For each item, find the text in the passage that will help you. Follow the directions for each item. Write on the lines provided.

1. Write the words that tell you that the speaker is talking directly to someone or something. *the pronouns you and your*

2. Circle the names that the speaker uses to address the subject of the poem.

3. Explain what the words you circled tell about Chicago. *They describe the work that goes on there and create an image of the city as a powerful, aggressive workman.*

4. Reread the lines that begin with "They tell me you are wicked" to the end of the passage above. Describe the speaker's feelings toward the city. *Possible answer: The speaker feels admiration for the city's vitality and accomplishment and fear or dislike for its dangerous and evil aspects.*

Name .... Class .... Date ....

from *Songs of Gold Mountain*

Interacting with Text Literal and Figurative Language

In **literal language**, the definitions of words let you know exactly what is meant. **Figurative language** expresses ideas beyond the literal meanings of the words.

EXERCISE A. Read the following passages from "Songs of Gold Mountain." In these poems, men express reactions to detention, some literally and some figuratively. Underline the descriptions that are literal. Circle the descriptions that are figurative.

Passage 1

Cruel treatment, not one restful breath of air.
Scarcity of food, severe restrictions—all
unbearable.
Here even a proud man bows his head low.

Passage 2

The Golden Gate firmly locked, without even a
crack to crawl through . . .
Though talented, how can we put on wings and
fly past the barbarians?

EXERCISE B. Now read the following questions. For each question, find the text in the passage that will help you answer it. Write the answers to the questions on the lines provided.

1. What conditions for the detained men are described in literal language? The men are treated cruelly. They are not given sufficient food. Their freedom is restricted.

2. Which line vividly describes the men's reaction to this treatment? "Here even a proud man bows his head low."

3. How do you know that the figurative language in the second passage shown above is not literally true? The Golden Gate is a strait, so it cannot be locked.

4. To what is the Golden Gate compared? Why is this comparison ironic, or the opposite of what is expected? It is compared to a locked door or gate. These men had hoped that this entrance to America would bring them freedom, wealth, and happiness instead of incarceration and misery.

5. What do you think the poet really means by the phrase "put on wings"? He may mean "escape detention" or "convince officials to let those detained enter the country."

Name .... Class .... Date ....

In Another Country

Interacting with Text: Analyzing Cause-and-Effect Relationships

A **cause** is an occurence that makes something else happen. An **effect** is an occurrence that is the result of an earlier event. Words such as *because*, *so*, *consequently*, and *as a result* signal a cause-and-effect relationship.

EXERCISE A. Read the following passage from "In Another Country." It explains the narrator's friendship with one young soldier. Underline any phrases that indicate causes and effects. Circle any words that signal cause-and-effect relationships.

. . . . But I stayed good friends with the boy who had been wounded his first day at the front, because he would never know now how he would have turned out; so he could never be accepted either, and I liked him because I thought perhaps he would not have turned out to be a hawk either.

EXERCISE B. Now read the following questions. For each question, find the text in the passage that will help you answer it. Answer the questions on the lines provided.

1. What does the boy's failure to be accepted cause the narrator to feel toward him?
It causes the narrator to feel fond of the boy because the two share a common bond.

2. Why does the narrator like the boy? The narrator feels that the other young soldier is like him, and would not have been a fierce "hawk."

EXERCISE C. Read the following passage and answer the question that follows. Write on the lines provided.

The boys at first were very polite about my medals and asked what I had done to get them. I showed them the papers, which . . . really said, with the adjectives removed, that I had been given the medals because I was an American. After that, their manner changed a little toward me. . . .

Why does the narrator believe he recieved his medals? He believes that he recieved his medals for being an American.

Name .... Class .... Date ....

Soldiers of the Republic

Interacting with Text — Making Inferences

To make **inferences** is to figure out the unstated, or implied, meaning of one or more statements in a literary work. Readers make inferences on the basis of the clues provided in the text and their own knowledge and experience.

EXERCISE A. Read the following passage from "Soldiers of the Republic." It is a lecture the narrator gives herself after she observes a poor family with a baby. Underline words that hint at the author's suggesting something beyond the surface meaning of the words.

"Oh, for God's sake, stop that!" I said to myself. "All right, so it's got a piece of blue ribbon on its hair. All right, so its mother went without eating so it could look pretty when its father came home on leave. All right, so it's her business, and none of yours. All right, so what have you got to cry about?"

EXERCISE B. Now read the following questions. For each question, review the text in the passage that will help you answer it. Then write the answers on the lines provided.

1. What phrase provides a clue that helps you make the inference that the narrator is experiencing inner conflict? She tells herself, "Oh, for God's sake, stop that!"

2. What repeated words show that the narrator is arguing against the part of herself that feels sorry for the people? "All right, so . . . "

3. What words show that she has been moved to tears? The narrator says to herself, "What have you got to cry about?"

4. What does the author suggest about the narrator by having her talk roughly to herself in this way? The author suggests that the narrator is angry with herself for showing that she feels sorry for those enduring poverty. She seems to wish that she could accept the family's circumstances without any emotional involvement.

Name .... Class .... Date ....

The Death of the Hired Man

Interacting with Text Analyzing Blank Verse

Blank verse is poetry written in unrhymed *iambic pentameter*. Each line has five pairs of syllables: the first syllable is unstressed and the second syllable is stressed in each pair. Because blank verse imitates the rhythms of speech, not every line follows this pattern exactly.

EXERCISE A. Read the following passage from "The Death of the Hired Man." In these lines, the characters Warren and Mary talk about Silas, an old farmhand who has returned to their farm. Add slash marks (/) to divide each line into units of stressed and unstressed syllables. Underline each syllable that should be stressed as you read the lines aloud.

"Sh! Not/so loud!/He'll hear/you," Mar/y said.

"I want/him to:/he'll have/to soon/or late."

"He's worn/out. He's/asleep/beside/the stove.
When I/came up/from Rowe's/I found/him here,
Huddled/against/the barn-/door fast/asleep,
A mis/erable sight,/and fright/ening, too—

EXERCISE B. Read the following questions. Use marks you made in the passage above to help you answer each question on the lines provided.

1. In most of the two-syllable units you marked, what is the pattern of stressed and unstressed syllables? An unstressed syllable is followed by a stressed syllable.

2. In what places is this pattern changed? What effect do these changes have?
"Sh! Not" has two stressed syllables; "huddled" stresses the first syllable rather than the second. The variations seem natural, like speech. "Miserable" and "frightening" are condensed into two syllables each—mis/erable and fright/ening.

3. How does the variation in the last line of the passage suit the meaning of the line?
The variation in this line serves to emphasize Silas's misery and the way it scares Mary.

Name .... Class .... Date ....

My City

Interacting with Text Visualizing

Visualizing means making mental images that are based on reading and on prior experiences. This technique helps readers to understand what they have read and to remember it later.

EXERCISE A. Read the following lines from "My City." Underline words that help you to form a mental picture of the city.

But, ah! Manhattan's sights and sounds,
her smells,
Her crowds, her throbbing force, the thrill
that comes
From being of her a part, her subtle spells,
Her shining towers, her avenues, her slums—

EXERCISE B. Now read the following questions. For each question, find the text in the passage that will help you answer it. Then answer the question. Write on the lines provided.

1. What picture comes to mind when you read the beginning two words of the excerpt, "But, ah!"? Possible answer: A person is talking about something he or she loves.
2. What words help you to visualize the people and the pace of Manhattan? "crowds" and "throbbing force"
3. What do these words suggest to you about life there? "Crowds" suggests many people packed together; "throbbing force" suggests a mass of people moving steadily, quickly, and energetically.
4. What words or phrases help you to visualize the physical structures of Manhattan? "shining towers," "avenues," "slums"
5. What kinds of buildings and surroundings do these words suggest? These words suggest clean, modern skyscrapers with many sparkling windows and broad streets, and shabby neighborhoods with rundown buildings.
6. How does visualizing help you understand the speaker's meaning? Possible answer: Visualizing helps me "see" different aspects of the city—good and bad, beautiful and ugly. It gives me a better understanding of the speaker's feelings about Manhattan.

Name .... Class .... Date ....

from *Dust Tracks on a Road*

Interacting with Text — Analyzing Cause-and-Effect Relationships

Some actions or circumstances, called **causes,** are responsible for other actions or occurrences, called **effects.** You can analyze cause-and-effect relationships to understand actions in a story.

EXERCISE A. Read the following passage from *Dust Tracks on a Road.* Underline the words that describe an event or action that causes something else to happen. Circle the words that reveal the effect of the action.

The whites who came down from the North were often brought by their friends to visit the village school. . . . Always, the room was hurriedly put in order, and we were threatened with a prompt and bloody death if we cut one caper while the visitors were present. We always sang a spiritual, led by Mr. Calhoun himself. Mrs. Calhoun always stood in the back, with a palmetto switch in her hand as a squelcher. We were all little angels for the duration, because we'd better be.

EXERCISE B. Read the following questions. Use the text you have marked to help you answer each question.

1. What event takes place at the school? Write your answer in the "cause" box in the following graphic organizer.
2. What three things occur in the school because of this event? Complete the cause-and-effect chart with information from the passage.

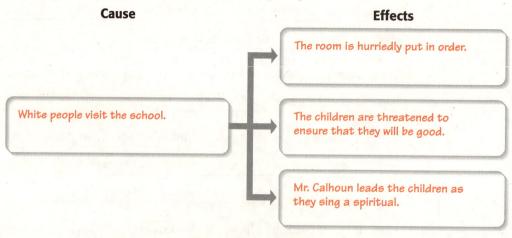

Cause	Effects
White people visit the school.	The room is hurriedly put in order.
	The children are threatened to ensure that they will be good.
	Mr. Calhoun leads the children as they sing a spiritual.

3. What is the cause-and-effect relationship in the last two sentences of the passage?
Mrs. Calhoun holds a switch to remind the children of what will happen if they behave badly. The effect is that the children are all "little angels."

Name .... Class .... Date ....

If We Must Die and *The Tropics in New York*

Interacting with Text Comparing and Contrasting

When we **compare** two things, we recognize how they are alike. When we **contrast** them, we recognize their differences.

EXERCISE A. Read the following lines from "If We Must Die" (passage 1) and "The Tropics in New York" (passage 2). Underline the rhyming words.

	Rhyme Scheme
Passage 1	
O kinsmen! we must meet the common foe!	a
Though far outnumbered let us show us brave,	b
And for their thousand blows deal one deathblow!	a
What though before us lies the open grave?	b
Passage 2	
My eyes grew dim, and I could no more gaze;	a
A wave of longing through my body swept,	b
And, hungry for the old, familiar ways,	a
I turned aside and bowed my head and wept.	b

EXERCISE B. Read and answer each of the following questions on the lines provided. Follow the directions for marking the text.

1. Look at the rhyming words that you have underlined. Assign each word that ends a line a letter of the alphabet, beginning with letter *a*. When two line-ending words rhyme, they share the same letter of the alphabet. For example, the pattern of passage 1 is *abab*. What is the rhyme scheme of passage 2? *abab*

2. Circle phrases in each passage that convey what the speaker is feeling. How does the speaker feel, according to passage 1? According to passage 2?
The first speaker is defiant and brave and cries out for action; the second speaker is so filled with longing that it makes him weep.

3. Compare and contrast the two passages. How are they alike and different? *Alike: They have the same rhyme scheme. Different: They have different subjects and convey different feelings.*

Name .... Class .... Date ....

I, Too

Interacting with Text Analyzing the Speaker

The **speaker** of a poem is its narrator. The speaker may be the poet, a fictional character, or even an object. The words the speaker uses help to create the tone of the poem. Remember that **tone** is a reflection of the writer's or speaker's attitude toward the subject matter.

EXERCISE A. Read the following lines from "I, Too." Underline once the words or phrases that describe the speaker's perspective. Double-underline the phrase that helps you identify the speaker.

I, too, sing America.

I am the darker brother.
They send me to eat in the kitchen
When company comes,
But I laugh,
And eat well,
And grow strong.

Tomorrow,
I'll be at the table
When company comes.

EXERCISE B. Read the following questions. Use the text you have marked to help you answer each question. Write your answers on the lines provided.

1. What words identify the speaker? What do they say about the identity of the speaker? About the speaker's attitude toward those addressed? "Darker brother" identifies the speaker. "Darker" tells that the speaker is African American. The word "brother" indicates that the speaker feels kinship with other Americans.

2. What words or phrases reveal the attitude of the speaker toward the injustice of being sent to the kitchen to eat? "laugh," "eat well," "grow strong," "Tomorrow I'll be at the table"

3. What attitude do these words suggest? The attitude suggests self-confidence, pride, strength, and hope.

4. To whom is this poem addressed? What motivates the speaker? The poem is addressed to the people of America. The speaker sees a need to proclaim the importance, strength, and beauty of his race.

Name .... Class .... Date ....

from *Songs for Signare*

Interacting with Text **Analyzing Connotations**

Connotations are the implied associations of a word beyond its dictionary definition. Thinking about what is suggested by a word's connotation helps readers interpret an author's underlying meaning.

EXERCISE A. Read the following lines from *Songs for Signare.* Underline the word in each line whose meaning is provided in parentheses.

On the walls, pure primordial masks distant and yet present.	(primitive)
Stools of honor for hereditary guests, for the	(genetic)
Princes of the High Lands.	
Wild perfumes, thick mats of silence	
Cushions of shade and leisure, the noise of a	
wellspring of peace.	(source)

EXERCISE B. Read the following questions. For each question, find the text in the lines that will help you answer it. Then answer the question on the lines provided.

1. What word has about the same meaning as *primitive?* What underlying associations does this word have that *primitive* does not? *Primordial suggests something as ancient as time itself and essential to the universe.*

2. What negative connotations might *primitive* suggest to readers? *Primitive implies lack of sophistication, something crude or not evolved.*

3. What word might be replaced by *genetic?* What associations would then be lost? *Hereditary suggests both biological and cultural inheritance and stresses forebears or ancestors, whereas genetic focuses on the biological aspect of inheritance.*

4. What word could be replaced by *source?* What connotations make the poet's word a better choice? *Wellspring suggests fresh, bubbling water that continually renews itself and promises refreshment and life itself; source is a much more neutral word.*

Name .... Class .... Date ....

Sonnet to a Negro in Harlem

Interacting with Text Analyzing Speaker's Viewpoint

The words in "Sonnet to a Negro in Harlem" are carefully balanced and structured. Analysis of this balance and structure can provide clues to the speaker's viewpoint.

EXERCISE A. Read the following lines from "Sonnet to a Negro in Harlem." It describes an African American walking on a crowded street. Underline once adjectives that describe the person admiringly. Underline twice those that assign to the person negative qualities.

You are disdainful and magnificent–
Your perfect body and your pompous gait,
. . .
Your head thrown back in rich, barbaric song,
. . .
I love your laughter arrogant and bold.

EXERCISE B. Read the following questions. Use a dictionary and your analysis of the text to help you answer the questions. Write on the lines provided.

1. Which words describe the person positively? What does each word suggest about him or her?

magnificent—The person is handsome and grand.

perfect—The person's body is without faults or defects.

rich—The voice has a full, resonant quality.

bold—The person's laughter shows fearlessness.

2. Which words connote unpleasant or negative qualities? What traits does each word suggest?

disdainful—The person is proud and judges others as worthless.

pompous—The person conveys a self-important aspect.

barbaric—The voice is unaffected, simple and rough.

arrogant—The person is proud and scornful of others.

3. What is the speaker's overall view of this person? How do you know? The speaker sees the person's good and bad points, rejoices in the positive and finds just cause for the negative. The speaker admires the total person.

Name .... Class .... Date ....

November Cotton Flower

Interacting with Text Analyzing Caesura

A **caesura** is a pause between lines or in the middle of a line of poetry. It can change the rhythm of a line and usually calls attention to the word at the breaking point. A caesura often signals a sudden change in thought.

EXERCISE A. Read the following lines from "November Cotton Flower." Three caesuras can be found in the passage. Place a slash mark (/) at each example. Underline the words that these pauses emphasize.

Drought fighting soil had caused the soil to take
All water from the streams;/dead birds were found A
In wells a hundred feet below the ground—
Such was the season when the flower bloomed.
Old folks were startled,/and it soon assumed B
Significance./Superstition saw C
Something it had never seen before.

EXERCISE B. Read the following items. Refer to the text in the passage that you have marked. Write on the lines provided.

Label A, B, and C the three caesuras in the passage. Then, after each corresponding letter below, identify the word or words that are emphasized in each caesura. Why may the poet have wanted to emphasize those words?

A. Emphasized word(s): "dead birds"

Reason for emphasis: The dead birds represent the hardship caused by the drought and the toll it has taken on living things.

B. Emphasized word(s): "startled"

Reason for emphasis: The word "startled" communicates the farmers' astonishment that the plant is flowering.

C. Emphasized word(s): "Significance"

Reason for emphasis: "Significance" emphasizes that something important is happening; it also conveys great meaning to this sign of hope. The blossom's appearing despite adversity symbolizes hope for the crops and for the famers' own survival.

Name .... Class .... Date ....

Any Human to Another

Interacting with Text Analyzing Figurative Language

Figurative language is language used for descriptive effect, in order to convey ideas or emotions. Symbolism is one type of figurative language. A **symbol** is any object, person, place, or experience that exists on a literal level but also represents something else.

EXERCISE A. Read the following lines from "Any Human to Another." Underline the words that name objects or items that may stand for larger ideas.

Let no man be so proud
And confident,
To think he is allowed
A little tent
Pitched in a meadow
Of sun and shadow
All his little own.

EXERCISE B. Read the following questions. Use the words you underlined to help you answer the questions on the lines provided.

1. What are the effects of being in a tent mentioned in the fourth line in the passage? Possible answer: A tent is put up to protect someone from the elements, but it also closes that person off from the world.

2. What larger ideas may the tent and the meadow represent? Possible answer: A tent may stand for a protective shell that surrounds an individual; the meadow could represent all of life's experiences.

3. What do "sun" and "shadow" represent in this passage? Possible answer: They represent the happiness and sorrows of a lifetime.

4. What does the word "little," in the fourth line, add to your understanding of the tent? Possible answer: The "little" tent suggests the futility of attempting to shelter oneself from the sorrow of others.

Name .... Class .... Date ....

The Second Tree from the Corner

Interacting with Text Making Inferences

Making inferences is the skill of using details from the text and personal knowledge and experiences to help interpret an idea that the author implies but does not directly state.

EXERCISE A. Read the follow passages from "The Second Tree from the Corner."

Passage 1

Trexler's gaze followed the smoke. He managed to make out one of the titles, *The Genito-Urinary System*. A bright wave of fear swept cleanly over him and he winced under the first pain of kidney stones.

Passage 2

"Look at the chair you've been sitting in!" [the doctor said] ". . . You kept inching away from me while I asked you questions. That means you're scared."

[On a later visit] . . . Trexler noticed that at this point the doctor's chair slid slightly backward, away from him. Trexler stifled a small, internal smile. Scared as a rabbit, he said to himself. Look at him scoot!

EXERCISE B. Now read the following items. Follow the directions for marking the passages. Then answer each question on the lines provided.

1. In passage 1, underline the name of the object that Trexler sees. What does Trexler see through the smoke? Trexler sees a medical book entitled *The Genito-Urinary System.*

2. Double-underline the text in the passage that tells of Trexler's physical reaction to what he sees. How does he react? Why? Trexler winces, as if he feels kidney stones. When he sees the book, he imagines that he has a disease that is probably included in the book.

3. In passage 2, underline the action that Trexler and then the doctor take. According to the doctor, what does the action mean? The action, pushing back the chair, suggests fear.

4. Circle the text that describes Trexler's reaction to the doctor's action. Is Trexler pleased or displeased with the doctor's action? Why? Trexler is pleased that the doctor is fearful. He probably feels pleased to know that the doctor is susceptible to the same emotions that Trexler himself is.

Name .... Class .... Date ....

Ode to My Socks

Interacting with Text **Analyzing**

Analyzing often requires readers to break a large idea into smaller parts, check understanding of the parts, and then review the meaning of the whole.

EXERCISE A. Read the following passage from "Ode to My Socks."

I resisted
the mad impulse
to put them
into a golden
cage
and each day give them
birdseed
and pieces of pink melon.
Like explorers
in the jungle who hand
over the very rare
green deer
to the spit
and eat it
with remorse,
I stretched out
my feet
and pulled on
the magnificent
socks

EXERCISE B. Read the following items. Follow the directions for marking the passage. Then answer the questions on the lines provided.

1. In lines 56–63, underline the text that tells how the speaker is tempted to treat his socks. How does he want to treat his socks? Why? The speaker wants to treat his socks as he would treasured birds—to put them into a "golden cage" and give them "birdseed and pieces of pink melon." He wants to give his socks special care because he values them.

2. Circle the words in the passage that indicate that the speaker did not treat his socks as he first suggested. What does he resist? The speaker resists the temptation to treat his socks like treasured birds. Instead, he puts his socks on.

3. In lines 64–70, underline the text that tells to what the socks are next compared. To what does the speaker compare the socks? He compares the socks to a rare deer in the jungle.

Name .... Class .... Date ....

Breakfast

Interacting with Text Analyzing Description

Description refers to a detailed portrayal of a person, a place, an object, or an event.

EXERCISE A. Read the following passages from "Breakfast."

Passage 1

The mother moved about, poking the fire, shifting the rusty lids of the stove to make a greater draft, opening the oven door; and all the time the baby was nursing, but that didn't interfere with the mother's work, nor with the light quick gracefulness of her movements. There was something very precise and practiced in her movements.

Passage 2

The elder man turned to me, "Had your breakfast?"

"No."

"Well sit down with us, then."

. . . The older man filled his mouth full and he chewed and chewed and swallowed. Then he said, "God Almighty, it's good," and he filled his mouth again.

EXERCISE B. Read the following items and follow the directions for marking the text. Write your answers to the questions on the lines provided.

1. In passage 1, underline the woman's activities. What is the woman doing? She is working at a wood cookstove to get it to cook more efficiently, while she is nursing her baby.

2. Double-underline the words that describe the woman's movements. In your own words, describe her actions. What do her actions suggest about her? The woman moves smoothly and easily. She appears to be agile and used to doing many things at one time.

3. What impression of the woman do you get from the manner in which she performs her tasks? She cares for her family expertly and with a natural grace.

4. In passage 2, underline the dialogue that shows what the elder man is like. What impression of the elder man do his words convey? The man is hospitable; he is thankful and happy that he has such wonderful food.

Name .... Class .... Date ....

A Rose for Emily

Interacting with Text Establishing Time Order

Events in a story are not always presented in chronological order. To understand when actions occur, look for clue words, such as *first, then, after, later,* and *finally*.

EXERCISE A. Read the following passage from "A Rose for Emily" about the events in Miss Emily's life.

So she vanquished [the town leaders], horse and foot, just as she had vanquished their fathers thirty years before about the smell. That was two years after her father's death and a short time after her sweetheart . . . had deserted her. After her father's death, she went out very little; after her sweetheart went away, people hardly saw her at all.

EXERCISE B. Read the following items and follow the directions for marking the text. Write your answers to the questions on the lines provided.

1. In the passage, which event happens first? Briefly describe the event. Miss Emily's father dies.

2. Underline five events in the passage with time-order word clues that indicate when the events occurred.

3. In the passage, double-underline the words and phrases that indicate the order of events. What are the words and phrases? The words and phrases that provide the reader with hints about the order of events are "thirty years before," "two years after," "a short time after," and "after."

4. Which event takes place two years after the death of Miss Emily's father? Circle the letter of the correct answer choice.
   a. Miss Emily deserts the town.
   b. Her sweetheart dies.
   (c.) She sends the town's leaders away.

5. According to the passage, what two events occur before Miss Emily becomes a recluse? In what order do these events occur? Explain. According to the passage, Miss Emily's father dies. Later, her sweetheart deserts her, resulting in her rarely leaving the house.

Name .... Class .... Date ....

Father's Bedroom

Interacting with Text **Making Inferences**

You **make inferences** about events and characters in a poem by combining what you already know with the clues that the poet provides. The details and images in a poem suggest more than they say literally.

EXERCISE A. Read the following lines from "Father's Bedroom." Underline the details that describe the room and double-underline the details that describe the book.

The broad-planked floor
had a sandpapered neatness.
The clear glass bed-lamp
. . . .
was still raised a few
inches by resting on volume two
of Lafcadio Hearn's
Glimpses of Unfamiliar Japan.
Its warped olive cover
was punished like a rhinoceros hide.
In the flyleaf:
"Robbie from Mother."

EXERCISE B. Read the following questions. For each question, find the marked text in the passage that will help you answer it. Write your answer on the lines provided.

1. What is the floor in the father's bedroom like? It is made of wide, thick planks of wood; it is bare and meticulously neat.

2. Which quality of the floor stands out the most? What do you infer that this quality suggests about the father? Possible answer: Its "sandpapered neatness" suggests a personality that rubs out any parts of life, such as emotions, that are not perfectly smooth and regular.

3. What do details and images tell you the book looks like? Possible answer: Its cover is drab, misshapen, and rough, with bumps and ridges.

4. What inference can you make about the father from the description of the book? Possible answers: Its condition suggests failure to take care of the book, even though it was a gift from his mother. An inference might be that the father was not sentimental or warm. Alternatively, the well-worn book accompanying the father on his travels may suggest that he treasured it but did not show his emotions.

Name .... Class .... Date ....

from *Black Boy*

Interacting with Text Analyzing Dialogue

Dialogue is conversation between characters. It offers clues to characters' feelings and motivations. In a narrative, dialogue is enclosed in quotation marks and is usually preceded or followed by a speaker tag that shows who is speaking.

EXERCISE A. Read the following passage from *Black Boy*.

"It's not for me," my mother was saying. "It's for your children that I'm asking you for money."

"I ain't got nothing," my father said, laughing.

"Come here, boy," the strange woman called to me.

I looked at her and did not move.

"Give him a nickel," the woman said.

"He's cute."

. . .

"You ought to be ashamed," my mother said to the strange woman. "You're starving my children."

"Now don't you-all fight," my father said, laughing.

"I'll take that poker and hit you!" I blurted at my father.

EXERCISE B. Read the following questions and follow the directions for marking the text.

1. How does the narrator's father respond to his mother's request for support? Underline the words in the speaker tags that show the manner in which he responds.
2. What does "the strange woman" tell the father to do? Double-underline the dialogue that shows the woman's command to the father.
3. What does the mother accuse the woman of? Circle the dialogue that shows the mother's accusation.

EXERCISE C. Read the following questions. Find the marked text in the passage that will help you answer the questions. Write your answers on the lines provided.

1. What does the father's response to the mother show about him? His laughing and saying that he has no money to give show that he does not care about his children's hunger.
2. What feelings are revealed through the mother's words? The mother shows anguish and outrage.

Name .... Class .... Date ....

A Worn Path

Interacting with Text Analyzing Figurative Language

Figurative language is used for descriptive effect, in order to convey ideas or emotions. A **simile** is a figure of speech, a kind of figurative language in which an author uses a word such as *like* or *as* in a comparison of seemingly unlike things.

EXERCISE A. Read the following passages from "A Worn Path." Each passage presents a scene that Phoenix Jackson passes on her journey. Underline the simile in each passage.

Passage 1

At last she was safe through the fence and risen up out in the clearing. Big dead trees, like black men with one arm, were standing in the purple stalks of the withered cotton field.

Passage 2

She followed the track, swaying through the quiet bare fields, through the little strings of trees silver in their dead leaves, past cabins silver from weather, with the doors and windows boarded shut, all like old women under a spell sitting there.

EXERCISE B. Read the following questions. For each question, use the text you underlined to help you answer it. Write on the lines provided.

1. To what are the dead trees compared? The dead trees are compared to one-armed "black men."

2. What effect does this comparison have? What does it add to the mood? Possible answer: It lends a solemn, foreboding mood to the scene, perhaps a reminder of the field laborers who lost their health and lives in those fields. The missing limbs suggest that life is crippling, but Jackson manages to fight death by following the track.

3. To what are the line of trees and abandoned cabins that she passes compared? They are compared to "old women under a spell."

4. What does this figurative language contribute to the atmosphere? Possible answer: It extends the portrait of Jackson as old and tired and adds a mythic quality.

Name .... Class .... Date ....

The Explorer

Interacting with Text Identifying Tone

Tone is a reflection of an author's or a speaker's attitude toward the subject matter. Studying an author's word choices helps the reader to determine the tone.

EXERCISE A. Read the following passage from "The Explorer."

Somehow to find a still spot in the noise
Was the frayed inner want, the winding, the frayed hope
Whose tatters he kept hunting through the din.
A satin peace somewhere.
A room of wily hush somewhere within.

EXERCISE B. Read the following items and follow the directions for marking the text. Write your answers to the questions on the lines provided.

1. Underline the words in the passage that mean "torn in shreds."
2. Circle the word in the passage that has the same meaning as the word *noise*.
3. What emotions do the phrases "frayed inner want" and "the winding, the frayed hope" suggest? Possible answer: The phrases suggest a strained nervousness, longing, and anxiety.
4. Double-underline three words or phrases in the passage that suggest the opposite of what *noise* suggests.
5. What do you think the speaker of the poem is searching for? The speaker is searching for inner peace.
6. Circle two words that suggest that the speaker has been searching a long time and is losing hope.
7. Review the words in the passage that you have marked. What is the overall tone of the poem? The tone is that of frustration and longing for inner peace.

Name .... Class .... Date ....

February

Interacting with Text Analyzing Symbols

A **symbol** is any object, color, person, place, or experience that exists literally but that also represents something else.

EXERCISE A. Read the following passage from "February," in which the author describes a scene in the woods.

And the birds: I descended into a little valley in the windless quiet and the smell of apples and saw the air erupt with red tracer-bullet streaks of flight—across the snows, a carnival of cardinals. The red birds zoomed, the flickers flew, pheasants roared up like gaudy Chinese kimono rags. My heart beat hard and I saw the single tree, black-limbed against the sky, here and there the miracle of a dark red apple still hanging after months of ice and snow.

EXERCISE B. Read the following items and follow the directions for marking the text. Write your answers and explanations on the lines provided.

1. In the passage, underline the names of two kinds of birds. Then underline what the speaker compares the birds to. Explain the comparisons on the lines provided.
Cardinals are compared to bullet streaks and a carnival; pheasants are compared to colorful, "Chinese kimono rags."

2. For what idea or quality might the birds be a symbol? Possible answer: The birds could be a symbol of life or proof of vitality in an otherwise dead place and time.

3. Why does the author's heart beat hard when he sees a "single tree, black-limbed against the sky"? Why does the tree seem miraculous to Ellison? The tree still has apples on it; by February, all the apples should have fallen and rotted.

4. For what idea or quality might the apples be a symbol? Possible answer: The apples might be a symbol for life, resiliency, and survival or the ability to persevere ("hang on"). The apples might represent the idea that even in the bleakest time, surprise, hope, and unexpected survival exist.

Name .... Class .... Date ....

The Portrait

Interacting with Text — Making Inferences from Dialogue

Dialogue is a conversation between characters in a literary work. Authors reveal the personalities of characters through what the characters say.

EXERCISE A. Read the following dialogue from "The Portrait," in which Don Mateo and his wife listen to a salesman's pitch and debate about whether to order a portrait of their son who has died.

"Well, sir, see, you give us a picture, any picture you may have, and we will not only enlarge it for you but we'll also set it in a wooden frame like this one and we'll shape the image a little, like this—three dimensional, as they say."

"And what for?"

"So that it will look real. That way . . . look, let me show you . . . see? Doesn't he look real, like he's alive?" . . .

"Yes, but it's much too expensive."

"Well, yes. But the thing is, this is very fine work. . . . "

" . . . What do you think, vieja?"

"Well, I like it a lot. Why don't we order one? And if it turns out good . . . my Chuy . . . may he rest in peace. It's the only picture we have of him. We took it right before he left for Korea. Poor m'ijo, we never saw him again. See . . . this is his picture. Do you think you can make it like that, make it look like he's alive?"

"Sure, we can. You know, we've done a lot of them in soldier's uniforms."

EXERCISE B. Read the following items and follow the directions for marking the text. Write your answers to the questions and your explanations on the lines provided.

1. Circle the statement of the salesman that is most effective in influencing the parents to buy the portrait. What words in the salesman's "pitch" appeal to the couple? Why? The salesman promises to make their son look as if he were alive. Their love for their dead son may be so strong that they cannot resist the lifelike portrait that may help to keep his memory alive.

2. Double-underline the part of the dialogue that shows the inquiry of Don Mateo's wife and the reply of the salesman. What do you infer about the couple from their dialogue? The loss of their son has been painful to them; his memory is more precious to them than the inflated fee for the portrait.

Name .... Class .... Date ....

The Death of the Ball Turret Gunner

Interacting with Text Analyzing Metaphor

A **metaphor** is a figure of speech in which two essentially unlike things are compared or equated. Although the things are basically unrelated, unexpected similarities are revealed through the metaphor.

EXERCISE A. Reread "The Death of the Ball Turret Gunner." Underline the metaphor that describes the gunner inside the ball turret.

From my mother's sleep I fell into the State,
And I hunched in its belly till my wet fur froze.
Six miles from earth, loosed from its dream of life,
I woke to black flak and the nightmare fighters.
When I died they washed me out of the turret with a hose.

EXERCISE B. Read the following items. Use the underlined words and phrases above to help you answer each question on the lines provided.

1. What is the gunner's position in the plane? Describe his physical position. He is crouched or curled up in a small round plastic space.

2. To what is the gunner being compared? Use words from the passage to support your answer. The gunner is compared to a fetus. The words "I hunched in its belly" bring to mind the image of a fetus in the womb.

3. How is the gunner's position like being in a womb? Explain. The gunner's position is a round, cramped space in the plane's "belly" into which he must curl his body so as to fit. The space in the bomber is cut off from earth, as a fetus is cut off from the outside world.

4. What is ironic, or the opposite of what is expected, about the comparison of the gunner and a fetus? A mother usually takes care that the fetus will be healthy and develop normally; the State is careless with the life of the gunner. A womb is warm and sustains life; the turret and war are cold and cause death.

Name .... Class .... Date ....

The Beautiful Changes

Interacting with Text Parts of Speech

A good clue to a word's meaning, when the word appears in context, is the word's part of speech. A **noun** names a person, a place, a thing, or an idea. A **verb** names an action. A **gerund** is a verb form than ends in *-ing* and is used the same way as a noun.

EXERCISE A. Read the following lines from "The Beautiful Changes."

Passage 1

One wading a Fall meadow finds on all sides
The Queen Anne's Lace lying like lilies
On water; it glides
So from the walker, it turns
Dry grass to a lake, as the slightest shade of you
Valleys my mind in fabulous blue Lucernes.

Passage 2

. . . the beautiful changes
In such kind ways,
Wishing ever to sunder
Things and things' selves for a second finding,
to lose
For a moment all that it touches back to
wonder.

EXERCISE B. Read the following items. Follow the directions for marking the text. Answer the questions and supply explanations on the lines provided.

1. Underline the nouns in passage 1.
2. Double-underline the verbs in passage 1.
3. List the verbs you underlined in the first passage. Which one is surprising? Why?
"lying," "glides," "turns," and "valleys." "Valleys" is surprising because the poet uses it as a verb.
4. How does the use of *valleys* as a verb affect the image of the mountain lakes in the poem? What is the effect of *valleys*, used as a verb, on the reader of the poem?
Possible answer: Use of valley as a verb makes the image of "fabulous blue Lucernes" more vivid. It causes the reader to picture a valley and a blue mountain lake in terms of a mental activity that has depth: immersing the mind in thoughts of love.
5. Circle the verb form that is used as a noun in passage 2.
6. Explain what you think the poet means by "a second finding." Possible answer: Sometimes when we look at an object or idea again, we gain a new depth of insight into its beauty.

Name .... Class .... Date ....

The Rockpile

Interacting with Text — Comparing and Contrasting Characters

To **compare** characters is to show how they are alike. To **contrast** them is to show how they are different.

EXERCISE A. Read the following passage from "The Rockpile." It describes the interaction between Roy and John when Roy decides to go to the rockpile. Underline parts of the text that give clues to Roy's character. Double-underline parts of the text that show John's character.

By and by Roy became bored and sat beside John in restless silence; and John began drawing into his schoolbook. . . . John looked up. Roy stood looking down at him.

"I'm going downstairs," he said.

"You better stay where you is, boy. You know Mama don't want you going downstairs."

"I be right *back*. She won't even know I'm gone, less you run and tell her."

. . .

"But Daddy's going to be home soon!"

"I be back before *that.* What you all the time got to be so *scared* for?"

EXERCISE B. Read the following questions. For each question, find the text in the passage that will help you answer it. Write your answers on the lines provided.

1. What details tell you that Roy craves action? Sitting makes him bored and restless; he decides to leave.

2. What contrasting detail shows that John is quieter and has more self-control than Roy? John finds a quiet activity—drawing—to occupy his time.

3. What reasons does John give Roy for not going downstairs? What do his reasons show about his character? John's reasons are that their mother does not want Roy to go downstairs and that their father will soon be home. John is obedient and seems fearful of his father.

4. What rationale does Roy give to justify his disobedience? What do his reasons show about his character? He says that his act will not be discovered and that he will be back before his father gets home; Roy is daring, confident, and careless of consequences.

Name .... Class .... Date ....

The Magic Barrel

Interactive Reading **Reading Guide**

KEY FIGURES

Leo Finkle–a young rabbinical student who wants to marry

Pinye Salzman–an elderly marriage broker

Lily Hirschorn–a possible wife for Leo

Stella–Pinye Salzman's daughter

KEY VOCABULARY AND TERMS

congregation–a religious community

tormented–distressed

portfolio–a case for carrying loose papers

inherently–innately, essentially

steadfastly–steadily, determinedly

imperceptible–not perceivable; very slight

mystical–of a spiritual nature that cannot be perceived by the senses or mind

mortified–embarrassed

sanctified–holy, blessed

THE QUEST

SORTING IT OUT

EXERCISE Read "The Magic Barrel" up to the paragraph that begins "He was infuriated with the marriage broker. . . ." Use information from the story to help you complete the following items on the lines provided.

1. After studying for six years, Leo Finkle was to be ordained, to become a rabbi.

2. Finkle thinks that marrying will improve his chances of getting a congregation.

3. Finkle engages the services of Pinye Salzman, the matchmaker, to help him find a wife.

4. Pinye Salzman's appearance is slight but dignified, with a few teeth missing, a wisp of a beard, and sad eyes. He smells of fish.

5. Although Finkle knows that matchmaking is an accepted practice in traditional Jewish culture, he feels ashamed and uncomfortable because of its loveless nature and the focus on appearance and money.

6. Finkle is not interested in any of the women the matchmaker suggests. Salzman says that he has more names at home in a magic barrel. Finkle is sorry he called the marriage broker.

Name .... Class .... Date ....

7. What is the last thing Salzman tells Finkle about Lily Hirschorn to pique Leo's interest in meeting her? Salzman tells Finkle that Lily Hirschorn is not yet married because she is particular and wants the best.

8. What does Hirschorn ask Finkle that makes him tremble with rage? Why does it affect him so? Hirschorn asks Finkle when he became "enamored of God." From hearing this question, Leo realizes that she and he himself have been "sold a bill of goods." She is interested in a "mythical figure," not himself, the real person.

THE DISCOVERY

Now read from the paragraph that begins "He was infuriated . . . " to the end of the story. Use the information from the story to help you complete the following items.

9. What insight does Finkle gain as a result of his conversation with Hirschorn? Explain. Finkle begins to understand the true nature of his relationship to God. He realizes that he has never loved anyone except his parents. He questions his love for God because he has not loved people.

10. After Finkle chastises the marriage broker for "overselling" Hirschorn, he tells Salzman that he is not interested in an arranged marriage because he wants to be in love with the woman he marries.

11. Finkle eventually examines the photographs of women that Salzman left in a packet on the table. While returning the photographs into the envelope, he finds a snapshot of a woman that deeply moves him.

12. Excited by his discovery, Leo sees a picture of someone whose "eyes are hauntingly familiar, yet absolutely strange." In her, he sees a trace of evil but knows she is "good for Leo Finkle", the one "who could understand him and help him."

13. Who is the girl in the photograph, and what is her relationship to Salzman? Stella Salzman is the girl in the picture. She is Pinye Salzman's daughter.

14. What does Finkle say to convince the matchmaker to arrange a meeting with Stella? Explain. He says, "Perhaps I can be of service," meaning that maybe he can help change Stella's evil ways. This gets the matchmaker's attention.

15. What does Finkle suspect about the matchmaker? Finkle suspects Salzman of planning for him to meet Salzman's daughter all along.

Name .... Class .... Date ....

from *Stride Toward Freedom*

Interacting with Text: Evaluating the Validity of Opinions

Writers attempt to persuade readers to accept different viewpoints by presenting opinions. **Opinions** reflect the writer's attitudes, feelings, or beliefs and cannot be proven to be true or false. However, opinions can be substantiated, or supported, with evidence (such as examples, statements by experts, facts, and logical arguments).

EXERCISE A. Read the following passage from *Stride Toward Freedom*.

To accept passively an unjust system is to cooperate with that system; thereby the oppressed become as evil as the oppressor. Noncooperation with evil is as much a moral obligation as is cooperation with good. The oppressed must never allow the conscience of the oppressor to slumber. Religion reminds every man that he is his brother's keeper. To accept injustice or segregation passively is to say to the oppressor that his actions are morally right. It is a way of allowing his conscience to fall asleep. At this moment the oppressed fails to be his brother's keeper. . . . The Negro cannot win the respect of his oppressor by acquiescing; he merely increases the oppressor's arrogance and contempt. Acquiescence is interpreted as proof of the Negro's inferiority.

EXERCISE B. Read the following items and follow the directions for marking the text. Write your answers and explanations on the lines provided.

1. Underline the text in the passage that shows how Martin Luther King Jr. views a person who passively accepts an unjust system.

2. Double-underline the text that shows what King thinks noncooperation with evil is. Why does King think that passive acceptance of oppression is wrong? King thinks that noncooperation with evil is a moral obligation.

3. What authority does King cite to support his opinion about passive acceptance? Circle the text that shows on what authority King bases his opinion. Explain. King cites religion as the moral authority that reminds all people to be each other's keepers.

4. Do you think King's opinion is valid? Why or why not? Explain. King's opinion is valid because he uses a logical argument, cites the authority of religion, and appeals to the better nature of human beings.

Name .... Class .... Date ....

Choice: A Tribute to Dr. Martin Luther King Jr.

Interacting with Text Cause-and-Effect Relationships

A **cause** is an action or occurrence that makes something happen. An **effect** is the result of that action or occurrence. One action may have several effects, and some events are the result of many causes. In addition, an effect may be the result of one action and become the cause of another action.

EXERCISE A. Read the following passage from "Choice: A Tribute to Dr. Martin Luther King Jr." It describes Alice Walker's feelings on first seeing King, when he was arrested at a demonstration.

He had dared to claim his rights as a native son, and had been arrested. He displayed no fear, but seemed calm and serene, unaware of his own extraordinary courage. His whole body, like his conscience, was at peace.

At the moment I saw his resistance I knew I would never be able to live in this country without resisting everything that sought to disinherit me, and I would never be forced away from the land of my birth without a fight.

He was The One, The Hero, The One Fearless Person for whom we had waited.

EXERCISE B. Read the following items and follow the directions for marking the passage. Write your answers and explanations on the lines provided.

1. Why was Martin Luther King Jr. arrested? Underline the part of the passage in which Alice Walker gives her opinion about why King was arrested.
2. Circle the words in the text that describe King's reaction to being arrested. How does King react? As he is arrested, King seems calm and unafraid.
3. How does King's arrest affect Walker? Underline twice the parts of the passage that contain Walker's vows for the future. Explain what she promises herself. She is inspired to resist injustice herself; she vows to fight for the land of her birth.
4. What does her new awareness cause Walker to understand about African American people? Walker's awareness causes her to see that African Americans have been waiting for a fearless, heroic leader.

Name .... Class .... Date ....

The Crucible

Interactive Reading Introductory Reading Guide

Act 1

EXERCISE A. Read the Key Characters and Key Vocabulary and Terms sections that follow. Then read act 1 of *The Crucible*.

KEY CHARACTERS

the Reverend Samuel Parris–a minister from Barbados, where he was a merchant

Betty Parris–the minister's ten-year-old daughter

Tituba–a woman in her forties from Barbados, an enslaved person owned by the Reverend Samuel Parris

Abigail Williams–a seventeen-year-old orphan, the Reverend Mr. Parris's niece

Susanna Walcott–a girl a bit younger than Abigail

Ann Putnam–a woman who seems to look for the worst in everyone and has borne many children who die shortly after birth

Thomas Putnam–the husband of Ann Putnam; a well-to-do landowner

Mercy Lewis–an eighteen-year-old servant of the Putnams

Mary Warren–a seventeen-year-old girl who works in the Proctor household

John Proctor–a man for whom Abigail Williams once worked

Rebecca Nurse–an elderly woman who has borne many healthy children, who have in turn provided her with many grandchildren

Giles Corey–an elderly man

the Reverend John Hale–a minister considered to be an authority on witchcraft

Elizabeth Proctor–the wife of John Proctor

Francis Nurse–the husband of Rebecca Nurse

Ezekiel Cheever–a clerk of the court

Marshal Herrick–a man of about thirty who works for the court

Judge Hathorne–a prosecutor of the court

Deputy Governor Danforth–a man in his sixties who is the authority in the court

Sarah Good–a woman in rags who is in jail

Hopkins–a guard in the jail

KEY VOCABULARY AND TERMS

Act 1

inert–lifeless

hearty–well, energetic

propriety–behavior accepted as proper

bid–told

quavering–trembling

gibberish–nonsense

stiff-necked–unyielding

sniveling–whimpering

begrudge–to give reluctantly

demonic–having to do with the devil

vengeful–wanting to take revenge

formidable–forceful; frightening

conjuring–calling forth a spirit by means of magic

contention–argument

notorious–widely and unfavorably known

baffled–confused and puzzled

peopled–added people to; inhabited

fathom–to understand

mortgages–loans against property

Quakers–members of a Christian group formally known as the Society of Friends; Quakers oppose all war and weaponry.

Name .... Class .... Date ....

SORTING IT OUT

EXERCISE B. Complete the sentences, or answer the questions that follow, on the lines provided.

1. Identify the setting of the play as it opens. The time is the spring of 1692.

   The place is a small bedroom in the house of Reverend Samuel Parris in Salem, Massachusetts.

2. List the characters that appear as the curtain rises and tell something about each one. Parris is praying and acts confused and frantic. Betty, his ten-year-old daughter, is lying on the bed and appears to be ill. Tituba, a woman in her forties who is an enslaved person in Parris's house, seems frightened.

3. Susanna Walcott brings news from the doctor, who has been consulting his medical books about Betty's illness. What does the doctor think may be causing the illness? The doctor suggests that the illness may have unnatural causes.

4. Why is Parris so afraid? He is fearful that the "unnatural causes" may be witchcraft, or the work of the devil.

5. What two people seem to be most eager to persuade others that the girls are engaging in witchcraft? Ann Putnam and her husband, Thomas, are eager to persuade others that the girls are engaging in witchcraft.

6. What seems to have been the relationship between Abigail Williams and John Proctor? Abigail, previously a servant in the Proctor home, and Proctor were involved romantically while she worked for his family. Consequently, Proctor's wife fired her. Now Proctor seems firm when he tells Abigail that his relationship with Abigail is over.

7. What do Abigail and Betty do at the end of act 1? They accuse many local women of having dealings with the devil.

Act 2

EXERCISE C. Read the following Key Vocabulary and Terms. Then read act 2 of *The Crucible*.

KEY VOCABULARY AND TERMS

Act 2

heifer–a young cow

draught–a draft, amount of something that is drunk

condemnation–the declaration of someone's guilt

naught–nothing

mock–to ridicule; treat with contempt

poppet–a doll

deference–respect

falter–to hesitate; act as if uncertain

flinch–to shrink away from something difficult, painful, or dangerous

quail–to lose courage or conviction

tonnage–weight, as measured in tons

calamity–a disaster

SORTING IT OUT

EXERCISE D. Answer the following questions. Write on the lines provided.

1. According to the stage directions at the beginning of act 2, what does Proctor do? When he hears Elizabeth coming, how does he respond? Why? Proctor puts seasoning into the stew. Then he quickly moves away from the pot because he does not want Elizabeth to know what he has done.

2. Why do Proctor and his wife seem so distant from each other as they talk at the beginning of act 2? She apparently has not forgiven him for his relationship with Abigail, although he insists that it is over and that his wife should trust him now.

3. Mary Warren brings news that Goody Osburn will hang but that Sarah Good will not. Why will one hang and the other be saved? Osburn has not confessed to witchcraft; because she is accused and, therefore, considered guilty, she will hang for it. On the other hand, Sarah Good, who has also been accused, has confessed. According to the court, a confession spares her from the death penalty.

4. Why does the Reverend John Hale visit the Proctors? Hale goes to the Proctors' to verify that the Proctors are good Christians.

5. Ezekiel Cheever arrives to arrest Elizabeth. What evidence of witchcraft does he believe he discovers in the Proctor house? The poppet, or rag doll, that Mary Warren has brought to Elizabeth has a needle in it, which he interprets as an instrument of witchcraft used to cause the pains that Abigail has suffered.

Name .... Class .... Date ....

The Crucible

Interactive Reading — Reading Guide for Act 3 and Act 4

Act 3

EXERCISE A. Read the following Key Vocabulary and Terms. Then read act 3 of *The Crucible*.

KEY VOCABULARY AND TERMS

Act 3

daft–crazy

contentious–quarrelsome

contemptuous–disdainful; feeling disgust

contention–belief; argument based on a belief

forfeit–to give up something as a penalty

prodigious–enormous

remorselessly–without pity or sadness

manifest–made real or evident

agape–with mouth wide open in astonishment

transfixed–motionless with shock

compacted–contracted

unintelligible–impossible to hear or understand

SORTING IT OUT

EXERCISE B. Complete the following sentences as you read act 3. In each blank, write the correct name from the following list. You may use a name more than once.

Francis Nurse	Thomas Putnam	Mary Warren
Abigail Williams	Giles Corey	John Proctor

1. As Judge Hathorne questions Martha Corey, Giles Corey shouts that he has evidence for the court.

2. Giles Corey accuses Thomas Putnam of wanting to get rid of people in order to obtain their land.

3. Francis Nurse claims that the girls who are accusing the women of witchcraft are frauds.

4. John Danforth brings in Mary Warren, who states that the accusations she has made are false, as are those of the other girls.

5. John Proctor is startled to hear Danforth claim that his wife is pregnant, which will remove her from the court for more than a year.

6. When Danforth tells the court that the girls have been acting, Abigail Williams denies the accusation and insists that her accusations against the women are true.

7. In order to try to prove that Abigail Williams is not sincere and credible, John Proctor reveals his romantic involvement with her.

8. Abigail leads the other girls in accusing Mary Warren of bewitching her by becoming a bird hovering around the ceiling.

9. At the end of act 3, two men have been arrested for witchcraft: John Proctor and Giles Corey.

Act 4

EXERCISE C. Read the following Key Vocabulary and Terms. Then read act 4 of *The Crucible*.

KEY VOCABULARY AND TERMS

Act 4

transformation–a profound change

rile–to stir up or irritate

Andover–a town near Salem, where accusations of witchcraft have begun

providence–God's protection

remedy–to fix or solve

beguile–to deceive; trick

belie–to contradict

wizard–a male witch

conspiracy–a secret plan of a group to commit immoral or illegal acts

empower–to give authority or power to someone

SORTING IT OUT

EXERCISE D. Answer these questions as you read act 4. Write on the lines provided.

1. As act 4 begins, how does Hale spend his time? He visits and prays with those condemned to death.

2. What is the problem with the cows? So many people are now in jail that the cows are roaming free, causing people to wonder to whom the cows belong.

3. What crime does Abigail commit against Parris, her uncle? What happens to Abigail and to Mercy Lewis? Abigail steals money from her uncle, and he suspects that the two girls have left town.

4. Why does Danforth allow the Proctors to meet before Proctor's execution? Danforth hopes and believes that Elizabeth will be able to persuade Proctor to confess, which will save him from execution.

5. Why is Giles Corey killed? He refuses to confess or to deny the charges against him. Therefore, he is killed without being condemned of witchcraft, and his sons are able to inherit his property.

6. Why does Proctor destroy his confession? He knows that Danforth will post it where the whole village will see it, and he does not want to ruin his own name with a lie, even though doing so would save his life.

Name .... Class .... Date ....

Nineteen Thirty-Seven

Interacting with Text Identifying Similes and Metaphors

Writers use **figurative language** to create vivid descriptions and comparisons. Two types of figurative language are similes and metaphors. A **simile** is a comparison that includes the word *like* or *as*. (For example: The kitten's fur was *as soft as velvet.*) A **metaphor** is a comparison in which one thing is said, or implied, to be another. (For example: My uncle is *the star of our family.*)

EXERCISE A. Read the following passages from "Nineteen Thirty-Seven."

Passage 1

Our mothers were the ashes and we were the light. Our mothers were the embers and we were the sparks. Our mothers were the flames and we were the blaze. We came from the bottom of that river where the blood never stops flowing. . . .

Passage 2

Jacqueline said nothing as she carefully walked around the women who sat like statues in different corners of the cell. There were six of them. They kept their arms close to their bodies, like angels hiding their wings. In the middle of the cell was an arrangement of sand and pebbles in the shape of a cross for my mother.

EXERCISE B. Read the following items and follow the directions for marking the passages. Write your answers to the questions on the lines provided.

1. Which passage contains two similes? Underline the two similes in the passage. Passage 2: The two similes are "the women . . . like statues" and "They . . . like angels hiding their wings."

2. What objects, people, or ideas are being compared in the two similes you have underlined? With what are they being compared? The women are being compared to statues and angels.

3. Which passage has three sentences containing metaphors? Double-underline each metaphor. Write the metaphors on the lines provided. Passage 1: The three sentences containing metaphors are "Our mothers were the ashes and we were the light." "Our mothers were the embers and we were the sparks." "Our mothers were the flames and we were the blaze."

Name .... Class .... Date ....

Snow

Interacting with Text Identifying Main Idea and Supporting Details

The **main idea** of a passage is the most important idea of the passage. Often the writer directly states the main idea. At other times, the writer merely suggests the main idea by providing facts and details.

EXERCISE A. Read the following passage from "Snow."

Sister Zoe explained to a wide-eyed classroom what was happening in Cuba. Russian missiles were being assembled, trained supposedly on New York City. President Kennedy, looking worried too, was on the television at home, explaining we might have to go to war against the Communists. At school, we had air-raid drills: an ominous bell would go off and we'd file into the hall, fall to the floor, cover our heads with our coats, and imagine our hair falling out, the bones in our arms going soft.

EXERCISE B. Now read the following questions. Mark the text in the passage that will help you answer each question. Then answer each question, using the lines provided.

1. Circle the hyphenated word that indicates how the narrator and her classmates feel as they listen to their teacher talk about the missiles in Cuba. What is their reaction? The class is "wide-eyed"—at full attention—because of the seriousness of what is happening. They are afraid of what may happen to the United States and to themselves as a result of the problem in Cuba.

2. Underline the word in the passage that describes the air-raid bell. What does the word mean? The word ominous means "threatening or foreboding."

3. Underline the words that describe the children's actions in response to the air-raid bell. What exactly are the children to do? The children are to go to the hall, fall to the floor, and cover their heads.

4. Double-underline the words that tell what the children picture happening to them as a result of the nuclear blast. What do the children picture as they wait in the hall? They imagine that the nuclear blast is making their hair fall out and their bones become soft.

5. What is the main idea of the passage? The main idea of the passage: We were frightened about a possible nuclear attack as we practiced protecting ourselves.

Name .... Class .... Date ....

from *The Woman Warrior*

Interacting with Text Comparing and Contrasting

To **compare,** one notes details that show how people, things, or ideas are alike.
To **contrast,** one notes details that show how people, things, or ideas are different.

EXERCISE A. Read the following passage below from *The Woman Warrior*. It describes the sisters Brave Orchid and Moon Orchid. Underline the words and phrases that show how the sisters are alike. Circle the words and phrases that show how they are different.

And at last Moon Orchid looked at her—two old women with faces like mirrors. Their hands reached out as if to touch each other's face, then returned to their own, the fingers checking the grooves in the forehead and along the side of the mouth. Moon Orchid, who never understood the gravity of things, started smiling and laughing, pointing at Brave Orchid. . . .

Brave Orchid had tears in her eyes. But Moon Orchid said, "You look older than I. You *are* older than I," and again she'd laugh. "You're wearing an old mask to tease me." It surprised Brave Orchid that after thirty years she could still get annoyed at her sister's silliness.

EXERCISE B. Now read the following questions. Use the marked text to help you answer each one. Write on the lines provided.

1. In what way are the sisters alike? They are two old women; they look alike; they reach toward each other in similar ways; they both have wrinkles and creases in their faces.

2. How are their reactions to seeing each other different? Brave Orchid is solemn and saddened and then annoyed; Moon Orchid is amused and jokes about how old her sister looks.

3. What personality differences do these different reactions suggest? Brave Orchid is serious and is easily annoyed, whereas Moon Orchid is more cheerful and laughs easily.

4. What detail suggests that their differences have caused conflict in the past? Brave Orchid is surprised that she "could still get annoyed at her sister's silliness," a feeling that reveals that she was often annoyed with her sister when they were younger.

Name .... Class .... Date ....

Son

Interacting with Text **Inferring Theme**

The **theme** of a story is the central idea or the message that the writer wants to communicate to readers.

EXERCISE A. Read the following passages from "Son." They reveal bonds between different fathers and sons in the story. Underline phrases that suggest the nature of the father-son connection.

He would be a better father than his father. But time has tricked him, has made him a son.

. . . . . .

My father cursed: his father's old sorrow bore him down into depression, into hatred of life.

. . . . . .

I asked him [my father], Had he ever received the call? He said No. He said No, he never had. Received the call. That was a terrible thing, for him to admit. And I was the one he told.

. . . . . .

I roll my weight toward him like a rock down a mountain, and knock the weapon [a cardboard mailing tube] from his hand. He smiles. Smiles! Because my facial expression is silly? Because he is glad that he can still be overpowered, and hence is still protected? Why? I do not hit him.

EXERCISE B. Read the following questions. Use the underlined text in the passages to help you answer each question. Write on the lines provided.

1. What words and phrases suggest tension in the father-son relationships? In the first passage, a son thinks he would be more understanding than his father; in the last passage, a father moves forward and knocks a "weapon" from his son's hands.

2. What details suggest closeness and sympathy between fathers and sons? In the second passage, a son is depressed as he remembers his father's sorrow; in the third passage, a father makes a humbling admission of failure to his son; in the last passage, a son smiles when his father disciplines him.

3. What idea or message about the lifelong bonds between father and son do these passages imply? Possible answer: There is both resentment and understanding between a father and son. Fathers and sons rely on each other in different ways and are connected throughout life.

Name .... Class .... Date ....

from *The Way to Rainy Mountain*

Interacting with Text Analyzing Imagery

Imagery is the "word picture" that writers create to evoke an emotional response in readers. Writers use rich, descriptive language and figures of speech to create imagery.

EXERCISE A. Read the following passage from *The Way to Rainy Mountain*. It describes the worn houses on the plain where Momaday's grandmother lived. Underline the words or phrases that help create a clear picture of the houses.

Houses are like sentinels in the plain, old keepers of the weather watch. There, in a very little while, wood takes on the appearance of great age. All colors wear soon away in the wind and rain, and then the wood is burned gray and the grain appears and the nails turn red with rust. The windowpanes are black and opaque; you imagine there is nothing within, and indeed there are many ghosts, bones given up to the land. They stand here and there against the sky, and you approach them for a longer time than you expect. They belong in the distance; it is their domain.

EXERCISE B. Read the following questions. Use text from the passage to help you answer each one. Write on the lines provided.

1. What image is suggested by the simile in the first sentence, "like sentinels in the plain"? Possible answer: The houses stand like silent guards, watching unmoved by the harsh weather.

2. What colors do the houses have? What do these colors suggest? How do they show "great age"? Possible answer: The colors "burned gray," "red with rust," and "black and opaque" suggest a stark and dreary mood. Gray hair denotes age; metals rust with age; opaque windowpanes are filmy like aged eyes.

3. What has happened to other colors? What turns the wood gray? What feelings do these actions heighten? The colors have faded or have been worn away by the weather. The wood is bleached by the hot sun. These actions add to the sense of harshness.

4. What does the emptiness of the houses remind the narrator of? They remind him of those who lived and died here.

Name .... Class .... Date ....

Ambush

Interacting with Text Making Inferences

Authors do not always directly state everything they want readers to know. They may instead provide clues and details. Readers use these clues and details to help them **make inferences,** or reasoned conclusions, concerning the author's full meaning and intent.

EXERCISE A. Read the following passage from "Ambush." It describes how the narrator views the enemy soldier. Underline words that suggest how the narrator feels about the experience.

His shoulders were slightly stooped, his head cocked to the side as if listening for something. He seemed at ease. . . . There was no sound at all—none that I can remember. In a way, it seemed, he was part of the morning fog, or my own imagination, but there was also the reality of what was happening in my stomach. . . . I did not hate the young man; I did not see him as the enemy; I did not ponder issues of morality or politics or military duty. . . . I tried to swallow whatever was rising from my stomach, which tasted like lemonade, something fruity and sour. I was terrified. There were no thoughts about killing. The grenade was to make him go away—just evaporate. . . . It occurred to me that he was about to die. I wanted to warn him.

EXERCISE B. Read the following items. Follow the directions in each one. Use the text you marked to help you answer each question. Write on the lines provided.

1. Double-underline the details that describe the enemy soldier. What details suggest that the narrator is still haunted by the appearance of the man? He remembers the exact positions of the man's shoulders and head, as if the man is listening intently; he recalls that the man seems relaxed and unafraid.

2. What details suggest that the narrator remembers the scene as being unreal, like a dream? There are no sounds, and the soldier seems to be "part of the morning fog," or just a part of the narrator's imagination.

3. What does the narrator feel toward this man? How do you know? The narrator views the man as just a problem to be dealt with. He says that he feels no hatred and does not regard him as an enemy. Instead, he just wants him to "go away."

4. Which detail proves that the narrator identifies himself with the soldier? The narrator wants to warn the enemy soldier so that he will not be killed.

Name .... Class .... Date ....

Rain Music

Interacting with Text Analyzing Figurative Language: Metaphors and Similes

A **simile** is a comparison of two things in which the word *like* or *as* appears. A **metaphor** is a direct comparison of two things; one thing or person is said to *be* another.

EXERCISE A. Read the following passage from "Rain Music." It describes the narrator's sister, Linh. Underline each simile. Circle each metaphor.

She [Linh] has wide almond-shaped eyes . . . velvet-smooth cheeks. . . . Her nose is just slightly upturned . . . her lips rosebud shaped, her chin small and delicate. . . . The vision, taken together as a whole, is breathtaking. There is something about it, a wistful, dandelion, orchid-like kind of beauty that feels like notes in a chord being played separately, finger by finger, harmonizing back and forth. I marvel even now.

My mother and father have polished her until she shines.

EXERCISE B. Read the following items. Refer to the passage in answering each question. Write on the lines provided.

1. To what two items is Linh's beauty compared? Are these comparisons similes or metaphors? Linh's beauty is compared to orchids and to separate but harmonizing musical notes. These comparisons are both similes.

2. What do these comparisons suggest about the nature of Linh's beauty? Possible answer: The comparisons suggest that Linh's beauty is delicate, like a perfect exotic flower, and that all aspects of her beauty fit together harmoniously.

3. What is suggested by the metaphor that compares Linh's face to a "vision"? Possible answer: Linh's beauty is almost perfect, too lovely to be real.

4. Sometimes metaphors or similes are implied rather than directly stated. The final line of the passage contains an implied metaphor. To what is Linh being compared in it? What does this comparison suggest about Linh? Linh is compared to an object made from a precious metal that, when polished, glows radiantly; this suggests that Linh's parents have nurtured and groomed her to be both physically beautiful and highly successful.

Name .... Class .... Date ....

Kitchens

Interacting with Text Analyzing Sensory Images

Sensory images are words and phrases that appeal to one or more of the readers' senses. The purpose of sensory language is to help the reader visualize the scene and feel as if he or she is experiencing it.

EXERCISE A. Read the following passage, from "Kitchens," which describes the cooking processes of Morales's grandmothers. Underline each detail that appeals to one or more of the five senses—sight, hearing, smell, taste, touch.

From the corner of my eye, I see the knife blade flashing, reducing mounds of onions, garlic, cilantro, and green peppers into *sofrito* to be fried up and stored, and best of all is the pound and circular grind of the *pilon:* . . . . *Pound, pound* (the garlic and oregano mashed together), THUMP! (the mortar lifted and slammed down to loosen the crushed herbs and spices from the wooden bowl), *grind* (the slow rotation of the pestle smashing the oozing mash around and around, blending the juices, the green stain of cilantro and oregano, the sticky yellowing garlic, the grit of black pepper).

EXERCISE B. Read the following questions. Use the text you underlined to help you answer each one. Write on the lines provided.

1. Which details appeal to the sense of sight? "I see the knife blade flashing"; "mounds of onions, garlic, cilantro, and green peppers"; "circular grind"; "mortar lifted and slammed down"; "slow rotation"; "green stain"; "yellowing garlic"; "black pepper"

2. Which details appeal to the sense of hearing? "Pound pound," "THUMP," "slammed down," "grind"

3. Which details appeal to the sense of touch? "garlic and oregano mashed together"; "the mortar lifted and slammed down"; "crushed herbs and spices"; "smashing the oozing mash"; "sticky garlic"; "grit of black pepper"

4. What overall impression do the sights, sounds, and textures create? Possible answer: Sights emphasize the speed, style, and power of the women's cooking; the sounds, feel, and textures emphasize the intermingling of ingredients and the sticky, rough, juicy feel of the resulting paste.

Name .... Class .... Date ....

Bread

Interacting with Text Identifying Tone

The **tone** of a piece of writing is a reflection of the writer's overall attitude toward the subject matter. Authors reveal the tone through word choice, sentence structure, sensory images, and figures of speech.

EXERCISE A. Read the following passage from "Bread." Underline words and phrases that suggest the author's attitude about the subject matter.

You are now lying on a thin mattress in a hot room. The walls are made of dried earth, and your sister, who is younger than you, is in the room with you. She is starving, her belly is bloated, flies land on her eyes; you brush them off with your hand. You have a cloth too, filthy but damp, and you press it to her lips and forehead. The piece of bread is the bread you've been saving, for days it seems. You are as hungry as she is, but not yet as weak.

EXERCISE B. Read the following questions. Use the text you marked in the passage to help you answer each one. Write on the lines provided.

1. What words suggest that the situation the author describes is extremely serious and harsh? "thin mattress," "hot room," "starving," "belly is bloated," "flies land on her eyes," "filthy but damp," "not yet as weak"

2. Considering the words that you underlined, how would you describe the tone of this passage? Possible answer: The tone is grave or somber.

3. The author's writing is a series of short, direct statements, such as "You brush [the flies] off with your hand." These cause the reader to envision himself or herself as part of specific, disturbing images of starvation. How do these statements contribute to the overall tone? Possible answer: The directness of the sentences makes the tone seem unemotional and matter-of-fact. The reader is a participant in the scene and feels almost clinically involved in the life-and-death struggle that is occurring.

4. What tone and underlying message are suggested by the final sentence in the passage? Possible answer: It suggests a tone of foreboding—the reader is "not yet as weak" as the starving sister, suggesting that soon the reader will also become weak from starvation.

Name .... Class .... Date ....

Picture Bride

Interacting with Text Analyzing Imagery

Imagery consists of "word pictures" that writers create to evoke an emotional response in readers. To create effective imagery, writers use **sensory details,** or descriptions that appeal to one or more of the five senses—sight, hearing, smell, taste, and touch.

EXERCISE A. Read the following lines from "Picture Bride." Underline the words that create a clear picture in your mind.

. . . on whose shore
a man waited,
turning her photograph
to the light when the lanterns
in the camp outside
Waialua Sugar Mill were lit
and the inside of his room
grew luminous
from the wings of moths
migrating out of the cane stalks?

EXERCISE B. Read the following questions. Refer to the lines you marked in the passage to help you answer each one on the lines provided.

1. Where is the man, and what is he doing? He is in his room at the sugar mill camp, looking at a woman's picture.

2. What is the time of day? What is it like in the room? How do you know? It is dusk, becoming dark; the room is also dark. To study the picture, he must turn it toward the light from the lamps outside.

3. What are the moths doing? What sights and sounds do the probable action of the moths suggest? Possible answer: The moths' whitened wings flicker in the lamplight as they flutter out of the tall cane stalks. The sounds of their wings beating and their bodies hitting the lights can be imagined.

4. Given his actions, how do you think the man feels? Possible answer: His studying the picture and turning it toward the light show that he is curious about the young woman who is about to arrive.

Name .... Class .... Date ....

Prime Time

Interacting with Text Distinguishing Between Facts and Opinions

A **fact** can be proven to be true by observation or by consulting a reference source. An **opinion** expresses a belief or feeling and so cannot be proven or disproven. However, opinions can be supported by evidence, such as facts, details, examples, and reasons.

EXERCISE A. Read the following passage from "Prime Time" in which the author, an African American, describes his experiences at a local restaurant. Underline all facts once. Underline all opinions twice.

Even when we were with Daddy, you see, we had to stand at the counter and order takeout, then eat on white paper plates using plastic spoons, sipping our vanilla rickeys from green-and-white paper cups through plastic flexible-end straws. Even after basketball games, when Young Doc Bess would set up the team with free Cokes after one of the team's many victories, the colored players had to stand around and drink out of paper cups while the white players and cheerleaders sat down in the red Naugahyde booths and drank out of glasses. Integrate? I'll shut it down first, Carl Dadisman had vowed. He was an odd-looking man, with a Humpty-Dumpty sort of head and bottom. . . . He ran the taxis service, too, and was just as nice as he could be, even to colored people.

EXERCISE B. Read the following questions. Use the text that you marked in the passage to help you answer each one. Write your answers on the lines provided.

1. What treatment did the author experience at the Cut-Rate? The author had to "stand at the counter and order takeout" and then eat while using disposable dishes and utensils.

2. Is the treatment he received a fact or an opinion? Why? The treatment he describes is a fact. Others who were with him can also verify his experiences.

3. What is the author's opinion on Carl Dadisman's appearance? He says that Dadisman was "odd looking."

4. What had Carl Dadisman vowed? Is it a fact or an opinion? Explain. Dadisman had vowed not to integrate. This statement is a fact because it can be proven that he made the statement. Others heard him make this vow.

Name .... Class .... Date ....

Se me enchina el cuerpo al oír tu cuento . . .

Interacting with Text Analyzing Problems and Solutions

Most story plots contain a **problem,** or conflict, that one or more characters must face. Much of the action in the story centers around finding a **solution** to this problem.

EXERCISE A. Read the following passages from "Se me enchina el cuerpo al oír tu cuento . . ." Underline once words or phrases that suggest a problem. Underline twice words or phrases that suggest the solution.

Passage 1

You take control and pack the family off. "No pay for all your work if you leave." And you say, "We're leaving." . . . And driving the Midwest farm road almost crossing the state line you spy a sign "Labor Relations," and you stop. And, yes, you are owed your wages, and the bosses pay reluctantly.

Passage 2

Years later a lover will wonder why you refuse to sleep on feather-filled pillows, and you want to tell, to spill your guts, but you can't, you refuse. You hold your words like caged birds.

Memory's wound is too fresh.

And more years later when you tell the story, I cringe and get goosebumps; you tell your story and are healed, but there's still a scar . . .

EXERCISE B. Read the following questions. Use the text you marked to help you answer each one. Write on the lines provided.

1. In passage 1, what problem is presented as a result of the main character's decision to pack up his family and leave the job site? The bosses tell him that he and his family will not be paid, in that case.

2. What is the main character's solution to this problem? He learns at the Labor Relations office that his family is entitled to be paid, and the family is paid.

3. In passage 2, what problem does the main character have? He cannot sleep on feather pillows. He is troubled by the memory of an incident but finds it too painful to talk about.

4. What is the solution to the problem? Why does this action help? The main character tells the narrator his story. This action "heals" the main character and relieves his rage and hurt.

Name .... Class .... Date ....

from *Kubota*

Interacting with Text Recognizing Cause-and-Effect Relationships

Many events in a selection are connected by cause-and-effect relationships. A **cause** is an action or occurrence that makes something else happen. An **effect** is the result or outcome. One cause can produce several effects. One effect may result from several causes.

EXERCISE A. Read the following passages, in which the narrator recalls hearing true stories of his grandfather's experiences during World War II. In the passages, underline once all phrases or sentences that refer to causes. Underline twice all phrases or sentences that represent effects.

Passage 1

[Kubota] told me about Pearl Harbor, how the planes flew in wing after wing of formations over his old house in La'ie in Hawaii, and how, the next day, after Roosevelt had made his famous "Day of Infamy" speech about the treachery of the Japanese, the FBI agents had come to his door and taken him in, hauled him off to Honolulu for questioning, and held him without charge for several days.

Passage 2

In session after session, for months it seemed, [Kubota] pounded away at his story. He wanted to tell me the names of the FBI agents. He went over their questions and his responses again and again. He'd tell me how one would try to act friendly toward him, offering him cigarettes while the other, who hounded him with accusations and threats, left the interrogation room. . . . I was not made yet, and he was determined that his stories be part of my making.

EXERCISE B. Read the following questions. Use the marked parts of the passages to help you answer each question. Write your answers on the lines provided.

1. According to information in passage 1, what events cause Kubota's being taken to Honolulu for questioning by the FBI? The bombing of Pearl Harbor and President Roosevelt's speech in which he speaks of the "treachery of the Japanese" are probable causes for Kubota's being taken to Honolulu for questioning.

2. Kubota had a reason for telling his grandson the details of his experiences. According to the narrator, why did Kubota tell his grandson of his experiences? The narrator writes that he was "not made yet, and [Kubota] was determined that his stories be part of my making." The narrator believes that Kubota wanted his stories to shape and influence his grandson as he grew up.

Name .... Class .... Date ....

apprenticeship 1978

Interacting with Text Analyzing Imagery

Poets use **imagery,** or language that creates word pictures, to enable the reader to visualize a character or a scene.

EXERCISE A. Read the following lines from "apprenticeship 1978." Underline words and phrases that create vivid pictures in your mind.

when I join my grandmother
for a tasa de café
and I listen to the stories
de su antepasado*

her words paint masterpieces
and these I hang
in the galleries of my mind:

I want to be an artist like her.

* "of her past"

EXERCISE B. Read the following questions. Use the text you marked in the passage to help you answer each question on the lines provided.

1. Where are the grandmother and granddaughter, and what are they doing? The grandmother and granddaughter are sitting at a table drinking coffee. The grandmother is talking. The granddaughter is listening intently.

2. What do you picture when you hear the word *masterpieces*? Possible answer: beautiful works of art by great and famous artists that are appreciated by countless people through the years.

3. What do you picture when you hear the word *galleries*? Possible answer: rooms with walls lined with paintings.

4. How are the grandmother's words like masterpieces? Possible answer: The speaker suggests that her grandmother's stories are classics: beautiful creations.

5. What does the imagery of stories hung as masterpieces suggest about their importance to the speaker? The speaker "hangs" the stories in her mind as an artist would hang pictures in a gallery. With this image, the speaker suggests that she will remember and cherish the stories. The speaker wants to be an artist too—one who creates with words rather than with paint.

Name .... Class .... Date ....

Prayer to the Pacific

Interacting with Text Analyzing Simile and Personification

A **simile** is a figure of speech in which two seemingly unlike things are compared, using the word *like* or *as*. **Personification** is a figure of speech in which human qualities are ascribed to an animal, an object, or an idea.

EXERCISE A. Read the following passage from "Prayer to the Pacific."

I traveled to the ocean
distant
from my southwest land of sandrock
to the moving blue water
Big as the myth of origin.

Pale
pale water in the yellow-white light of
sun floating west
to China
where ocean herself was born.
Clouds that blow across the sand are wet.

EXERCISE B. Read the following items. Follow the directions for marking the passage and then for answering the questions.

1. Underline the simile in the first stanza. Which two things are being compared?
The simile compares "the moving blue water" of the ocean and "the myth of origin."

2. What idea does the poet convey through the comparison in the simile? Circle the letter before the correct answer.
   a. The ocean is larger than the mind can imagine.
   b. The ocean is far away from the myth of origin.
   (c.) The ocean has a mythical quality.
   d. The vastness of the "land of sandrock" is like the vastness of the ocean.

3. Underline the example of personification in the second stanza. Which of the following is assigned human characteristics?
   a. The sun is assigned human characteristics.
   (b.) The ocean is assigned human characteristics.
   c. The sand is assigned human characteristics.
   d. China is assigned human characteristics.

4. Explain the personification in the second stanza. To the ocean is ascribed the human experience of having been born.

Name .... Class .... Date ....

Riding the Elevator into the Sky

Interacting with Text Interpreting Poetry

When you **interpret** something you read, your knowledge of the world, your direct experience, and your understanding of other works help to create personal meaning.

EXERCISE A. Read the following passages from "Riding the Elevator into the Sky."

Passage 1

As the fireman said:
Don't book a room over the fifth floor
in any hotel in New York.
They have ladders that will reach further
but no one will climb them.
. . . .
These are the warnings
that you must forget
if you're climbing out of yourself.
If you're going to smash into the sky.

Passage 2

Floor five hundred:
messages and letters centuries old,
birds to drink,
a kitchen of clouds.
Floor six thousand:
the stars,
skeletons on fire,
their arms singing.

EXERCISE B. Read the following items. Follow the directions for marking the passages. Answer the questions on the lines provided.

1. In passage 1, underline the fireman's warning. Why does the speaker ignore the warning? What might the fireman's warning symbolize? Possible answer: The speaker ignores the warning because the speaker wants to "smash into the sky." The fireman's warning may symbolize being careful and not taking risks.

2. In passage 2, underline three details that seem surreal, or like images from a dream. Why could the lines "Floor five hundred" and "Floor six thousand" be considered surreal? Possible answers: (1) "Floor five hundred," (2) "birds to drink," (3) "a kitchen of clouds," (4) "Floor six thousand," (5) "skeletons on fire, / their arms singing"; the lines "Floor five hundred" and "Floor six thousand" seem surreal because no actual building is high enough to require elevators that go that high.

Name .... Class .... Date ....

Game

Interacting with Text Noun-Forming Suffixes

A **noun-forming suffix** is a group of letters that, when added to the end of a word, transforms the word into a noun. For instance, when the suffix *-ness* is added to the adjective *good*, a noun—*goodness*—is formed.

EXERCISE A. Read the following passages from "Game." Underline five nouns containing suffixes in which the base word is a verb. Then double-underline two nouns containing suffixes in which the base word is an adjective.

Passage 1

In the beginning I took care to behave normally. So did Shotwell. Our behavior was painfully normal. Norms of politeness, consideration, speech, and personal habits were scrupulously observed.

Passage 2

Definitions of normality were redrawn in the agreement of January 1, called by us, The Agreement. Uniform regulations were relaxed, and mealtimes are no longer rigorously scheduled.

EXERCISE B. Complete the following chart. In the first column, list the words that you underlined. (Use the suffixes listed in column 4 to guide you.) In the second column, write the base word for each word you underlined. In the third column, write the base word's part of speech.

Word Containing Noun-Forming Suffix	Base Word	Part of Speech of Base Word	Noun-Forming Suffix
beginning	begin	verb	-ing
politeness	polite	adjective	-ness
consideration	consider	verb	-ation
definitions	define	verb	-tion
normality	normal	adjective	-ity
agreement	agree	verb	-ment
regulations	regulate	verb	-ion

Name .... Class .... Date ....

Waiting for the Barbarians

Interacting with Text Using Context Clues

Use **context clues,** hints in the words and sentences that surround an unknown word, to help you make a reasoned guess about the meaning of the word.

EXERCISE A. Read the passages from "Waiting for the Barbarians."

Why are the senators sitting there without legislating?

. . . .

Why are they carrying elegant canes
beautifully worked in silver and gold?

. . . .

Why don't our distinguished orators turn up as usual
to make their speeches, say what they have to say?

EXERCISE B. Read the following items. Then follow the directions in each item for marking the poetry. Write answers or explanations on the lines provided.

1. Underline the word *legislating*. Underline another word in the same sentence that gives you a clue about the meaning of *legislating*. Write the clue word. senators
What does *legislating* mean? Legislating means making laws.

2. How does the second word you underlined help explain the meaning of *legislating*?
Senators make laws, so legislating is likely to have to do with making laws.

3. Underline the word *worked*. What do you think *worked* means in this line?
Worked means "decorated" in the context of the line.

4. Which context clues help you to know the meaning? The cane is elegant and has silver and gold on it, so worked must be the way the silver and gold are applied to it.

5. Underline the word *orator*. What is an orator? An orator is someone who makes speeches.

6. Underline the context clues that help you to know the meaning. Explain.
The word "usual" implies a typical activity. That activity is making "their speeches."

Name .... Class .... Date ....

Mirror

Interacting with Text Analyzing a Poem

Analyzing a poem is looking carefully at its elements. Identifying the topic and key words and interpreting the figurative language are all part of analyzing a poem.

EXERCISE A. Read the following stanza from the poem "Mirror."

Now I am a lake. A woman bends over me,
Searching my reaches for what she really is.
Then she turns to those liars, the candles or the moon.
I see her back, and reflect it faithfully.
She rewards me with tears and an agitation of hands.
I am important to her. She comes and goes.
Each morning it is her face that replaces the darkness.
In me she has drowned a young girl, and in me an old
woman
Rises toward her day after day, like a terrible fish.

EXERCISE B. Read the following items. Mark the passage as directed. Answer the questions on the lines provided.

1. Underline the sentence in which the speaker identifies itself. Who or what is the speaker? The speaker is a lake.

2. Underline the two objects that the speaker calls liars. Why does the speaker call the objects liars? The speaker calls the candle and the moon liars, possibly because they light people's faces in a flattering way.

3. Underline the words that tell how the woman reacts to her reflection. Why does she react this way? She is unhappy with her reflection in the mirror.

4. Reread the last two lines. Underline the simile. What two things are compared? The woman's fear of her aging reflection is compared to the fear she would feel if a "terrible fish" swam toward her.

Name .... Class .... Date ....

Traveling Through the Dark

Interacting with Text Summarizing

To **summarize** is to retell the main ideas and important details about a passage in logical sequence and in your own words.

EXERCISE A. Read the following passages from "Traveling Through the Dark."

Passage 1

By glow of the tail-light I stumbled back
of the car
and stood by the heap, a doe, a recent
killing;
she had stiffened already, almost cold.
I dragged her off; she was large in the
belly.

Passage 2

My fingers touching her side brought me
the reason—
her side was warm; her fawn lay there
waiting,
alive, still, never to be born.
Beside that mountain road I hesitated.

EXERCISE B. Read the following items. Follow the directions for marking the passages. Answer the questions and supply explanations on the lines provided.

1. Underline one word that shows who or what passage 1 is about. What is passage 1 about? The passage is about a doe.

2. Double-underline three details about the main subject of passage 1. What details describe the subject? Explain. "A recent killing" and "she had stiffened already, almost cold" mean that the doe is dead; "large in the belly" means that the doe was pregnant.

3. Read the following summaries. Circle the letter before the better summary of passage 1.
   a. The speaker saw a dead, pregnant doe at the side of a road and dragged her away.
   b. The speaker ran over a large deer at twilight and dragged its cold, stiff carcass off the road.

4. Underline the parts of the text that show what passage 2 is about. Summarize passage 2. The speaker touches the doe's side, realizes that the fawn is alive, and hesitates.

Name .... Class .... Date ....

Frederick Douglass

Interacting with Text **Analyzing and Interpreting**

To **analyze** a poem is to study its elements separately and then consider their overall effect. To **interpret** a poem is to use one's knowledge and experience to help one construct meaning.

EXERCISE A. Read the following poem, "Frederick Douglass."

When it is finally ours, this freedom,
this liberty, this beautiful
and terrible thing, needful to man as air,
usable as earth; when it belongs at last to all,
when it is truly instinct, brain matter,
diastole, systole,
reflex action; when it is finally won; when
it is more
than the gaudy mumbo jumbo of politicians:
this man, this Douglass, this former slave,
this Negro
beaten to his knees, exiled, visioning a world
where none is lonely, none hunted, alien,
this man, superb in love and logic, this man
shall be remembered. Oh, not with
statues' rhetoric,
not with legends and poems and wreaths
of bronze alone,
but with the lives grown out of his life,
the lives
fleshing his dream of the beautiful,
needful thing.

EXERCISE B. Now read the following items. For each item, find the part of the poem that will help you respond to it. Follow the directions with each item.

1. Underline, in the first sentence of the poem, each clause that begins with the word *when*.
2. Circle the subject of the first sentence.
3. Double-underline the verb of the first sentence.
4. Underline the part of the poem in the last sentence that tells exactly how Frederick Douglass will be remembered, according to Hayden.
5. Now consider the poem as a whole. Think about what you know about Douglass and the history of African American people in the United States. Briefly interpret the message of the poem on the lines provided. Possible answer: Frederick Douglass's work and person will best be honored by the lives of people coming after him who live in the freedom for which Douglass worked so tirelessly.

Name .... Class .... Date ....

#2 Memory and Poem

Interacting with Text **Responding**

Use everything you know and feel to help you **respond** to poetry. Decide what the speaker is saying and why he or she is saying it. Focus on your own reactions to what the speaker is saying.

EXERCISE A. Read the following poems, "#2 Memory" and "Poem."

#2 Memory

Don Arturo says:
You have to know
what you once said
Because it could
travel in the air
for years
And return in different
clothes
And then you have to
buy it.

Poem

Think with your body
And dance with your mind.

EXERCISE B. Now read the following items. Mark the passages as indicated. Write your answers to the questions on the lines provided.

1. Underline the part of the poem that tells you who is giving advice in "#2 Memory." Who is that person? What advice does he give? How do you react to the advice? Don Arturo gives advice. His advice is to watch what you say, because it could come back later to haunt you. Possible response: The advice is realistic. I believe it.

2. Underline the verbs in "Poem." What is the advice to the reader in "Poem"? How do you react to it? "Think with your body and dance with your mind" is the advice. Possible response: The poem is like a riddle. I have to think about it to understand it.

3. What does the advice in the poem mean? Possible answer: The verbs *think* and *dance* are used unexpectedly to suggest actions that cannot literally be performed. The advice, written creatively, is to be creative and to be guided by instincts as well as by intellect.

Name .... Class .... Date ....

Weaver

Interacting with Text — Analyzing Sensory Imagery

Often poets use **sensory images,** language that appeals to one or more of the five senses: taste, smell, hearing, sight, and touch.

EXERCISE A. Read the following stanzas from "Weaver." Underline words and phrases that appeal to one or more of the senses.

Weave us a red of fire and blood
that tastes of sweet plum
fishing around the memories of the dead
following a scent wounded
our spines bleeding with pain

. . . .

And weave us a white song to hold us
when the wind blows so cold to make our
children wail
submerged in furious ice
a song pure and raw
that burns paper
and attacks the colorless venom stalking
hidden
in the petal softness of the black night.

EXERCISE B. Classify the sensory images in the passage. Decide which of the five senses each image appeals to. Write the descriptive words in the image under the heading that names the sense. Some images may be recorded more than once.

1. Touch
   "spines bleeding with pain," "wind blows so cold,"
   "submerged in furious ice," "petal softness"
2. Taste
   "tastes of sweet plum"
3. Sight
   "red of fire and blood," "white song," "colorless venom,"
   "petal softness of the black night"
4. Hearing
   "white song," "children wail," "song pure and raw," "burns paper"
5. Smell
   "a scent wounded," "burns paper"

Name .... Class .... Date ....

For Georgia O'Keeffe

Interacting with Text Visualizing

Visualizing is forming mental pictures of people, places, and things while reading.

EXERCISE A. Read the following passage from "For Georgia O'Keeffe."

I want
. . . .
to stand near
you straight
as a Spanish Dagger,
to see your fingers
pick a bone bouquet
touching life
where I touch death,
to hold a warm, white
pelvis up
to the glaring sun
and see
your red-blue world
to feel you touch
my eyes
as you touch canvas.

EXERCISE B. Read the following items. Follow the directions for marking the passage. Answer the questions on the lines provided.

1. Double-underline the text that describes the desired posture of the speaker. How does the speaker want to stand? How do you picture her? The speaker wants to stand "straight as a Spanish Dagger." Possible visualization: I picture the speaker standing tall; she is respectful and silent beside Georgia O'Keeffe.

2. Circle the text that tells what the speaker imagines finding. What do you picture the speaker and O'Keeffe doing with what they find as they walk? Possible answer: I picture O'Keeffe delicately picking up a warm, sun-bleached pelvic bone from the sandy desert and turning it over in her hands.

3. How do you visualize O'Keeffe touching the speaker's eyes? What does this text mean? Possible answer: O'Keeffe lovingly touches the speaker's eyes, as she would touch a canvas on which she would create her art. This act symbolizes O'Keeffe's helping the speaker see as O'Keeffe sees.

Name .... Class .... Date ....

Geometry

Interacting with Text Analyzing Figurative Language

Metaphor and personification are two types of figurative language. In **metaphor** a direct comparison is made between two seemingly unlike things. In **personification** human characteristics are attributed to animals, objects, and ideas.

EXERCISE A. Read the following poem, "Geometry."

I prove a theorem and the house expands:
the windows jerk free to hover near the
ceiling,
the ceiling floats away with a sigh.

As the walls clear themselves of everything
but transparency, the scent of carnations
leaves with them. I am out in the open

and above the windows have hinged into
butterflies,
sunlight glinting where they've intersected.
They are going to some point true and
unproven.

EXERCISE B. Now read the following items. Mark the poem as directed. Then answer the questions–on the lines provided or by circling the letter of the correct answer choice.

1. Underline two examples of personification in the first stanza. What objects are being personified? What human characteristics are attributed to the personified objects? Examples of personification: "windows jerk free to hover" and "ceilling floats away with a sigh." The windows "jerk free," or pull away, and the ceiling sighs.

2. What does the poet's use of personification tell the reader about the speaker's feelings? Circle the letter before the correct answer choice.
   - **a.** The speaker feels free or liberated. (circled)
   - **b.** The speaker feels anxious.
   - **c.** The speaker is distressed.

3. What extended metaphor can you find in the poem? Explain. Proving a theorem is compared to a house's expanding. After solving the problem, the speaker describes standing out in the open after the windows of the expanding house jerk free and turn into butterflies, and the ceiling is no longer a restriction.

Name .... Class .... Date ....

The Welder

Interacting with Text Comparing and Contrasting

Comparing is looking for similarities. **Contrasting** is examining differences.

EXERCISE A. Read the following stanzas from "The Welder."

I am a welder.
Not an alchemist.
I am interested in the blend
of common elements to make
a common thing.

. . . .

We plead to each other,
we all come from the same rock
we all come from the same rock
ignoring the fact that we bend
at different temperatures
that each of us is malleable
up to a point.

. . . .

I am the welder.
I understand the capacity of heat
to change the shape of things.
I am suited to work
within the realm of sparks
out of control.

EXERCISE B. Read the following items. Follow the directions for marking the passage. Then answer the questions on the lines provided.

1. In the passage, underline three ways in which the speaker and a welder are alike. In what three ways are the speaker and a welder compared? (1) They are interested in blending common elements. (2) They both understand that heat can change the shape of things. (3) They are both suited to dealing with sparks out of control.

2. In the second stanza of the passage, underline the parts of the text that indicate what the speaker compares and contrasts. What is like rock? What is not like rock? Explain. The speaker compares rock to humanity: "we all come from the same rock," and the speaker contrasts people with rock by pointing out the differences. People "bend at different temperatures," or have real differences and thus can be joined only to a limited extent.

Name .... Class .... Date ....

The House/La Casa

Interacting with Text Using Language Clues

When you encounter words from a language that is unfamiliar, look for similarities between the foreign words and English words. Your knowledge of English may help you to interpret words from some languages.

EXERCISE A. Read the following passages from "The House" and "La Casa." Underline words in each passage that have similar spellings.

I see you standing	Te veo parada
desolate	desolada
with the sun's rays	con los rayos del sol
spattered	salpicados
on your hair	en tu cabellera
of black roof-tiles.	de tejas negras.
Dark	Oscura
alone	sola
you remain like the cave	quedas como la cueva
of a hermit	de un hermitaño
whose	al cual se le ha
fire has died down.	apagado su fuego.

EXERCISE B. Now read the following items. Write your responses on the lines provided.

1. List the pairs of English and Spanish words that have similar spellings.
Words with similar spellings: desolate/desolada, rays/rayos, cave/cueva, hermit/hermitaño.

2. Look carefully at each line of the poem in English and then at the matching line in Spanish. Write the Spanish word for each of the following English words.
sun sol   your tu
dark oscura   alone sola

3. Which Spanish word in the first line of the passage means "see"? veo

4. Which Spanish word in the last line of the passage means "fire"? fuego

Name .... Class .... Date ....

Salvador Late or Early

Interacting with Text Analyzing Characterization

Characterization is the author's methods of revealing the personality of a character.

EXERCISE A. Read the following passages from "Salvador Late or Early."

Passage 1

Salvador with eyes the color of caterpillar, Salvador of the crooked hair and crooked teeth, Salvador whose name the teacher cannot remember, is a boy who is no one's friend, runs along somewhere in that vague direction where homes are the color of bad weather, lives behind a raw wood doorway, shakes the sleepy brothers awake, ties their shoes, combs their hair with water, feeds them milk and corn flakes from a tin cup in the dim dark of the morning.

Passage 2

Salvador inside that wrinkled shirt, inside the throat that must clear itself and apologize each time it speaks, inside that forty-pound body of boy with its geography of scars, its history of hurt, limbs stuffed with feathers and rags, in what part of the eyes, in what part of the heart, in that cage of the chest where something throbs with both fists and knows only what Salvador knows . . .

EXERCISE B. Now read the following items. Follow the directions for marking the passages. Write on the lines provided.

1. In passage 1, underline the parts of the text that describe Salvador's physical appearance. What do you think Salvador looks like? He has yellow/brown eyes with uneven teeth and unruly hair.

2. In passage 1, double-underline the parts of the text that suggest that Salvador does not stand out and is probably lonely. Explain. His teacher cannot remember his name, and he has no friends.

3. In passage 1, circle the parts of the text that let you know that Salvador is a responsible person.

4. In passage 2, underline the parts of the text that let you know that Salvador lacks self-confidence. Explain. Salvador clears his throat and apologizes when he speaks. These behaviors suggest a lack of self-confidence.

Name .... Class .... Date ....

Embroidering: A Response to "Somnad" by Carl Larsson

Interacting with Text Analyzing Sensory Imagery

Poets often use **sensory imagery,** or descriptions, words, and phrases that appeal to the five senses: sight, hearing, taste, smell, and touch.

EXERCISE A. Read the following passages from "Embroidering: A Response to 'Somnad' by Carl Larsson."

Passage 1

One is pale green
like a single blade of weed
at the edge of a small pond. Another
strand is the color of deep wood
roses, wild and very sweet.
Also, threads like filaments
of fish tails, gold
and a blue string curled
like a child's ball, color
of sky on early desert mornings.

Passage 2

This afternoon, pale
and warm, the daughter listens
to her mother's breath, soft
and steady like a small animal
full of milk, nearly asleep,
this rhythm of breathing and needles
sliding slowly through the cloth.
They have planned this thing,
a tablecloth to spread out
for guests who will come
to this room, who will sit
and bow their heads to the white
plates of food.

EXERCISE B. Read the following items. Follow the directions for marking the passages. Write on the lines provided.

1. In passage 1, underline the words and phrases that refer to colors. To what sense do do these phrases appeal? *The phrases referring to color appeal to the sense of sight.*

2. In your own words, describe the sensory imagery in passage 1. *Possible answer: The threads are pale green, brownish red, gold, and blue—all sparkling or glowing as the filaments of fish tails do.*

3. In passage 2, underline the words and phrases that appeal to the sense of hearing. What two things are compared? *The sound of the mother's breathing is compared to that of a sleepy and contented small animal.*

Name .... Class .... Date ....

The Names of Women

Interacting with Text Homographs and Homophones

Homographs are words that are spelled the same way but have different meanings and may have different pronunciations. **Homophones** are words that sound the same but have different meanings and usually different spellings.

EXERCISE A. Read the following passages from "The Names of Women." Underline words that have homographs or homophones. (Do not underline the word *in* or *I*.)

Passage 1

Shortly after the first tribal roll, the practice of renaming became an ecclesiastical exercise, and, as a result, most women in the next two generations bear the names of saints particularly beloved by the French.

Passage 2

The owner of the other cart, Virginia Grandbois, died when I was nine years old. . . . Forty years before I was born, she was photographed on her way to fetch drinking water at the reservation well.

EXERCISE B. Fill in the chart. List the words you underlined in the passages. Write one homograph or homophone for each word you underlined. Then write one meaning for each word. Consult a dictionary as necessary.

Word from Passage	Meaning in the Context of the Passage	Homograph or Homophone	Meaning
roll	list of people	roll; role	small bread; to turn over; part played by an actor
two	number after one	to, too	toward; also
bear	have; carry	bear, bare	animal; give birth to; without covering
by	according to	buy; bye	purchase; farewell
died	ceased to exist	dyed	tinted; colored
born	come into existence	borne	carried
well	place to get water from the ground	well	not sick; interjection

Name .... Class .... Date ....

Naming Myself

Interacting with Text Summarizing

Summarizing is stating the most important ideas in a passage in one's own words and in a logical order.

EXERCISE A. Read the following passage from "Naming Myself."

I knew my first ancestor.
. . . .
the grandfather
whose people owned slaves and cotton.
He was restless in Virginia
among the gentleman brothers, until
one peppered, flaming autumn he stole a
horse,
rode over the mountains to marry
a leaf-eyed Cherokee.

EXERCISE B. Read the following items. Then mark the passage as directed. Follow the directions for each item. Write on the lines provided.

1. Underline the word that indicates whom the passage is about. Who does the passage describe? The passage describes the speaker's grandfather.

2. Underline four details that describe whom the passage is about. List four details that provide information about the subject or the subject's actions. Possible answers: (1) had a family that "owned slaves and cotton"; (2) was "restless"; (3) "stole a horse"; (4) "rode over the mountains to marry / a leaf-eyed Cherokee"

3. Which is the best summary of the passage? Circle the letter before the best answer choice.
   a. My grandfather left his well-to-do family in Virginia and married a Cherokee woman.
   b. My grandfather fell in love with a Cherokee woman and wanted to marry her.
   c. My grandfather did not believe in slavery, so he abandoned his slave-holding brothers.

Name .... Class .... Date ....

Emily Dickinson

Interacting with Text Analyzing and Interpreting

Analyzing is looking critically at what you read. **Interpreting** is attaching meaning to what you have read, using personal experiences and knowledge.

EXERCISE A. Read the following poem, "Emily Dickinson."

Like you, I belong to yesterday,
to the bays where
day is anchored to
wait for its hour.

Like me, you belong to today,
the progression of that hour
when what is unborn
begins to throb.

We are cultivators of
the unsayable weavers
of singulars, migrant
workers in search of
floating gardens as yet
unsown, as yet unharvested.

EXERCISE B. Read the following items. Follow the directions for marking the text. Write your answers and your description on the lines provided.

1. Underline words that indicate that the poem is addressed to someone. Whom is the poem addressed to? How do you know? The poem is addressed to Emily Dickinson. The poem's title is "Emily Dickinson."

2. According to stanzas 1 and 2, in what ways are the speaker and the "you" of the poem alike? Possible answer: Both the speaker and Emily Dickinson belong to the past, when time moved more slowly. Both have messages for modern times.

3. In stanza 3, what does the speaker imply about her own job or vocation? How is the speaker's job like the job of Emily Dickinson? The speaker implies that she is a poet, just as Emily Dickinson was.

4. In stanza 3, double-underline the word that indicates how the speaker views her own and Emily Dickinson's jobs. Describe that job, using your own words. Possible answer: Both poets are gardeners ("cultivators") who interpret human experiences; their gardens are their own imaginations ("floating gardens as yet / unsown . . . unharvested").